AROUND PARLIAMENT
See pages 104–119.

*Around
Városliget*

Central Pest

AROUND VÁROSLIGET
See pages 140–151.

CENTRAL PEST
See pages 120–139.

EYEWITNESS *Travel Guides*

BUDAPEST

EYEWITNESS *TRAVEL GUIDES*

BUDAPEST

Main Contributor: TADEUSZ OLSZÁNSKI

DORLING KINDERSLEY
LONDON • NEW YORK • SYDNEY • MOSCOW
www.dk.com

A DORLING KINDERSLEY BOOK

www.dk.com

Produced by Wydawnictwo Wiedza i Życie, Warsaw
SERIES EDITOR Ewa Swagrzyk
CONSULTANTS András Hadik, Małgorzata Omilanowska,
Katalin Szokolay
EDITORS Joanna Egert, Anna Kożurno-Królikowska,
Bożena Leskowicz
DESIGNER Paweł Pasternak

Dorling Kindersley Ltd
PROJECT EDITOR Jane Oliver
EDITORS Felicity Crowe, Nancy Jones

SENIOR MANAGING EDITOR Vivien Crump
DEPUTY ART DIRECTOR Gillian Allan

PRODUCTION Jo Blackmore, David Proffit
DTP DESIGNERS Lee Redmond, Ingrid Vienings

MAIN CONTRIBUTOR
Tadeusz Olszański

TRANSLATORS
Magda Hannay, Anna Johnson, Ian Wisniewski

MAPS
Maria Wojciechowska, Dariusz Osuch
(D Osuch i Spółka)

PHOTOGRAPHERS
Gábor Barka, Dorota and Mariusz Jarymowiczowie

ILLUSTRATORS
Paweł Mistewicz, Piotr Zubrzycki

Text film output by Graphical Innovations, London
Printed and bound in China by L Rex Printing Company Limited

First published in Great Britain in 1999
by Dorling Kindersley Limited
9 Henrietta Street, London WC2E 8PS

A CIP CATALOGUE RECORD IS AVAILABLE FROM THE BRITISH LIBRARY.

ISBN 0 7513 1150 2

**The information in every
Eyewitness Travel Guide is checked annually**.
Every effort has been made to ensure that this book is as up-to-
date as possible at the time of going to press. Some details,
however, such as telephone numbers, opening hours, prices,
gallery hanging arrangements and travel information are liable to
change. The publishers cannot accept responsibility for any
consequences arising from the use of this book.
We value the views and suggestions of our readers very highly.
Please write to: Senior Managing Editor, Eyewitness Travel Guides,
Dorling Kindersley, 9 Henrietta Street, London WC2E 8PS.

<| The Parliament building *(see pp108–9)*, standing on the Danube

CONTENTS

HOW TO USE
THIS GUIDE *6*

Pallas Athene on the Old Town Hall

INTRODUCING
BUDAPEST

PUTTING BUDAPEST ON
THE MAP *10*

THE HISTORY OF
BUDAPEST *16*

BUDAPEST
AT A GLANCE *36*

BUDAPEST THROUGH
THE YEAR *58*

**Hungarian crest adorning a wall
close to the Tunnel *(see p100)***

The Hungarian National Gallery *(see pp74–7)*, in the former Royal Palace

View across the Danube towards
St Stephen's Basilica *(see p116–17)*

Porcelain in the Museum of
Applied Arts *(see pp136–7)*

Barrel-organ player in the historic
Castle District *(see pp68–85)*

The landmark domes and towers of four of Budapest's most striking places of worship

HOW TO USE THIS GUIDE

THIS EYEWITNESS Travel Guide helps you get the most from your stay in Budapest with the minimum of difficulty. The opening section, *Introducing Budapest*, locates the city geographically, sets modern Budapest in its historical context and describes events through the entire year. *Budapest at a Glance* is an overview of the city's main attractions. *Budapest Area by Area* starts on page 66. This is the main sightseeing

Plotting the route

section, which covers all of the important sights, with photographs, maps and illustrations. It also includes day trips from Budapest and two walks around the city. Information about hotels, restaurants, shops and markets, entertainment and sports is found in *Travellers' Needs*. The *Survival Guide* has advice on everything from using the postal service and telephones to Budapest's public transport system and medical services.

FINDING YOUR WAY AROUND THE SIGHTSEEING SECTION

Each of six sightseeing areas in Budapest is colour-coded for easy reference. Every chapter opens with an introduction to the area of the city it covers, describing its history and character, and has one or two *Street-by-Street* maps

illustrating typical parts of that area. Finding your way around the chapter is made simple by the numbering system used throughout. The most important sights are covered in detail in two or more full pages.

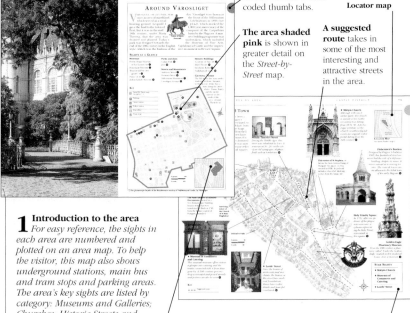

Each area has colour-coded thumb tabs.

Locator map

The area shaded pink is shown in greater detail on the *Street-by-Street* map.

A suggested route takes in some of the most interesting and attractive streets in the area.

1 Introduction to the area
For easy reference, the sights in each area are numbered and plotted on an area map. To help the visitor, this map also shows underground stations, main bus and tram stops and parking areas. The area's key sights are listed by category: Museums and Galleries; Churches; Historic Streets and Squares; Palaces and Historic Buildings; Hotels and Baths and Parks and Gardens.

A locator map shows where you are in relation to the other areas in the city centre.

2 Street-by-Street map
This gives a bird's-eye view of interesting and important parts of each sightseeing area. The numbering of the sights ties up with the area map and the fuller description on the pages that follow.

The list of star sights recommends the places that no visitor should miss.

BUDAPEST AREA MAP

The COLOURED AREAS shown on this map *(see inside front cover)* are the six main sight-seeing areas used in this guide. Each is covered in a full chapter in *Budapest Area by Area (pp66–167)*. They are highlighted on other maps throughout the book. In *Budapest at a Glance*, for example, they help you locate the top sights. They are also used to help you find the position of the two walks *(pp168–73)*.

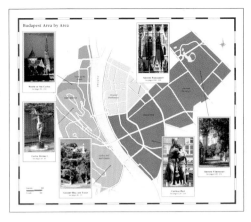

Numbers refer to each sight's position on the area map and its place in the chapter.

Practical information provides everything you need to know to visit each sight. Map references pinpoint the sight's location on the *Street Finder* map *(pp234–47)*.

Façades of important buildings are often shown to help you recognize them quickly.

The visitors' checklist provides all the practical information needed to plan your visit.

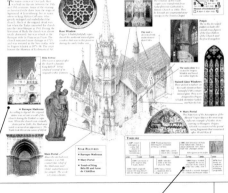

3 Detailed information on each sight
All the important sights in Budapest are described individually. They are listed in order following the numbering on the area map at the start of the section. Practical information includes a map reference, opening hours, telephone numbers and admission charges. The key to the symbols used is on the back flap.

Stars indicate the features no visitor should miss.

4 Budapest's major sights
Historic buildings are dissected to reveal their interiors; museums and galleries have colour-coded floorplans to help you find important exhibits.

A timeline charts the key events in the history of the building.

INTRODUCING
BUDAPEST

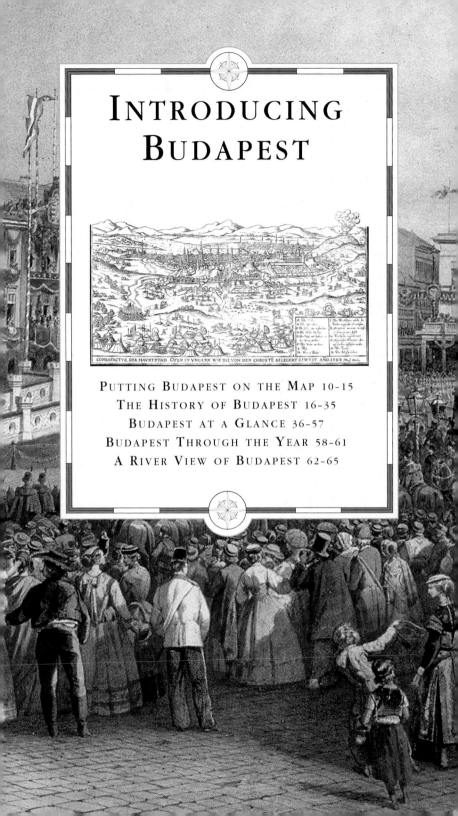

CONRATACTVR. DER HAVBTSTAD OFEN IN VNGERN WIE DIE VON DEN CHRISTE BELEGERT GEWEST. ANO.1598

Putting Budapest on the Map

THE CAPITAL OF the Republic of Hungary, Budapest has over two million inhabitants, a fifth of the country's total population. The city is situated on the Danube and covers an area of 525 sq km (200 sq miles). One third of the city is taken up by hilly Buda and Óbuda, on the western bank of the Danube, and the remaining two thirds by flat Pest, on the eastern bank. Budapest has a pivotal location at the heart of central Europe. From here one can easily reach other major cities such as Vienna, Zagreb, Bratislava, Belgrade, Bucharest and Prague.

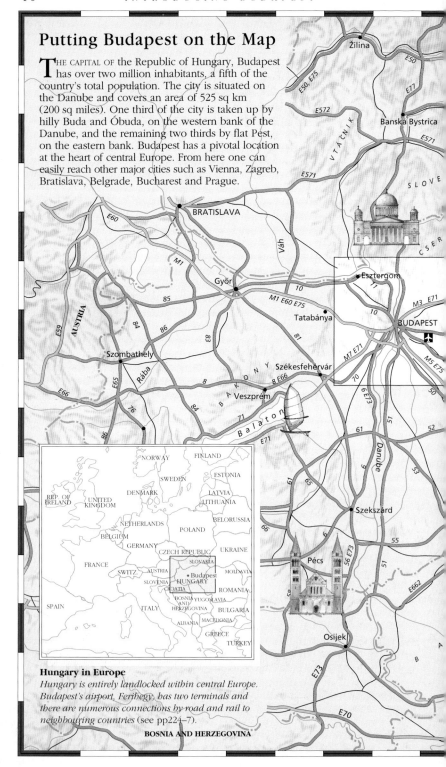

Hungary in Europe

Hungary is entirely landlocked within central Europe. Budapest's airport, Ferihegy, has two terminals and there are numerous connections by road and rail to neighbouring countries (see pp224–7).

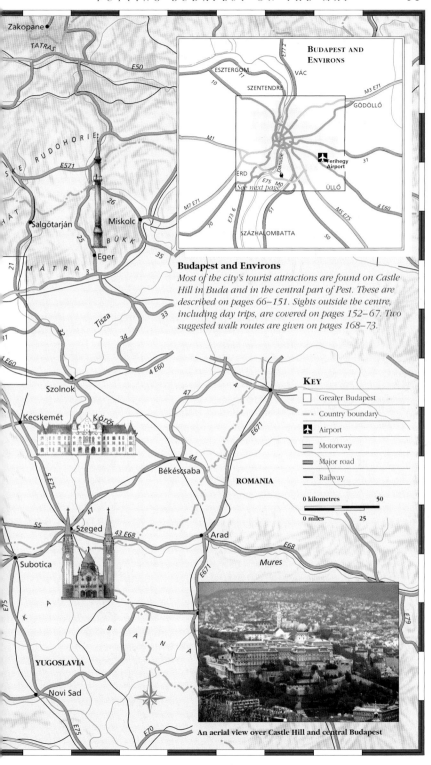

Budapest and Environs

Most of the city's tourist attractions are found on Castle Hill in Buda and in the central part of Pest. These are described on pages 66–151. Sights outside the centre, including day trips, are covered on pages 152–67. Two suggested walk routes are given on pages 168–73.

KEY

☐ Greater Budapest

– – Country boundary

✈ Airport

▬ Motorway

▬ Major road

▬ Railway

0 kilometres   50

0 miles   25

An aerial view over Castle Hill and central Budapest

Greater Budapest

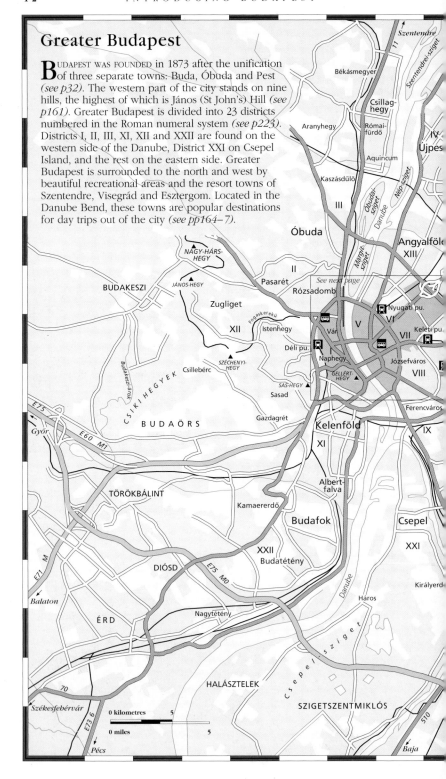

BUDAPEST WAS FOUNDED in 1873 after the unification of three separate towns: Buda, Óbuda and Pest (*see p32*). The western part of the city stands on nine hills, the highest of which is János (St John's) Hill (*see p161*). Greater Budapest is divided into 23 districts numbered in the Roman numeral system (*see p223*). Districts I, II, III, XI, XII and XXII are found on the western side of the Danube, District XXI on Csepel Island, and the rest on the eastern side. Greater Budapest is surrounded to the north and west by beautiful recreational areas and the resort towns of Szentendre, Visegrád and Esztergom. Located in the Danube Bend, these towns are popular destinations for day trips out of the city (*see pp164–7*).

Szentendre

Békásmegyer

Csillag-hegy

Aranyhegy

Rómaifürdő

IV
Újpes

Aquincum

Kaszásdűlő

III

Óbuda

Angyalfölc
XIII

NAGY-HÁRS-HEGY

II

Pasarét

See next page

BUDAKESZI

JÁNOS-HEGY

Rózsadomb

Nyugati pu.

Zugliget

V
VI

Istenhegy

XII

Vár

Keleti pu.

Déli pu.

SZÉCHENYI-HEGY

Csillebérc

Naphegy

VII

Józsefváros

SAS-HEGY

GELLÉRT-HEGY

VIII

Sasad

CSIKI HEGYEK

Gazdagrét

Ferencváros

Győr

BUDAÖRS

Kelenföld

IX

XI

Albert-falva

TÖRÖKBÁLINT

Kamaererdő

Budafok

Csepel

DIÓSD

XXII
Budatétény

XXI

Balaton

Királyerd

Háros

ÉRD

Nagytétény

Székesfehérvár

0 kilometres   5

0 miles   5

HALÁSZTELEK

SZIGETSZENTMIKLÓS

Pécs

Baja

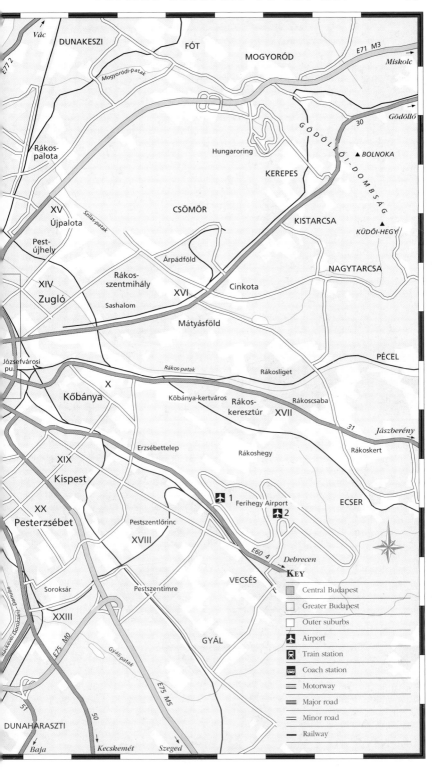

Vác

DUNAKESZI

FÓT

MOGYORÓD

E71 M3
Miskolc

Mogyoródi-patak

E71 2

GÖDÖLLŐI-DOMBSÁG

30

Gödöllő

Rákos-palota

Hungaroring

KEREPES

▲ BOLNOKA

XV
Újpalota

CSÖMÖR

KISTARCSA

Szilas-patak

KÜDŐI-HEGY ▲

Pest-újhely

Árpádföld

NAGYTARCSA

XIV
Zugló

Rákos-szentmihály

Sashalom

XVI

Cinkota

Mátyásföld

Józsefvárosi pu.

PÉCEL

X

Rákos-patak

Rákosliget

Kőbánya

Kőbánya-kertváros

Rákos-keresztúr

Rákoscsaba

XVII

31

Jászberény

Erzsébettelep

Rákoshegy

Rákoskert

XIX
Kispest

XX
Pesterzsébet

Pestszentlőrinc

XVIII

1 Ferihegy Airport
2

ECSER

E60 4

Debrecen

Soroksár

Pestszentimre

VECSÉS

Ráckevei (Soroksári) Danube

XXIII

E75 M0

GYÁL

Gyáli-patak

E75 M5

KEY

Central Budapest

Greater Budapest

Outer suburbs

Airport

Train station

Coach station

Motorway

Major road

Minor road

Railway

51

DUNAHARASZTI

50

Baja

Kecskemét

Szeged

Central Budapest

Detail on the Stock Exchange

THE CENTRE OF TOWN includes Castle Hill (district I) on the western bank of the Danube and districts V, VI, VII, VIII and IX of Pest on the river's eastern bank, bounded by the city's original tram line. The Roman numerals denote the official administrative districts *(see p223)*. For the purposes of this guide, the centre is divided into six areas. Each area has its own chapter containing a selection of sights that convey its character and history. Sights on the outskirts of the city, and suggested day trips and walks, are covered in separate chapters.

Calvinist Church
Situated close to the Danube, this church is distinguished by its eye-catching, polychromatic roof (see p100).

Royal Palace
The Royal Palace has been destroyed and painstakingly rebuilt many times. It was last meticulously reconstructed after World War II, to the form that the Habsburgs had given it (see pp70–71).

Liberation Monument
This statue of a woman holding aloft the palm of victory was created by the Hungarian sculptor Zsigmond Kisfaludi Stróbl. Situated in a park on Gellért Hill, the monument is visible from all over the city. It is now one of the symbols of Budapest (see p92).

0 metres   500
0 yards   500

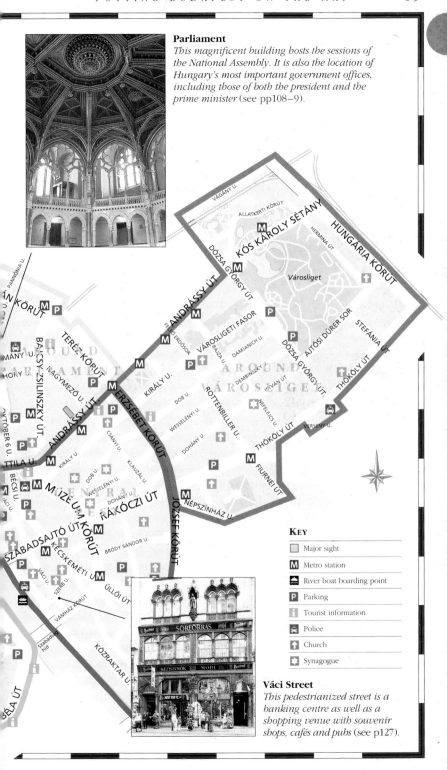

Parliament
This magnificent building hosts the sessions of the National Assembly. It is also the location of Hungary's most important government offices, including those of both the president and the prime minister (see pp108–9).

VÁGÁNY U.

ÁLLATKERTI KÖRÚT

KÓS KÁROLY SÉTÁNY

HUNGÁRIA KÖRÚT

HERMINA ÚT

Városliget

PANNÓNIA U.

...ÁN KÖRÚT

DÓZSA GYÖRGY ÚT

AJTÓSI DÜRER SOR

STEFÁNIA ÚT

TERÉZ KÖRÚT

BAJCSY-ZSILINSZKY ÚT

...MÁNY U.

NAGYMEZŐ U.

...HORY

ANDRÁSSY ÚT

FERDINÁND...

FERDINÁND...

ANDRÁSSY ÚT

VÁROSLIGETI FASOR

BAJZA U.

DAMJANICH U.

DÓZSA GYÖRGY ÚT

THÖKÖLY ÚT

...OKTÓBER 6 U.

KIRÁLY U.

ERZSÉBET KÖRÚT

DOB U.

ROTTENBILLER U.

DEMBINSZKY U.

IVÁN U.

...ATTILA U.

KIRÁLY U.

CSÁNYI U.

WESSELÉNYI U.

NEFELEJCS U.

BÉCSI U.

...VÁCI U.

MÚZEUM KÖRÚT

DOB U.

WESSELÉNYI U.

KLAUZÁL U.

DOHÁNY U.

DOHÁNY U.

THÖKÖLY ÚT

VERSENY U.

FIUMEI ÚT

RÁKÓCZI ÚT

JÓZSEF KÖRÚT

NÉPSZÍNHÁZ U.

SZABADSAJTÓ ÚT KÖRÚT

KECSKEMÉTI U.

BRÓDY SÁNDOR U.

...VÁCI U.

SZERB U.

ÜLLŐI ÚT

VÁMHÁZ KÖRÚT

Szabadság híd

KÖZRAKTÁR U.

BÉLA ÚT

KEY

▢	Major sight
Ⓜ	Metro station
⛴	River boat boarding point
P	Parking
ℹ	Tourist information
🚓	Police
✝	Church
✡	Synagogue

SÖRFORRÁS

KÉZISZOVÖK

MODL

JUST DO IT

Váci Street
This pedestrianized street is a banking centre as well as a shopping venue with souvenir shops, cafés and pubs (see p127).

THE HISTORY OF BUDAPEST

AS EARLY AS THE Palaeolithic era, there were settlements in the area of Budapest: the narrowing of the Danube made the crossing of the river easy at this particular spot. In around AD 100, the Romans established the town of Aquincum here. Their rule lasted until the early 5th century AD, when the region fell to Attila the Hun. It was subsequently ruled by the Goths, the Longobards and, for nearly 300 years, by the Avars.

The ancestors of modern Hungarians, the Magyars, migrated from the Urals and arrived in the Budapest region in 896. They were led by Prince Árpád, whose dynasty ruled until the 13th century. At the turn of the first millennium, St István, whose heathen name was Vajk, accepted Christianity for the Hungarians. As their first crowned king, István I also laid the basis of the modern Hungarian state.

It was Béla IV who, in 1247, after the Mongol invasion, moved the capital to Buda. Much of the expansion of Buda took place under kings from the dynasty of the Angevins. Buda reached a zenith during the reign of Mátyás Corvinus in the 15th century, but further development was hindered by the advancing Turks, who took the region and ruled Buda for 150 years.

Crest of the Hunyadis

Liberation by the Christian armies resulted in the submission of the country as a whole to the Habsburgs. They suppressed all nationalist rebellions, but at the same time took care of economic development. Empress Maria Theresa and Archduke Joseph, the emperor's governor, made particular contributions to the modernization of both Buda and Pest. Yet, the slow pace of reforms led to an uprising in 1848, which was brutally crushed by Franz Joseph I. Compromise in 1867 and the creation of an Austro-Hungarian Empire stimulated economic and cultural life once more. Soon after, in 1873, Buda and Pest were united to create the city of Budapest.

Following World War I, the monarchy fell and Hungary lost two thirds of its territory. The desire to regain this contributed to its support of Germany in World War II. However, Budapest was taken by Russian troops in 1945 and large sections of it levelled. Under the subsequent Communist rule, the popular uprising of 1956 was ruthlessly suppressed by Soviet tanks but it initiated a crisis that shook the regime. Free elections took place in 1990, resulting in the victory of the democratic opposition, and the emergence of a new bourgeoisie.

Dating from 1686, when the Turks were expelled, this map shows the fortified towns of Pest and Buda

◁ Gyula Benczúr's *The Baptism of Vajk*, displayed in the Hungarian National Gallery *(see pp74–7)*

The City's Rulers

IN THE 13TH CENTURY, Béla IV built a castle in Buda and designated the town as his new capital. Until that time, the Árpád dynasty, the first family of Hungarian kings, had ruled their domain from elsewhere. When, at the beginning of the 14th century, there were no male heirs to the Árpád throne, Hungary began a long period during which it was mainly ruled by foreign kings including the French Angevins and the Polish Jagiełłos. Under Mátyás Corvinus, a great Hungarian king, Buda became one of Europe's most impressive cities. The Habsburgs, while suppressing national insurrections, rebuilt Buda and Pest after the devastation left by the Turks, adding fine pieces of architecture.

LADISLAUS HUN BOHEM REX

1440–44
Władysław (Ulászló) I
of Poland

1272–90
Ladislas IV,
"the Cuman"

1270–72
István V

1301–5
Wenceslas II of Bohemia

1385–6
Charles II
of Durazzo

1386–95
Maria
(crowned)

1437–9
Albert of
Austria

1307–42
Charles I Robert
of Anjou

1541–66
Sultan Süleyman,
"the Magnificent"

1490–1516
Władysław
(Ulászló) II

1526–64
Ferdinand I

1200	1300	1400	1500
ÁRPÁDS	**ANGEVINS**	**JAGIEŁŁOS**	**OTTOMANS**
1200	1300	1400	1500

1290–1301
András III

1382–5
Maria (un-
crowned)

1445–57
Ladislas V,
"Posthumus"

1235–70
Béla IV

1458–90
Mátyás I, "Corvinus"

1516–26
Louis II

1526–40
János I
Zápolyai

1564–76
Maximilian I

1576–1608
Rudolf I

1342–82
Louis I (Lajos),
"the Great"

1305–7
Otto Wittelsbach
of Bavaria

1387–1437
Sigismund of Luxembourg
(initially as Maria's consort)

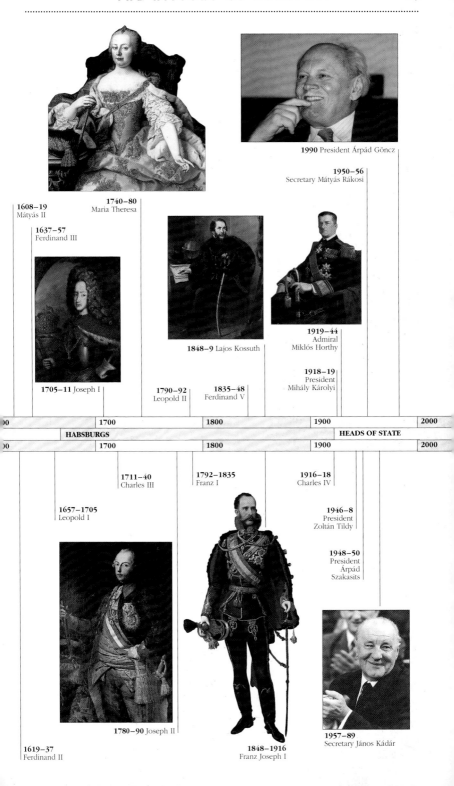

1990 President Árpád Göncz

1950–56
Secretary Mátyás Rákosi

1608–19
Mátyás II

1740–80
Maria Theresa

1637–57
Ferdinand III

1848–9 Lajos Kossuth

1919–44
Admiral
Miklós Horthy

1705–11 Joseph I

1790–92
Leopold II

1835–48
Ferdinand V

1918–19
President
Mihály Károlyi

)0	1700	1800	1900	2000
	HABSBURGS		**HEADS OF STATE**	
)0	1700	1800	1900	2000

1711–40
Charles III

1792–1835
Franz I

1916–18
Charles IV

1657–1705
Leopold I

1946–8
President
Zoltán Tildy

1948–50
President
Árpád
Szakasits

1780–90 Joseph II

1619–37
Ferdinand II

1848–1916
Franz Joseph I

1957–89
Secretary János Kádár

Early Settlers

TRACES OF SETTLEMENTS in the region by the Scythians and the Celtic Eravi date from around 400 BC onwards. In the 1st century AD, the Romans conquered the area as their province of Pannonia and soon established Aquincum *(see pp162–3)* within the limits of the modern city. Little evidence remains of the next rulers, the Huns, who were followed by the Goths and the Longobards. For nearly three centuries, starting in around AD 600, the Avars were pre-eminent. In 896, the Magyars swept into the region and laid claim to what would later become the Hungarian state.

Bronze Age vessel

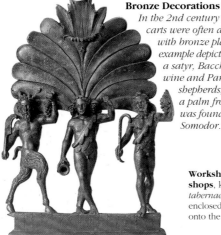

Bronze Decorations
In the 2nd century AD, Roman carts were often decorated with bronze plaques. This example depicts (from left): a satyr, Bacchus, god of wine and Pan, god of shepherds, under a palm frond. It was found in Somodor.

Workshops and shops, known as *tabernae*, were enclosed and faced onto the street.

The Sun God Mithras
The Persian god Mithras was adopted by the Eravi and his cult survived into the Roman period. This bronze image dates from 2nd–3rd centuries AD.

RECONSTRUCTION OF THE MACELLUM
This solidly built, square market hall was the focus for trade in the Roman town of Aquincum. At its centre was a courtyard with stalls, shops and workshops built around.

TIMELINE

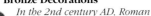

10,000 BC Remains dating from the Palaeolithic era indicate the existence of a settlement in the Remeda Cave in Buda.

Silver Celtic coin dating from the 4th century BC

c. 50 BC Celtic Eravi settlement on Gellért Hill *(see pp88–9)*

c. AD 100 The town of Aquincum is established by the Romans

800 BC Tombs with Iron Age urns at Pünkösdfürdő

400 BC Scythians in the region

10,000	5000	1000	AD 1

5000 BC Stone Age settlements in Talxina and along the Danube

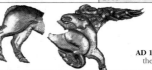

Scythian ornamental gold stag

AD 89 Romans establish a permanent army camp in modern-day Óbuda

AD 106 Aquincum becomes the capital of the Roman province of Lower Pannonia

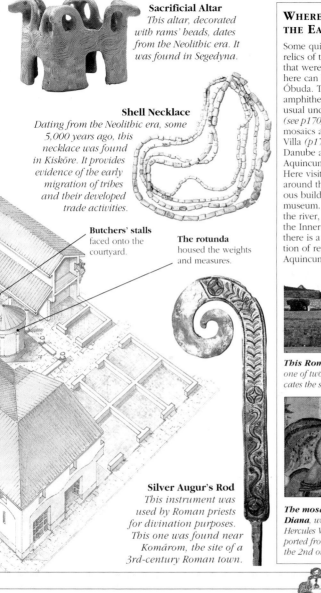

Sacrificial Altar
This altar, decorated with rams' heads, dates from the Neolithic era. It was found in Segedyna.

Shell Necklace
Dating from the Neolithic era, some 5,000 years ago, this necklace was found in Kiskőre. It provides evidence of the early migration of tribes and their developed trade activities.

Butchers' stalls
faced onto the courtyard.

The rotunda
housed the weights and measures.

Silver Augur's Rod
This instrument was used by Roman priests for divination purposes. This one was found near Komárom, the site of a 3rd-century Roman town.

WHERE TO SEE THE EARLY CITY

Some quite considerable relics of the Roman legions that were once stationed here can be seen in modern Óbuda. The remains of an amphitheatre are near an un-usual underground museum *(see p170)*, while magnificent mosaics adorn the Hercules Villa *(p171)*. Further up the Danube are the ruins of Aquincum itself *(pp162–3)*. Here visitors can wander around the remains of vari-ous buildings and enter a museum. On the Pest side of the river, just to the north of the Inner City Parish Church, there is a small, open-air sec-tion of remains from Contra Aquincum *(p122)*.

This Roman amphitheatre, one of two in Aquincum, indi-cates the status of the town.

The mosaic of Hercules and Diana, which survives at the Hercules Villa, was probably im-ported from Alexandria during the 2nd or 3rd century AD.

c. 140–60 Two amphi-theatres are built to serve Aquincum's growing population

409 The Huns, under Attila, conquer Aquincum

c. 600–896 The Avars rule the region

Ornate earring from the 7th century AD

200	400	600	800

194 Aquincum is promoted to the status of a Roman colony

294 Contra Aquincum is founded on the eastern bank of the Danube

453 Collapse of the Huns' domination

Carving of the Sun God Mithras

896 Magyar (Hungarian) tribes take over Pannonia

The Árpád Dynasty

Hair clasp from the 9th century

AFTER A LONG JOURNEY beginning in the Urals region in Russia, nomadic tribes of Magyars eventually settled in Pannonia in AD 896. Following a period of internal disputes, the tribes made a blood-bonded alliance and chose one leader, Árpád. While Géza I made contact with missionaries, it was his son, István I, who accepted Christianity for his people. Their first crowned king, István organized the state according to the European, feudal model. Initially under the Árpáds, Esztergom *(see p164)* was the country's capital and later Székesfehérvár. The development of Buda, Pest and Óbuda began in the second half of the 12th century, but was interrupted by the Mongol invasion of 1241.

EXTENT OF THE CITY
⬛ *1300*   ☐ *Today*

Christ is depicted twice in the middle section of the coat; in each case He is larger than the surrounding figures.

Trinity of Hungarian Saints
The figures of three saints, King István, his son Emeric and Bishop Gellért, are presented on this colourful triptych in the Chapel of St Emeric in Mátyás Church (see pp82–3).

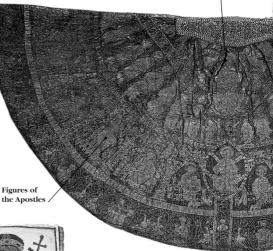

Figures of the Apostles

Prince Géza
Géza I, the father of King István, is represented on an enamel plaque decorating the Crown of the Árpáds.

CORONATION COAT
This silk coronation coat was made in 1031 for the Árpád kings. It has a pearl-beaded collar and is embroidered with the figures of Christ, Mary, the Apostles and the Prophets.

TIMELINE

c.900 Árpád settles on Csepel Island (in modern-day Budapest) and his brother Kurszán in Óbuda

Sword of an Árpád king

850	900	950	1000	1050

973 Prince Géza invites missionaries into the region

Sculpture of King István I by Imre Varga

1001 Coronation of István (Stephen) I

1046 Revolt by pagans and the martyr's death of Bishop Gellért, thrown in a barrel into the Danube

Crown of the Árpáds
This gold crown, ornamented with jewels, pearls and enamel, was created by joining two existing crowns. The lower, Byzantine one was known as the "Greek crown" and the upper one as the "Latin crown".

Bone artifacts
Bone items such as shepherds' staffs often had carved handles.

Figures of the Prophets

King István's coin
The first Hungarian coin, the denar, *was produced soon after AD 1000, during King István's reign.*

Tympanum
This 11th-century church tympanum, from Gyulafehérvár in modern Romania, is in the Hungarian National Gallery (see pp74–7).

WHERE TO SEE THE MEDIEVAL CITY

Only a few monuments survive from the Middle Ages. Among the notable ones that still remain are the crypts in Mátyás Church *(see pp82–3)*, and the elevations and cellars of some historic houses in the Castle District (a few of which are now converted into wine bars). The reconstructed lower chambers of the Royal Palace *(pp70–71)* and parts of its fortifications also date from the medieval era.

This 19th-century copy of the Romanesque Ják Chapel (see p143) reveals how the Árpáds adopted European styles.

Gothic niches can be seen by the entrances to many houses in the Old Town (see pp78–9).

1188 Béla III moves his headquarters to Óbuda and sets out on Frederick Barbarossa's crusade

1222 "Golden Bull" grants nobility privileges including tax exemption

1241 Mongol invasion

1247 Béla IV builds castle in Buda, which becomes capital of Hungary

1267 Béla IV announces new "Golden Bull"

1100	1150	1200	1250	1300

Magyar belt buckle dating from the 10th century

1244 The citizens of Pest are granted civic rights

1255 The citizens of Buda get civic rights

1301 Death of King András III, last king of the Árpád dynasty

Gothic and Renaissance Eras

Tabernacle of the Inner City Parish Church

As a result of the efforts of the Angevins and Sigismund of Luxembourg, the Gothic style reached Buda in the 14th century. Buda's palace and the summer palace in Visegrád were both extensively rebuilt. Shortly after defeat by the Turks at Varna, Hungary regained control of Belgrade and, for a while at least, halted their invasion. Mátyás Corvinus, the son of hetman János Hunyadi, the victor of Belgrade, became king. Under Mátyás's rule Hungary was turned into the greatest monarchy of Middle Europe, and, as a result of his marriage to Beatrice, a Neapolitan princess, the Renaissance began to blossom in the country.

EXTENT OF THE CITY

 c. 1480   ☐ Today

Castellan Ferenc Sárffy was the commander of Győr Castle.

Hungarian soldier

Illuminated letter from the Philostratus Codex
This illuminated letter depicts King Mátyás I after he took Vienna. Part of his own library, it is today housed in the Széchenyi National Library (see p72).

Royal Medallion
An unknown master from Lombardy commemorated King Mátyás I in this marble silhouette dating from the 1480s.

Gold Seal
This gold seal, which belonged to King Mátyás I, is indicative of the affluence enjoyed by Hungary while he was on the throne.

Ulrik Czettrich, an officer of the royal household, discovered the body of Louis II on the marshy bank of the Csele river.

TIMELINE

1355 Óbuda's citizens gain civic rights	**1370** Louis I enters a political union and becomes king of Poland	**1385** Sigismund of Luxembourg marries Maria	
Ciborium dating from the 14th century		**1395** University established in Óbuda	
1350	**1375**	**1400**	**1425**
		1387–1437 Rule of Sigismund of Luxembourg. He enlarges the Royal Palace *(see pp70–71)*	
1342 Louis I, "the Great", becomes king			
1335 Treaty on co-operation and succession signed by the kings of Hungary, Poland and Czechoslovakia in Visegrád		**1382** After death of Louis I, one daughter, Maria, becomes queen of Hungary and another, Jadwiga, queen of Poland	

Wine Cups
This pair of elaborate Renaissance wine cups, dating from the 16th century, is designed to fit together to form a covered receptacle.

Crest of King Mátyás Corvinus
Inscribed with the date 1470, this crest commemorates the building of significant additions to Mátyás Church (see pp82–3), which was then renamed after the king.

King Louis II

Hungarian knight

WHERE TO SEE THE GOTHIC AND RENAISSANCE CITY

The full bloom of the Gothic period took place in Hungary in the 14th century. Mátyás Church *(see pp82–3)* has portals that survive from this era. Renaissance art reached Hungary thanks to Italian masters brought by Mátyás's second wife, Beatrice. Both the Royal Palace *(pp70–71)* and the summer palace at Visegrád *(p164)* were outstanding pieces of Renaissance architecture. Since the storming of Buda by the Turks, only a few remnants of the former splendour have remained.

A royal chamber from the period of Angevin rule can be seen in the Budapest History Museum (see p72).

This portal of Mátyás Church dates from the 14th century. In the 19th century, a Neo-Gothic porch was built around it.

THE DISCOVERY OF LOUIS II'S BODY
At the Battle of Mohács, on 29 August 1526, King Louis II lost his life together with thousands of Hungarian and Polish knights. The tragic scene of the finding of his body was recreated by Bertalan Székely in 1859.

1440 Władysław III of Poland is Władysław I of Hungary

1444 Władysław I is killed during the Battle of Varna

1456 Victory over Turks at the Battle of Belgrade

1458–1490 Reign of Mátyás Corvinus

1473 *Chronica Hungarorum*, the first book to be published in Hungary, is printed by András Hess

1478 Law is passed threatening landlords who fail to maintain their buildings with dispossession

1514 Peasant revolt under György Dózsa

Sword of Władysław II

1526 Defeat by the Turks at the Battle of Mohács. King Louis II perishes during the fighting

Shield of soldier in the army of Mátyás Corvinus

1450	1475	1500	1525	1550

The Turkish Occupation

Ottoman plate

AFTER THE BATTLE OF MOHÁCS, the Turks razed Buda, but they temporarily turned their attention elsewhere and did not return to occupy it until 1541. When they then moved into the Royal Palace *(see pp70–71)*, Buda became the capital of Ottoman Hungary, while eastern Hungary and Transylvania were feudal suzerains. The Ottomans soon converted the city's churches, including Mátyás Church, into mosques and also built numerous Turkish baths *(see pp50–53)*. The Habsburgs tried relentlessly to recover Buda during this period. Their sieges destroyed the city progressively and when, in 1686, the Christian armies eventually recovered it the scene was one of devastation.

EXTENT OF THE CITY

☐ *1630*   ☐ *Today*

Turkish fortress on Gellért Hill

The Rudas and Rác Baths

The Liberation of Buda in 1686
After a bloody siege, the Christian army, led by Prince Eugene of Savoy, entered Buda and liberated it from the Turks. This painting by Gyula Benczúr, dating from 1896, depicts the event.

Ottoman Tombstones
A few inscribed Ottoman tombstones, topped by distinctive turbans, remain to this day in Tabán (see p94).

PEST AND BUDA IN 1617

Georgius Hurnagel's copperplate print shows the heavily-fortified towns of Pest and Buda in a period when much of Hungary was firmly under Turkish rule.

TIMELINE

1526–41 Turks conquer Buda on three occasions	**1541–66** Reign of Sultan Süleyman I, "the Magnificent", who considered himself the Turkish king of Hungary	**1602–3** Austrians, led by General Herman Russworm, fail in attempts to storm Pest and Buda
1529 János I Zápolyai, the Hungarian monarch, pays homage to Sultan Süleyman I		

1525	1545	1565	1585	1605

1530–40 János I Zápolyai rebuilds Buda

1542 The Austrians lay siege to Buda

Austrian siege of Buda

1594 Bálint Balassi, Hungary's first great lyric poet, is killed taking part in a battle against the Turks at Esztergom *(see p164)*

Campaign Tent
Taken during the siege of Vienna in 1683, this Turkish leader's tent is decorated with appliqué work. It is on show in the Hungarian National Museum (see pp130–33).

Mátyás Church *(see pp82–3)* was converted into a mosque.

Ottoman Coat
This 16th-century leather coat was supposedly taken from the battlefield of Mohács (see p25).

Ottoman Jug
Dating from the 17th century, this copper vessel was found in Buda during the reconstruction of the Royal Palace (see pp70–71).

WHERE TO SEE THE TURKISH CITY

Almost all Turkish buildings were razed by their successors, the Habsburgs, during or after the recapture of the city. Churches which the Turks had used as mosques were converted back again, although some *mihrabs*, the niches pointing towards Mecca, were left. These can be seen in the Inner City Parish Church *(see pp124–5)* and in the Capuchin Church *(p100)*. Among the few wonderful examples of classical Ottoman architecture to survive are the Rudas, Rác *(p95)* and Király Baths, and the Tomb of Gül Baba, a Turkish dervish *(p101)*.

The Király Baths, *built in the 16th century by Arshlan Pasha, remain an impressive Ottoman monument (see p101).*

The Rudas Baths *have an original Turkish dome covering their central chamber (see p93).*

Ottoman tablet with calligraphy

1634 György I Rákóczi, prince of Transylvania, joins an anti-Habsburg alliance with France and Sweden

1684 Start of ultimately successful siege of Buda by the Austrians

Viennese sword dating from the 17th century

1625	1645	1665	1685	

1624 Signing of the Treaty of Vienna

1648 Death of György I Rákóczi

Gold five-ducat coin from 1603, showing the prince of Transylvania's crest

1686 Christian troops enter Buda. The end of Turkish rule in Hungary

Habsburg Rule

Order created by Maria Theresa

IN ORDER TO GAIN CONTROL of Hungary, the Habsburgs encouraged foreign settlers, particularly Germans, to move into the country. This policy led to a national uprising in 1703–11, led by the prince of Transylvania, Ferenc II Rákóczi. Only in the second half of the 18th century, particularly under Empress Maria Theresa, did the reconstruction of Buda, Óbuda and Pest begin in earnest. This was accompanied by economic development and a further increase in the country's population. The university at Nagyszombat (now Trnava in the Slovak Republic) moved to Buda in 1777, and subsequently to Pest in 1784, and was an important factor in their expansion.

EXTENT OF THE CITY

☐ *1770*   ☐ *Today*

Maria Theresa holds the infant Joseph, the successor to her throne.

The Return of the Crown to Buda *(1790)*
A vast ceremonial procession of commissioners marked the arrival in Hungary of royal insignias from Vienna, a sign of peace between the two countries.

Ferenc II Rákóczi
This fine portrait by Ádám Mányoki depicts Ferenc II Rákóczi, the leader of the national uprising of 1703–11 and a figure much loved by the Hungarian people.

"VITAM ET SANGUINEM"
In 1741, the Hungarian states swore on "life and blood" their loyalty to the Habsburg Empress Maria Theresa. This copperplate print by Joseph Szentpetery depicts the scene of the oath-taking.

TIMELINE

1687 Under Austrian pressure, the Hungarian parliament gives up its right to elect a king and accedes to the inheritance of the throne by the Habsburgs	**1702** The Jesuits open a college and theological seminary	
	1703 The Prince of Transylvania, Ferenc II Rákóczi, leads a rebellion by the Hungarians against the Habsburgs	**1729** The start of the reconstruction of Pest's suburbs

1690	1705	1720	1735

1689 Bubonic plague devastates the population of Buda and Pest	**1711** Suppression of Rákóczi's rebellion; a second bubonic plague decimates the city	**1724** The population of Buda and Pest reaches 12,000 people
Royal postal carriage		**1723** Great Fire of Buda

Triple-jug of the Andrássy family
These silver jugs are joined by a miniature of the castle belonging to the Andrássy family, at what is now Krásna Hůrka in the Slovak Republic.

Hungarian aristocrats swear on their lives to protect Maria Theresa's throne.

Dress *(c. 1750)*
This dress, typical of Hungarian style with its corset which was tightened by golden cords, was worn by a lady from the noble Majtényi family.

Ferenc II Rákóczi's Chair
Richly upholstered, this graceful 18th-century chair from Regéc Castle is typical of the style of the period.

WHERE TO SEE THE HABSBURG CITY

Having taken Buda and Pest from the Turks in the late 17th century, the Habsburgs set about rebuilding them in the 18th century, mainly in the Baroque style. Famous buildings from this era include the Municipal Council Offices, St Anne's Church *(see pp102–3)*, St Elizabeth's Church *(p101)* and the University Church *(p139)*.

St Anne's Church, *which was built between 1740–1805, astonishes visitors with its magnificent Baroque interior.*

The Municipal Council Offices *in the heart of Pest have a portico decorated with allegorical figures by Johann Christoph Mader (see p127).*

1745–71 Building of the Habsburg Royal Palace

The magnificent Habsburg Royal Palace

1788 First Hungarian newspaper, *Magyar Merkurius*, begins printing

1778 Roman remains are discovered in Óbuda

A hussar, or soldier

1750	1765	1780	1795

1752 A regular postal service operates between Buda and Vienna

1746–57 Construction of the Zichy Palace in Óbuda *(see p171)*

1766 A floating bridge links Buda and Pest

1777 University moves from Nagyszombat to Buda; later relocates to Pest

1792 Convocation of parliament and the coronation of Franz I

1784 Establishment of Ferenc Goldberger's textile factory in Óbuda

National Revival and the "Springtime of Revolutions"

Hungarian crest

THE DYNAMIC ECONOMIC development of Buda and Pest began at the start of the 19th century. Pest, in particular, benefited from favourable circumstances for the grain trade and became, in the Napoleonic Wars, an important centre for the Habsburg monarchy. A national revival and rekindling of cultural life took place after the Napoleonic Wars. The Hungarian National Museum and many other public and private buildings were built at this time. Yet, Hungarian reformers were hampered by the Viennese royal court and an uprising erupted in the spring of 1848. This rebellion was suppressed by the Habsburgs, with the help of the Russian army, and a period of absolutism followed.

EXTENT OF THE CITY

▨ *1848*   ☐ *Today*

Count György Andrássy, offered 10,000 forints towards the building of the Hungarian Academy of Sciences.

The Advance of the Hussars
In this watercolour, painted in 1850, Mór Than depicts fighting in the Battle of Tápióbicske of 1849. The Hungarian side was led by a Polish general, Henryk Dembiński.

The Great Flood
This bas-relief, made by Barnabás Holló in 1900, shows a heroic rescue by Count Miklós Wesselényi during the Great Flood of 1838.

THE FOUNDING OF THE ACADEMY

In 1825, István Széchenyi put up 60,000 forints towards the building of Hungarian Academy of Sciences *(see p114)*, a move which led to a national effort to collect funds for it. Barnabás Holló created this bas-relief depicting the major donors.

TIMELINE

1802 Count Ferenc Széchenyi donates collections which will form the basis for Széchenyi National Library *(see p72)* and Hungarian National Museum *(see pp130–33)*	**1809** Royal court moves from Vienna to Buda as Napoleon advances. Despite his offer of Hungarian independence, the Hungarians back the Habsburgs	**1817** First steamboat sails on Danube in the environs of Buda and Pest

1800	1805	1810	1815	1820

1808 Establishment of the Embellishment Commission, led by Governor Archduke Joseph

Boats on the Dan

Lajos Batthyány Eternal Flame

This lamp, designed by Móric Pogány, has burnt since 1926 in Liberty Square (see p110). It was there that the Austrians shot Lajos Batthyány, the first prime minister of liberated Hungary, on 6 October 1849.

Count István Széchenyi, an energetic force for change, is regarded as the one of the greatest Hungarians.

National Song

The 1848 uprising was sparked on 15 March when Sándor Petőfi recited his poem, Nemzeti Dal *(National Song), outside the Hungarian National Museum.*

WHERE TO SEE THE NEO-CLASSICAL CITY

In the early 19th century, the Embellishment Commission, set up by Archduke Joseph and led by architect János Hild, prepared a plan for the development of Pest in which its centre was redesigned on a pattern of concentric streets. Monumental Neo-Classical buildings were built here and to this day they form the heart and the character of this area. Structures to look for in particular include the Hungarian National Museum, the Chain Bridge and several houses located on Jószef Nádor Square *(see p126)*.

György Károlyi

*The **Hungarian National Museum**, which was built in 1836–46, is among Hungary's finest examples of Neo-Classical architecture (see pp74–7).*

*The **Chain Bridge**, the first permanent bridge over the Danube, was built by Adam Clark in 1839–49 (see p63).*

Buda and Pest in 1838

Seen here in the year before the construction of the Chain Bridge, the Danube was an important means of transport.

1825–48 Period of major projects: establishment of the Hungarian Academy of Sciences, Hungarian National Museum and National Theatre	*Poet Sándor Petőfi (1823–49)*	**1840** Language Act: Hungarian takes over from Latin as the official language of the nation	**1847** Death of Archduke Joseph, emperor's governor	**15 March 1848** Uprising begins
1825	**1830**	**1835**	**1840**	**1845**
	1830 István Széchenyi publishes his book, *On Credit*. It is seen as the manifesto for the fight for modern Hungary	*The Great Flood* **1838** Catastrophic Great Flood results in destruction of half of Pest's buildings	**1846** First railway line in the city, linking Pest and Vác	**1849** After stout resistance, the Russian army, under the command of General Ivan Paskievicz, suppresses uprising

Compromise and the Unification of Budapest

Maria Theresa

AFTER SUFFERING A DEFEAT by Prussia in 1866, the Habsburgs realized the necessity of reaching an agreement with Hungary and the Compromise brokered in 1867 proved to be of tremendous importance for the future of Buda and Pest. The option of uniting the two cities had been considered since the opening of the Chain Bridge in 1849. It eventually came about in 1873 and Budapest soon found itself among Europe's fastest growing metropolises. In 1896, Városliget was the focal point for Hungary's Millennium Celebrations *(see p142)*.

EXTENT OF THE CITY
☐ *1873*   ☐ *Today*

The Citadel *(see p92)* on Gellért Hill

Castle District

Hungarian Wine Cup
This 19th-century wine cup is embellished with the Hungarian crest, which incorporates the Crown of the Árpáds (see p23).

Today's Boráros tér, where goods were once traded.

Ferenc Deák
(1803–76)
A great statesman, Deák was an advocate of moderate reforms. He argued persuasively in favour of accepting the Compromise reached with the Habsburgs in 1867.

Decorative Pipe *(1896).*
Made in the year of Hungary's Millennium Celebrations, this pipe of "heavenly peace" includes figures of the Árpád kings and Emperor Franz Joseph.

TIMELINE

1854 Martial law ends five years after 1848–9 uprising

1856 Tunnel *(see p100)* built by Adam Clark under Castle Hill
Entrance to the Tunnel

1875 Opening of the Franz Liszt Academy of Music *(see p129)*, with the composer as its principal

1850	1860	1870	1880

1859 Synagogue on Dohány utca *(see p134)* completed

1864 Opening of the Great Market Hall *(see p203)*

1873 The unification of Buda, Óbuda and Pest as one city, with a total of 300,000 inhabitants

1867 Compromise with Austria, giving Hungary independence in its internal affairs. Creation of the Dual Monarchy; Emperor Franz Joseph accepts the Hungarian crown

Monument to Hungarian Soldiers Killed in World War I
This bas-relief, by János Istók, commemorates the dead of World War I, in which Hungary fought on the German side. It is located next to the main entrance to the Servite Church (see p128).

"Handcuff" Bracelet
Following the defeat of the national uprising of 1848–9, Hungarians sought to symbolize their oppression even in pieces of jewellery.

WHERE TO SEE THE HISTORICIST CITY

Historicism had a profound influence on the form of the rapidly developing metropolis at this time. A wonderful example of the style is the Hungarian Academy of Sciences. Among others are Parliament *(see pp108–9),* St Stephen's Basilica *(pp116–17),* the Museum of Fine Arts *(pp146–7),* the New York Palace *(p129)* and many of the buildings that stand on Andrássy Street *(p144).*

The Hungarian Academy of Sciences is housed in this fine Neo-Renaissance palace dating from 1864 (see p114).

St Stephen's Basilica was built over a period of 60 years by three architects. It was finished in 1905 (see pp116–17).

TRADING ON THE PEST EMBANKMENT
Completed in 1887, this painting by Antal Ligeti shows the Pest embankment at a time when the city was booming. Manufactured goods and grain were sent along the Danube for sale in Germany and the Balkans.

1894 Body of Lajos Kossuth *(see p106)* is returned from Turin	**1904** Grand opening of Parliament *(see pp108–9)*	*Congress Hall in Parliament*	**1916** Franz Joseph dies and Charles IV becomes king of Hungary
1890	**1900**	**1910**	**1920**
1896 First metro line and several museums opened	**1909** Airport opened in Rákos, now Kőbánya — **1900** With a population of 773,000, Budapest is Europe's fastest growing city	**1914** Hungary enters World War I on the German side	**1918** Abdication of Charles IV marks end of the Austro-Hungarian Empire

Modern Budapest

Poster for Unicum liqueur *(see p193)*

1944 Efforts to withdraw from World War II end with German troops entering the country. A ghetto is established in Budapest and the extermination of Hungarian Jews begins. As the Russian army approaches the city, all bridges across the Danube are blown up

HUNGARY PAID A HIGH price for its alliances first with Austria and later with Nazi Germany. Following defeat in both World Wars, the country had lost a large portion of its territory. As a result of the Yalta Agreement of 1945, it then found itself within the Soviet-controlled zone of Europe. Stalinism took on a particularly ruthless form here and led to the 1956 Uprising, which was brutally put down by Soviet tanks on the streets of Budapest. Efforts towards reform, undertaken by János Kádár, brought some changes but political opposition was not tolerated. In 1989, the Communists were ousted and Hungary at last regained control of its own affairs.

1945 After a siege lasting six weeks, the Russian army takes Budapest

1946 Proclamation of Republic of Hungary. Smallholders' Party wins elections

1947 After falsification of election results, Communists control the whole country

1919 Communists take over government and declare the Hungarian Soviet Republic

1941 Hungary enters World War II on Germany's side

1939 Hungary neutral at beginning of World War II. Accepts refugees after capitulation of Poland

1957 János Kádár is first secretary of Hungarian Socialist Workers' Party

1949 Stalinist terror prevails. Cardinal Mindszenty *(see p111)* goes on trial. László Rajk, secret police chief, sentenced to death by Moscow loyalists

1922 Reopening of the State Opera House *(see pp118–19)* after World War I

1928 Budapest is a free port on Danube

1937 Sixth and last visit of author Thomas Mann

1920	1930	1940	1950

1920	1930	1940	1950

1935 Tabán *(see p94)* levelled and transformed into a park

1938 Eucharistic Congress

1953 The national football team beats England 6–3 at Wembley

1925 Radio Budapest broadcasts its first programme

1948 Mátyás Rákosi leads Hungarian Socialist Workers' Party, created by Communists

1919 Admiral Miklós Horthy enters Budapest; many killed in the period of "White Terror". Horthy becomes regent

1945–1 August 1946 Monetary reform. Banknotes valued at one billion pengő are printed during rampant inflation. There is not enough room for all the zeros to be shown on the notes

1918 Democratic revolution; Hungary declared a republic. Mihály Károlyi selected as the country's first president

1956 National uprising is suppressed through Soviet intervention

1958 The leader of the 1956 Uprising, Prime Minister Imre Nagy, is executed

1960–66 Rebuilding of Castle District *(see pp68–85),* including Royal Palace, and the Danube bridges

1964 The Elizabeth Bridge *(see p63)* reopens to traffic, having been totally reconstructed

October 1989 Republic of Hungary is proclaimed once more. The national emblem is changed

September 1989 Hungary opens its borders to allow refugees to flee from East Germany to the West

February 1989 Round-table talks between opposition parties and ruling socialist government

1981 Director István Szabo receives an Oscar for his film *Mefisto*

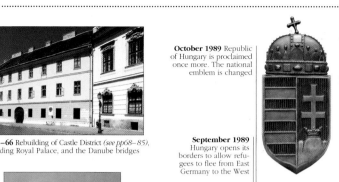

1991 Warsaw Pact is dissolved. Russian army leaves Hungary

1994 Second free elections are won by Socialist Hungarian Party. Coalition government led by Gyula Horn

1998 Third free elections won by Viktor Orbán of the Citizens' Party

	1970	1980	1990	2000

	1970	1980	1990	2000

1968 Introduction of new economic system known as "goulash-Communism"

1987 UNESCO places the historic centre of Budapest on its list of world monuments

June 1989 Ceremonial funeral for Imre Nagy and rehabilitation for other leaders of 1956 Uprising

1990 The Democratic Hungarian Forum wins free elections. József Antall becomes the first prime minister to be elected in a democratic process; Árpád Göncz is elected president

1993 Pope John Paul II visits Hungary

1970 Opening of a new metro line

1991 Václav Havel, József Antall and Lech Walesa sign an agreement in Visegrád *(see p164)* between Czechoslovakia, Hungary and Poland

BUDAPEST AT A GLANCE

OFTEN DESCRIBED as the "Little Paris of Middle Europe", Budapest is famous not only for the monuments reflecting its own 1,000-year-old culture, but also for the relics of others who settled here. Remains from both Roman occupation, and, much later, rule by the Turks can still be seen in the city. After Turkish rule, union with Austria had a particular influence on the city's form and style. Descriptions of nearly 150 places of interest can be found in the *Area by Area* section of the book. However, to help you make the most of your stay, the following 20 pages are a guide to the best Budapest has to offer. Museums and galleries, churches and synagogues, palaces and historic buildings, baths and pools are presented, together with the influence of Secession in the city. Each sight is is cross-referenced to its main entry. Below are the sights not to be missed.

BUDAPEST'S TOP TEN SIGHTS

Gellért Monument
See p93.

Zoo
See pp150–51.

Váci Street
See p127.

Parliament
See pp108–9.

National Museum
See pp130–33.

State Opera House
See pp118–19.

Margaret Island
See pp172–3.

Chain Bridge
See p62.

Mátyás Church
See pp82–3.

National Gallery
See pp74–7.

◁ **The Neo-Renaissance façade of the City Council Chamber** *(see p138)* in the centre of Pest

Budapest's Best: Museums and Galleries

UNLIKE MANY OTHER European cities – such as
Paris with the Louvre and Madrid with the
Prado – Budapest does not have a museum
founded from a royal treasury because Hungary
was for so long ruled by foreign powers. In
the early 19th century, however, the modern
aristocracy, backed by an increasingly affluent
middle class, began to take an interest in pre-
serving historic objects for the nation. Today,
there are over 60 museums and galleries in
Budapest, ranging from those with collections
of international significance to others of much
more local interest. For more information on
museums and galleries see pages 40–41.

Museum of Military History
*This museum has interesting
displays illustrating the history of
Hungarian weaponry.*

**Hungarian
National Gallery**
*The Hungarian art
displayed here dates
from the Middle Ages
right through to the
20th century. The
Yawning Journeyman
(1868), by the great
Mihály Munkácsy, is
among the highlights
of the collection.*

*North of
the Castle*

DANUBE

Castle District

Budapest History Museum
*This Gothic work is one
of the medieval treasures
of the Budapest History
Museum. The oldest ex-
hibits are located in the
original, lower-floor
rooms of the Renais-
sance Royal Palace.*

*Gellért Hill
and Tabán*

| 0 metres | 500 |
| 0 yards | 500 |

**Semmelweis Museum of
Medical History**
*Doctor Ignác Semmelweis,
famous for his discovery of the cure for
puerperal fever, was born in 1818 in the
house where the museum is now situated.*

Ethnographical Museum

Among the exhibits at this museum illustrating the material culture of the Hungarians is this jug, dating from 1864, made by György Mantl. There are also impressive displays concerning tribal societies in other parts of the world.

Museum of Fine Arts

The wonderful Portrait of a Man *(c.1565), by Paolo Veronese, is one of many Old Masters in this splendid collection of paintings and sculpture.*

Around Parliament

Around Városliget

Central Pest

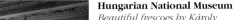

Jewish Museum

Located in several rooms in the Great Synagogue, this museum covers the Holocaust in this country and displays religious objects.

Hungarian National Museum

Beautiful frescoes by Károly Lotz and Mór Than decorate the elegant staircase of Budapest's oldest museum.

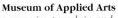

Museum of Applied Arts

Precious ceramics, porcelain and furnishings are housed in a building that is itself a work of art, surmounted by a magnificent, oriental-style dome.

Exploring the Museums and Galleries

Crest of the Museum of Commerce

MOST OF the city's museums and galleries are located in historic buildings. These include the spacious chambers of the restored Royal Palace, which in the 1970s and 1980s were designated as the premises of several museums, including the Hungarian National Gallery. The largest museums – including the Hungarian National Museum and Budapest History Museum – also stage temporary exhibitions that are popular with both locals and tourists.

Sculpture of Imre Varga at the gallery named after him *(see p171)*

HUNGARIAN PAINTINGS AND SCULPTURE

THERE ARE TWO important venues that should be on the itinerary of anyone interested in viewing the finest examples of Hungarian art.

At the **Hungarian National Gallery**, seven chronological sections present paintings and sculpture dating from the Middle Ages up until modern times. The sequence begins in the Lapidarium, where fragments of recovered medieval stone sculptures from the castles of the first Hungarian kings are exhibited.

As a rule, very few examples of Gothic and Renaissance art survive in Budapest because of the pillage inflicted by the Turks during their rule. However, a fine collection of altar retables from the 15th and 16th centuries are on display

in the Hungarian National Gallery. In the 19th century, Hungarian painting developed and flourished, at the same time reflecting all the major international modern art movements. The Hungarian style can be seen particularly in the works of Pál Szinyei-Merse, Mihály Munkácsy and László Paál. For sculpture, meanwhile, the main names to look out for are István Ferenczy, Zsigmond Kisfaludi Stróbl and Imre Varga.

It is portraits, rather than paintings and sculpture, that are shown at the **Hungarian National Museum**. These provide a fascinating insight into the country's history.

The **Vasarely Museum** has a collection of 300 works by Hungarian-born artist Victor Vasarely. He moved to Paris in 1930 and became famous as one of the main exponents of the Op Art movement.

EUROPEAN PAINTINGS AND SCULPTURE

MASTERPIECES BY the finest European artists, from medieval times to the modern day, are also divided between two museums in Budapest.

The **Museum of Fine Arts** has a magnificent collection of Italian paintings, dating from the 14th century up to the Baroque period, by masters such as Titian, Antonio Correggio, Paolo Veronese, Giambattista Tiepolo and Jacopo Tintoretto. However, it is the *Esterházy Madonna* (1508) by Raphael, that is the jewel of the Italian collection. Equally splendid is the exhibition of Spanish paintings, which is one of the largest in the world after that of the Prado in Madrid. Works by Goya include *The Water Seller* (c.1810). There are seven canvases by El Greco and others by Francisco de Zurbarán and Bartolomé Esteban Murillo. Other galleries within the museum represent artists of the Netherlands and Germany, as well as British, French and Flemish masters. The museum also owns more than 100,000 drawings and engravings by the Old Masters, while its modern art collection includes some notable works.

Modern European paintings can also be viewed in the **Ludwig Collection**. All the canvases belong to the Peter Ludwig Foundation based in Germany. Highly prized works here include two paintings by Pablo Picasso, *Mother and Child* and *Musketeer*.

Pablo Picasso's *Musketeer* (1967), in the Ludwig Collection

Interior of the Jewish Museum, located in the Great Synagogue

HISTORY

THE HISTORY of Budapest, and that of Hungary as a whole, is illustrated in several museums. Relics from the Roman era can be found at the **Aquincum Museum** and at a handful of museums, including the **Roman Camp Museum**, in Óbuda.

The most important national historic treasures are housed in the **Hungarian National Museum**. Royal insignia, crowns and coronation robes dating back to the 11th century are included in the collection.

Medieval seals and Gothic statuary are among the exhibits at **Budapest History Museum**. At the **Museum of Military History**, displays chart various Hungarian struggles for liberty, including the 1956 Uprising *(see p34)*.

The **Jewish Museum** has a room covering the Holocaust, as well as many ritual objects. The collection of the **Lutheran Museum**, situated next to the Lutheran Church, includes a copy of Martin Luther's will.

MUSIC

TWO OF the museums featured in this book are dedicated to internationally re-nowned composers: the **Franz Liszt Museum** and the **Zoltán Kodály Museum**. In each case, the apartment where the composer

Beer mug at the Lutheran Museum

lived and worked is the setting, and visitors can see the musical instruments that they played, scores, photographs and correspondence.

A more general view of Hungarian music is on offer at the **Museum of Musical History**, located in a Baroque palace. Displays feature the development of instruments, folk music and the musical scene of the 18th and 19th centuries; a special section is dedicated to Béla Bartók.

ETHNOGRAPHY AND ORIENTAL CRAFTS

LAVISH FOLK costumes, as well as many other everyday items that belonged to the people of the region, can be viewed in the beautiful interiors of the **Ethnographical Museum**. The museum also has a section that focuses on the primitive tribes of Africa, America and, particularly, Asia. It is in Asia that the Hungarians seek their roots as it is from there that the Magyars are thought to have come.

This fascination with the Orient has led to the foundation of two other museums displaying Eastern artifacts. The **György Rath Museum** has items such as fans and combs from China and Japan, while the **Ferenc Hopp Museum** has assorted Indian objects.

Roling pin at the Museum of Commerce

DECORATIVE ARTS

HOUSED IN an extraordinary building designed by Ödön Lechner *(see p56)*, the **Museum of Applied Arts** gives an impressive overview of the development of crafts from the Middle Ages onwards. Meissen porcelain is exhibited alongside oriental carpets and Hungarian pieces. The display relating to the Secession *(see pp54–7)* is striking and there are usually also temporary shows.

The decorative arts, paintings and architectural plans that are gathered at the **Kiscelli Museum** give a flavour of life in Budapest in the 18th and 19th centuries. Other exhibits in this varied museum include an antique printing press.

SPECIALIST MUSEUMS

ANYONE INTERESTED in the history of gastronomy should head for one of Budapest's more unusual museums, the **Museum of Commerce and Catering**. It boasts a varied selection of exhibits connected with the food trade.

The **Semmelweis Museum of Medical History** explores the work of a doctor called Ignác Semmelweis, who discovered the cure for puerperal fever. This affliction had previously been a serious threat for women who had recently given birth. The **Golden Eagle Pharmacy Museum** is situated in a building that first opened as a pharmacy in 1681. Many original fixtures are intact and pharmaceutical exhibits are displayed.

Railway enthusiasts will appreciate the **Transport Museum** with its enormous collection of model trains.

Budapest's Best: Churches and Synagogues

THERE ARE VERY FEW medieval and Renaissance churches still standing in Budapest. This is mainly due to the fact that the Turks, during their 150-year rule, turned all churches into mosques, which were later destroyed during the attacks on Buda and Pest by the Christians. The reconstruction of old churches and the building of new ones started in the late 17th century, hence the prevalence of Baroque and Neo-Classical styles.

Capuchin Church
Two Turkish windows remain from the time when this church was used as a mosque, alongside fragments of its medieval walls.

St Anne's Church
Built in the mid-18th century, this is one of the most beautiful Baroque churches in the city. The joined figures of St Anne and Mary decorate the centre of its façade.

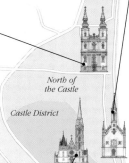

North of
the Castle

DANUBE

Castle District

Mátyás Church
Romanesque and Gothic styles are both evident in the coronation church of the Hungarian kings. The Neo-Gothic altar dates from the 19th century.

Gellért Hill
and Tabán

Cave Church
In the rocky interior of St István's Cave, on the south side of Gellért Hill, the priests of the Pauline order established a church in 1926. It was designed to imitate the holy grotto at Lourdes.

| 0 metres | 500 |
| 0 yards | 500 |

St Stephen's Basilica
A bas-relief by Leó Feszler, representing the Virgin Mary surrounded by Hungarian saints, decorates the main tympanum of St Stephen's Basilica. This imposing church was built between 1845–1905.

Lutheran Church
This Neo-Classical church was completed by Mihály Pollack in 1808. The impressive façade was added half a century later by József Hild.

Around Városliget

Around Parliament

Central Pest

Great Synagogue
Two Moorish-style minarets, each topped by an onion-shaped dome, dominate the exterior of the largest synagogue in Europe.

Franciscan Church
The magnificent 19th-century paintings that decorate the interior of this Baroque church are by Károly Lotz.

Inner City Parish Church
Dating from 1046, this church is Pest's oldest building. A figure of St Florian, the patron saint of fire fighters, was placed on the wall beside the altar after the church survived the great fire of 1723.

Exploring the Churches and Synagogues

MOST OF THE CITY's churches are found around the centres of Buda and Pest. Only a few sacred buildings of architectural interest are situated on the outskirts of the city. The greatest period of construction took place in the 18th century, after the final expulsion of the Turks. Another

Detail on St Elizabeth's Church

phase occurred in the second half of the 19th century, producing two of Budapest's grandest places of worship: St Stephen's Basilica and the Great Synagogue. Religious buildings were neglected after World War II, but thanks to restoration some have now regained their former splendour.

Reconstructed Gothic window of the Church of St Mary Magdalene

MEDIEVAL

BOTH **Mátyás Church** and the **Inner City Parish Church** date originally from the reign of Béla IV in the 13th century. Glimpses of their original Romanesque style can be seen, although each church was subsequently rebuilt in the Gothic style. After being sacked by the Turks in 1526,

Mátyás Church was given a Baroque interior by the Jesuits who had at that time taken it over. Finally, the church was returned to a likeness of its medieval character between 1874–96, when all Baroque elements were systematically removed and it was given a Neo-Gothic shape.

The **Church of St Mary Magdalene**, built in 1274 in the Gothic style, was almost completely destroyed in 1945. All that remains intact today is the 15th-century tower with its two chapels. A Gothic window has also been rebuilt.

St Michael's Church, founded in the 12th century on Margaret Island, was completely destroyed by the Turks. However, in 1932 it was reconstructed from its original Romanesque plans.

BAROQUE

IN THE 18TH CENTURY, 17 churches were built in Pest, Buda and Óbuda, all of them in the Baroque style. The influence of the Italian architectural school is visible in many of them, although only

University Church was built by an Italian architect, Donato Allio. Under Habsburg rule, the leading architects working in the city, András Meyerhoffer, Mátyás Nepauer and Kristóf Hamon, often chose to follow Austrian examples.

University Church and **St Anne's Church** are generally considered to be the most beautiful buildings in the city dating from this era. The former astonishes visitors with its beautifully carved stalls and pulpit, and with the paintings by Johann Bergl adorning its vaults. St Anne's Church has a magnificent Baroque façade and reveals the influence of southern German Baroque in its oval floor plan. Inside, there is a lavish altar and pulpit designed by Károly Bebó.

The **Franciscan Church**, which is situated in the centre of Budapest and dates from 1758, has a wide Baroque nave and a main altar created by Antal Grassalkovich.

The interior of the Servite Church (1725), with its Baroque altar

SPIRES AND DOMES

The Gothic spire belonging to the Church of St Mary Magdalene and the Neo-Gothic spire of Mátyás Church are among Budapest's main landmarks. The twin Baroque towers of St Anne's Church and the soaring spire of the Calvinist Church rise above the Danube in Buda. On the Pest side, the dome of St Stephen's Basilica and the minarets of the Great Synagogue dominate.

Gothic spire of the Church of St Mary Magdalene

Baroque towers of St Anne's Church

Neo-Gothic spire of the Calvinist Church

NEO-CLASSICAL AND HISTORICIST

IN 1781, JOSEPH II passed an edict permitting the building of Protestant churches. The city already had many Catholic churches and Protestant communities now started to build their own places of worship in the prevailing style of the time, Neo-Classicism.

One of the first to go up was the **Lutheran Church**, on Deák Ferenc tér, completed in 1808 by Mihály Pollack, a gifted master of Neo-Classical architecture. The white, ascetic interior of the church, with its two-floor gallery, was ideally suited to the nature of this place of worship. The majesty and simplicity of the Neo-Classical style corresponded with the more austere nature of Protestant belief. József Hild, another master of the style, later extended the church. He added the portico with its Doric columns, linking the church with the presbytery and a school. The complex as a whole is one of the best examples of Neo-Classical architecture in Budapest.

On a more modest scale is the **Calvinist Church**, built in the Neo-Gothic style between 1893–6.

When plans for it were drawn up by József Hild in 1845, **St Stephen's Basilica** was intended to be the pinnacle of Neo-Classical architecture. However, several delays, including the collapse of its dome at one point, meant

Baptismal font at the Lutheran Church

that the realization of the original design was impossible. Following Hild's death in 1867, Miklós Ybl continued the project. He departed from Hild's plan, incorporating Renaissance-style features. The Basilica was finally completed by a third architect, József Kauser, in 1905.

LATE 19TH- AND 20TH-CENTURY

THE TWO MOST stunning synagogues in Budapest were designed by Viennese architects in the second half of the 19th century.

Ludwig Förster constructed the **Great Synagogue** in Byzantine-Moorish style in 1859 and Otto Wagner, an important Secession architect *(see pp54–7)*, realized one of his first projects in 1872. This was the **Orthodox Synagogue** on Rumbach utca, which also incorporated Moorish ideas.

Closely linked to the Secession style is the Hungarian National Style, based on an idiosyncratic combination of ethnic motifs and elements from folk art. This style is most visible in two churches by Hungarian architects. Ödön Lechner, the originator of the Hungarian National Style, completed **Kőbánya Parish Church**, on the outskirts of Budapest, in 1900. Meanwhile, Aladár Árkay built **Városliget Calvinist Church** in 1913. These two churches display a striking combination

Carvings and an inscription adorning the Great Synagogue

of colourful ceramics, Eastern-style ornamentation and also Neo-Gothic elements.

Moorish-style towers of the Great Synagogue

Dome of the eclectic St Stephen's Basilica

Budapest's Best: Palaces and Historic Buildings

Detail on the façade of Károly Palace

BUDAPEST boasts historic buildings and palaces in a broad range of architectural styles. The majority represent the Neo-Classicism, Historicism and Secession of the 19th and early 20th centuries, when a dynamic development of the capital took place. All but a few Gothic and Renaissance details were lost in the destruction of Buda and Pest by Christian troops in 1686, but some examples of its Baroque heritage remain. This map gives some highlights, with a more detailed look on pages 48–9.

Royal Palace
This palace has a turbulent history dating back to the 13th century. Its present form, however, reflects the opulence of the 19th century. Today the palace houses some of the city's finest museums.

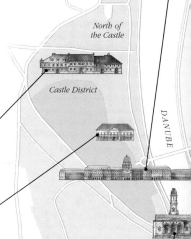

North of the Castle

Castle District

DANUBE

Gellért Hill and Tabán

Houses on Vienna Gate Square
This charming row of four houses was built in the late 18th and early 19th centuries on the ruins of medieval dwellings. The houses are adorned with decorative motifs in the Baroque, Rococo and Neo-Classical styles.

Sándor Palace
The original friezes, by Anton Kirchmayer, that decorated this 19th-century palace were destroyed in 1945, when the building suffered severe damage. They were recreated by Hungarian artists as part of its restoration.

Várkert Kiosk
This Neo-Renaissance pavilion was built by Miklós Ybl (see p119) as a pump house for the Royal Palace. It now houses the luxurious Várkert Casino and Casino-Valentina Restaurant (see p196).

Hungarian Academy of Science
The façade of the academy is adorned with statues by Emil Wolff and Miklós Izsó, symbolizing major fields of knowledge: law, natural history, mathematics, philosophy, linguistics and history.

Gresham Palace
This splendid example of Secession design was built in 1905–7 by Zsigmond Quittner as the headquarters of a London insurance firm.

0 metres 500

0 yards 500

Around Parliament

Around Városliget

Central Pest

Pallavicini Palace
Gustáv Petschacher built this Neo-Renaissance mansion on Kodály körönd in 1882. The inner court-yard was copied from the Palazzo Marini in Milan.

Ervin Szabó Library
The grand, Neo-Baroque palace that now houses this library was originally built in 1887 for the Wenckheims, a family of rich industrialists.

Péterffy Palace
This plaque, commemorating a flood of 1838, was placed on one of the few Baroque mansions that remain in Pest. The house was built in 1756.

Exploring the Palaces and Historic Buildings

LITTLE MORE THAN FRAGMENTS remain of Budapest's Gothic and Renaissance past. However, some Baroque buildings have survived in Buda's Castle District and Víziváros. Neo-Classicism, on the other hand, has a much wider presence; there are many apartment buildings, palaces and secular monuments built in this style, especially around the old fortification walls of Pest on the eastern side of the Danube. Historicism dominated the architecture of the second half of the 19th century. It played a vital role in the enlargement of the city as it expressed and celebrated the optimism of the era.

Façade of the Gross Palace, built by Jószef Hild in 1824

BAROQUE PALACES AND BUILDINGS

MANY BUILDINGS in the Castle District and neighbouring Víziváros, around Fő utca, have retained their original Baroque façades. The main entrance of the **Hilton Hotel**, formerly a 17th-century Jesuit college, is a fine example.

Other outstanding instances of this style are the four houses on **Vienna Gate Square**, the **Batthyány Palace** on Parade Square and the **Erdődy Palace** on Mihály Táncsics Street, now the Museum of Musical History.

The **Zichy Palace** in Óbuda is a splendid Baroque edifice, and the buildings of the former **Trinitarian Monastery**, now the Kiscelli Museum, stand as significant models of the style.

There are only two Baroque monuments remaining in Pest. The **Péterffy Palace**, a mansion that stands below the current street level, dates from 1755. Pest's other Baroque edifice was, however, the first to be built in either Buda or Pest. The huge complex of the **Municipal County Offices**, formerly a hospital for veterans of the Turkish wars, was constructed by the Italian master Anton Erhard Martinelli. It was greatly admired by Empress Maria Theresa, who declared it to be more beautiful than the Schönbrunn Palace in Vienna.

NEO-CLASSICAL PALACES AND BUILDINGS

NEO-CLASSICISM, influenced by ancient Greco-Roman design, was popular in the first half of the 19th century as it reflected the confidence of this period of national awakening and social reform. Many monumental Neo-Classical structures were produced, including the Chain Bridge, built in 1839–49. The leading Neo-Classical architect was Mihály Pollack, who built the **Hungarian National Museum**.

Two stunning Neo-Classical palaces deserve particular mention – **Sándor Palace** in Buda and **Károlyi Palace** in Pest. The first stands on Castle Hill, by the top of the funicular railway, and impresses visitors with its harmonious elegance. The second, now housing the Petőfi Literary Museum, gained its present form in 1834 after considerable reconstruction.

A group of particularly attractive Neo-Classical houses is situated on **József Nádor Square**. Some of their features, such as the pillars, projections and tympanums, merit individual attention.

In 1808, the Embellishment Commission was set up by the Austrian architect János Hild to develop Pest. He and his son, Jószef Hild, who built the **Gross Palace** in 1824, were both involved in the general restoration of the city. Having studied architecture in Rome, they created many splendid Italianate buildings.

Baroque balcony and carved crest above the entrance to Erdődy Palace

HISTORICIST PALACES AND BUILDINGS

IN THE SECOND HALF of the 19th century, Historicism took precedence over Neo-Classicism. After the unification of Buda, Óbuda and Pest in 1873, Historicism had a significant influence on the city's architectural development. In this period Budapest gained an eclectic mix of new apartment buildings and palaces, as Historicist architects sourced different genres for inspiration. Miklós Ybl, whose work includes the **State Opera House** and the expansion of the **Royal Palace**, looked to the Renaissance, while Imre Steindl designed a Neo-Gothic **Parliament** (to which a Neo-Renaissance dome was added). Frigyes Schulek's **Fishermen's**

Sculptures on the Vigadó façade

Bastion features Neo-Gothic and Neo-Romanesque designs.

The **Vigadó**, a concert hall built by Frigyes Feszl between 1859 and 1864, is often thought of as the most magnificent Historicist building, with its façade richly decorated with relief sculptures and busts of the great Hungarians. However, the complex of three French-style, Neo-Renaissance palaces, Festetics, Károly and Esterházy, in **Mihály Pollack Square**, is also considered by many to be a fine example.

The **Drechsler Palace** in Andrássy út is a marvellous model of Neo-Renaissance design, while the **Divatcsarnok** department store features Lotz's Hall, stunningly decorated with paintings and gold. The twin apartment buildings known as the **Klotild Palaces** incorporate Spanish-Baroque motifs

Beautiful Neo-Baroque interior of the New York Palace

and can be admired near the Elizabeth Bridge. Perhaps one of the most extravagant of all the examples of Historicism in the city is the Neo-Baroque **New York Palace** by Alajos Hauzmann, which has a luxurious interior of twisting marble columns and rich colour.

DECORATIVE FEATURES

The façades of many palaces and buildings still display the rich sculptural decoration characteristic of the various styles of architecture prevalent in the city. These features include coves, cartouches, finials, relief sculptures and ornamental window frames.

Regrettably, almost no original Gothic detail remains in Budapest, but niches or pointed arches decorating old apartment buildings can be spotted in the Old Town.

Baroque elements are still evident in fine buildings such as the Zichy Palace and the Erdődy Palace.

Decorative Neo-Classical features, such as borders and tympanums, are visible on many buildings from the first half of the 19th century.

A finial with cartouche on the Neo-Classical Károlyi Palace

Relief on the Hungarian National Bank (1905)

Cove detail on the façade of the Staffenberg House

Ornate window frame adorning the house at 21 József Nádor utca

Budapest's Best: Baths and Pools

BUDAPEST IS ONE OF the great spa cities of Europe. Numerous natural hot springs pour out over 80 million litres (18 million gal) of richly mineralized water every day. The greatest concentrations of natural springs are situated in Óbuda, near Gellért Hill, on the Buda embankment near Margaret Bridge and on Margaret Island itself. Baths have existed here since Roman times, but it was the Turks who best exploited Budapest's natural resources. Today there is a wide choice of therapeutic and recreational baths and pools.

Palatinus Strand
With seven swimming pools, hot springs, water slides and a restful location on Margaret Island, this spa is perhaps the most beautiful in Europe.

Hajós Olympic Pool
The pool was designed by Alfréd Hajós, who won Hungary's first Olympic gold medal in 1896 and on the walls of the swimming hall hang gold-engraved marble plaques citing Hungary's numerous Olympic champions.

North of the Castle

Castle District

DANUBE

Lukács Baths
These 19th-century thermal pools are open all year round, and attract both tourists and the locals of Budapest.

Gellért Hill and Tabán

Király Baths
Dating from 1566, these baths were built by the Turks and have many authentic Ottoman features.

Rác Baths
An ornate side room at these baths has been turned into a gymnasium.

Dagály Strand
Half a century ago, it was discovered that the water in a pond on this site was beneficial to health. Now a huge open-air complex of swimming pools, children's pools and a hydrotherapy and fitness centre is located here.

Around Parliament

Around Városliget

Central Pest

Széchenyi Baths
This spa has the hottest thermal baths in Budapest and the added attraction of magnificent Neo-Baroque architecture. The warmth of the water is such that these baths are popular even during the winter season.

Rudas Baths
The most famous of the Turkish baths were constructed during the 16th century. They still have an original Ottoman cupola and octagonal pool.

Gellért Baths
The main indoor swimming pool of this popular Buda spa delights bathers with its beautiful Secession interior, marble columns and colourful mosaics.

0 metres	500
0 yards	500

Exploring Budapest's Baths and Pools

HEATED DEEP INSIDE THE EARTH, the waters of the mineral-rich hot springs which bubble up through fractures in the rocky hills of Buda and Óbuda have given the city a Turkish-influenced bathing culture which has survived even the rigours of Communism. A total of 31 spa-water pools and thermal baths, with entrance fees kept low by generous government subsidies, make taking the waters an unmissable treat for visitors to Budapest.

THE TURKISH INFLUENCE

ALTHOUGH THE ruins of Roman thermal baths dating from the 2nd century AD have been found in Óbuda, it was only under the Ottoman occupation of the 16th–17th centuries (see pp 26–7), that the bathing culture really took hold in Budapest.

Four stunning Turkish-built baths, some of the few remaining examples of Ottoman architecture in Budapest, are still in operation. The **Rudas**, the **Rác**, the **Király** and the **Császár Baths** were all built in the 16th century, and are constructed on a single model. A marble staircase leads into a chamber containing a dome-topped, octagonal thermal pool, which is surrounded by smaller dome-covered pools at temperatures ranging from icily cold to roastingly hot. The most beautiful and the most atmospheric are almost certainly the Rudas Baths, followed closely by the Király Baths. Though not without their charms, the Rác Baths are heavily restored and are less spectacular than

the Rudas and Király Baths. The Császár Baths have been absorbed into the Lukács Baths complex (see below).

Many of the city's newer baths are for both men and women. The Turkish baths, however, owe much of their unique atmosphere to the fact that they remain resolutely single-sex. The Rudas Baths are for men only, while the Rác and the Király Baths are open to men and women on alternate days. There is no need to wear a bathing suit, as a small apron is provided.

AFTER THE TURKS

THE LATE 19TH and early 20th century was a new golden age for Budapest (see pp32–3), and saw the building of a number of splendid baths. Many have spring-water swimming pools attached.

Opened in 1894 the Neo-Classical **Lukács Baths** offer two outdoor swimming pools as well as the 16th-century Császár thermal pool. The **Széchenyi Baths**, opened 20 years later on the Pest side of the river, make up the biggest

bathing complex in Europe. In addition to the usual indoor thermal pools, they also boast outdoor thermal and swimming pools, complete with sun terraces. With the hottest spa-water in the city, the outdoor thermal pool is popular even in the depths of winter.

As well as the thermal pools, Budapest's bathing establishments also include a steam room and sauna. Professional massages are almost always available for a small fee. Some places offer medicinal mud and sulphur baths. You will be invited to take a shower, and a short nap in the rest room before you leave.

Swim in style at the Gellért Hotel

SPA HOTELS

NESTLING AT THE foot of Gellért Hill, the beautiful **Gellért Hotel and Baths Complex** is the oldest and most famous of a handful of luxury hotels in Budapest offering swimming and thermal pools, steam rooms, sauna and massage. The renowned Gellért Baths were opened to the general public in 1927, and include a fabulous, marble-columned indoor swimming pool, a labyrinth of thermal baths (one set for men and one for women), single-sex nudist sun-bathing areas and an outdoor swimming pool. A hugely popular wave machine is switched on in the latter for ten minutes in every hour.

A second wave of spa-hotels were built in the 1970s and '80s. Set on leafy Margaret Island, the modern, squeaky-clean and extremely luxurious **Thermal Hotel**, is linked by an underground passage to the older **Ramada-Grand Hotel**. In addition to the usual range of baths and pools, services on offer here include

Outdoor pool at the Gellért Hotel and Baths Complex

Széchenyi Baths, the biggest bathing complex in Europe

manicure, pedicure and a solarium. The late 1980s saw the arrival of two new spa hotels, the **Thermal Hotel Helia** not far from the Pest riverbank and, on the Buda side, the **Hotel Aquincum**, facing north towards Óbuda. Both make use of the hot springs on Margaret Island, and offer gyms, bars and restaurants as well as swimming pools and thermal baths.

THE HEALING WATERS

The citizens of Budapest are great believers in the medical benefits of the thermal baths. Most of the baths employ staff who can offer advice on the most appropriate pools and special treatments for a particular ailment. The spa waters are extremely good for general relaxation. They can also be helpful in the relief of a number of specific complaints, including post-traumatic stress, joint and muscle damage, rheumatism and menstrual pain.

An ornamental tap, typical of the architectural detail found in Budapest's historic baths

SWIMMING AS SPORT

MANY HUNGARIANS are excellent swimmers, and the country has achieved great success in competitive water sports. In addition to Budapest's many recreational pools, sports pools include the **Hajós Olympic Pool** complex on Margaret Island. The complex consists of three sports pools, two outdoor, including one at full Olympic size, and one indoor. The pools are used for professional training, but are also open to the public. Together with the Komjádi Béla Swimming Stadium on Árpád Béla Fejedelem útja, the Hajós Olympic Pool is the place to see professional swimming, diving or water polo.

A DAY AT THE STRAND

DESIGNED AS A complete bathing day out, the strands of Budapest are a phenomenon not to be missed. A total of 12 strands in the city testifies to their popularity. Outdoor swimming and thermal pools are surrounded by grassy sunbathing areas. Trampolines and ping-pong and pool tables offer a change from the water, while ice creams, beers and hot dogs add to the summer-holiday atmosphere.

The lovely **Palatinus Strand**, set in a large area of parkland on Margaret Island, boasts seven outdoor pools, some thermal and some for swimming, complete with water slides and wave machines. Just east of the Pest river bank is the vast, modern **Dagály Strand** complex. Built after World War II, it includes 12 pools, with space for up to 12,000 people. Other strands worth visiting include **Római Strand** in Óbuda in the north of the city. Three pools have been carefully rebuilt here, on the site of some Roman baths, together with a not-so-Roman water chute. To the north of the city at Csillaghegy on the HÉV suburban train line, **Csillaghegy Strand** consists of four pools set in picturesque grounds, and includes a popular south-facing nudist beach.

Sculpture at the Római Strand

WHERE TO FIND THE BATHS AND POOLS

Császár Baths, part of Lukács Baths *p101*
Gellért Hotel and Baths Complex *pp90–91*
Hajós Olympic Pool *p172*
Király Baths *p101*
Lukács Baths *p101*
Palatinus Strand *p172*
Rác Baths *p94*
Ramada-Grand Hotel *p185*
Rudas Baths *p93*
Széchenyi Baths *p151*
Thermal Hotel *p173*
Thermal Hotel Aquincum *p185*
Thermal Hotel Helia *p185*

Budapest's Best: the Secession

VISITORS TO BUDAPEST are often impressed by its wonderful late 19th and early 20th century buildings. The majority of these are found in central Pest and around Városliget; Buda was already developed at this stage and so boasts few examples. The

Decoration on a house on Áldás utca

movement started among groups of avant-garde artists in Paris and Vienna, from where the term Secession comes. In Budapest, the Secession style was also the inspiration for the development of the Hungarian National Style. Further details are given on pages 56–7.

The School on Rose Hill
Károly Kós and Dezső Zrumeczky used motifs from village houses in Transylvania to give this building on Áldás utca its character.

Woman with a Birdcage (1892)
This painting by József Rippl-Rónai has an atmosphere of mystery and in- timacy typical of Hungarian art of the period. It hangs in the Hungarian National Gallery (see p77) today.

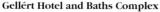

North of the Castle

Castle District

DANUBE

Gellért Hill and Tabán

Ironwork Gates of Gresham Palace
Two intricately crafted peacocks, a classic Secession motif, decorate the wrought-iron gates of Gresham Palace. This block of offices was built by Zsigmond Quittner and the Vágó brothers between 1905–7.

Gellért Hotel and Baths Complex
Supported by flattened arches, a glass roof adds to the tranquil appeal of this hall in the famous spa at the Gellért Hotel. The Secession interiors created here are among the most splendid to be found in Budapest.

Post Office Savings Bank
The main staircase of this building by Ödön Lechner is embellished by fine balusters, rounded lamps and decorative windows.

Entrance to the Zoo
Kornel Neuschloss made ingenious use of elements of Hindu architecture when he created this amusing gate guarded by two elephants.

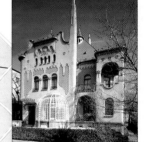

Around Parliament

Around Városliget

Central Pest

Sipeky Balázs Villa
Built between 1905–6, this fanciful villa is perhaps the most representative example of the Secession style in Budapest. It was designed by Ödön Lechner.

Philanthia Florist's
This extraordinary florist's is on Váci utca. The interior of the shop is in the Secession style, while the building itself is Neo-Classical.

| 0 metres | 500 |
| 0 yards | 500 |

Apartments on Bartók Béla Utca
Ödön Lechner was the leading exponent of the Hungarian National Style. He built this apartment block, with a studio for himself on the fourth floor, in 1899. The block is at 40 Bartók Béla utca.

Exploring Secession Budapest

Secession ornament

THE SECESSION MOVEMENT crossed artistic boundaries, influencing painting and the decorative arts as well as architecture. Colourful, sometimes fantastical designs are instantly recognizable hallmarks of the style. The Hungarian National Style drew heavily on this general trend, incorporating motifs from old Hungarian architecture, particularly that of Transylvania, folk art and even oriental features.

Vase designed by István Sovának, in the Museum of Applied Arts

József Rippl-Rónai's *Lady in a White Polka-dot Dress* (1899), in the Hungarian National Gallery

PAINTINGS AND DRAWINGS

THE MAIN EXPONENTS of Secession art in Hungary were József Rippl-Rónai, János Vaszary and Lajos Gulácsy.

Rippl-Rónai spent many years in Paris, at the time when the Art Nouveau movement was beginning to flourish. *Lady in a White Polka-dot Dress*, which he painted in 1899, was the first Hungarian painting in the Secession style. Many of Rippl-Rónai's works are on show in the **Hungarian National Gallery**. There is also a tapestry version of *Lady in a White Polka-dot Dress* in the **Museum of Applied Arts**.

The work of János Vaszary was heavily influenced by both German and English art. His finest pictures, which include *Gold Century* and the mysterious *Adam and Eve*, can be admired in the Hungarian National Gallery. Lajos Gulácsy was influenced by the Pre-Raphaelite movement and his pictures are often symbolic. Many of his paintings, too, can now be viewed in the Hungarian National Gallery.

The artists' colony based at Gödöllő was an important centre for painters working in the new Secession style. Its founder, Aladár Körösfői-Kriesch, created numerous works, including a fresco entitled *The Fount of Youth* which decorates the **Franz Liszt Academy of Music**.

DECORATIVE ARTS

NEW IDEAS in the decorative arts at this time were closely related to architectural developments. Ödön Lechner began to make use of colourful ceramic tiles, acquired from his father-in-law's brickyard in Pécs in southern Hungary, not only to cover roofs but also as a decorative element.

The owner of this brickyard, Vilmos Zsolnay, discovered an innovative method of glazing tiles and ceramics. This proved so successful that the brickyard was turned into a factory specializing in their production. Zsolnay's factory eventually made most of the vivid and distinctive ceramic tiles covering the Secession buildings in the city.

Zsolnay also employed leading designers to create ranges of dinner services, vases and candlesticks. For these he was awarded the Gold Medal of the Legion of Honour at the World Fair in Paris. A wonderful collection of his Secession china is displayed in the Museum of Applied Arts, where beautiful

ÖDÖN LECHNER (1845–1914)

Portrait of Lechner

The most influential architect of the Hungarian Secession, Ödön Lechner trained in Berlin before completing his apprenticeship by working in both Italy and France. His quest was to create an identifiable Hungarian National Style, by combining Secession motifs with elements from Hungarian folk art and Hindu designs. The colourful ceramics that he often used became his signature. Among the buildings that Budapest owes to him are the Museum of Applied Arts, the Post Office Savings Bank and the Institute of Geology. Behind the ingenious and fantastical exteriors, Lechner's buildings have wonderfully simple, functional and superbly lit interiors.

Secession glass, lamps and decorative ironwork are also exhibited. **Gresham Palace** and the **Gellért Hotel and Baths Complex** are among the many buildings in the city that are embellished by ornamental wrought-iron gates, gratings and banisters that incorporate Secession motifs.

INTERIOR DECORATION

AMONG THE INTERIORS of the era, those of the **New York Palace** are a real jewel. Ostentatiously decked out in the best materials, including bronze and marble, they retain the splendour of their original, Neo-Baroque form.

Also worth visiting are the **Hungarian National Bank** and the **Post Office Savings Bank**, with their furnished secure rooms and ornate door and window frames. The interior of Philanthia, a florist's shop, is another wonderfully

Window created by Miksa Róth, at the Hungarian National Bank

preserved example of decor from the Secession.

Exhibitions of attractive Secession furniture are a feature of both the Museum of Applied Arts and also the **Nagytétény Palace**.

ARCHITECTURE

HUNGARIAN architecture of the *fin de siècle* is characterized not only by decorative forms using glazed ceramics, but, more fundamentally, by the implementation of modern technical solutions. Reinforced concrete, steel and glass were used together, and large, light-filled interiors were often achieved. The central hall of the Museum of Applied Arts is a fine example of this.

Aside from Ödön Lechner, the most important of the Hungarian Secession architects, others who contributed significant buildings in the prevailing style included Béla Lajta, Aladár Árkay, Károly Kós and István Medgyaszay.

Béla Lajta, a pupil of Lechner, designed the **Rózsavölgyi Building**, with its distinctive geometrical ornamentation, on Martinelli tér. Also among his buildings is the extraordinary former **Jewish Old People's Home**, at No. 57 Amerikai út. With sophisticated ornamental details based on folk designs, **Városliget Calvinist Church** was the creation of Aladár Árkay.

Károly Kós was a highly original member of this set. Fascinated by the traditional architecture of Transylvania, he trawled the whole of that region, making drawings of the village churches and manor houses he encountered. Motifs from these buildings were later transferred to the aviary at Budapest's **Zoo** and the houses of the **Wekerle Estate**.

Frieze on the Rózsavölgyi Building

A Secession cabinet, displayed in the Museum of Applied Arts

DECORATIVE MOTIFS

Stylized folk motifs derived from embroidery and also oriental patterns were often employed in Budapest's decorative arts during this period. Secession motifs such as feline forms, based on Viennese and Parisian examples, also feature.

Sunflower motif adorning the Post Office Savings Bank

Secession lettering on the sign of Philanthia Florist's

Colourful mosaic at No. 3 Aulich utca

BUDAPEST THROUGH THE YEAR

SET IN THE MIDDLE OF the Great Hungarian Plain, Budapest enjoys a continental climate with sharply defined seasons, each of which brings its own attractions, from traditional feast days to cultural and sporting events. Historically a centre of cultural, and especially musical, activity, Budapest continues the tradition

Spring Festival logo

with many musical events including the Spring Festival, an international celebration of classical music and ballet, and the smaller Budapest Contemporary Music Weeks, devoted to contemporary classical music. Many hotels and tourist offices provide a programme of the events taking place in the city, as do English-language weeklies.

SPRING

SPRING MAKES A welcome return to the city in March, with sunshine and fresh, warm days. Budapest turns green and the Spring Festival sees the arrival of some of the year's first tourists.

MARCH

The Spring Uprising *(15 Mar)*. A public holiday marks the day in 1848 when the youth of Buda, led by the poet Sándor Petőfi, rebelled against the Habsburg occupation of Hungary *(see pp30–31)*. Thousands of people take to the streets to lay wreaths and light eternal flames, wearing the national colours of red, white and green. There are speeches and street theatre, especially in front of the Hungarian National Museum *(see pp130–33)*.
  Spring Festival *(last two weeks of Mar– mid-Apr)*. Top musicians from Hungary and

Parade in the Castle District during the Spring Festival

the rest of the world gather in Budapest for several weeks of music and dance in churches and concert halls all over the city. The emphasis of the festival is on the classical tradition, but also in evidence are folk music and dance, as well as pop and jazz.

APRIL

Easter is an important religious event in Hungary and the Easter service is well worth attending in one of the city's many churches. On the

morning of Easter Monday young men roam the streets, spraying girls and young women with perfume or water, a ritual which is said to keep them beautiful until the following year. Painted eggs are given in return.
  Horse Racing *(Sun, Apr–Oct)*. April sees the beginning of the flat-racing season. Place your bets every Sunday at the busy and charmingly down-at-heel Kincsem Park race course on Albertirsai út.
  Budapest Marathon *(last Sun in Apr)*. Crowds line the streets to cheer on the runners in this popular event.

MAY

May Day *(1 May)*. No longer a compulsory display of patriotism, May Day celebrations take place in public parks all over the city and involve craft markets, street performers and sausage and beer tents. A dip in the local thermal bath or swimming pool *(see pp50–53)*, is another popular May Day tradition.
  IFABO *(May)*. Held at the Budapest Exhibition Centre *(see p156)*, the city's major venue for international trade fairs, IFABO is Hungary's largest computer fair where you can see and buy a huge array of computer equipment at very competitive prices.
  Book Week *(last week in May or 1st week in Jun)*. Hungarian publishers display their new books along the streets of central Pest, between the river and Nagykörút (Outer Ring). Open-air theatre often takes place on Mihály Vörösmarty Square *(see p126)*.

Springtime magnolia blossom on Margaret Island

AVERAGE DAILY HOURS OF SUNSHINE

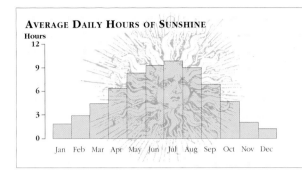

Hours

Jan Feb Mar Apr May Jun Jul Aug Sep Oct Nov Dec

Sunshine Chart

Budapest enjoys some of the sunniest weather in Europe, with an average of eight hours of sunshine each day from April to September. During the sticky months of high summer (June, July and August), the Buda hills provide a welcome refuge from the heat of the city.

SUMMER

THE LONG HOT DAYS of summer are made for relaxing on Margaret Island or sun-bathing at some of the city's twelve open-air pools.

JUNE

Open-Air Theatre Festival
(Jun–Aug). Margaret Island and Óbuda Island, two quiet parks in the middle of the Danube, provide two of the major venues for this summer-long, open-air arts festival. Despite the name, not just theatre, but opera, ballet, orchestral and folk music are all on offer. Do not miss the puppet theatre performances for children.
Budapesti Búcsú *(last weekend in Jun).* This is the weekend when the people of Budapest celebrate the long-

Formula One racing in the Hungarian Grand Prix

awaited departure, in 1991, of the last Soviet troops from Hungarian soil. An eclectic mixture of music, dance and theatre is performed in parks and squares around the city.

JULY

Concerts in St Stephen's Basilica *(Jul–Aug).* Monday evening organ concerts in the city's largest church *(see*

Fireworks on Gellért Hill to celebrate St István's Day

pp116–17) provide a perfect opportunity to study the lavish interior decoration of this extraordinary building.
Opera and Ballet Festival *(Jul or Aug).* Look out for the ten-day series of performances that makes up the short summer season at the magnificent State Opera House *(see pp118–19)* on Andrássy út.

AUGUST

Hungarian Grand Prix *(2nd Sun in Aug).* Otherwise known as the *Hungororing*, the biggest event in the Hungarian sporting calendar takes place 20 km (13 miles) east of the city, at the Mogyoród race track.
St István's Day *(20 Aug).* St István, the patron saint of Hungary, is celebrated with mass in St Stephen's Basilica followed by a huge procession. The day ends with a fireworks display on Gellért Hill *(see pp88–9)*, best viewed from the Pest embankment.
Diáksziget *(3rd week in Aug).* Ten stages and a camp site are set up on Óbuda Island for this popular week-long festival of rock, folk and jazz.

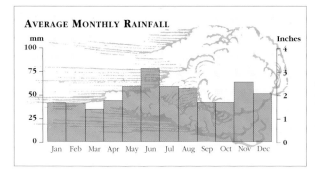

AVERAGE MONTHLY RAINFALL

(Rainfall bar chart showing mm on left axis (0–100) and Inches on right axis (0–4) for months Jan through Dec)

Rainfall Chart
Budapest is a fairly dry country. Typically, it rains very heavily for two days or so, then is dry for several weeks. June is the wettest month, with May, July, August and November only slightly dryer. Autumn is usually the dryest season, while there is some snowfall in the winter months.

AUTUMN

O NE OF THE MANY TREATS of autumn in Budapest is a visit to one of the city's fruit and vegetable markets, where you can feast your eyes on a vast array of jewel-coloured vegetables and fruit.

SEPTEMBER

Budapest Wine Festival
(2nd week of Sep). After the late-August grape harvest, wine makers set up their stalls for wine tastings and folk dancing on Mihály Vörösmarty Square *(see p126)* and other squares around the city.

Budapest Contemporary Music Weeks *(25 Sep–end Oct)*. The anniversary of the death of the great Béla Bartók marks the start of this festival of 20th-century classical music. **Architectural Heritage Days** *(3rd or 4th weekend in Sep)*. Organized once a year by the Ödön Lechner Foundation, this is an opportunity to see inside such spectacular buildings as the Ministry of Finance.

OCTOBER

Autumn Festival *(late Sep– mid-Oct)*. Several weeks of contemporary film, dance and theatre at a number of venues across the city.

A colourful food stall in one of Budapest's covered markets

Remembrance Day *(23 Oct)*. This is a national day of mourning to remember the 1956 Uprising, when 30,000 people were killed by Soviet tanks and 200,000 fled the country. Wreaths are laid in Municipal Cemetery *(see pp158– 9)*, on the grave of the executed leader Imre Nagy *(see p34)*.

NOVEMBER

International Table Tennis Tournament *(Nov)*. The nominal entrance fee (and the low winter temperatures) make this tournament a great opportunity to discover the joys of watching table tennis. Check the Hungarian-language daily newspaper *Nemzeti Sport* for details.
Outdoor Ice-Skating *(5 Nov– 8 Mar)*. The outdoor ice-skating season begins in November at the skating rink next door to the People's Stadium on Népstadion út.
Vox Pacis *(Nov)*. A festival of choral music featuring choirs from all over the world.

Performers take part in the Open-Air Theatre Festival

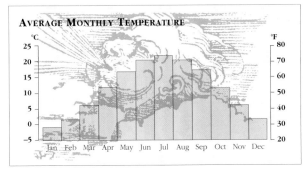

AVERAGE MONTHLY TEMPERATURE

Temperature Chart
*Seasons in Budapest
are sharply defined.
Daytime temperatures
rise rapidly from
March onwards. By
June, the thermometer
often reaches 30°C
(90°F) and more.
September sees cooler
weather, with temper-
atures falling rapidly
to lows of well below
freezing in January.*

WINTER

DESPITE THE COLD weather,
winter can be an exciting
time to visit Budapest. Open-
air ice-skating takes place from
November, roast-chestnut sel-
lers appear on the streets and
a Christmas tree is erected in
Mihály Vörösmarty Square.

DECEMBER

Silver and Gold Sunday
*(2nd-to-last Sunday before
Christmas).* All the city's shops
stay open for this Sunday of
serious Christmas shopping.
Mikulás *(6 Dec).* On *Mikulás,*
or St Nicholas Day, children
leave their shoes on the window sill for Santa Claus to fill
with sweets and presents.
Christmas *(25–26 Dec).* The
city shuts down for two days
from lunchtime on Christmas
Eve. Celebrations begin with a
family meal of carp on 24 Dec.
Szilveszter *(31 Dec).* The
whole of Budapest celebrates
in style on New Year's Eve,
taking to the streets for champagne and kisses at midnight.
Public transport is free and
runs all night.

**Seeing in the New Year, a stylish
affair in Budapest**

**Christmas tree in Mihály
Vörösmarty Square**

JANUARY

New Year's Day Concert *(1
Jan).* This traditional concert
of popular Hungarian classics
takes place in the Vigadó
concert hall *(see p208).*
Pig-Killing Festival *(Jan).*
Pig-killing parties begin with
the slaughter of the pig, which
is then distributed among the
guests. Look out for delicious
sausages and pork dishes on
the menus of city restaurants.

FEBRUARY

Hungarian Film Festival
(early Feb). This two-day
celebration of Hungarian film
has been run by the *Magyar
Filmszemle* since 1969, in an
attempt to attract funding to a
hard-pressed industry. Many
of the films are subtitled.
Masked-Ball Season *(Feb).*
Budapest forgets the cold

weather to welcome the arrival
of the *farsang,* or fancy dress
masked-ball season, with
many companies holding
their own event. The climax
of the season is a masked
procession on Carnival
Sunday, which is the last
Sunday before Lent.

Shopping for Christmas

PUBLIC HOLIDAYS

Public holidays mainly
follow the Christian calendar. Two days mark cata-
clysmic events in Magyar
history, while one, May
Day, is a reminder of the
country's socialist past.

New Year's Day (1 Jan)
Spring Uprising (15 Mar)
Easter Sunday (variable)
Easter Monday (variable)
Whit Monday (variable)
May Day (1 May)
St István's Day (20 Aug)
Remembrance Day
(23 Oct)
Christmas Day (25 Dec)
Boxing Day (26 Dec)

Margaret Bridge to Elizabeth Bridge

Crown on Elizabeth Bridge

A TRIP ON A river boat along the Danube provides a unique panorama of the city. Most major cities have a river at their heart. However, the Danube historically played a different role in this case, for centuries dividing the separate towns of Buda and Pest. Several road bridges today link the two halves of the modern city. All had to be reconstructed this century after being destroyed by the retreating Nazi army towards the end of World War II.

Centenary Monument
This monument was erected in 1973 to commemorate the centenary of the joining of Buda, Óbuda and Pest as Budapest. It stands on Margaret Island (see pp172–3), close to Margaret Bridge.

MARGIT H

St Elizabeth's Church
This Baroque church was built for an order of nuns, with its front facing away from the Danube. The hospital and hostel run by the sisters face the river (see p101).

BATTHYÁNY TÉR

M

Mátyás Church
With medieval origins, the tower of this church has been rebuilt several times. It overlooks the Hilton Hotel and the Fishermen's Bastion (see pp82–3).

St Anne's Church
can be recognized by its twin, slender Baroque towers.

LÁNCHID

Chain Bridge was built between 1839–49 at the initiative of Count István Széchenyi *(see p31)*. It was designed by Englishman William Tierney Clark and completed by the unrelated Adam Clark. The bridge extends for 380 m (1,250 ft), supported by two towers – a major feat of engineering at the time.

KEY

 Metro

 River boat boarding point

Margaret Bridge was built by the French engineer Ernest Gouin, at the point where the Danube becomes a single body once more after dividing to flow around Margaret Island. The bridge is distinguished by its unusual chevron shape. It was erected in 1872–6, and between 1899–1900 access from the bridge onto the island was added. Sculptures by Adolphe Thabart decorate its columns.

Parliament
The magnificent, high dome of the Parliament building is visible from every point along the Danube in central Budapest (see pp108–9).

Much of the eastern bank of the river is characterized by fairly uniform architecture. Variation is provided here by the dome and towers of St Stephen's Basilica *(see pp116–17).*

0 metres	300
0 yards	300

Hungarian Academy of Sciences

Elizabeth Bridge, constructed in 1897–1903, was at that time the longest suspension bridge in the world. Destroyed in 1945, it was rebuilt in its current form by Pála Sávolya.

The bridgehead of Chain Bridge is guarded by two vast stone lions sculpted by János Marschalkó. According to an anecdote János was heartbroken because he forgot to give the lions any tongues, so he drowned himself in the river. In fact the lions do have tongues, but they are not easily visible.

VÖRÖSMARTY TÉR

FERENCIEK TERE

Piers, from which passenger cruises operate daily in summer, are spaced frequently along the Danube in central Budapest.

RZSÉBET HÍD

Elizabeth Bridge to Lágymányosi Bridge

LIKE PARIS, BUDAPEST has fully exploited the opportunities given by its river. The most important and beautiful buildings of Buda and Pest crowd along the banks of the Danube. These include the Royal Palace, churches, historic palaces and houses, and Hungary's Parliament.

VÖRÖSMARTY TÉR Ⓜ

FERENCI TÉRE

ERZSÉBET HÍD

SZABADSÁ H

Royal Palace
From the Danube the lower sections of the defensive walls, with fragments dating from the Middle Ages, can be seen. The enormous mass of the Habsburg Royal Palace was built within these (see pp70–71).

Inner City Parish Church
This church was built in the 12th century on the ruins of Roman Contra Aquincum's walls. The spot was, from early times, an important place for crossing the river (see pp124–5).

Gellért Hotel and Baths Complex
The architects of this hotel maximized its river façade to make it as imposing as possible (see pp90–91).

Technical University
The campus of Hungary's largest educational institution occupies almost the entire space between Liberty Bridge and Petőfi Bridge (see p157).

An embankment walk extends along the length of the Danube on the Pest side. It is a favourite place to meet or to go for a stroll and is lined by up-market hotels and restaurants.

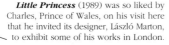

Little Princess (1989) was so liked by Charles, Prince of Wales, on his visit here that he invited its designer, László Marton, to exhibit some of his works in London.

K Á L V I N
T É R
Ⓜ

Liberty Bridge was built between 1894–9 by Hungarian engineer János Feketeházy. Opened by Emperor Franz Joseph, it initially took his name. All its original features were retained when it was rebuilt after World War II: on top of the bridge there are legendary Hungarian *turul* birds and royal crests.

P E T Ő F I   H Í D

University of Economics

Formerly a customs' headquarters, this building has an elegant façade decorated with ten allegorical figures. These are the work of German sculptor August Sommer (see p138).

L Á G Y M Á N Y O S I
H Í D

Lágymányosi Bridge, Budapest's most modern and southernmost bridge, is pictured here under construction. Opened in 1996, it is designed to carry traffic on a ring road bypassing the city centre.

BUDAPEST AREA
BY AREA

CASTLE DISTRICT

THE HILL TOWN of Buda grew up around its castle and Mátyás Church from the 13th century onwards. At 60 m (197 ft) above the Danube, the hill's good strategic position and natural resources made it a prize site for its earliest inhabitants. In the 13th century, a large settlement arose when, after a Tartar invasion, King Béla IV decided to build his own defensive castle and establish his capital here. The reign of King Mátyás Corvinus in the 15th century was an important period in the evolution of

Bas-relief on the Eugene of Savoy monument

Buda, but it suffered neglect under Turkish rule during the next century and was then destroyed by Christian troops. The town was reborn, however, and assumed an important role during the 18th and 19th centuries under the Habsburgs. By the end of World War II, the Old Town had been almost utterly destroyed and the Royal Palace burnt to the ground. Since the war the Royal Palace and Old Town have been reconstructed, restoring the original allure of this part of the city.

SIGHTS AT A GLANCE

Churches
Buda Lutheran Church **17**
Mátyás Church pp82–3 **11**
Church of St Mary
Magdalene **20**

Museums and Galleries
Budapest History Museum **1**
Golden Eagle Pharmacy
Museum **9**
Hungarian National Gallery
pp74–7 **4**
Museum of Commerce and
Catering **18**

Museum of Contemporary
History and Ludwig
Collection **5**
Museum of Military History **21**
Széchenyi National Library **2**

Historic Streets and Squares
András Hess Square **14**
Holy Trinity Square **10**
Lords' Street **22**
Mihály Táncsics Street **15**
Parade Square **8**
Parliament Street **19**
Vienna Gate Square **16**

**Palaces, Historic Buildings
and Monuments**
Castle Theatre **7**
Fishermen's Bastion **12**
Hilton Hotel **13**
Mátyás Fountain **3**
Sándor Palace **6**

GETTING THERE

Castle Hill and the Old Town are largely pedestrianized, but there are a couple of car parks where cars and coaches can park for a fee, allowing visitors to walk to the area. Bus 16 runs from Clark Ádám tér to Dísz tér, and a funicular railway (Sikló) connects Clark Ádám tér to Szent György tér. There is also a minibus (Várbusz) that arrives at this square from Moszkva tér to the north.

KEY

▨	Street-by-Street map *See pp70–71*
▨	Street-by-Street map *See pp78–9*
P	Parking
i	Tourist information

0 metres 400
0 yards 400

◁ **Fountain on Tárnok utca in the Old Town**

Street-by-Street: The Royal Palace

T HE ROYAL PALACE has borne many incarnations
during its long life. Even now it is not known
exactly where King Béla IV began building his
castle, though it is thought to be nearer the site of
Mátyás Church *(see pp82–3)*. The Holy Roman
Emperor Sigismund of Luxembourg built a Gothic
palace on the present site, from which today's
castle began to evolve. In the 18th century, the
Habsburgs built their monumental palace here.
The current form dates from the rebuilding
of the 19th-century palace after its destruction in February 1945. During this work,
remains of the 15th-century Gothic palace
were uncovered. Hungarian archeologists
decided to reveal the recovered defensive
walls and royal chambers in the reconstruction.

An ornamental gateway,
dating from 1903, leads
from the Habsburg Steps
to the Royal Palace. Nearby, a bronze sculpture of
the mythical *turul* bird
guards the palace. This
statue marks the millen-
nium anniversary of the
Magyar conquest in 896.

★ **Mátyás Fountain**
*In the northwest courtyard of the Royal
Palace stands the Mátyás Fountain. It
was designed by Alajos Stróbl in 1904
and depicts King Mátyás Corvinus and
his beloved Ilonka* ❸

Lion Gate, leading to a
rear courtyard of the Royal
Palace, gets its name from
the four lions that watch
over it. These sculptures
were designed by János
Fadrusz in 1901.

TIMELINE

1255 First written document, a letter by King Béla IV, refers to building a fortified castle	**c.1400** Sigismund of Luxembourg builds an ambit-ious Gothic pal-ace on this site	**1541** After captur-ing Buda, the Turks use the Royal Palace to stable horses and store gunpowder	**1719** The building of a small palace begins on the ruins of the old palace, to a design by Hölbling and Fortunato de Prati	**1881** Miklós Ybl *(see p119)* begins programme to re-build and expand the Royal Palace

1200	**1400**	**1600**	**1800**

c.1356 Louis I builds a royal castle on the southern slopes of Castle Hill	**1686** The assault by Christian soldiers leaves the palace completely razed to the ground	**1849** Royal Palace is destroyed again, during an un-successful attack by Hungarian insurgents	Turul *bird*
1458 A Renaissance palace evolves under King Mátyás	**1749** Maria Theresa builds a vast palace comprising 203 chambers		

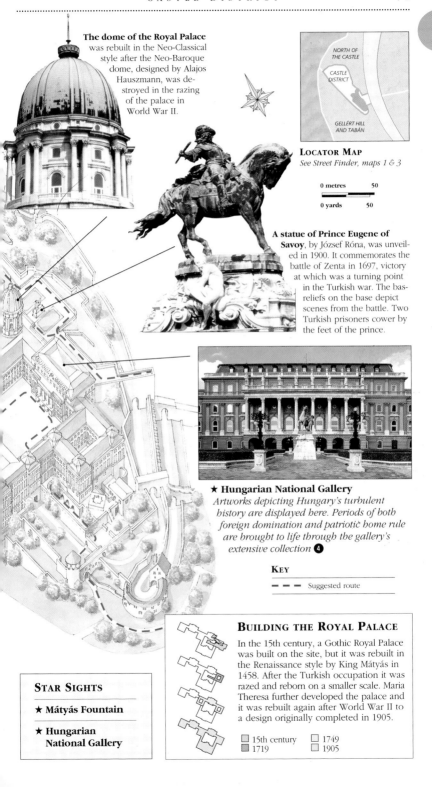

The dome of the Royal Palace was rebuilt in the Neo-Classical style after the Neo-Baroque dome, designed by Alajos Hauszmann, was destroyed in the razing of the palace in World War II.

NORTH OF THE CASTLE

CASTLE DISTRICT

GELLÉRT HILL AND TABÁN

LOCATOR MAP
See Street Finder, maps 1 & 3

| 0 metres | 50 |
| 0 yards | 50 |

A statue of Prince Eugene of Savoy, by József Róna, was unveiled in 1900. It commemorates the battle of Zenta in 1697, victory at which was a turning point in the Turkish war. The bas-reliefs on the base depict scenes from the battle. Two Turkish prisoners cower by the feet of the prince.

★ **Hungarian National Gallery**
Artworks depicting Hungary's turbulent history are displayed here. Periods of both foreign domination and patriotic home rule are brought to life through the gallery's extensive collection ❹

KEY

– – – Suggested route

BUILDING THE ROYAL PALACE

In the 15th century, a Gothic Royal Palace was built on the site, but it was rebuilt in the Renaissance style by King Mátyás in 1458. After the Turkish occupation it was razed and reborn on a smaller scale. Maria Theresa further developed the palace and it was rebuilt again after World War II to a design originally completed in 1905.

| | 15th century | | 1749 |
| | 1719 | | 1905 |

STAR SIGHTS

★ **Mátyás Fountain**

★ **Hungarian National Gallery**

Renaissance majolica floor from the 15th century, uncovered during excavations on Castle Hill and displayed at the Budapest History Museum

Budapest History Museum ❶

BUDAPESTI TÖRTÉNETI MÚZEUM

Szent György tér 2. **Map** 3 C1.
📞 375 75 33. 🚌 16, Várbusz.
🕐 Apr– Oct: 10am–6pm Wed–Mon;
Nov– Mar: 10am–4pm Wed–Mon.
🎫 free Wed.

SINCE THE UNIFICATION of Budapest in 1873, historic artifacts relating to Hungary's capital have been collected. Many are now on show at the Budapest History Museum (also called the Castle Museum).

During the rebuilding that followed the destruction suffered in World War II, chambers dating from the Middle Ages were uncovered in the south wing (wing E) of the Royal Palace. They provide an insight into the character of a much earlier castle within today's Habsburg reconstruction.

These chambers, including a tiny prison cell and a chapel, were recreated in the basement of the palace. They now house an exhibition, the Royal Palace in Medieval Buda, which displays authentic weapons, seals, tiles and other early artifacts.

On the ground floor, the Budapest in the Middle Ages exhibit illustrates the evolution of the town from its Roman origins to a 13th-century Hungarian settlement. The reconstructed defensive walls, gardens and keep on this level are further attractions. Also on the ground floor are

the Gothic Statues from the Royal Palace, dating from the 14th and 15th centuries. These were uncovered by chance in the major excavations of 1974.

The first-floor exhibit, Budapest in Modern Times, traces the history of the city from 1686 to the present day.

Széchenyi National Library ❷

NEMZETI SZÉCHENYI KÖNYVTÁR

Szent György tér 6. **Map** 3 C1. 📞 375 75 33, ext 384. 🚌 16, Várbusz.
🕐 1–6pm Mon, 9am– 6pm Tue–Sat (exhibitions: until 5:30pm).

A MAGNIFICENT COLLECTION of books has been housed, since 1985, in wing F of the Royal Palace, built in 1890– 1902 by Alajos Hauszmann and Miklós Ybl (see p119).

Corviniani illuminated manuscript in the Széchenyi National Library

Previously, the library was part of the Hungarian National Museum (see pp130–33).

Among the library's most precious treasures is the *Corviniani*, a collection of ancient books and manuscripts that originally belonged to King Mátyás Corvinus (see p24–5). His collection was one of the largest Renaissance libraries in Europe. Also of importance are the earliest surviving records in the Hungarian language, dating from the early 13th century.

The library was established by Count Ferenc Széchenyi in 1802. He endowed it with 15,000 books and 2,000 manuscripts. The collection now comprises five million items; everything that has been published in Hungary, in the Hungarian language or that refers to Hungary is here.

Crest on the Mátyás Fountain in a courtyard at the Royal Palace

Mátyás Fountain ❸

MÁTYÁS KÚT

Royal Palace. **Map** 1 C5.
🚌 16, Várbusz.

THE ORNATE FOUNTAIN in the northwest courtyard of the Royal Palace (situated between wings A and C) was designed by Alajos Stróbl in 1904. The statue is dedicated to the great Renaissance king, Mátyás, about whom there are many popular legends and fables.

The Romantic design of the bronze sculptures takes its theme from a 19th-century ballad by the poet Mihály Vörösmarty. According to the tale, King Mátyás, while on a hunting expedition, meets a beautiful peasant girl, Ilonka, who falls in love with him.

This representation shows King Mátyás disguised as hunter, standing proudly with his kill. He is accompanied by his chief hunter and several hunting dogs in the central part of the fountain. Beneath the left-hand columns sits Galeotto Marzio, an Italian court poet, and the figure of the young Ilonka is beneath the columns on the right.

In keeping with the romantic reputation of King Mátyás, a new tradition has grown up concerning this statue. The belief is that anyone wishing to revisit Budapest should throw some coins into the fountain to ensure their safe return.

Hungarian National Gallery ❹

MAGYAR NEMZETI GALÉRIA

See pp 74–7.

Museum of Contemporary History and Ludwig Collection ❺

LEGÚJABBKORI TÖRTÉNETI MÚZEUM ÉS LUDWIG MÚZEUM

Disz tér 17. **Map** 3 C1. ☎ 375 75 33. 🚌 16, Várbusz. ◯ Apr–Oct: 10am–6pm Tue–Sun; Nov–Mar: 10am–4pm Tue–Sun. 🅿 free Tue.

SINCE 1991, WING A of the Royal Palace has been the home of both the Museum of Contemporary History and the Ludwig Collection.

The former was previously the Museum of the Hungarian Workers' Movement. It now has exhibitions on the recent

The western elevation of the Neo-Classical Sándor Palace

social history of Hungary, and includes documents and exhibits dating from the early 20th century to the present day.

The Ludwig Collection is located on the second floor and displays a collection of 150 modern works of art. These were donated, originally loaned, by German patrons Peter and Irene Ludwig in 1989. There is a permanent exhibition showing work by Hungarian artists from the 1960s onwards and another that includes works by artists such as Pablo Picasso.

Sándor Palace ❻

SÁNDOR PALOTA

Szent György tér 1–3. **Map** 1 C5. 🚌 16, Várbusz. ◯ to the public.

BY THE TOP OF the cog-wheel railway stands the grand Neo-Classical mansion, Sándor Palace. It was commissioned in 1806 by Count Vincent Sándor from architects Mihály Pollack and Johann Aman.

The bas-reliefs that decorate the palace are the work of Richárd Török, Miklós Melocco and Tamás Körössényi. The decoration on the western elevation depicts Greek gods on

Mount Olympus. The southern elevation shows Count Sándor being knighted and the northern elevation features a 1934 sculpture of Saint George by Zsigmond Kisfaludi Stróbl.

Sándor Palace functioned as the prime minister's official residence from 1867 to 1944, when it was severely damaged in World War II. It was restored during the 1980s but still remains unoccupied and is closed to the public today.

Castle Theatre ❼

VÁRSZINHÁZ

Szinház utca 1–3. **Map** 1 C5. ☎ 375 86 49. 🚌 16, Várbusz. ◯ 2–6pm Mon–Sat, 10am–6pm Sun.

AN UNLIKELY assortment of institutions have stood on the site now occupied by the Castle Theatre. The church of St John the Evangelist, founded by King Béla IV, stood here in the 13th century. This church was then used as a mosque under Ottoman rule, and in 1686 it was demolished by the Christian armies that retook the city. In 1725 the Carmelite order built a Baroque church in its place, and it is this building that was first converted into a theatre in 1786, during the reign of Emperor Joseph II.

Farkas Kempelen, a famous Hungarian designer, undertook the conversion of the church, adding a Rococo façade and seats for 1,200 spectators. The first plays were in German and it was not until 1790 that any work was staged in Hungarian. Beethoven's concert of 1800 is commemorated by a plaque.

The building suffered considerable damage in World War II and was restored in 1978. Its reopening as a theatre was inaugurated with a performance by the Royal Castle Ensemble.

Imre Bukta's *Pig Killing* (1993) on display in the Ludwig Collection

Hungarian National Gallery ❹

ESTABLISHED IN 1957, the Hungarian National Gallery houses a comprehensive collection of Hungarian art from medieval times to the 20th century. Gathered by various groups and institutions since 1839, these works had previously been exhibited at the Hungarian National Museum *(see pp130–33)* and the Museum of Fine Arts *(see pp146–9)*. The

Sisters by **Erzsébet Schaár**

collection was moved to the Royal Palace (wings B, C and D) in 1975. There are now six permanent exhibitions, presenting the most valuable and critically acclaimed Hungarian art in the world.

St Anne Altarpiece
(1510–20)
Elaborately decorated, this folding altarpiece is one of the Gothic highlights in the gallery.

Madonna of Toporc
(c. 1420)
This is a captivating example of medieval wood sculpture in the Gothic style. It was originally crafted for a church in Spiz (now part of Slovakia).

First floor

Madonna of Bártfy
(1465–70)
This painting of a Madonna and Child is from a church in Bártfy (now in Slovakia). It is thought to have been painted in Cracow, Poland.

★ The Visitation *(1506)*
This painting by Master MS is a delightful example of late Gothic Hungarian art. It is a fragment of a folding altarpiece from a church in Selmecbánya in modern-day Slovakia.

Ground floor

Main entrance

KEY

☐	Stone sculptures and artifacts
☐	Gothic works
☐	Late Gothic altarpieces
☐	Renaissance and Baroque works
☐	19th-century works
☐	Early 20th-century works
☐	Temporary exhibitions

STAR EXHIBITS

★ The Visitation

★ Picnic in May

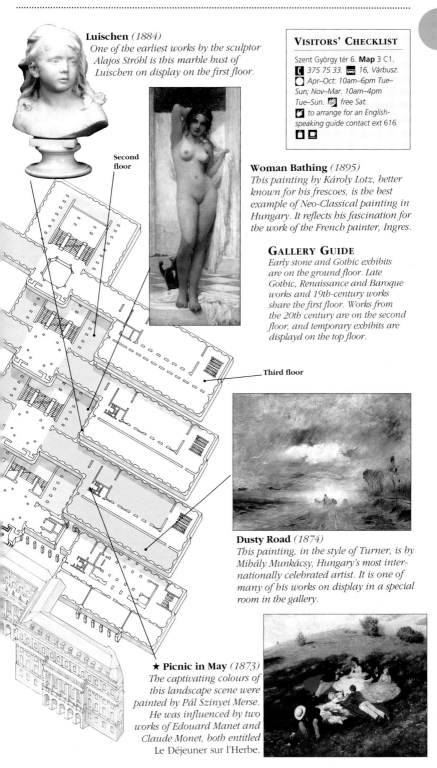

Luischen (1884)
One of the earliest works by the sculptor Alajos Stróbl is this marble bust of Luischen on display on the first floor.

Second floor

Woman Bathing (1895)
This painting by Károly Lotz, better known for his frescoes, is the best example of Neo-Classical painting in Hungary. It reflects his fascination for the work of the French painter, Ingres.

GALLERY GUIDE
Early stone and Gothic exhibits are on the ground floor. Late Gothic, Renaissance and Baroque works and 19th-century works share the first floor. Works from the 20th century are on the second floor, and temporary exhibits are displayd on the top floor.

Third floor

Dusty Road (1874)
This painting, in the style of Turner, is by Mihály Munkácsy, Hungary's most internationally celebrated artist. It is one of many of his works on display in a special room in the gallery.

★ **Picnic in May** (1873)
The captivating colours of this landscape scene were painted by Pál Szinyei Merse. He was influenced by two works of Edouard Manet and Claude Monet, both entitled Le Déjeuner sur l'Herbe.

Exploring the Hungarian National Gallery

T HE WORKS ARE DISPLAYED in six permanent exhibitions and give a thorough insight into Hungarian art from the early Middle Ages to the present day. Although one-and-a-half centuries of Turkish occupation and wartime destruction interrupted the development of Hungarian art, the birth of national pride in the 19th century allowed a new indigenous style to develop. Among the most interesting are the Hungarian paintings of the late 19th century, when a greater diversity of styles came to the fore.

The Habsburg Crypt, with the sarcophagus of Palatine Archduke Joseph

THE LAPIDARIUM

O N THE GROUND FLOOR, to the left of the main entrance, is a display of stone objects discovered during the reconstruction of the Royal Palace *(see p70)*. Called the Lapidarium, it includes sculptures and fragments of architectural features, such as balustrades and windows, that decorated the royal chambers during the Angevin and Jagiełło eras *(see p18)*. The most valuable exhibit, however, is a sculpture of King Béla III's head, which dates from around 1200.

Also in this first section are two marble bas-reliefs of King Matthias and his wife Beatrice, by an unknown Renaissance master from Lombardy.

The second section exhibits late Gothic and Renaissance artifacts from other palaces in Hungary. There are pillars and balustrades from the palace at Visegrád and bas-reliefs from a chapel in Esztergom.

King's head sculpted from black marble

GOTHIC WORKS

A COLLECTION OF painted panels, sculptures and fragments of altar decoration is opposite the Lapidarium. Note, however, the image of the *Madonna of Bártfy*, which is a rare complete example from the Gothic period.

The sculptures of the "Beautiful Madonnas" are executed in the Soft Style. This style is

characterized, as its name suggests, by the sentimental and gentle imagery of the Madonna playing with the Christ child.

The Annunciation, a magnificent late Gothic work by Master GH, is, in fact, only the main section of an altar; the other pieces are now in Esztergom *(see p164)*.

RENAISSANCE AND BAROQUE WORKS

T HE EXHIBITION BEGINS with a still life by Jakab Bogdány (1660–1724) and portraits by Ádám Mányoki (1673–1757) *(see p28)*, who actually settled outside Hungary. As a result of the powerful influence of the Habsburgs during this period *(see pp28–9)*, Baroque art was overwhelmingly dominated by Austrian artists. Painters such as Joseph Dorfmeister and Franz Anton Maulbertsch and sculptors Georg Raphael Donner and Philipp Jakob Straub were the acknowledged masters. Jan Kupetzky's portraits are also exemplary models of this era.

The sculptures by Donner and the sacred paintings of Dorfmeister conclude this section of the gallery.

LATE GOTHIC ALTARPIECES

O NE OF THE STAR exhibits of this collection is the imposing late Gothic altarpiece. Arranged in the Great Throne Room, the majority of these vast altarpieces date from the 15th and early 16th centuries.

The Great Throne Room, displaying the collection of folding altarpieces

Architecturally these altarpieces are pure Gothic, while adorned with sculptures and paintings revealing a Renaissance influence. This is evident in the altars of St Anne and St John the Baptist from a church in Kisszeben (now Sabinov in Slovakia), which date from 1510–16. The most recent altarpiece dates from 1643 and is from the church of Our Lady Mary in Csíkmenaság.

Lebanese Cedar **by Tivadar Kosztka Csontváry (1907)**

Bertalan Székely's *Women of Eger* (1867), depicting the Turkish wars

19TH-CENTURY WORKS

THE WONDERFUL collection of works from this period reflects the rise of fine art in Hungary in the 19th century.

Historicist art developed during this period. Among those distinguishing themselves in particular were Gyula Benczúr and Bertalan Székely, who produced the epic works *The Return of Buda in 1686* (1896) and *Women of Eger* (1867) respectively. The latter depicts the women of the town defending the Castle of Eger against the Turks.

Viktor Madarász's work *The Mourning of László Hunyadi* (1859) refers to the execution of László Hunyadi by the Habsburgs in 1457. It alludes, too, to the execution of many Hungarians after the crushing of the uprising against Austria in 1849 *(see pp30–31).*

European developments in fine art can also be seen in Hungarian painting from the late-19th century. The influence of Impressionism, for example, is best seen in Pál Szinyei Merse's *Picnic in May* (1873).

Hungarian Realism is expressed in the work of Lászlo Paál and Mihály Munkácsy, the latter being widely regarded as the country's greatest artist. Paintings by Munkácsy which deserve particular attention are *The Yawning Traveller* (1869), *Woman Carrying Brushwood* (1870), *Dusty Road* (1874), and the still life *Flowers* (1881).

It is also worth spending a few moments seeing the paintings of the Neo-Classical artists. The work of Károly Lotz, who is perhaps better known for his frescoes that can be seen on walls and ceilings around Budapest, is exhibited here.

20TH-CENTURY WORKS

EXAMPLES OF WORK from the Secession era through to Expressionism and Surrealism, and even contemporary art are exhibited here. They provide a comprehensive review of 20th-century Hungarian art.

The work of József Rippl-Rónai, who studied in France, shows the influence of the Secession style in *The Palace in Körtvélyes* and *Woman with a Birdcage*. But one of the most engaging artists from the early-20th century is Károly Ferenczy whose *The Painter* (1923) exemplifies the serene qualities of his work.

Tivadar Kosztka Csontváry is an artist whose work did not follow any conventional style but was greatly admired, even by Pablo Picasso. Two paintings in particular capture

his abstract interpretation of the world: the *Ruins of the Greek Amphitheatre in Taormina* (1905) and the well-known *Lebanese Cedar* (1907).

The Eight, a group of artists who set up the first Hungarian avant-garde school, were active between the two world wars. Notable examples of their work are *Young Girl with a Bow* by Béla Czóbel, *Woman Playing a Doublebass* by Róbert Berény, *The Oarsmen* by Ödön Marffy, *Walking by the Water Tower* by István Farkas and *Riders at the Edge* by Károly Kernstok.

The best works of Hungarian Expressionism can be seen in the paintings *Along the Tracks*, *For Bread* and *Generations*, by Gyula Derkovits.

Among the sculptures on display, the most interesting are *Raising Oneself* and *The Sower*, by Ferenc Medgyessy, and *Standing Girl*, by Béni Ferenczy. The exhibition is completed by a section on contemporary artists.

The Painter **by Károly Ferenczy (1923), a typically peaceful work**

Street-by-Street: the Old Town

Bas-reliefs on a house on Fortuna utca

BUDA'S OLD TOWN has been a barometer of Hungary's changing fortunes. It developed, to the north of the Royal Palace, from the 13th century. Under kings such as Sigismund, it flourished, and wealthy German merchants set up shops in Lords' Street (Úri utca) to supply the court. The area was later destroyed by the Turks and again by their evictors. It was most recently rebuilt after World War II, but genuine relics can be hunted out in its cobbled streets and squares.

Mihály Táncsics Street
During the Middle Ages, this street was inhabited by Jews. A museum at No. 26, on the site of an old synagogue, displays finds such as tombstones **⑮**

The State Archive of Historic Documents, located in a Neo-Romanesque building, houses items that were transferred to Buda in 1785 from the former capital of Hungary, Bratislava.

Surviving tower of the Church of St Mary Magdalene

Defensive walls

0 metres	50
0 yards	50

★ **Museum of Commerce and Catering**
This unusual museum offers visitors a glimpse into catering and the trades connected with it from days gone by. A 19th-century grocer's shop is recreated and period utensils and posters can also be seen **⑱**

★ **Lords' Street**
Once the homes of aristocrats and merchants, the houses on this street have medieval foundations. Many have Gothic details and peaceful courtyards **㉒**

KEY

– – – Suggested route

★ Mátyás Church
Although with much earlier parts, this church is mainly a Neo-Gothic reconstruction dating from 1874–96. A picturesque vestibule on the church's southern façade covers an original Gothic portal dating from the 14th century ⑪

LOCATOR MAP
See Street Finder, map 1

This statue of St Stephen, or István, the first crowned king of Hungary *(see pp22–3)*, was erected in 1906. Its pedestal includes a bas-relief showing scenes from the king's life.

Fishermen's Bastion
Designed by Frigyes Schulek in 1905, this fantastical structure never had the role of a defensive building, despite its name. It serves instead as a viewing terrace. The conical towers are an allusion to the tribal tents of the early Magyars ⑫

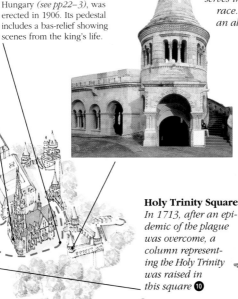

Holy Trinity Square
In 1713, after an epidemic of the plague was overcome, a column representing the Holy Trinity was raised in this square ⑩

Golden Eagle Pharmacy Museum
From the 18th century a pharmacy called "Under the Golden Eagle" traded in this medieval house, now a museum ⑨

STAR SIGHTS

- ★ **Mátyás Church**
- ★ **Museum of Commerce and Catering**
- ★ **Lords' Street**

Batthyány Palace on Parade Square

Parade Square ❽

DÍSZ TÉR

Map 1 B5. 🚌 *Várbusz.*

PARADE SQUARE IS named after the military parades held here in the 19th century. At the northern end of the square is the Honvéd Monument, built in 1893 by György Zala. It honours and commemorates those who died during the recapture of Buda from Austria in 1848.

The house at No. 3 was built between 1743–8, by József Giessl. This two-floor Baroque palace was the home of the Batthyány family until 1945. Although the building has been frequently remodelled, the façade has remained intact.

A few houses on Parade Square were built incorporating medieval remains. Such houses can be seen at Nos. 4–5 and 11, built by Venerio Ceresola. The former has seat niches dating from the 13th century.

Golden Eagle Pharmacy Museum ❾

PATIKAMÚZEUM

Tárnok utca 18. **Map** 1 B5. 📞 *375 97 72.* 🚌 *16, Várbusz.* ⏰ *10:15am– 5:30pm Tue–Sun.* 🕹

THIS PHARMACY WAS opened in 1688 by Ferenc Ignác Bösinger and traded under the name the "Golden Eagle" from 1740. It moved to this originally Gothic building, with its Baroque interior and Neo-Classical façade, in the 18th century.

The museum opened here in 1974. It displays pharmaceutical items from the Renaissance and Baroque eras, including a collection of china instruments.

Holy Trinity Square ❿

SZENTHÁROMSÁG TÉR

Map 1 B4. 🚌 *Várbusz from Moszkva tér.*

THIS SQUARE IS the central point of the Old Town. It takes its name from the Baroque Holy Trinity Column, originally sculpted by Philipp Ungleich in 1710–13, and restored in 1967. The column commemorates the dead of two outbreaks of the plague, which struck the inhabitants of Buda in 1691 and 1709.

The pedestal of the column is decorated with bas-reliefs by Anton Hörger. Further up are statues of holy figures and at the summit is a magnificent composition of the figures of the Holy Trinity. The central section of the column is decorated with angelic figures surrounded by clouds.

Buda's Old Town Hall, a large Baroque building with two courtyards, was also built on the square at the beginning of the 18th century. It was designed by the imperial court architect, Venerio Ceresola, whose architectural scheme incorporated the remains of medieval houses. In 1770–74 an east wing was built, and bay windows and a stone balustrade with Rococo urns, by Mátyás Nepauer, were also added. The corner niche, opposite Mátyás Church, houses a small statue by Carlo Adami of Pallas Athene.

Near Holy Trinity Square, at No. 7 Trinity utca, is the patisserie Ruszwurm, *(see p201)*. Opened in 1827, it has retained its original Empire styling.

Mátyás Church ⓫

MÁTYÁS TEMPLOM

See pp82–3.

Fishermen's Bastion ⓬

HALÁSZBÁSTYA

Szentháromsag tér. **Map** 1 B4.

FRIGYES SCHULEK DESIGNED this Neo-Romanesque monument to the Guild of Fishermen in 1895. It occupies the site of Buda's old defensive walls and a medieval square where fish was once sold. This building, from which a beautiful view of the Danube and Pest can be seen, is a purely aesthetic addition to Castle Hill.

In front of the bastion is a statue of St István, the king who first introduced Hungary to Christianity.

Buda's Old Town Hall, its clock tower crowned with an onion-shaped dome, on Holy Trinity Square

Bas-relief depicting King Mátyás on the façade of the Hilton Hotel

Hilton Hotel ⓭

HILTON SZÁLLÓ

Hess András tér 1–2. **Map** 1 B4.
📞 214 30 00. 🚍 Várbusz.

B UILT IN 1976, the Hilton Hotel is an rare example of modern architecture in the Old Town. Controversial from the outset, the design by the Hungarian architect Béla Pintér combines the historic remains of the site with contemporary materials and methods.

From 1254 a Dominican church, to which a tower was later added, stood on this site, followed by a late-Baroque Jesuit monastery. The remains of both these buildings are incorporated into the design. For example, the remains of the medieval church, uncovered during excavations in 1902, form part of the Dominican Courtyard, where concerts and operettas are staged during the summer season.

Similarly, the main façade, overlooking the Danube, comprises part of the façade of the Jesuit monastery. To the left of the entrance is St Nicholas's Tower. In 1930, a replica of the 15th-century German bas-relief of King Mátyás, considered to be his most authentic likeness, was added to this tower.

András Hess Square ⓮

HESS ANDRÁS TÉR

Map 1 B4.
🚍 Várbusz from Moszkva tér.

T HIS SQUARE IS NAMED after the Italian-trained printer who printed the first Hungarian book, *Chronica Hungarorum*, in a printing works at No. 4 in 1473. The house was rebuilt at the end of the 17th century as an amalgamation of three medieval houses, with quadruple seat niches, barrel-vaulted cellars and ornamental gates.

The former inn at No. 3 was named the Red Hedgehog in 1696. This one-floor building has surviving Gothic and Baroque elements.

The square also features a statue by József Damkó of Pope Innocent XI, who was involved in organizing the armies who recaptured Buda from the Turks. It was built to mark the 250th anniversary of the liberation, in 1936.

Hedgehog on the façade of No. 3 András Hess Square

Mihály Táncsics Street ⓯

TÁNCSICS MIHÁLY UTCA

Map 1 B4. 🚍 Várbusz.
Museum of Musical History
📞 375 9011. 🕐 May–Oct:
10am–6pm Wed–Sun, 4–8pm Mon.

S TANDING AT NO. 7 is Erdődy Palace, built in 1750–69 for the Erdődy family by Mátyás

Nepauer, the leading architect of the day. It features outstanding Baroque façades on its Danube, courtyard and street sides. Like many houses on this street, it was erected on the ruins of medieval houses.

In 1800, Ludwig van Beethoven, who was then giving concerts in Budapest, resided here for a short period.

The palace now houses the Museum of Musical History and the Béla Bartók archives. A permanent exhibition illustrates musical life in Budapest from the 18th to 20th centuries, and includes the oldest surviving Hungarian musical instruments.

The Royal Mint stood on the site of No. 9 during the Middle Ages, and, in 1810, the Joseph Barracks were built here. These were later used by the Habsburgs to imprison leaders of the 1848–9 uprising, including Mihály Táncsics himself.

An original mural has survived on the façade of the house at No. 16, which dates from around 1700. It depicts Christ and the Virgin Mary surrounded by saints. The bas-reliefs on the gateway are, however, from a Venetian church.

Relics of Buda's Jewish heritage can be found at Nos. 23 and 26. The remains of a 15th-century synagogue stand in the garden of the mansion at No. 23. During archeological excavations, tombs and religious items were also found in the courtyard of No. 26.

The Museum of Musical History on Mihály Táncsics Street

Mátyás Church ⓫

THE PARISH CHURCH of Our Lady Mary was built on this site between the 13th and 15th centuries. Some of the existing architectural style dates from the reign of Sigismund of Luxembourg, but its name refers to King Mátyás Corvinus, who greatly enlarged and embellished the church. Much of the original detail was lost when the Turks converted the church into the Great Mosque in 1541. During the liberation of Buda the church was almost totally destroyed, but was rebuilt in the Baroque style by Franciscan Friars. The church sustained more damage in 1723, and was restored in the Neo-Gothic style by Frigyes Schulek in 1873–96. The crypt houses the Museum of Ecclesiastical Art.

Rose Window
Frigyes Schulek faithfully reproduced the medieval stained-glass window that was in this position during the early Gothic era.

Béla Tower
This tower is named after the church's founder, King Béla IV. It has retained several of its original Gothic features.

★ Baroque Madonna
According to legend, the original statue was set into a wall of the church during the Turkish occupation. When the church was virtually destroyed in 1686, the Madonna made a miraculous appearance. The Turks took this as an omen of defeat.

Main Portal
Above the arched west entrance is a 19th-century bas-relief of the Madonna and Child, seated between two angels. The work is by Lajos Lantai.

STAR FEATURES

★ Baroque Madonna

★ Mary Portal

★ Tomb of King Béla III and Anne de Châtillon

★ Tomb of King Béla III and Anne de Châtillon
The remains of this royal couple were transferred from Székesfehérvár Cathedral to Mátyás Church in 1860. They lie beneath an ornamental stone canopy in the Trinity Chapel.

VISITORS' CHECKLIST

Szentháromság tér. **Map** 1 B4.
🚌 Várbusz. ⏰ 6am–8pm. ✝
7am, 8:30am, 6pm daily. ♿ 📷
Museum of Ecclesiastical Art
⏰ 9:30am–5:30pm daily. 📷

Pulpit
The richly decorated pulpit includes the carved stone figures of the four Fathers of the Church and the four Evangelists.

The roof is decorated with multicoloured glazed tiles.

The main altar was created by Frigyes Schulek and based on Gothic triptychs.

Stained-Glass Windows
Three arched windows on the south elevation have beautiful 19th-century stained glass. They were designed by Frigyes Schulek, Bertalan Székely and Károly Lotz.

★ Mary Portal
This depiction of the Assumption of the Blessed Virgin Mary is the most magnificent example of Gothic stone carving in Hungary. Frigyes Schulek reconstructed the portal using fragments that remained after World War II.

TIMELINE

1250	1350	1450	1550	1650	1750	1850	1950

c.1387 Church redesigned as Gothic hall-church by Sigismund of Luxembourg

1458 Thanksgiving mass following the coronation of Mátyás Corvinus

1541 Turks convert church into a mosque

1686 After liberation of Buda from Turkish rule, church is almost destroyed. New church built with a Baroque interior

Holy figures on the pulpit

1309 Coronation of the Angevin king Charles Robert

1526 Cathedral burnt in the first attack by Turks

1896 Frigyes Schulek completes the reconstruction of the church in the Neo-Gothic style

1970 Final details are completed in post-war rebuilding programme

1255 Church originally founded by King Béla IV after the Mongol invasion

1470 Mátyás Tower is completed after its collapse in 1384

1945 Church is severely damaged by German and Russian armies

Vienna Gate, rebuilt in 1936, commemorating the liberation of Buda

In 1966 the world's first catering museum opened here. Small but charming, this exhibition displays, among other items, the interior of a Buda pâtisserie from 1870 and the bust of Emil Gerbeaud, the founder of Pest's most famous coffee shop, by Alajos Stróbl.

Vienna Gate Square ⑯

BÉCSI KAPU TÉR

Map 1 B4.
Várbusz from Moszkva tér.

THE SQUARE TAKES its name from the gate that once led from the walled town of Buda towards Vienna. After being damaged several times, the old gate was demolished in 1896. The current gate, based on a historic design, was erected in 1936 on the 250th anniversary of the liberation of Buda from the Turks.

The square has a number of interesting houses. Those at Nos. 5, 6, 7 and 8 were built on the ruins of medieval dwellings. They are Baroque and Rococo in design and feature sculptures and bas-reliefs. The façade of No. 7 has medallions with the portraits of Classical philosophers and poets; Thomas Mann, the German novelist, lodged here between 1935–6. No. 8, meanwhile, is differentiated by its bay windows, attics and the restored medieval murals on its façade.

On the left-hand side of the square is a vast Neo-Romanesque building with a beautiful multicoloured roof, built in 1913–20 by Samu Pecz. This building houses the National Archive, which holds documents dating from before the battle of Mohács in 1526 and others connected with the Rákóczi and Kossuth uprisings (see pp 25, 31 and 38).

A monument built in honour of Mihály Táncsics, the leader of the Autumn Uprising, also stands in Vienna Gate Square. It was unveiled in 1970.

Buda Lutheran Church ⑰

BUDAVÁRI EVANGÉLIKUS TEMPLOM

Bécsi kapu tér. **Map** 1 B4.
Várbusz.

FACING THE VIENNA GATE is the Neo-Classical Lutheran church, built in 1896 by Mór Kollina. A plaque commemorates pastor Gábor Sztéhló, who saved 2,000 children during World War II.

At one time, a painting by Bertalan Székely, called *Christ Blessing the Bread*, adorned the altar, but it was unfortunately destroyed during the war.

Museum of Commerce and Catering ⑱

KERESKEDELMI ÉS VENDÉGLÁTÓIPARI MÚZEUM

Fortuna utca 4. **Map** 1 B4.
375 62 49. Várbusz.
10am–5pm Wed–Fri, 10am–6pm Sat–Sun.

FORMERLY THE Fortuna Inn from 1784–1868, this building was erected on the ruins of three medieval houses in the 17th and 18th centuries. The façade has original Gothic niches and a Baroque gate.

Parliament Street ⑲

ORSZÁGHÁZ UTCA

Map 1 A4 & 1 B4.

THIS STREET was once inhabited by Florentine artisans and craftsmen working on King Mátyás' Royal Palace (see pp70–71) and was known for a time as Italian Street. Its present name comes from the building at No. 28, where the Hungarian parliament met from 1790–1807. This building was designed in the 18th century by the architect Franz Anton Hillebrandt as a convent for the Poor Clares. However, Emperor Joseph II dissolved the order before the building was completed.

Numerous houses on this street have retained attractive Gothic and Baroque features. No. 2, now with a Neo-Classical façade, is the site of the Alabárdos Étterem (see p196), but its history dates back to the late 13th century. In the 15th century, Sigismund of Luxembourg built a Gothic mansion here and some details, such as the colonnade around the courtyard and the murals on the second floor, have survived until the present day. The entrance to No. 9 features the Gothic traceried seat niches popular in Buda at this time.

In front of the Neo-Classical house at No. 21 is a statue of Márton Lendvay (1807–58), a famous Hungarian actor and member of the Hungarian National Theatre.

An enamelled box from the Gerbeaud Pâtisserie

The reconstructed Baroque tower of the Church of St Mary Magdalene

Church of St Mary Magdalene **⑳**

MÁRIA MAGDOLNA TEMPLOM TORNYA

Kapisztrán tér 6. **Map** 1 A4.
🚌 *Várbusz.*

N OW IN RUINS, this church was built in the mid-13th century. During the Middle Ages, Hungarian Christians worshipped here as Mátyás Church was only for use by the town's German population.

The church did not become a mosque until the second half of the Turkish occupation, but was severely damaged in 1686 during the liberation of Buda. A Baroque church and tower were then built by the Franciscans who took it over.

After World War II, all but the tower and the gate were pulled down. These now stand in a garden, together with the reconstructed Gothic window.

Museum of Military History **㉑**

HADTÖRTÉNETI MÚZEUM

Kapisztran tér 2–4. **Map** 1 A4.
📞 356 95 86. 🚌 *Várbusz.*
🕐 *Apr–Sep: 10am–6pm Tue–Sun; Oct–Mar: 10am–4pm Tue–Sun.* 📷
📷 *by arrangement.*

T HE MUSEUM IS LOCATED in a wing of the former Palatine barracks. It houses a wide range of military items relating to the skirmishes and wars that have afflicted Budapest from before the Turkish occupation to the 20th century. Uniforms, flags, weapons, maps and ammunition from as far back as the 11th century give an insight into the long, turbulent history of Budapest.

Of particular interest is the exhibit concerning the 1956 Uprising. Photographs illustrate the 13 days of demonstrations that ended in a Soviet invasion and a huge civilian death toll.

Lords' Street **㉒**

ÚRI UTCA

Map 1 A4, 1 B4 and 1 B5.
🚌 *Várbusz.* **Telephone Museum**
📞 *201 81 88.* 🕐 *Apr–Oct: 10am–6pm Tue– Sun; Nov–Mar 10am–4pm Tue–Sun.* 📷 **Labyrinth** 📞 *375 68 58.* 🕐 *9:30am– 7:30pm daily.*

T HE BUILDINGS IN Lords' Street were destroyed first in 1686 and again in 1944. Reconstruction in 1950 –60 restored much of their original medieval character. Almost all have some remnant of a Gothic gateway or hall, while the façade is Baroque or Neo-Classical.

An excellent example of a Gothic façade can be seen on Hölbling House at No. 31. Enough of its original features survived the various wars and renovations to enable architects to reconstruct the façade in considerable detail. The first-floor window is a particularly splendid Gothic feature. The houses opposite are also examples of this restoration work.

The building at No. 53 was rebuilt between 1701–22 as a Franciscan monastery, but in 1789 it was restyled for use by Emperor Joseph II. In 1795, Hungarian Jacobites, led by Ignác Martinovics, were imprisoned here; a plaque records this event. A well featuring a copy of a sculpture of Artemis, the Greek goddess of hunting, by Praxiteles, was set in front of the house in 1873.

There are two museums located on Lords' Street. The Telephone Museum, at No. 49, is a former telephone exchange and one of the most fun and interactive museums in the city. At No. 9 is the entrance to the Labyrinth. Visitors to this new attraction can explore a section of the expansive complex of cellars, dungeons, springs and caves that run beneath Castle Hill. Within the Labyrinth is an exhibition focusing on the early period of Hungarian history and on the legends, such as that of the Magic Stag, that are connected with this era.

Lords' Street, which runs the full length of the Old Town

GELLÉRT HILL AND TABÁN

ISING STEEPLY beside the Danube, Gellért Hill is one of the city's most attractive areas. From the top, at a height of 140 m (460 ft), a beautiful view of the whole of Budapest unfolds. The Celtic Eravi, who preceded the Romans, formed their settlement on the hill's northern slope *(see p94)*. Once called simply Old Hill, many superstitions and tales are connected

Carving on the altar in the Cave Church

with it. In 1046, heathen citizens threw a sealed barrel containing Bishop Gellért, who was trying to convert them to Christianity, from the hill to his death. Afterwards, the hill was named after this martyr. Gellért Hill bulges out slightly into the Danube, which narrows at this point. This made the base of the hill a favoured crossing place, and the settlement of Tabán evolved as a result.

KEY

- ▢ Street-by-Street map *See pp88–9*
- P Parking
- M Metro
- Police station
- ✕ Post office
- Bus stop

0 metres   300
0 yards   300

SIGHTS AT A GLANCE

Museums
Semmelweis Museum of Medical History ⑫

Churches
Cave Church ②
Tabán Parish Church ⑩

Historic Buildings
Citadel ④
Golden Stag House ⑬

Hotels and Baths
Gellért Hotel and Baths Complex pp90–91 ①
Rác Baths ⑨
Rudas Baths ⑥

Districts, Squares and Monuments
Empress Elizabeth Monument ⑦
Gellért Monument ⑤
Liberation Monument ③
Miklós Ybl Square ⑪
Tabán ⑧

GETTING THERE

The easiest ways to ascend Gellért Hill are to drive up, or to take bus 27, which makes its way from Móricz Zsigmond körtér right up to the top of the hill. Tram 19 travels to Tabán along the Danube from the tram station at Batthyány tér, while bus 86 stops there on its route from Óbuda. Buses 5, 7, 8, 78, 112 and 116, all originating in Pest, also make stops in Tabán.

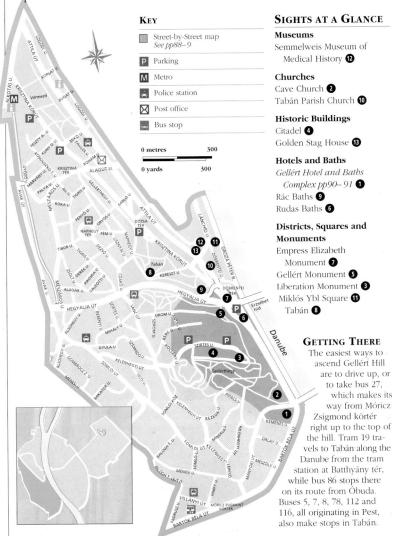

◁ **The Gellért Monument, dedicated to a murdered 11th-century bishop**

Street-by-Street: Gellért Hill

THE HILL TO THE SOUTH OF CASTLE HILL was long regarded as a notorious spot. In the 11th century, Prince Vata, brother of King István, incited a heathen rebellion here that resulted in the death of Bishop Gellért. During the Middle Ages, witches were even reputed to celebrate their sabbath here. Under the Turks, a small strong-hold was first built on the hill to protect Buda. In 1851, the Austrians placed their own bleak and intimidating Citadel at the summit. Not until the end of the 19th century did the popular image of Gellért Hill begin to change, when it became a venue for picnicking parties. In 1967, the area around the Citadel was made into an attractive park.

★ Gellért Monument
Blessing the city with his uplifted cross, the martyred Bishop Gellért is the patron saint of Budapest ❺

Empress Elizabeth Monument
Close to the entrance to Elizabeth Bridge stands this statue of Emperor Franz Joseph's wife, who was popular with the Hungarians ❼

HEGYALJA ÚT

Citadel
Once a place to inspire terror, the Citadel now hosts a hotel, restaurant and wine bar, where people can relax and enjoy the view ❹

0 metres		500
0 yards		500

KEY

- - - Suggested route

Liberation Monument
At the foot of the Liberation Monument, towering above the city, are two sculptures, one representing the battle with evil ❸

STAR SIGHTS

★ **Gellért Monument**

★ **Cave Church**

The observation terraces on Gellért Hill provide those who climb up to them with a beautiful panorama over the southern part of Buda and the whole of Pest.

LOCATOR MAP
See Street Finder, maps 3 and 4

★ **Cave Church**
This church was established in 1926 in a holy grotto. Under the Communists, the Pauline order of monks was forced to abandon the church, but it was reopened in 1989 ❷

Gellért Hotel and Baths Complex
One of a number of bath complexes built at the beginning of the 20th century, this magnificent spa hotel was erected here to exploit the natural hot springs ❶

Rudas Baths
These famous Turkish baths, which date from the 16th century, have a characteristic Ottoman cupola ❻

SZENT GELLÉRT RAKPART

THE RESERVOIR

In 1978, a reservoir for drinking water was established close to the Uránia Observatory on Gellért Hill. The surface of the reservoir is covered over and provides a point from which to observe the Royal Palace *(see pp70–71)* to the north. A sculpture by Márta Lessenyei decorates the structure.

Sculpture by Márta Lessenyei on Gellért Hill's reservoir

Gellért Hotel and Baths Complex ❶

Bᴇᴛᴡᴇᴇɴ 1912–18, this hotel and spa was built in the modernist Secession style *(see pp54–7)* at the foot of Gellért Hill. The earliest reference to the existence of healing waters at this spot dates from the 13th century, during the reign of King András II and in the Middle Ages a hospital stood on the site.

Stained-glass window by Bózó Stanisits

Baths built here by the Ottomans were referred to by the renowned Turkish travel writer of the day, Evliya Çelebi. The architects of the hotel were Ármin Hegedűs, Artúr Sebestyén and Izidor Sterk. Destroyed in 1945, it was rebuilt and modernized after World War II. The hotel has several restaurants and cafés. The baths include an institute of water therapy, set within Secession interiors, but with modern facilities.

Outdoor Wave Pool
An early swimming pool with a wave mechanism, built in 1927, is situated at the back of the complex, looking towards Gellért Hill behind.

★ Baths
Two separate baths, one for men and one for women, are identically arranged. In each there are three plunge pools, with water at different temperatures, a sauna and a steam bath.

Balconies
The balconies fronting the hotel's rooms have fanciful Secession balustrades that are decorated with lyre and bird motifs.

★ Entrance Hall
The interiors of the hotel, like the baths, have kept their original Secession decor, with elaborate mosaics, stained-glass windows and statues.

Sun Terraces
Situated in the sunniest spot, these terraces are a popular place for drying off in the summer.

VISITORS' CHECKLIST

Szent Gellért tér. **Map** 3 C3.
☎ 466 61 66. 🚌 7, 7A, 86.
🚋 18, 19, 47, 49. ⊘ 🛗 🖥 🍴
🛁 **Baths** Entrance on Kelenhegyi
út. 🕐 6am–7pm Mon–Fri,
6am–5pm Sat & Sun. 🛀 ⊘ 🛗

Hot pool with medicinal spa water

Eastern-Style Towers
The architects who designed the hotel gave its towers and turrets a characteristically oriental, cylindrical form.

Main Staircase
The landings of the main staircase have stained-glass windows by Bózó Stanisits, added in 1933. They illustrate an ancient Hungarian legend about a magic stag, recorded in the poetry of János Arany.

Restaurant Terrace
From this first-floor terrace, diners can appreciate a fine view of Budapest. On the ground and first floors of the hotel there are a total of four cafés and restaurants.

★ Main Façade
Behind the hotel's imposing façade are attractive recreational facilities and a health spa that is also open to non-guests. The entrance to the baths is around to the right from the main entrance, on Kelenhegyi út.

STAR FEATURES

★ **Entrance Hall**

★ **Baths**

★ **Main Façade**

Gellért Hotel and Baths Complex ❶
GELLÉRT SZÁLLÓ ÉS FÜRDŐ

See pp90–91.

Cave Church ❷
SZIKLATEMPLOM

Gellért rakpart 1a. **Map** 4 E3. 🚌 7, 7A, 86. 🚋 18, 19, 47, 49.

ON THE SOUTHERN slope of Gellért Hill, the entrance to this grotto church is a short walk from the Gellért Hotel and Baths Complex. Based on the shrine at Lourdes, the church, designed by Kálman Lux, was established in 1926.

The church was intended for the Pauline order of monks, which was founded in the 13th century by Eusebius of Esztergom. In 1934, 150 years after Joseph II had dissolved the order in Hungary, 15 friars arrived back in the city from exile in Poland. However, their residence lasted only until the late 1950s, when the Communist authorities suspended the activities of the church, accusing the monks of treasonable acts, and sealed the entrance to the grotto.

The church and adjoining monastery were reopened on 27 August 1989, when a papal blessing was conferred on its beautiful new granite altar, designed by Győző Sikot. To the left within the grotto is a copy of the *Black Madonna of Czestochowa* and a depiction of a Polish eagle. Visitors will also see a painting of St Kolbe, a Polish monk who gave his

life to protect other inmates at Auschwitz concentration camp. A memorial plaque lists the names of the camps where Polish soldiers were interned during World War II, together with the towns and schools where Polish refugees were sheltered in those years.

The monastery can be reached through the Chapel of St István inside the church. While in this chapel it is worth pausing to look at Béli Ferenc's exquisite wooden sculptures.

Liberation Monument ❸
FELSZABADULÁSI EMLÉKMŰ

Map 4 D3. 🚌 27.

POSITIONED HIGH on Gellért Hill, this imposing monument towers over the rest of the city. It was designed by the outstanding Hungarian sculptor Zsigmond Kisfaludi Stróbl and set up here to commemorate the liberation of Budapest by the Russian army in 1945 *(see p34)*. The monument was, the story persists, originally intended to honour the memory of István, son of the Hungarian Regent Miklós Horthy, who disappeared in 1943 on the eastern front. However, after the liberation of the city by Russian troops, Marshal Klimient Woroszyłow spotted it in the sculptor's workshop and re-assigned it to this purpose.

The central figure on the monument is a woman holding aloft a palm leaf. Standing on

The Liberation Monument, standing at the top of Gellért Hill

its pedestal, this reaches a height of 14 m (46 ft). At the base of the monument there are two allegorical compositions, representing progress and the battle with evil.

The arrival of the Russians in Budapest was a liberation but also the beginning of Soviet rule. After Communism's fall, a figure of a Russian soldier was removed from the monument and a plaque listing Russian war casualties was also transferred elsewhere.

Citadel ❹
CITADELLA

Map 4 D3. 🚌 27. 🔲 daily. 🏨 Hotel Citadella 🔲 466 57 94. Citadella Discotheque 🔲 386 47 97. 🔲 10pm–4am daily. **Restaurant** 🔲 466 77 36. 🔲 10am–11pm daily.

AFTER THE SUPPRESSION of the uprising of 1848–9 *(see pp30–31)*, the Habsburgs decided to build a fortification on this strategically important site. Constructed in 1850–54, the Citadel housed 60 cannons, which could, in theory, fire on the city at any time. In reality, from its very inception the Citadel did not fulfil any real military requirements, but served rather as a means of intimidating the population.

The Citadel is some 220 m (720 ft) long by 60 m (200 ft) wide, and has walls 4 m (12 ft) high. After peace was agreed with the Habsburgs, Hungarian society continually demanded the destruction of the Citadel, but it was not until 1897 that the Austrian soldiers left their barracks here. A section of its

Entrance to the Cave Church, run by the Pauline order of monks

entrance gateway was then symbolically ripped out.

After much discussion in the early 1960s, the Citadel was converted into a leisure complex. A restaurant (see p196), hotel (see p182) and even a nightclub now attract customers up Gellért Hill. From the old defensive walls of the Citadel there is a spectacular panorama of the city.

Gellért Monument ❺

SZENT GELLÉRT EMLÉKMŰ

Map 4 E3. 🚌 27.

I N 1904 A VAST monument was established on the spot where Bishop Gellért was supposedly murdered in the 11th century. According to the tale, the bishop was thrown into the Danube in a barrel, by a mob opposed to the adoption of Christianity. St Gellért holds a cross in his outstretched hand and a Hungarian convert to Christianity is depicted kneeling at his feet.

The statue was designed by Gyula Jankovits, while the semi-circular collonade behind it is by Imre Francsek. A water source that bubbles up here was used to create the fountain. Overlooking the Elizabeth Bridge, the monument can be seen from virtually every part of the city. It is an especially impressive spectacle at night, when it is illuminated.

The main plunge pool at the Rudas Baths, covered by a Turkish cupola

Rudas Baths ❻

RUDAS GYÓGYFÜRDŐ

Döbrentei tér 9. Map 4 D2.
📞 375 83 73. Spa Baths (men only) 🕐 6am–6pm Mon–Fri, 6am–noon Sat–Sun. Swimming pool 🕐 6am–5pm Mon–Fri, 6am–noon Sat–Sun.

D ATING ORIGINALLY from 1550, these baths were greatly extended in 1566 by Sokoli Mustafa, an Ottoman pasha. The main part of the baths dates from this period. In this section there are an octagonal plunge pool and four small corner pools with water of varying temperatures. An Ottoman cupola provides the roof over the baths.

In more recent years the baths have been extensively modernized and in 1952 a covered swimming pool was added to the complex.

While the swimming pool is mixed, the warm, healing spa water (principally used to remedy rheumatic illnesses) is reserved exclusively for men.

Empress Elizabeth Monument ❼

ERZSÉBET KIRÁLYNÉ SZOBRA

Döbrentei tér. Map 4 D2.

T HIS MONUMENT TO Empress Elizabeth, wife of Habsburg Emperor Franz Joseph, was created by György Zala.

The statue was erected in its present location in 1986. It stands close to the Elizabeth Bridge (see p63), which was also named after the empress, who showed great friendship to the Hungarians. The statue stood on the opposite side of the river from 1932 until 1947, when the Communists ordered it to be taken down.

The Gellért Monument, a landmark of Budapest overlooking the Elizabeth Bridge

Tabán ❽

Map 3 C1 and 3 C2, 3. 🚇 18, 19. 🚌 5, 78, 112.

THE TABÁN now consists of a pleasant park and a few historic buildings, but was once very different. In the early 20th century, this district, nestling in between Castle Hill and Gellért Hill, was a slum which was cleared as part of a programme to improve the city. Only a few buildings, including Tabán Parish Church, escaped the demolition.

Natural conditions ensured that this was one of the first places in the area where people chose to live. The Celtic Eravi were the first to establish a settlement here, while the Romans later built a watchtower from which they could observe people using a nearby crossing point over the river. The first reference to bathing in thermal waters in Tabán dates from the 15th century. The Turks took advantage of this natural asset and built two magnificent baths here, the Rác Baths and the Rudas Baths *(see p93)*, around which a blossoming town was established. Apart from the baths, virtually everything was destroyed in the recapture of Buda in 1686 *(see p26)*.

In the late 17th century, a large number of Serbs, referred to in Hungarian as Rácami, moved into the Tabán after fleeing from the Turks. They were joined by Greeks and Gypsies. Many of the inhabitants of the Tabán at this stage were tanners or made their living on the river. On the hillside above grapevines were cultivated. By the early 20th century, though picturesque, the district was still without proper sanitation. The old, decaying Tabán, with its numerous bars and gambling dens, was demolished and the present green space established in its place.

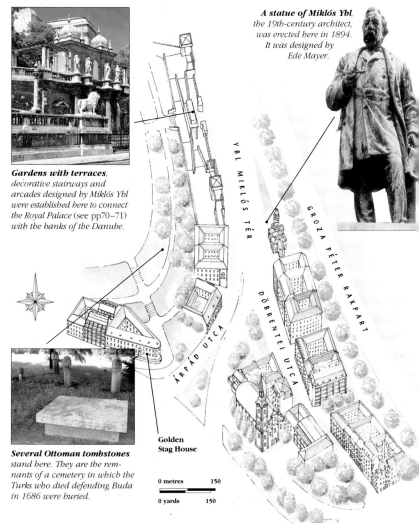

Gardens with terraces,
decorative stairways and
arcades designed by Miklós Ybl
were established here to connect
the Royal Palace (see pp70–71)
with the banks of the Danube.

A statue of Miklós Ybl,
the 19th-century architect,
was erected here in 1894.
It was designed by
Ede Mayer.

YBL MIKLÓS TÉR

GROZA PÉTER RAKPART

DÖBRENTEI UTCA

ÁRPÁD UTCA

Several Ottoman tombstones
stand here. They are the rem-
nants of a cemetery in which the
Turks who died defending Buda
in 1686 were buried.

Golden
Stag House

0 metres   150

0 yards   150

Rác Baths ❾

RÁC GYÓGYFÜRDŐ

Hadnagy utca 8–10. **Map** 3 C2.
📞 *375 83 73.* 🚊 *18, 19.*
🕐 *6:30am–6pm Mon, Wed, Fri
(women); 6:30am–6pm Tue, Thu,
Sat (men).* 📷 📵 *except by special
permission.*

TAKING THEIR name from the
Serbian, or Rác, people
who once lived here, the baths
date back to the Turkish era
(see pp26–7). This is not clear
from the outside, as the baths
were redeveloped in 1869 to
a design by Miklós Ybl. Inside,
however, original Ottoman
features include an octagonal
pool and cupola. Many locals
take the waters for their
believed therapeutic benefits.

The façade of the Rác Baths

Tabán Parish Church ❿

TABÁNI PLÉBÁNIATEMPLOM

Attila út 11. **Map** 3 D1. 📞 *375 54 91.*
🚊 *18, 19.*

A TEMPLE IS thought to have
stood on this site even in
the reign of Prince Árpád. In
the Middle Ages a church was
built here, which was converted into a mosque by the
Turks and subsequently destroyed. In 1728–36, after the
Habsburgs had taken control
of the city, a second church
was erected to a design by
Keresztély Obergruber. Mátyás
Nepauer added the tower in
the mid-18th century. In 1881
the façade was extended and
the tower crowned by a Neo-
Baroque dome.
    Inside the church, on the
right-hand side under the
choir gallery, is a copy of a

**Tabán Parish Church, with its
Neo-Baroque domed tower**

12th-century carving entitled
Christ of Tabán; the original
is now in the collection of the
Budapest History Museum
(see p72). The altar, pulpit and
several paintings adorning the
walls of the church all date
from the 19th century.

Miklós Ybl Square ⓫

YBL MIKLÓS TÉR

Map 4 D1. 🚊 *19.*

IT IS NO COINCIDENCE that the
important architect Miklós
Ybl *(see p119)* is commemorated by a statue in this square,
close to many of his buildings.
Among Ybl's most monumen-
tal projects were the State
Opera House *(see pp118–19),*
St Stephen's Basilica *(see
pp116–17)* and also a large-
scale rebuilding of the Royal
Palace *(see pp70–71).*
    The Várkert Kiosk, on the
square, was also built by Ybl.
Initially it pumped water up
to the Royal Palace, but in
1903 it was converted into a
café. Since 1992 the building
has contained the Casino-
Valentine Restaurant *(see p196).*

Semmelweis Museum of Medical History ⓬

**SEMMELWEIS ORVOSTÖRTÉNETI
MÚZEUM**

Apród utca 1–3. **Map** 3 D2.
📞 *375 35 33.* 🚊 *18, 19.*
🕐 *10:30am–5:30pm Tue–Sun.*
📷 📹 📵

THIS MUSEUM is located in the
18th-century house where
Dr Ignáz Semmelweis was
born in 1818. He is renowned
for his discovery of an
antiseptic-based treatment for
puerperal fever, a fatal condition common among women
who had recently given birth.
    The history of medicine from
ancient Egypt onwards is portrayed in the museum, which
includes a replica 19th-century
pharmacy. Semmelweis's
surgery can also be seen with
its original furniture. In the
courtyard is a monument called
Motherhood by Miklós Borsos.

Golden Stag House ⓭

SZARVAS HÁZ

Szarvas tér 1. **Map** 4 D1.
📞 *375 64 51.* 🚊 *19.*

STANDING AT the foot of
Castle Hill is this distinctive early 19th-century house.
It received its name from the
inn that opened here called
"Under the Golden Stag" –
above the entrance you will
see a bas-relief depicting a
golden stag pursued by two
hunting dogs. The building
still accommodates a restaurant of that name, Aranyszarvas
(see p196), which specializes
in game dishes. There is also
a separate wine bar located
in the cellar.

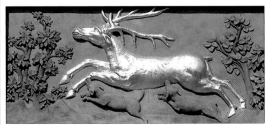

Bas-relief above the entrance to Golden Stag House

★ St Anne's Church

Characteristic of the late Baroque period, the interior of this church is quite stunning. The main portal is decorated with allegorical sculptures of Faith, Hope and Charity ❹

LOCATOR MAP
See Street Finder, map 1

Calvinist Church

The roof of this church, built in 1893–6, is covered with colourful ceramic tiles from the Zsolnay factory (see p56). They are a strong focal point in the panorama of Buda ❸

A Monument to Samu Pecz
stands beside one of his most important buildings, the Calvinist Church. Pecz was a follower of the Neo-Gothic movement and constructed many other important buildings in the city.

Capuchin Church

In its original medieval form, this church underwent conversion into a mosque at the hands of the Turks. Many Gothic elements have survived, however. Its present structure dates from 1854–6 ❷

To Clark Ádám tér and the Chain Bridge

Kapisztory House, at No. 20 Fő utca, was built in 1811 for the Greek merchant, Joseph Kapisztory. Its unusual turretted cylindrical window is an attractive feature of this street.

The imposing entrance to the Tunnel on Clark Ádám tér

Tunnel ❶
ALAGÚT

Clark Ádám tér. **Map** 1 C5. 🚌 *16, 86.*

T HE BRITISH ENGINEER Adam
Clark settled in Hungary
after completing the Chain
Bridge *(see p62)*. One of his
later projects, in 1853–7, was
building the Tunnel that runs
right through Castle Hill, from
Clark Ádám tér to Kristinaváros.

The Tunnel measures 350 m
(1,150 ft) long, 9 m (30 ft) wide
and 11 m (36 ft) in height.

The entrance on Clark Ádám
tér is flanked by two pairs of
Doric columns supporting the
massive entablature. This
square is the city's official
centre because of the location
here of the Zero Kilometre
Stone, from which all distances
from Budapest are calculated.

The Tunnel's western
entrance was originally ornamented with Egyptian motifs.
However, it was rebuilt without these details after it was
damaged in World War II.

Capuchin Church ❷
KAPUCINUS TEMPLOM

Fő utca 32. **Map** 1 C4. ☎ *201 47
25.* 📷 *by arrangement.*

T HE ORIGINS OF this church
date from the 14th century,
when the mother of Louis I,
Queen Elizabeth, decided to
establish a church here. Fragments of walls on the northern
façade survive from this time.

During the Turkish occupation *(see pp26–7)*, the church
was converted into a mosque.
Features from this period, such

as the window openings and
and the doorway on the southern façade, have remained
despite the fighting of 1686.

Between 1703–15 the
church was rebuilt, following
a Baroque design created by
one of the Capuchin Fathers.

In 1856 the church was again
restyled, by Ferenc Reitter and
Pál Zsumrák, who linked the
differently styled façades har-
moniously together. The statue
of St Elizabeth on the mid-
19th-century Romantic façade
also dates from 1856.

The altar of the Capuchin Church

Calvinist Church ❸
REFORMÁTUS TEMPLOM

Szilágyi Dezső tér 3. **Map** 1 C4.
☎ *201 37 25.*

O NE OF BUDAPEST'S more
unusual churches, the
Calvinist Church was built by
Samu Pecz between 1893–6
on the site of a former medieval market. It is one of the
major examples of his work.

Despite the use of modern
tiles on the roof, the church is

Neo-Gothic in style. It is also
interesting to note that Pecz
used this traditional design of
medieval Catholic churches
for a Calvinist church, which
has very different liturgical
and ecclesiastical needs.

St Anne's Church ❹
SZENT ANNA TEMPLOM

See pp102–3.

Batthyány Square ❺
BATTHYÁNY TÉR

Map 1 C3. Ⓜ *Batthyány tér.*

B ATTHYÁNY SQUARE is one
of the most interesting
squares on the Danube's western bank. Beautiful views of
Parliament and Pest on the opposite bank unfold from here.

In 1905 the square was
renamed after Count Lajos
Batthyány, the prime minister
during the Hungarian uprising
of 1848–9 *(see pp30–31)*, who
was shot by the Austrian army.

The square features buildings
in many different styles. The
Hikisch House, at No. 3, dating
from the late 18th century, is
late Baroque. It is notable for
the bas-reliefs on its façade
depicting the four seasons. The
White Cross Inn, at No. 4, also
late Baroque, features Rococo
decoration. On the western
side of the square is the first
covered market in Buda,
dating from 1902. It was damaged in World War II and did
not reopen until 1975.

The Hikisch House, with bas-reliefs
representing the four seasons

St Elizabeth's Church ❻

ERZSÉBET APÁCÁK TEMPLOMA

Fő utca 41–43. **Map** 1 C3.
🄲 201 80 91. Ⓜ Batthyány tér.
Király Baths 🄲 202 36 88.
⊙ 6:30am–6pm Mon, Wed, Fri (men);
6:30am–6pm Tue, Thu, Sat (women).

IN 1731–57 A CHURCH was built for the Franciscan order on the ruins of a former mosque, to a design by Hans Jakab. In 1785, after he had dissolved the Franciscan order, Emperor Joseph II gave the church to St Elizabeth's Convent.

The Baroque interior is adorned with late 19th-century frescoes, including one of St Florian protecting Christians from a fire in 1810. Their resonance is due to their recent restoration. The original pulpit and pews, carved by the friars, have remained intact.

In the early 19th century, a hospital and hostel were built adjacent to the church. These were run by the Elizabeth Sisters.

Further along Fő utca, at No. 84, are the 16th-century Király Baths, one of the city's few Turkish baths (see p50).

Capital on Hospital of St Elizabeth

József Bem Monument ❼

BEM JÓZSEF SZOBRA

Bem József tér. **Map** 1 C2.

JÁNOS ISTÓK'S monument to Josef Bem was unveiled in 1934. Bem, a Polish general and hero of the 1848–9 uprisings, is depicted with his arm in a sling. It was in this state, in the front line of the Battle of Pisk, that he inspired the Hungarian troops to attack the bridge and achieve victory over the Habsburg armies.

Memorable words, which he uttered during the battle, are engraved on the base of the monument. They read: "I will recapture the bridge or perish"; "Forward, Hungary"; "If there is no bridge, there is no homeland". Engravings of all the battles fought by the general are also on the monument.

Tiles on the Tomb of Gül Baba

Tomb of Gül Baba ❽

GÜL BABA TÜRBÉJE

Mecset utca 14. **Map** 1 B1.
🄲 355 88 49. ⊙ May–Oct: 10am–6pm Tue–Sun. 🚋 4, 6.

GÜL BABA WAS a Muslim dervish and member of the Bektashi order, who died in 1541, just after the capture of Buda. He was one of the few Turks who was respected and revered by the people of Hungary. His remains now lie in a tomb built between 1543–8. According to legend, it was Gül Baba who introduced roses to Budapest. From this came both the name

of this area, Rózsadomb, meaning Rose Hill, and Gül Baba's own name, which in English means Father of Roses.

A 400-year-old dome covers the octagonal tomb. Inside, the sarcophagus is draped in green cloth with gold citations from the Koran. Pictures, religious items and beautiful rugs also adorn the tomb.

Lukács Baths ❾

LUKÁCS GYÓGYFÜRDŐ

Frankel Leo út 25–9. **Map** 1 B1.
🄲 326 16 95. ⊙ 6am – 6pm daily.
🚋 17.

THIS FAMOUS SPA is named after St Luke. Although the Neo-Classical complex was established in 1894, the baths are one of a number still operating in the city (see pp50–53) that date back to the period of Turkish rule.

Set in peaceful surroundings, the complex comprises the 16th-century Császár thermal baths and two outdoor swimming pools. Natural hot springs keep these pools heated all year round, allowing locals and tourists alike to bathe in comfort even in winter.

It is also worth entering the overgrown courtyard to see a statue of St Luke, dating from 1760, and the plaques inscribed with thanks by bathers from around the world who benefited from the healing waters.

Lukács Baths, with beautiful old plane trees growing outside

St Anne's Church ❹

Budapest is home to many churches, but the twin-towered parish church of Vízíváros is one of its most beautiful Baroque examples. Initially a Jesuit church, the architect who first designed it is unknown. Building was begun in 1740 by Kristóf Hámon and completed after his death by Mátyás Nepauer. In 1763 an earthquake seriously damaged the building and the dissolution of the Jesuit order ten years later further delayed the completion of the church. Thus it remained unconsecrated until 1805. The rectory now houses the Angelika café.

Crucifix on the St Cross altar

The twin towers are crowned by magnificent Baroque spires.

Façade
Buda's coat of arms appears in the centre of the tympanum. The symbol of the Trinity is above this, between two kneeling angels.

★ Pulpit
This magnificent, late Baroque pulpit was created by Károly Bebó in 1773. It features gilded details and angels that embody theological virtues. The reliefs were added at a later date.

Main entrance

Organ
The organ case from a former Carmelite church on Castle Hill was transferred to St Anne's Church in the late 18th century, after the dissolution of the order by Emperor Joseph II.

★ Painted Ceiling
The painted ceiling in the cupola of the chancel depicts the Holy Trinity. It was painted in 1771 by Gergely Vogl. There are also Neo-Baroque frescoes in the nave dating from 1938.

VISITORS' CHECKLIST

Batthyány tér 7. **Map** 1 C3.
201 34 04. Ⓜ Batthyány tér.
only for services. daily.
Angelika café 201 48 47.
10am–10pm daily.

★ High Altar
The sculptures depict Mary, as a child, being brought into the Temple of Jerusalem by St Anne, her mother. Completed in 1773, it is regarded as one of the most beautiful works of Károly Bebó.

Church Pew
The choir pews are decorated with intricately carved wooden panels which feature figurative scenes.

Baptismal Font
Concealed behind a pillar, this baptismal font has a carved pedestal and a simply, but beautifully, decorated cover.

Side Altar
This late Baroque altar of St Francis the Saviour, like the altar of St Cross on the opposite side of the church, is the work of Antal Eberhardt and dates from 1768. The picture in the centre was, however, executed by Franz Wagenschön.

STAR FEATURES

★ Painted Ceiling

★ High Altar

★ Pulpit

AROUND PARLIAMENT

OWARDS THE END of the 18th and throughout the 19th century Pest underwent a series of huge changes. In 1838 a flood destroyed most of the rural dwellings that had occupied the area until that time. The unification of Budapest in 1873 and the 1,000-year anniversary, in 1896, of the Magyar conquest also boosted the city's development. The medieval walls that originally

An ornate lantern on the Parliament

marked Pest's limits were crossed as the area was gradually urbanized. This period produced a number of the most important buildings in Hungary, including St Stephen's Basilica, Parliament and the Hungarian Academy of Sciences, which were built in a variety of revivalist styles. Many Neo-Classical residences were also built, particularly on Nádor utca, Akadémia utca and Október 6 utca.

SIGHTS AT A GLANCE

Historic Buildings and Palaces
Drechsler Palace **12**
Gresham Palace **8**

Hungarian Academy of Sciences **9**
Ministry of Agriculture **3**
Parliament pp108–9 **1**
Post Office Savings Bank **5**
Radisson Béke Hotel **13**
University of Central Europe **6**

Museums
Ethnographical Museum **2**

Squares
Liberty Square **4**
Roosevelt Square **7**

Theatres
Capital Operetta Theatre **14**
State Opera House pp118–19 **11**

Churches
St Stephen's Basilica pp116–17 **10**

GETTING THERE
The M2 metro line (red) runs to Kossuth Lajos tér and the M3 metro line (blue) runs to Arany János utca. Tram 2 runs north along the Danube and terminates past Parliament at Margaret Bridge. Buses 70 and 78 also serve this area.

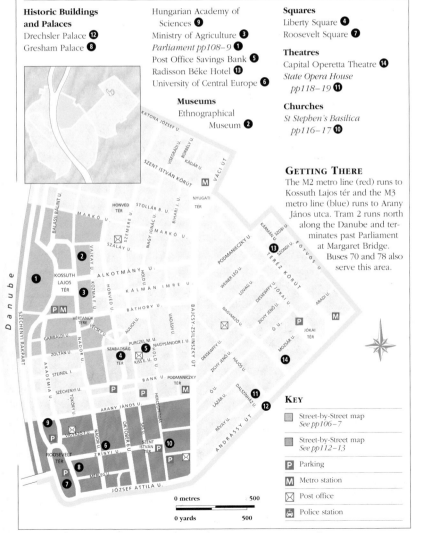

KEY

	Street-by-Street map *See pp106–7*
	Street-by-Street map *See pp112–13*
P	Parking
M	Metro station
⊠	Post office
	Police station

0 metres   500
0 yards   500

◁ **Neo-Gothic spires, flying buttresses and stained-glass windows on Hungary's Parliament**

Street-by-Street: Kossuth Square

Brigadier Woroniecki

THIS SQUARE expresses well the pomp and pride with which Pest was developed during the 19th and early 20th centuries. Pàrliament dominates the square on the Danube side, but equally imposing are the Ministry of Agriculture and the Ethnographical Museum on the opposite side. Several monuments commemorate nationalist leaders and provide a visual record of Hungary's recent political history.

★ **Ethnographical Museum**
Among 170,000 exhibits amassed in the museum's collection is a captivating collection of folk costumes representing the various nationalities and ethnic groups in Hungary ❷

★ **Parliament**
This building has become the recognized symbol of democracy in Hungary, despite the dome being crowned by a red star during the Communist period ❶

Attila József was a radical poet whose work sensitively explored the human condition. In 1937 he committed suicide, aged 32. This statue by László Marton dates from 1980.

LAJOS KOSSUTH (1802–94)

The popularity of Lajos Kossuth among the Hungarian people is immense. He led the 1848–9 uprising against Austrian rule *(see pp30–31)*, and was one of the most oustanding political figures in Hungary. He was a member of the first democratic government during the uprising, and briefly became its leader before being exiled after the revolt was quashed in 1849.

Stained-glass window depicting Lajos Kossuth

| 0 metres | 150 |
| 0 yards | 150 |

BALASSI BÁLINT U

Ferenc II Rákóczi, the prince of Transylvania, led one of the earliest revolts for independence against the Habsburgs in 1703–11. This bronze equestrian monument can be seen in front of Parliament. It was completed by János Pásztor in 1937.

LOCATOR MAP
See Street Finder, map 3

Ministry of Agriculture
A massive Corinthian collonade, supporting an entablature, lends this Neo-Classical building a dignified character ❸

This monument to Imre Nagy symbolizes the insurgent prime minister's 1956 defection from the side of Communism to the side of the people – a protest that cost him his life.

The Hungarian TV headquarters were designed in the Neo-Classical style by Ignác Alpár. Constructed in 1905, the building originally housed the Stock Exchange.

Plaque commemorating Brigadier Woroniecki, hero of the uprising of 1948–9

KEY

– – – Suggested route

STAR SIGHTS

★ **Parliament**

★ **Ethnographical Museum**

Parliament ❶

Hungary's parliament is the country's largest building and has become a symbol of Budapest. A competition was held to choose its design, the winner being Imre Steindl's rich Neo-Gothic masterpiece, built between 1884–1902. Based on the Houses of

One of the pair of lions at the main entrance

Parliament in London, completed by Charles Barry in 1835–6, it is 268 m (880 ft) long and 96 m (315 ft) high, and comprises 691 rooms.

Aerial View
The magnificent dome marks the central point of the Parliament building. Although the façade is elaborately Neo-Gothic, the ground plan follows Baroque conventions.

★ Domed Hall
Adorning the massive pillars that support Parliament's central dome are figures of some of the rulers of Hungary.

Danube façade

★ National Assembly Hall
Formerly the upper house, this hall is now where the National Assembly convenes. Its paintings include Mihály Munkácsy's The Magyar Conquest *(1893).*

South wing

Gables
Almost every corner of the Parliament building features gables with pinnacles based on Gothic sculptures.

Lobby
Lobbies, the venues for political discussions, are to be found along the corridors beneath stained-glass windows.

Dome
The ceiling of the 96-m (315-ft) high dome is covered in an intricate design of Neo-Gothic gilding combined with heraldic decoration.

Gobelin Hall
This hall is decorated with a Gobelin tapestry illustrating Prince Árpád, with seven Magyar leaders under his command, signing a peace treaty and blood oath.

North wing

Congress Hall
This vast hall is virtually a mirror image of the National Assembly Hall. Both halls have public galleries running around a horseshoe-shaped interior.

The main entrance on Kossuth Lajos tér

Main Staircase
The best contemporary artists were invited to decorate the interior. The sumptuous main staircase features ceiling frescoes by Károly Lotz and sculptures by György Kiss.

STAR FEATURES

★ **National Assembly Hall**

★ **Domed Hall**

The magnificent hall of the Ethnographical Museum

Parliament ❶
ORSZÁGHÁZ

See pp108–9.

Ethnographical Museum ❷
NÉPRAJZI MÚZEUM

Kossuth Lajos tér 12. **Map** 2 D3.
🄲 *332 63 40.* Ⓜ *Kossuth Lajos tér.*
🄾 *Nov–Mar: 10am–4pm Tue–Sun.*
🄵 *free Tue.* 🄵 🄿

THIS BUILDING, designed by Alajos Hauszmann and constructed between 1893–6, was built as the Palace of Justice and, until 1945, served as the Supreme Court.

The building was designed in the Historicist style, linking elements of Renaissance, Baroque and Classicism. The façade is dominated by a vast portico crowned by two towers. It also features a gable crowned by the figure of the Roman goddess of justice in a chariot drawn by three horses, by Károly Senyei. The grand hall inside the main entrance features a marvellous staircase and frescoes by Károly Lotz.

The building was first used as a museum in 1957, housing the Hungarian National Gallery *(see pp74–7),* which was later transferred to the Royal Palace. The Ethnographical Museum has been here since 1973.

The museum's collection was established in 1872 in the Department of Ethnography at the Hungarian National Museum *(see pp130–33).* There are now around 170,000 exhibits, although the majority are not currently on display.

The collection includes artifacts reflecting the rural folk culture of Hungary from the prehistoric era to the 20th century. A map from 1909 shows the settlement of the various communities who came to Hungary. Ethnic items relating to these communities, as well as primitive objects from North and South America, Africa, Asia and Australia, can also be seen.

The museum has two very informative permanent displays: Traditional Culture of the Hungarian Nation, on the first floor, and From Primeval Communities to Civilization, on the second floor.

Ministry of Agriculture ❸
ÉLELMEZÉSÜGYI MINISZTÉRIUM

Kossuth Lajos tér 11. **Map** 2 D3.
Ⓜ *Kossuth Lajos tér.*

ON THE SOUTHEAST side of Kossuth Square is this huge building, bordered by streets on all its four sides. It was built for the Ministry of Agriculture by Gyula Bukovics at the end of the 19th century.

The façade is designed in a manner typical of late Historicism, drawing heavily on Neo-Classical motifs. The columns of the colonnade are echoed in the fenestration above the well-proportioned pedimented windows.

On the wall to the right of the building two commemorative plaques can be seen. The first is dedicated to the commanding officer of the Polish Legion, who was also a hero of the 1948–9 uprising *(see p30–31).* Brigadier M Woroniecki, who was renowned for his bravery, was shot down on this spot by the Austrians in October 1849.

The second plaque honours Endre Ságvári, a Hungarian hero of the resistance movement, who died in the fighting against the Fascists in 1944.

The two sculptures in front of the building are by Árpád Somogyi. The *Reaper Lad* dates from 1956 and the *Female Agronomist* from 1954.

Liberty Square ❹
SZABADSÁG TÉR

Map 2 E4. Ⓜ *Kossuth Lajos tér, Arany János utca.*

AFTER THE enormous Neugebäude Barracks were demolished in 1886, Liberty Square was laid out in its place. The barracks, built for the Austrian troops, once dominated the southern part of Lipótváros (Leopold Town). It was here that Hungary's first independent prime minister, Count Lajos Batthyány was executed on 6 October 1849. Since 1926, an eternal flame *(see p31)* has been burning in the square to honour all those executed during the uprising.

Two particularly impressive buildings by Ignác Alpár are on opposite sides of the square. The former Stock Exchange, now the Hungarian TV headquarters (Magyar Televízió székháza), dates from 1905 and shows the influence of the Secession style. The Hungarian National Bank (Magyar Nemzeti Bank) is decorated in a pastiche of Historicist styles and also dates from 1905.

Bas-reliefs on the former the Stock Exchange

Beautiful Secession interior of the Post Office Savings Bank

An obelisk by Károly Antal stands at the northern end of the square commemorating the Red Army soldiers who died during the siege of Budapest in 1944–5. A second statue is to the US general Harry Hill Bandholtz. He led the allied forces that thwarted the Romanian troops looting the Hungarian National Museum.

Post Office Savings Bank ❺
POSTATAKARÉK PÉNZTÁR

Hold utca 4. **Map** 2 E3. Ⓜ Kossuth Lajos tér.

A MASTERPIECE BY Ödön Lechner, the former Post Office Savings Bank was built between 1900– 1901. Chiefly a Secession architect, Lechner (see p56) combined the curvilinear motifs of that style with motifs from Hungarian folk art to produce a unique visual style for his work.

Approaching the Post Office Savings Bank, one can see glimpses of the details that

have made this building one of Pest's most unusual sights. The construction methods, interior design and exterior detailing of the building are remarkable. Lechner commissioned the tiles used in the design, including the vibrant roof tiles, from the Zsolnay factory (see p56). The façades are decorated with floral

tendrils and icons taken from nature. The bees climbing up the gable walls represent the bank's activity and the pinnacles, which look like hives, represent the accumulation of savings. These features were intended to be accessible to the people who banked here.

The building is not officially open to the public, but it is possible to see the Cashiers' Hall during office hours.

University of Central Europe ❻
KÖZÉP-EURÓPAI EGYETEM

Nádor utca 9. **Map** 2 E5.
Ⓒ 312 94 30. Ⓜ Kossuth Lajos tér.

THIS NEO-CLASSICAL palace can be found on Nádor utca, in the direction of Roosevelt Square. It was built in 1826 by Mihály Pollack for Prince Antal Festetics. Since 1993 it has housed the University of Central Europe.

Founded by the American millionaire George Soros, who was born in Budapest, this international educational establishment is open to students from central and eastern Europe and the former USSR.

The university offers postgraduate courses in subjects ranging from history and law to political and environmental sciences. In Budapest, the Soros Foundation finances numerous other ventures and it has branches in all the central European countries.

THE AMERICAN EMBASSY

This beautiful house, at No. 12 Liberty Square, was designed by Aladár Kálmán and Gyula Ullmann and built between 1899–1901. The façade is decorated with bas-reliefs featuring motifs typical of the Secession style.

By the entrance to the embassy is a plaque with an image of the Catholic Primate, Cardinal Joseph Mindszenty, who was part of the movement seeking to liberate

Plaque commemorating Joseph Mindszenty

Hungary from the Communists after World War II. He was imprisoned by the regime in 1949 and was mistreated for many years. Released during the 1956 uprising, he asked for political asylum in the embassy. He lived here for 15 years in internal exile until, in 1971, the Vatican finally convinced him to leave Hungary.

Street-by-Street: Roosevelt Square

IN 1867, A CERMONIAL MOUND was made of earth from all over the country to celebrate the coronation of Franz Joseph as king of Hungary. Today, the historic earth has been dug into the ground where Roosevelt Square now stands. At the head of the Chain Bridge on the eastern bank of the Danube, it features many of Pest's most beautiful buildings, such as the Hungarian Academy of Sciences, to the north of the square, and Gresham Palace, to the east. The square was named after American president Franklin D Roosevelt in 1947.

No. 1 Akadémia utca was built in the Neo-Classical style by Mátyás Zitterbarth the younger, in 1835. A plaque shows that in November 1848 General József Bem *(see p101)* stayed here when it was the Prince Stephen Hotel.

★ **Gresham Palace**
This 1907 building is one of the most expressive examples of Secession architecture in Budapest **8**

House designed by József Hild in 1836

★ **Hungarian Academy of Sciences**
The debating hall of the Hungarian Academy of Sciences is decorated with sculptures by Miklós Izsó and ceiling paintings by Károly Lotz **9**

The Chain Bridge *(see p62)* was built between 1839–49 and was the city's first permanent river crossing. It was destroyed by the German forces in World War II and was reopened in 1949, 100 years after it was first finished.

AKADEMIA UTCA

NADOR UTCA

ROOSEVELT TÉR

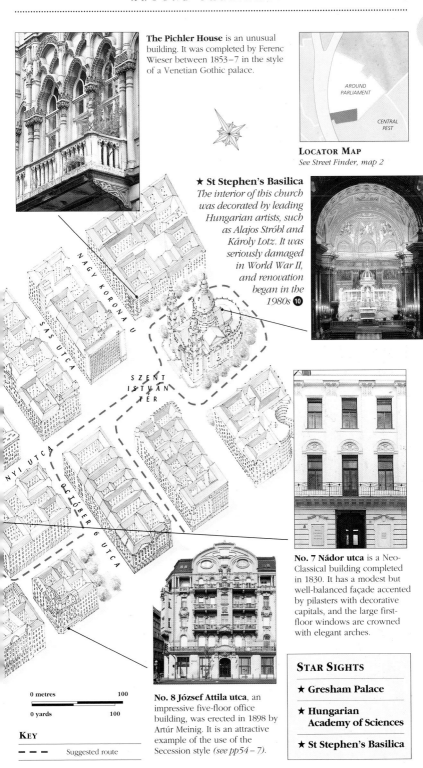

The Pichler House is an unusual building. It was completed by Ferenc Wieser between 1853–7 in the style of a Venetian Gothic palace.

LOCATOR MAP
See Street Finder, map 2

★ St Stephen's Basilica
The interior of this church was decorated by leading Hungarian artists, such as Alajos Stróbl and Károly Lotz. It was seriously damaged in World War II, and renovation began in the 1980s ⑩

No. 7 Nádor utca is a Neo-Classical building completed in 1830. It has a modest but well-balanced façade accented by pilasters with decorative capitals, and the large first-floor windows are crowned with elegant arches.

No. 8 József Attila utca, an impressive five-floor office building, was erected in 1898 by Artúr Meinig. It is an attractive example of the use of the Secession style *(see pp54–7)*.

0 metres   100

0 yards   100

KEY

– – – Suggested route

STAR SIGHTS

★ **Gresham Palace**

★ **Hungarian Academy of Sciences**

★ **St Stephen's Basilica**

Monument to Ferenc Deák, dating from 1887, in Roosevelt Square

Roosevelt Square ❼
ROOSEVELT TÉR

Map 2 D5. 🚊 16. 🚋 2.

PREVIOUSLY, Roosevelt Square was known by several different names – Franz Joseph Square and Unloading Square among others – but it received its current title in 1947. It is located at the head of the Pest side of the Chain Bridge, and is home to many beautiful and important buildings.

At the beginning of the 20th century the square was lined with various hotels, the Diana Baths and the Lloyd Palace designed by József Hild. The only building from the previous century still standing today is the Hungarian Academy of Sciences. The other buildings were demolished and replaced by the Gresham Palace and the Bank of Hungary, on the corner of Attila József utca. Two large modern hotels, the Atrium Hyatt *(see p183)* and the Inter-Continental *(see p183)*, stand on the southern side of the square.

There is a statue to Baron József Eötvös (1813–71), a reformer of public education, in front of the Inter-Continental. Situated in the centre of the square are monuments to two politicians who espoused quite different ideologies: Count István Széchenyi (1791–1860), the leading social and political reformer of his age, and Ferenc Deák (1803–76), who was instrumental in the Compromise of 1867, which resulted in the Dual Monachy *(see p32).*

Gresham Palace ❽
GRESHAM PALOTA

Roosevelt tér 5–6. **Map** 2 D5.
🚊 16. 🚋 2.

THIS SECESSION PALACE aroused both controversy and praise from the moment it was built. One of Budapest's most distinctive pieces of architecture, it was commissioned by the London-based Gresham Life Assurance Company from Zsigmond Quittner and the brothers József and László Vágó, and completed in 1907.

This enormous edifice enjoys an imposing location directly opposite the Chain Bridge. The crumbling façade features characteristic Secession motifs *(see pp54–7)*, such as curvilinear forms and organic themes. The ornately carved window surrounds appear as though they are projecting from the walls, blending seamlessly with the architecture. The bust by Ede Telcs, at the top of the façade, is of Sir Thomas Gresham. He was the founder of the Royal Exchange in London and of Gresham's Law: "bad money drives out good". Stone sculptures arranged on the cornices, small towers and alcoves complete the faded sophistication of the exterior.

On the ground floor of the palace there is a T-shaped arcade, covered by a multi-coloured glazed roof, which is occupied by shops and a restaurant. The entrance to the arcade is marked by a beautiful wrought-iron gate

Bust of Sir Thomas Gresham on the façade of the Gresham Palace

with peacock motifs. Still the original gate, it is widely regarded as one of the most splendid examples of design from the Secession era. Two plaques inside the entrance list the directors of the London and Hungarian offices. Inside the building, the second floor of the Kossuth stairway has a stained-glass window by Miksa Róth, featuring a portrait of Lajos Kossuth *(see p106).*

Miklós Izsó's sculptures inside the Hungarian Academy of Sciences

Hungarian Academy of Sciences ❾
MAGYAR TUDOMÁNYOS AKADÉMIA

Roosevelt tér 9. **Map** 2 D5. 🚊 16.

BUILT BETWEEN 1862–4, this Neo-Renaissance building was designed by the architect Friedrich August Stüler.

The statues adorning the façade represent six disciplines of knowledge – law, history, mathematics, sciences, philosophy and linguistics – and are the works of Emil Wolf and Miklós Izsó. On the Danube side of the façade there are allegories of poetry, astronomy and archeology, and on the corners of the building stand statues of renowned thinkers, including Isaac Newton, René Descartes and Miklós Révay.

The beautifully decorated interior features statues by Miklós Izsó, and the library, on the ground floor, has a priceless collection of academic books.

The Neo-Renaissance façade of the Drechsler Palace

St Stephen's Basilica ⑩

SZENT ISTVÁN BAZILIKA

See pp116–17.

State Opera House ⑪

MAGYAR ÁLLAMI OPERAHÁZ

See pp118–19.

Drechsler Palace ⑫

DRECHSLER PALOTA

Andrássy út 25. **Map** 2 F4.
Ⓜ Opera.

Now Housing the State Ballet Institute, the Drechsler Palace was originally built as Neo-Renaissance apartments for the Hungarian Railways Pension Fund in 1883. It was designed by Gyula Pártos and Ödön Lechner, more famous for their Secession work, to harmonize with the façade of the State Opera House opposite (see pp118–19).

Its name derives from the Drechsler Café, which occupied the ground floor of this building towards the end of the 19th and in the early 20th century.

Radisson Béke Hotel ⑬

BÉKE RADISSON HOTEL

Teréz körút 43. **Map** 2 F3.
☎ 301 16 00. Ⓜ Oktogon.

This is one of the most elegant of Budapest's historic hotels. It was built in 1896 as an apartment building, and in 1912 it was restyled by Béla Malmai as the Hotel Brittania. A mosaic, created by György Szondi, was added to the façade at this time.

In 1978 the hotel was taken over by the Radisson group, which restored the rich interiors. Notable features are the stained-glass windows in the Szondi Restaurant, by Jenő Haranghy, which illustrate the works of Richard Wagner. The Romeo and Juliet conference room and the Shakespeare Restaurant are named after the murals that decorate them. The Zsolnay Café serves cake and coffee on porcelain from the Pécs factory (see p56).

Capital Operetta Theatre ⑭

FŐVÁROSI OPERETT SZINHÁZ

Nagymező utca 17. **Map** 2 F4.
☎ 269 38 70. ☷ 4, 5, 6.

Budapest has a good reputation for musical entertainment, and its operetta scene (see p208) is over 100 years old. Operettas were first staged on this site in the Orfeum Theatre, designed in the Neo-Baroque style by the Viennese architects Fellner and Helmer, in 1898. The project was financed by the impressario Károly Singer-Somossy.

In 1922, the American entrepreneur Ben Blumenthal redeveloped the building and opened the Capital Operetta Theatre, which then specialized in the genre. After 1936, this theatre became the only venue for operetta in Budapest.

The repertoire of the theatre includes the works of both international and Hungarian composers of this genre, including Imre Kálmán, Ferenc Lehár and Pál Ábrahám, who wrote The Csardas Princess.

Entrance to the Capital Operetta Theatre on Nagymező utca

St Stephen's Basilica ⑩

DEDICATED TO ST STEPHEN, or István, the first Hungarian Christian king *(see p22)*, this church was designed by József Hild in the Neo-Classical style, using a Greek cross floor plan. Construction began in 1851 and was taken over in 1867 by Miklós Ybl *(see p119)*, who added the Neo-Renaissance dome after the original one collapsed in 1868. József Kauser completed the church in 1905. It received the title of Basilica Minor in 1938, the 900th anniversary of St István's death.

St István's coronation

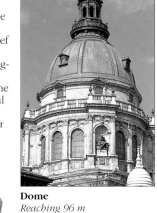

St Matthew
St Matthew is one of the four Evangelists represented in the niches on the exterior of the dome. They are all the work of the sculptor Léo Feszler.

Dome
Reaching 96 m (315 ft), the dome is visible from all over Budapest.

Observation point

Tower
A bell, weighing 9,144 kg (9 tons) is housed in this tower. It was funded by German Catholics to compensate for the original bell, which was looted by the Nazis in 1944.

Main Portal
The massive door is decorated with carvings depicting the heads of the 12 Apostles.

Mosaics
The dome is decorated with mosaics designed by Károly Lotz.

VISITORS' CHECKLIST

Szent István tér. **Map** 2 E4.
332 17 90. **M** Deák Ferenc tér. **Treasury** 9am–5pm daily (winter: 10am–4pm). daily.

★ Main Altar
In the centre of the altar there is a marble statue of St István by Alajos Stróbl. Scenes from the king's life are depicted behind the altar.

★ Holy Right Hand
Hungary's most unusual relic is the mummified forearm of King István. It is kept in the Chapel of the Holy Right Hand.

Figures of the 12 Apostles, by Léo Feszler, crown the exterior colonnade at the back of the church.

St Gellért and St Emeryka
This portrayal of St Gellért and his pupil, St Emeryka, is the work of Alajos Stróbl.

★ Paintng by Gyula Benczúr
This image shows King István, left without an heir, dedicating Hungary to the Virgin Mary, who became Patrona Hungariae, *the country's patron.*

STAR FEATURES

★ Main Altar

★ Holy Right Hand

★ Painting by Gyula Benczúr

State Opera House ⑪

OPENED IN September 1884, the State Opera House in Budapest was built to rival those of Paris, Vienna and Dresden. Its beautiful architecture and interiors were the life's work of the great Hungarian architect, Miklós Ybl. The interior also features ornamentation by Hungarian artists, including Alajos Stróbl and Károly Lotz. During its lifetime, the State Opera House has seen some influential music directors, including, Ferenc Erkel, composer of the Hungarian opera *Bánk Bán*, Gustav Mahler and Otto Klemperer.

Decorative lamp with putti

Façade
The decoration of the symmetrical façade follows a musical theme. In niches on either side of the main entrance there are figures of two of Hungary's most prominent composers, Ferenc Erkel and Franz Liszt (see p144). Both were sculpted by Alajos Stróbl.

Murals
The vaulted ceiling of the foyer is covered in magnificent murals by Bertalan Székely and Mór Than. They depict the nine Muses.

★ Foyer
The foyer, with its marble columns, gilded vaulted ceiling, murals and chandeliers, gives the State Opera House a feeling of opulence and grandeur.

Main entrance
Wrought-iron lamps illuminate the wide stone staircase and the main entrance.

★ Main Staircase
Going to the opera was a great social occasion in the 19th century. A vast, sweeping staircase was an important element of the opera house as it allowed ladies to show off their new gowns.

Chandelier
The main hall is decorated with a bronze chandelier that weighs 3,050 kg (3 tons). It illuminates a magnificent fresco, by Károly Lotz, of the Greek gods on Olympus.

Central Stage
This proscenium arch stage employed the most modern technology of the time. It featured a revolving stage and metal hydraulic machinery.

The side entrance has a loggia that reflects the design of the main entrance.

★ **Royal Box**
The royal box is located centrally in the three-storey circle. It is decorated with sculptures symbolizing the four operatic voices – soprano, alto, tenor and bass.

MIKLÓS YBL (1814–91)

The most prominent Hungarian architect of the second half of the 19th century, Miklós Ybl had an enormous influence on the development of Budapest. He was a practitioner of Historicism, and tended to use Neo-Renaissance forms. The State Opera House and the dome of St Stephen's Basilica are examples of his work. Ybl also built apartment buildings and palaces for the aristocracy in this style. A statue of the architect stands on the western bank of the Danube, in Miklós Ybl Square *(see p95).*

**Bust of
Miklós Ybl**

STAR FEATURES

★ **Foyer**

★ **Royal Box**

★ **Main Staircase**

CENTRAL PEST

A T THE END OF the 17th century much of Pest was in ruins and few residents remained. Within the next few decades, however, new residential districts were established, which are today's mid-town suburbs. In the 19th century, redevelopment schemes introduced grand houses and apartment blocks, some

Bas-relief on the façade of the City Council Chamber

with shops and cafés, as well as secular and municipal buildings. Perhaps the most prominent example of this work is the Hungarian National Museum. At this time Pest surpassed Buda as a centre for trade and industry. This was partly due to the area's Jewish community, who played an active role in its development.

SIGHTS AT A GLANCE

Streets and Squares

Jewish Quarter **16**
József Nádor Square **3**
Mihály Pollack Square **19**
Mihály Vörösmarty Square **4**
Váci Street **5**
Vigadó Square **2**

Churches

Calvinist Church **22**
Chapel of St Roch **18**
Franciscan Church **31**
Great Synagogue **17**
Inner City Parish Church pp124–5 **1**
Lutheran Church **11**
Serbian Church **26**
Servite Church **10**
University Church **28**

Historic Buildings and Monuments

City Council Chamber **25**
Danube Fountain **12**
Ervin Szabó Library **21**
Franz Liszt Academy of Music **14**
Károlyi Palace **29**
Klotild Palaces **6**
Lóránd Eötvös University **27**
Municipal Council Offices **8**
New Theatre **13**
New York Palace **15**
Pest County Hall **7**
Turkish Bank **9**
University Library **30**
University of Economics **24**

Museums

Hungarian National Museum pp130–33 **20**
Museum of Applied Arts pp136–7 **23**

KEY

	Street-by-Street map See pp122–3
M	Metro station
P	Parking
⊠	Post Office

0 metres   400
0 yards   400

⊲ **The well of Danaid, who was condemned to carry water to a leaking barrel, in Szomory Dezső tér**

Street-by-Street: Around Váci Street

T HE NOTHERN SECTION of Váci Street has been Budapest's
fashionable area for walking, meeting in cafés and
shopping in elegant boutiques since the early 19th century. Its attractive promenade is an enjoyable place for
an evening stroll, when it is stylishly illuminated.

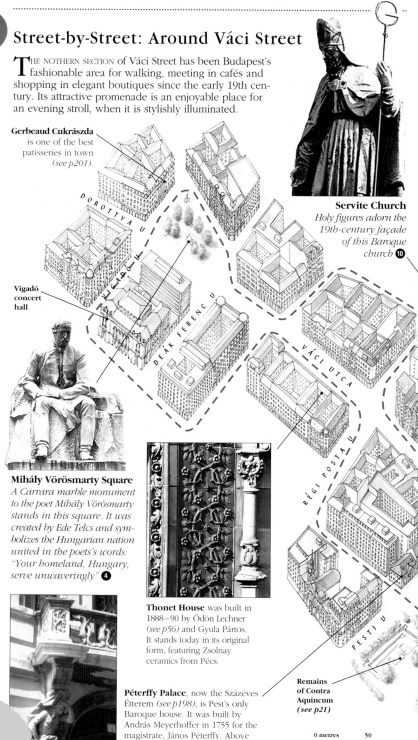

Gerbeaud Cukrászda
is one of the best
patisseries in town
(see p201).

Servite Church
*Holy figures adorn the
19th-century façade
of this Baroque
church* ❿

**Vigadó
concert
hall**

Mihály Vörösmarty Square
*A Carrara marble monument
to the poet Mihály Vörösmarty
stands in this square. It was
created by Ede Telcs and symbolizes the Hungarian nation
united in the poets's words:
"Your homeland, Hungary,
serve unwaveringly"* ❹

Thonet House was built in
1888–90 by Ödön Lechner
(see p56) and Gyula Pártos.
It stands today in its original
form, featuring Zsolnay
ceramics from Pécs.

Péterffy Palace, now the Százéves
Étterem *(see p198)*, is Pest's only
Baroque house. It was built by
András Meyerhoffer in 1755 for the
magistrate, János Péterffy. Above
the gateway there is a beautiful balcony supported by atlantes.

**Remains
of Contra
Aquincum**
(see p21)

0 metres	50
0 yards	50

★ Váci Street
Budapest's most elegant promenade and shopping area is lined with fashion boutiques, cafés, fountains and statues. Off the street there are old courtyards and shopping arcades ❺

LOCATOR MAP
See Street Finder, maps 4 & 5

Párizsi Udvar *(see p205)* is found on the corner of Kígyó utca and Petőfi Sándor utca. The arcade, which features shops, bookshops and a cafe, is decorated with beautiful wrought-iron work.

★ Klotild Palaces
This beautifully decorated block is one of two buildings, which together form a magnificent gateway to the Elizabeth Bridge ❻

KEY

– – – Suggested route

★ Inner City Parish Church
This white limestone and red marble tabernacle, in the church, dates from the early 16th century ❶

STAR SIGHTS

★ Inner City Parish Church

★ Váci Street

★ Klotild Palaces

Inner City Parish Church ❶

THIS CHURCH IS THE oldest building in Pest. It was first established during the reign of St István, the first king of Hungary *(see pp22–3)*, on the burial site of the martyred St Gellért. In the 14th century, a large Gothic church was built, which was used as a mosque under the Turks. Damaged by the Great Fire of 1723, the church was partly rebuilt in the Baroque style by György Pauer in 1725–39. The interior also features Neo-Classical elements by János Hild, as well as some 20th-century works.

The south tower includes one of the surviving walls of the Romanesque church.

★ Pulpit
This Neo-Gothic pulpit is beautifully carved from wood. It was produced in 1808 by Fülöp Ungradt.

Main Portal
The late Baroque portal is crowned by a sculpture of the Holy Trinity, inlaid with gold.

A fragment of a wall from the Romanesque church is visible in the lower section of the façade.

Nave
The interior of the church reflects the Gothic and Baroque periods in which it was built. The nave, in the western section of the church, is Baroque in design.

STAR FEATURES

★ **Pulpit**

★ **Fresco**

★ **Gothic Chapel**

★ **Fresco**
This fragment of a 15th-century Italianate fresco depicts the crucifixion of Christ. It was transferred from the cloister to its current location in the choir.

VISITORS' CHECKLIST

Március 15 tér 2. **Map** 4 E1
318 31 08. **M** *Ferenciek tere.* for services. daily.

Reconstructed Gothic tabernacle

Main Altar
The original altar was destroyed in World War II, and the current one, by Károly Antal and Pál C Molnar, dates from 1948.

Turkish Prayer Niche
One of the few remnants of the Turkish occupation (see pp26–7) is this mihrab, *or prayer niche, indicating the direction of Mecca.*

★ **Gothic Chapel**
This vaulted chapel is entered through a painted archway. It features recreated tracery windows.

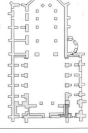

Crest of Pest
The crest of Pest adorns the pedestal of a Renaissance tabernacle, which was commissioned by Pest's city council in 1507. It is the work of a 16th-century Italian artist.

HISTORICAL FLOORPLAN OF THE CHURCH

Nothing remains of the first church: the oldest sections date from the 12th-century Romanesque church.

KEY

▨	Romanesque church
☐	Gothic church
☐	Baroque church

The opulent façade of the Vigadó concert hall, decorated with figures and busts of statesmen, leaders and other prominent Hungarians

Inner City Parish Church ❶

BELVÁROSI PLÉBÁNIA TEMPLOM

See pp124–5.

Vigadó Square ❷

VIGADÓ TÉR

Map 4 D1. 🚋 *2.*

THE VIGADÓ concert hall dominates the square with its mix of eclectic forms. It was built by Frigyes Feszl in 1859–64 to replace a predecessor destroyed by fire during the uprising of 1848–9 *(see pp30–31)*. The façade includes features such as folk motifs, dancers on columns and busts of former monarchs, rulers and other Hungarian personalities. An old Hungarian coat of arms is also visible in the centre.

The Budapest Marriott Hotel *(see p184)*, located on one side of the square, was designed by József Finta in 1969. It was one of the first modern hotels to be built in Budapest.

On the Danube promenade, in front of the square, there is a statue of a childlike figure sitting on the railings. Entitled *Little Princess (see p65)*, it is the 1989 work of László Marton. The square also has craft stalls, cafés and restaurants.

József Nádor Square ❸

JÓZSEF NÁDOR TÉR

Map 2 E5. Ⓜ *Vörösmarty tér.*

ARCHDUKE JÓZSEF, after whom this square is named, was appointed as the emperor's Palatine for Hungary in 1796 at the age of 20. He ruled the country for 51 years until his death in 1847. One of the few Habsburgs sympathetic to the Hungarian people, he was instrumental in the development of Budapest and, in 1808, he initiated the Embellishment Commission *(see p30)*.

A statue of Archduke József, by Johann Halbig, stands in the middle of the square. It was erected in 1869.

Some of the houses on the square are worth individual mention. The Neo-Classical Gross Palace at No. 1 *(see p48)* was built in 1824 by József Hild. Once a café, it now houses a bank. The building at Nos. 5–6, which overlooks the southern end of the square, dates from 1859 and was built by Hugó Máltás. At No. 11 is a shop run by the Herend company *(see p205)*. Its factory in southwest Hungary has produced world-renowned porcelain for almost 200 years.

Mihály Vörösmarty Square

VÖRÖSMARTY MIHÁLY TÉR ❹

Map 2 E5. Ⓜ *Vörösmarty tér.*

IN THE MIDDLE of the square stands a monument depicting the poet Mihály Vörösmarty (1800–55). Unveiled in 1908, it is the work of Ede Telcs. Behind the monument, on the eastern side of the square, is the Luxus department store *(see p205)*. It is located in a three-floor corner building dating from 1911 and designed by Kálmán Giergl and Flóris Korb.

On the northern side of the square is a renowned pâtisserie, which was opened by Henrik Kugler in 1858. It was taken over by the Swiss *patissière* Emil Gerbeaud, who was responsible for the richly decorated interior which survives to this day.

Sculpture in Vigadó Square

Terrace of the Gerbeaud pâtisserie, on Mihály Vörösmarty Square

A tempting selection of coffee, cakes, pastries and desserts are on offer. In summer, these can be taken on a terrace overlooking the square.

Thonet House, decorated with Zsolnay tiles, at No. 11 Váci Street

Váci Street ❺

VÁCI UTCA

Map 2 F1 & 2 F2.
Ⓜ Ferenciek tere.

ONCE TWO separate streets, which were joined at the beginning of the 18th century, Váci Street still has two distinct characters. Today, part of the southern section is open to traffic, while the northern end is pedestrianized and has long been a popular commercial centre. Most of the buildings lining the street date from the 19th and early 20th centuries. More recently, however, modern department stores, banks and shopping arcades have sprung up among the older original buildings.

Philantia, a Secession style florist's shop opened in 1905, now occupies part of the Neo-Classical block at No. 9, built in 1840 by József Hild. No. 9 also houses the Pest Theatre, where classic plays by Anton Chekhov, among others, are staged. The building was once occupied by the Inn of the Seven Electors, which had a large ballroom-cum-concert hall. It was here that a 12-year-old Franz Liszt performed.

Thonet House, at No. 11, is most notable for the Zsolnay tiles (see p56) from Pécs, which decorate its façade.

No. 13 is the oldest building on Váci Street and was built in 1805. In contrast, the post-modern Fontana department store (see p205) at No. 16, was built in 1984. Outside the store there is a bronze fountain with a figure of Hermes, dating from the mid-19th century.

The Nádor Hotel once stood at No. 20 and featured a statue of Archduke Palatine József in front of the entrance. Today the Taverna Hotel (see p183), designed by József Finta and opened in 1987, stands here.

In a side street off Váci Street, at No. 13 Régi posta utca, is a building from the Modernist period. An unusual sight in Pest, this Bauhaus-influenced building dates from 1937 and is by Lajos Kozma.

Klotild Palaces ❻

KLOTILD PALOTÁK

Szabadsajtó utca. **Map** 4 E1.
Ⓜ Ferenciek tere.

FLANKING Szabadsajtó utca, on the approach to the Elizabeth Bridge, stand two massive apartment blocks built in 1902. The buildings were commissioned by the daughter-in-law of Palatine József, Archduchess Klotild, after whom they were named.

They were designed by Flóris Korb and Kálmán Giergl in the Historicist style, with

One of the twin Klotild Palaces, from 1902, by the approach to the Elizabeth Bridge (see p63)

elements of Rococo decoration. Once all rented apartments, now only the upper floors remain residential. The ground floor is occupied by shops, a café and the Budapest Gallery with its exhibition space.

Pest County Hall ❼

PEST MEGYEI ÖNKORMÁNYZAT

Városház utca 7. **Map** 4 E1.
Ⓒ 318 01 11. Ⓜ Ferenciek tere.
Ⓞ 8am–4pm Wed.

BUILT IN SEVERAL stages, this is one of Pest's most beautiful, monumental Neo-Classical civic buildings. It was erected during the 19th century, as part of the plan for the city drawn up by the Embellishment Commission.

A seat of the Council of Pest has existed on this site since the end of the 17th century. By 1811, however, the building included two conference halls, a prison and a prison chapel. In 1829–32, a wing designed by József Hofrichter was added on Semmelweis utca, which was used to accommodate council employees.

In 1838 another redevelopment programme was begun, this time employing designs by Mátyás Zitterbarth Jr, a highly regarded exponent of Neo-Classical architecture. Completed in 1842, it included an impressive façade, which overlooks Városház utca. This features a portico with six Corinthian columns supporting a prominent tympanum.

Pest County Hall was destroyed in the course of World War II. During post-war rebuilding it was enlarged, with the addition of three internal courtyards, the first of which is surrounded by atmospheric cloisters. Due to the excellent acoustics, concerts are often held here during the summer.

Between Pest County Hall and the Municipal Council Offices building (see p128), in the small Kamermayer Károly tér, there is a monument to the first mayor of Budapest. Károly Kamermayer (1829–97) took office in 1873 after the unification of Óbuda, Buda and Pest. The aluminium monument was designed in 1942 by Béla Szabados.

Municipal Council Offices ❽

FŐVÁROSI ÖNKORMÁNYZAT

Városház utca 9–11. **Map** 4 E1 & F1.
🔲 327 10 00. Ⓜ *Ferenciek tere.*

THE LARGEST BAROQUE building in Budapest, this edifice was completed in 1735 to a design by the architect Anton Erhard Martinelli. It originally functioned as a hospital for veterans of the war between the Christian and Turkish armies at the end of the 17th century *(see pp26– 7)*.

In 1894 the city authorities bought the building in order to convert it into council offices. Ármin Hegedűs was commissioned to refurbish the building and a new southern wing was built to his design.

Most notable are the bas-reliefs decorating the gates on the Városház utca side of the building. The scenes depicted in the bas-reliefs commemorate a victory of Charles III *(see p19)* and Prince Eugene of Savoy's role in the war against the Turks *(see p71)*. These are thought to be the work of the Viennese sculptor Johann Christoph Mader.

Turkish Bank ❾

TÖRÖK BANKHÁZ

Szervita tér 3. **Map** 4 E1.
Ⓜ *Deák Ferenc tér.*

DATING FROM 1906 and designed by Henrik Böhm and Ármin Hegedűs, the building that formerly housed the Turkish Bank is a wonderful example of the Secession style.

The exterior used modern construction methods to create the glass façade, which is set in reinforced concrete. Above the fenestration, in the gable, is a magnificent colourful mosaic by Miksa Róth. Entitled *Glory to Hungary*, it depicts Hungary paying homage to the Virgin Mary, or *Patrona Hungariae (see p117)*. Angels and shepherds surround the Virgin, along with figures of Hungarian political heroes, such as Prince Ferenc Rákóczi *(see p28)*, István Széchenyi *(see pp30– 31)* and Lajos Kossuth *(see p106)*.

Glory to Hungary, the mosaic on the façade of the Turkish Bank

Servite Church ❿

SZERVITA TEMPLOM

Szervita tér 7. **Map** 4 E1.
Ⓜ *Deák Ferenc tér.*

THIS BAROQUE CHURCH was built between 1725– 32 to a design by János Hölbling and György Pauer. In 1871, the façade was rebuilt and the tower was covered with a new roof, designed by József Diescher.

Above the doorway there are figures of St Peregrin and St Anne, and above them sit St Philip and St Augustine. To the right of the entrance there is a bas-relief by János Istók, dating from 1930. It is dedicated to the heroes of the VIIth Wilhelm Hussar Regiment who gave their lives in World War I.

Lutheran Church ⓫

EVANGÉLIKUS TEMPLOM

Deák tér 4. **Map** 2 E5. 🔲 317 34 13.
Ⓜ *Deák Ferenc tér.* ♿ **National Lutheran Museum** ◯ 10am–6pm Tue– Sun. 🚫 ♿ *by arrangement.*

MIHÁLY POLLACK designed this Neo-Classical church, built between 1799– 1808. A portico, which features a tympanum supported by Doric columns, was added to the façade in 1856 by József Hild. The church is characterized by its simplicity, which is typical of early Neo-Classicism. It also reflects the notion of minimal church decoration, which was upheld by this branch of Protestantism. Above the modest main altar is a copy of Raphael's *Transfiguration* by Franz Sales Lochbihler, made in 1811. Organ recitals are often held in the church, which has excellent acoustics.

Another Neo-Classical building by Mihály Pollack adjoins the church. Constructed as a Lutheran school, it is now the National Lutheran Museum. The museum illustrates the history of the Reformation in Hungary, with the most interesting exhibit being a copy of Martin Luther's last will and testament. The original document, dating from 1542, is held in the Lutheran Archives.

Neo-Classical main altar in the Lutheran Church

The Danube Fountain, built in 1880–83 by Miklós Ybl

Danube Fountain ⑫
DANUBIUS KÚT

Erzsébet tér. **Map** 2 E5.
Ⓜ Deák Ferenc tér.

THIS FOUNTAIN, which once stood in Kálvin tér, was designed and built by Miklós Ybl (see p94) in 1880–83. It is decorated with copies by Deszö Györi of original sculptures, by Béla Brestyánszky and Leó Feszler, which were damaged in World War II.

The figure at the top of the fountain is Danubius, representing the Danube. The three female figures below symbolize Hungary's three principal rivers after the Danube: the Tisza, the Dráva and the Száva.

New Theatre ⑬
ÚJ SZÍNHÁZ

Paulay Ede utca 35. **Map** 2 F5.
Ⓒ 269 60 21. Ⓜ Opera.

ORIGINALLY completed in 1909, this building has undergone many transformations. It was designed by Béla Lajta in the Secession style, and, as the home of the cabaret troupe Parisian Mulató, became a shrine to frivolity.

In 1921 it was completely restyled by Lászlo Vágó, who turned it into a theatre. After World War II, the theatre gained a glass-and-steel façade, and a children's theatre company was based here.

Between 1988–90 the building was returned to its original form using Lajta's plans. Gilding, stained glass and marble once more adorn this unusual building. Hungary's New Theatre is now in residence.

Franz Liszt Academy of Music ⑭
LISZT FERENC ZENEAKADÉMIA

Liszt Ferenc tér 8. **Map** 7 A1.
Ⓒ 341 47 88. 🚋 4, 6 to Király utca.

THE ACADEMY is housed in a late Historicist palace, built between 1904–7 by Kálmán Giergl and Flóris Korb. Above the main entrance there is a statue of Franz Liszt, by Alajos Stróbl. The six bas-reliefs above its base are by Ede Telcs, and depict the history of music.

The Secession interiors of this building have remained intact and deserve particular attention. The Fount of Youth fresco, in the first floor foyer, is by Aladár Körösfői-Kriesch, who was a member of the Gödöllő school. The academy has two auditoriums. The first seats 1,200 people and features allegories of musical movements. The second seats 400 and is used for chamber music.

New York Palace ⑮
NEW YORK PALOTA

Erzsébet körút 9–11. **Map** 7 B2.
Ⓒ 322 38 49. Ⓜ Blaha Lujza tér.
Café and restaurant ⏰ 10am–midnight.

BUILT BETWEEN 1891–5 to a design by the architect Alajos Hauszmann, this building was initially the offices of an American insurance firm.

This five-floor edifice displays an eclectic mix of Neo-Baroque and Secession motifs. The decorative sculptures that animate the façade are the work of Károly Senyei.

On the ground floor is a renowned restaurant and café, called the New York Café (see p200). On the walls are paintings by Gusztav Mannheimer and Károly Lotz. The beautiful, richly gilded Neo-Baroque interior, with its magnificent chandeliers and marble pillars, now attracts tourists, just as it once attracted the literary and artistic circles in its heyday.

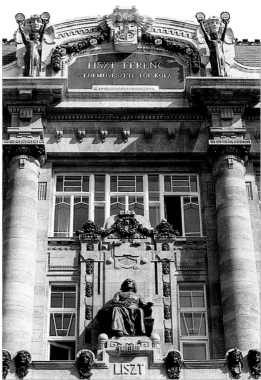

Statue of Franz Liszt above the entrance to the Academy of Music

Hungarian National Museum ⓴

Seal from Esztergom

THE HUNGARIAN National Museum is the country's richest source of art and artifacts relating to its own turbulent history. Founded in 1802, the museum owes its existence to Count Ferenc Széchényi, who offered his collection of coins, books and documents to the nation. The museum's constantly expanding collection of art and documents is exhibited in an impressive Neo-Classical edifice built by Mihály Pollack.

Placing the Cornerstone *(1864)*
This painting by Miklós Barabás shows the ceremony that marked the beginning of construction of the Chain Bridge (see p62) in 1842.

Campaign Chest
This carved Baroque campaign chest features the prince regent's decoration and the Hungarian crest. It dates from the insurrection led by Ferenc Rákóczi II (see p28).

★ Armchair
Adorned with multi-coloured fruit and floral ornamentation, this armchair dates from the early 18th century. It is the work of Ferenc II Rákóczi, who learnt carpentry during his exile in Turkey.

★ Royal Insignia
Decorated with filigree, this sceptre dates from around the end of the 12th century, while the simply designed orb dates from the 14th century.

Main entrance

KEY

- ☐ Royal insignia
- ☐ Roman mosaics
- ☐ 11th – 17th-century exhibits
- ☐ 18th – 19th-century exhibits
- ☐ 20th-century exhibits

MUSEUM GUIDE

On the ground floor on the left-hand side, past the Roman mosaics, are the royal insignia. The first floor exhibits comprise Hungarian artifacts from 11th–20th centuries. An exhibition of prehistoric finds is also planned.

Millennium Plate

This plate was produced in 1896 for the Hungarian Millennium Celebrations (see p33). It is decorated with historic scenes, inscriptions and crests.

VISITORS' CHECKLIST

Múzeum körút 14–16.
Map 4 F1. 338 21 22.
Apr–Sep: 10am–6pm Tue–Sun; Oct–Mar: 10am–5pm Tue–Sun. Kálvin tér.

First floor

★ Funeral Crown

This magnificent 13th-century golden crown was found in the ruins of the Dominican Church and Convent on Margaret Island in the Danube (see pp172–3).

Pelisse

This short leather jacket is typical of Hungarian national costume. It belonged to Gábor Bethlen, a prince of Transylvania, and dates from around 1620.

Ground floor

Gothic Well

These reconstructed fragments are part of a well from the Royal Palace at Visegrád (see p164). The well dates from the 14th-century rule of the Angevin dynasty.

STAR EXHIBITS

- ★ **Royal Insignia**
- ★ **Funeral Crown**
- ★ **Armchair**

Exploring the Museum's Collection

A 13th-century coin

THE STEPS OF THE Hungarian National Museum were the scene of a significant event in Budapest's history. It was from these steps that, in 1848, the poet Sándor Petőfi first read his *National Song*, which sparked the uprising against Habsburg rule *(see p30–31)*. This moment is commemorated each year on 15 March, when the museum is decorated in the national colours and a re-enactment is performed. Items from the museum's rich collection, including works of art and craft, historical documents and photographs, vividly illustrate this and other events from Hungary's varied and fascinating past.

in error as St István's Crown, though it post-dates him by some 70 years. It is decorated with precious stones, pearls and enamel work, and is composed of two sections. The lower, Byzantine section – the *corona graeca* – dates from around 1074 and is thought to have been a gift from the Byzantine emperor to Prince Géza I *(see p22)*. The upper, Roman section – the *corona latina* – which depicts eight of the 12 Apostles, was added during the 12th century.

Other treasures include a sceptre dating from the late 12th century, whose crystal head is thought to date from the 10th century. The gold-plated bronze royal orb was created in the 14th century, while the Renaissance sword, which was probably produced in Venice, is thought to date from the 16th century.

Completing the collection of royal insignia is a magnificent liturgical gown, dating from 1031 but refashioned in the 13th century. The now-faded silk cloth features an intricate embroidered design of fine gold thread and pearls.

Monument to poet János Arany in front of the Neo-Classical façade

MUSEUM BUILDING

BUILT BETWEEN 1837–47, according to a design by Mihály Pollack, this imposing Neo-Classical building is one of the finest manifestations of that architecural epoch.

The façade is preceded by a monumental portico, which is crowned by a tympanum by Raffael Ponti. The composition depicts the figure of Pannonia *(see p20)* among personifications of the arts and sciences.

In the gardens surrounding the museum there are statues of prominent figures from the spheres of literature, science and art. A monument to the poet János Arany, author of the *Toldi Trilogy*, stands in front of the main entrance. This bronze and limestone work dates from 1893 and is by Alajos Stróbl.

The notable features of the interior include the magnificent paintings by Mór Than and Károly Lotz in the main hall and a 3rd-century AD Roman mosaic integrated into the floor of the domed hall.

ROYAL INSIGNIA

SOME OF THE most important Hungarian treasures, the royal insignia of the Árpáds *(see pp22–3)*, are exhibited in a separate hall. Remarkably, these insignia have survived Hungary's dramatic history. Discovered by the American forces during World War II, they were removed and stored in Fort Knox before being returned to Hungary in 1978.

Among these items is an unusually beautiful gold crown, which at one time was known

11TH–17TH-CENTURY EXHIBITS

THE EXHIBITION begins in the Árpád era, the country's early history, and features one of the museum's most valuable exhibits, the crown of Constantine IX Monomachus, decorated with enamel work. Also on display in this section are the funeral decorations of Béla III, Romanesque sacred

Carved base of a chalice dating from the 15th century

vessels, weapons and an interesting collection of coins.

The period of Angevin rule *(see p18)* coincided with the birth of the Gothic style, which is represented here by some excellent examples of gold work. The next two halls explore the reign of Sigismund of Luxembourg *(see p24)* and the achievements of János Hunyadi *(see p24)*. On display here are copies of portraits of King Sigismund by Albrecht Dürer and a richly decorated ceremonial saddle. There are also several platinum and gold pieces, illuminated manuscripts and documents. The lifestyle of peasants from this era is illustrated, as well as the history of the royal court.

The reign of Mátyás Corvinus *(see pp24–5)* and the Jagiełło dynasty *(see p18)* marks the decline of the Gothic period and the birth of the Renaissance. Exhibits from this era include a 15th-century glass goblet belonging to King Mátyás, late Gothic pews from a church in Bártfie, armour and weapons, as well as a 16th-century dress belonging to Queen Maria.

Magnificent examples of sculpture, art and artifacts from the 16th and 17th centuries follow. Of particular interest are items that survived the Turkish occupation *(see pp26–7)*, especially the everyday objects and weapons.

A separate hall is dedicated to the Transylvanian dukedom and the important historical role that it played. Exhibited here are vessels and jewellery elaborately crafted in gold, 12th-century costumes, and original ceramics produced by the people of Haban, who settled there in the early 17th century. This last section of the exhibition ends in 1686, at the time of the liberation of Budapest by the Christain armies after the Turkish occupation. In this part of the museum there are also portraits of influential Hungarians from the period, and an interesting exhibition of jewellery dating from the 17th century.

Printing press used in 1848 to print nationalist propaganda

18TH–19TH-CENTURY EXHIBITS

THIS PART OF the museum covers Habsburg rule, a period of great civil unrest. The exhibition begins with artifacts connected to the Rákóczi insurrection of 1703–11 *(see pp28–9)*. Weapons, as well as furniture from Ferenc II Rákóczi's palace, are exhibited here. One item of particular interest is the armchair produced by Rákóczi himself. The next hall is dedicated to 18th-century Hungarian art and culture.

Brooch from the 18th-century

The following rooms portray the Hungarian history of the first half of the 19th century. Artworks, including magnificent portraits and historic paintings, such as *Placing the Cornerstone of the Chain*

Guild chest from the 20th century

Bridge, are assembled along with important documents and memoirs from that time.

The central section, dedicated to the uprising of 1848–9 *(see pp30–31)*, features a printing press on which were printed leaflets outlining the 12 demands in Hungary's fight for independence from Austria.

The exhibits from the second half of the 19th century include collections of masonic items, official decorations, coins and historic manuscripts. Items relating to the coronation of Franz Joseph in 1867 and the Millennium Celebrations of 1896 are also displayed here.

20TH-CENTURY EXHIBITS

REFLECTING THE technical developments of this century, Hungary's recent history is presented in a documentary style. Photographs, rather than works of art, and documents are widely used to illustrate the events of this period. Artifacts relating to World War I and the era of revolution between the wars, and shocking documents from World War II can be found here. The post-war history of Hungary is depicted mainly from a political perspective. Emphasis is placed on significant episodes, such as the uprising of 1956 and the events of 1989, which signalled the end of Communism in Eastern Europe *(see p35)*.

Jewish Quarter 16
ZSIDÓ NEGYED

Király utca, Rumbach Sebestyén utca,
Dohány utca & Akácfa utca.
Map 2 F5 & 7 A2. **M** Deák Ferenc tér.

JEWS FIRST CAME to Hungary in the 13th century and settled in Buda and Óbuda. In the 19th century, a larger Jewish community was established outside the Pest city boundary, in a small area of Erzébetváros.

In 1251, King Béla IV gave the Jews of Buda certain privilges, including freedom of

Window of the Great Synagogue

HOLOCAUST MEMORIAL

This sculpture of a weeping willow, designed by Imre Varga, was unveiled in 1991 in memory of the 600,000 Hungarian Jews killed by the Nazis in World War II. It was partly funded by the Hungarian-American actor Tony Curtis.

---

religion. The Jewish community became well integrated into Hungarian society, until in 1941, a series of Nazi anti-Semitic laws were passed and the wearing of the Star of David was made compulsory. In 1944, a ghetto was created in Pest and the deportation of thousands of Jews to camps, including Auschwitz, was implemented. After heavy fighting between the Russian and German armies, the Soviet Red Army liberated the ghetto on 18 January 1945. In total, 600,000 Hungarian Jews were victims of the Holocaust. This fact is commemorated by a plaque at the Orthodox Synagogue on Rumbach utca.

In the late 19th century, three synagogues were built and many Jewish shops and workshops were established. Kosher establishments, such as the Hanna Étterem *(see p197)* in the courtyard of the Orthodox Synagogue, and the butcher at No. 41 Kazinczy utca, were a common feature. Shops are now being reconstructed to recreate the pre-ghetto character of the Jewish Quarter.

Great Synagogue 17
ZSINAGÓGA

Dohány utca 2. **Map** 7 A3.
C 342 89 49. **M** Astoria.
O 10am–3pm Mon–Fri, 10am–1pm Sun.

THIS SYNAGOGUE is not only the largest of the three synagogues in this area, but it is also the largest in Europe. It was built in a Byzantine-Moorish style by the Viennese architect Ludwig Förster between 1854–9.

The synagogue has three naves and, following orthodox tradition, separate galleries for women. Together the naves and galleries can accommodate up to 3,000 worshippers. Interestingly, some features, such as the postion of the bimah, reflect elements of Judaic reform. The interior has valuable decorative fittings, particularly those by Aron Hakodesz and Frigyes Feszl.

In 1931, a museum was established within the synagogue, in which a vast collection of Judaic artifacts from ancient Rome to the present day has been assembled. The large collection includes the book of Chevra Kadisha from 1792, and documentation of the persecution of the Jews.

A large rose window is the façade's main ornamentation. It is located between two richly decorated towers crowned with distinctive onion domes.

The façade is composed of white and red brick and intricately designed ceramic friezes.

A Hebrew inscription from the second book of Moses is situated under the rose window.

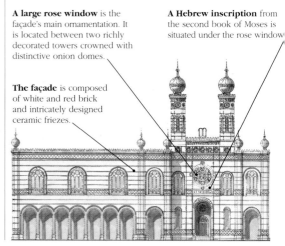

Chapel of St Roch **❽**

SZENT RÓKUS-KÁPOLNA

Gyulai Pál u 2. **Map** 7 A3. **C** 338 22 69. **M** Astoria or Blaha Lujza tér.

PEST TOWN COUNCIL built this chapel in what was then an uninhabited area. It was dedicated to St Roch and St Rozali, who were believed to provide protection against the plague, which afflicted Pest in 1711.

In 1740 the chapel was extended to its present size, and a tower was added in 1797. The façade is decorated with Baroque figures of saints, although the originals were replaced with copies in 1908.

Inside, on the right-hand wall of the chapel's nave, is a painting of the Virgin Mary from 1740. A painting by Jakab Warsch, depicting the Great Flood of 1838, is in the oratory.

Mihály Pollack Square **❾**

POLLACK MIHÁLY TÉR

Map 7 A4. **M** Kálvin tér.
Festetics Palace **C** 266 52 22.
🔲 by prior arrangement.

AT THE REAR of the Hungarian National Museum (see pp130–33) is a square named after Mihály Pollack, the architect of several Neo-Classical buildings such as the museum and Sándor Palace (see p73).

In the late 19th century, three palaces were built side by side on this square for the aristocratic elite of Hungary: Prince Festetics, Prince Esterházy and Count Károlyi. The beautiful façades makes this one of the city's most captivating squares.

Miklós Ybl (see p94) built the French-Renaissance style palace at No. 6 for Lajós Károlyi, in 1863–5. The façade is decorated with sculptures by Károly Schaffer. There is also a covered driveway for carriages. Next door, at No. 8, is a small palace, which was built in 1865 for the Esterházy family by Alájos Baumgarten. At No. 10 is the palace built for the Festetics family in 1862, again by Miklós Ybl. The interior, especially the Neo-Baroque staircase, is splendid.

Magnificent staircase inside the Festetics Palace on Mihály Pollack Square

Hungarian National Museum **❷⓪**

NEMZETI MÚZEUM

See pp130–33.

Ervin Szabó Library **❷①**

SZABÓ ERVIN KÖNYVTÁR

Szabó Ervin tér 1. **Map** 7 A4.
C 338 49 33. **M** Kálvin tér.
🕙 10am–3pm Mon, Tue, Thu & Fri, 9am–1pm Sat & Sun.

IN 1887, the wealthy industrialist Wenckheim family commissioned the architect Artur Meining to build a Neo-Baroque and Rococo style palace. The result was the former Wenckheim Palace, regarded as one of the most beautiful palaces in Budapest. The magnificent wrought-iron

Spiral staircase in one of the rooms of the Ervin Szabó Library

gates, dating from 1897, are the work of Gyula Jungfer. Also worth particular attention are the richly gilded salons on the first floor, as well as the dome above an oval panel of reliefs.

In 1926, the city council acquired the building and converted it into a public lending library, whose collection focuses on the city itself and the social sciences.

The Ervin Szabó Library was named after the politician and social reformer Ervin Szabó (1877–1918), who was the library's first director. It has over a hundred branches throughout Budapest and some three million books.

Calvinist Church **❷②**

REFORMÁTUS TEMPLOM

Kálvin tér 7. **Map** 7 A4.
C 217 67 69. **M** Kálvin tér.

THIS SINGLE NAVE church was designed by József Hofrichter and built between 1816–30. In 1848 József Hild designed the four-pillared façade and tympanum, and a spire was added in 1859.

Inside the church it is worth seeing the pulpit and choir gallery, designed by Hild in 1831 and 1854 respectively. The stained-glass windows were the work of Miksa Róth. Sacred artifacts from the 17th and 18th centuries are kept in the church treasury.

Museum of Applied Arts ㉓

O PENED IN 1896 by Emperor Franz Joseph as part of the Millennium Celebrations, this collection is housed not within a Neo-Classical building, but within an outstanding Secession building designed by Gyula Pártos and Ödön Lechner (see p56). The exterior incorporated elements inspired by the Orient as well as the Zsolnay ceramics characteristic of Lechner's work. Damaged in 1945 and again in 1956, the building only recently regained its original magnificence. The collection, founded in 1872, includes many examples of arts and crafts workmanship.

A Lalique pendant

Renaissance Tile
This tile, which dates from around 1530, depicts Queen Anne, wife of Ferdinand I.

Silver Plate
This magnificent Baroque plate depicts the Battle of Vezekény. It was crafted in 1654 in Augsburg by Philip Jacob Drentwett.

Ground floor

Inner Courtyard
This courtyard, covered by a glazed roof, is surrounded by cloisters with arcades designed in an Indian-Oriental style.

KEY

- ☐ Ceramics and glassware
- ☐ Leather and paper crafts
- ☐ Textiles
- ☐ Furniture and carving
- ☐ Metalwork
- ☐ Secession artifacts
- ☐ Temporary exhibitions

Main entrance

MUSEUM GUIDE

The first floor of the museum's left wing displays individual handicrafts, such as ceramics and glass, furniture and carving, and metalwork and textiles. An exhibition of Secession artifacts surrounds the inner courtyard on the first floor. The museum also has many temporary exhibitions.

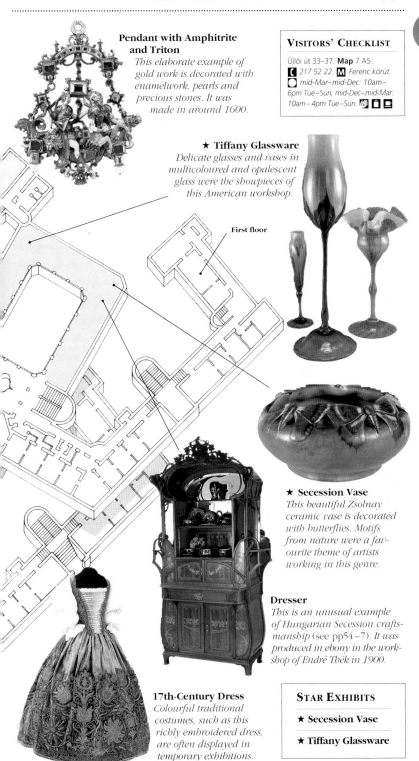

Pendant with Amphitrite and Triton
This elaborate example of gold work is decorated with enamelwork, pearls and precious stones. It was made in around 1600.

★ Tiffany Glassware
Delicate glasses and vases in multicoloured and opalescent glass were the showpieces of this American workshop.

First floor

★ Secession Vase
This beautiful Zsolnay ceramic vase is decorated with butterflies. Motifs from nature were a favourite theme of artists working in this genre.

Dresser
This is an unusual example of Hungarian Secession crafts-manship (see pp54–7). It was produced in ebony in the work-shop of Endré Thék in 1900.

17th-Century Dress
Colourful traditional costumes, such as this richly embroidered dress, are often displayed in temporary exhibitions.

STAR EXHIBITS

★ **Secession Vase**

★ **Tiffany Glassware**

University of Economics ❷

KÖZGAZDASÁGTUDOMÁNYI EGYETEM

Fővám tér 8. **Map** 4 F3.
🚋 47, 49.

F ACING THE DANUBE, this Neo-Renaissance edifice was designed by Miklós Ybl *(see p94)* and built as the Main Customs Office in 1871–4.

The façade is 170 m (560 ft) long and features a colonnade supporting a balcony. On the balustrade stand ten allegorical figures by August Sommer.

In 1951, this building opened as a university specializing in economics and management. There is a statue of Karl Marx, after whom the university was once named, in the atrium.

Decorative element on the façade of the City Council Chamber

City Council Chamber ❷

ÚJ VÁROSHÁZA

Váci utca 62–64. **Map** 4 F2.
Ⓜ Deák tér. 📞 327 10 00.
☑ by prior arrangement.

T HIS THREE-FLOOR edifice was built between 1870–75 as offices for the newly unified city of Budapest *(see p32)*. Its architect, Imre Steindl, was also responsible for designing Parliament *(see pp108–9)*.

The building is a mix of styles. The exterior is a Neo-Renaissance design in brick, with grotesques between the

Façade of the University of Economics, designed by Miklós Ybl

windows, while the interior features cast-iron Neo-Gothic motifs. The Great Debating Hall is decorated with mosaics designed by Károly Lotz.

Many antiquarian bookshops and galleries have now opened around here. Fashionable bars, restaurants and cafés, and the recent pedestrianization, make this a very charming area.

Serbian Church ❷

SZERB TEMPLOM

Szerb utca 2–4. **Map** 4 F2.
Ⓜ Kálvin tér.

S ERBS SETTLED IN the now largely residential area around the church as early as the 16th century. The end of the 17th century brought a new wave of Serb immigrants, and by the early 19th century Serbs comprised almost 25 per cent of Pest's home-owners.

In 1698, the Serb community replaced an earlier church on the site with this Baroque one. The church gained its final appearance after a rebuilding project that lasted until the mid-18th century, which was probably undertaken by András Meyerhoffer.

The interior of the church is arranged according to Greek Orthodox practice. A section of the nave, which is entered from the vestibule, is reserved for women. This

Ceramic tile from the Serbian Church

area is divided from the men's section by a partition, and the division is further emphasized by the floor, which has been lowered by 30 cm (1 ft). The choir gallery is enclosed by an iconostasis that divides it from the sanctuary. This iconostasis dates from around 1850. The carving is by the Serb sculptor Miahai Janich and the Italian Renaissance-influenced paintings are the work of the Greek artist Károly Sterio.

Lóránd Eötvös University ❷

EÖTVÖS LÓRÁND TUDOMÁNY EGYETEM KÖZPONTJA

Egyetem tér 1–3. **Map** 4 F2.
Ⓜ Ferenciek tere, Kálvin tér.

I N 1635, Cardinal Péter Pázmány, the leader of the Counter-Reformation, established a university in Nagyszombat (now Trnava in Slovakia). It moved to Buda in 1777, nearly a century after the end of the Turkish occupation *(see pp26–7)*, during the reign of Maria Theresa. Emperor Joseph II subsequently transferred the university to Pest, to the environs of the Pauline Church, now called the University Church.

It was not until 1889 that the university was endowed with a permanent home. This Neo-Baroque building, now the Law Faculty, was designed by architects including Sándor Baumgarten and Fülöp Herzog. Another wing was later added by Antal Weber.

The university is named after the noted physicist Lóránd Eötvös (1848–1919).

University Church 🕭

EGYETEMI TEMPLOM

Papnövelde utca 9. **Map** 4 F2.
☎ 318 05 55. Ⓜ *Kálvin tér.*

Tympanum adorning the façade of the University Library

THIS SINGLE-NAVE church, with a richly decorated façade, is considered one of the most impressive Baroque churches in the city. It was built for the Pauline Order in 1725–42, and was probably designed by András Meyerhoffer. The tower was added in 1771. The Pauline Order, founded in 1263 by Canon Euzebiusz, was the only religious order to be founded in Hungary.

The magnificent exterior features a tympanum and a row of pilasters that divide the façade. Figures of St Paul and St Anthony flank the emblem of the Pauline Order, which crowns the exterior. The carved-wood interior of the main vestibule is also worth particular mention.

Inside the church a row of side chapels stand behind unusual marble pilasters. In 1776 Johann Bergl painted the vaulted ceiling with frescoes depicting scenes from the life of Mary. Sadly, these frescoes are now in poor condition.

The main altar dates from 1746, and the carved statues behind it are the work of József Hebenstreit. Above it is a copy of the painting *The Black Madonna of Czestochowa*, which is thought to date from 1720. Much of the Baroque interior detail of the church is the work of the Pauline monks, for example the balustrade of the organ loft, the confessionals and the carved pulpit on the right.

Sculptures decorating the pulpit in the University Church

Károlyi Palace 🕭

KÁROLYI PALOTA

Károlyi Mihály utca 16. **Map** 4 F2.
☎ 317 36 11. Ⓜ *Ferenciek tere, Kálvin tér.* **Petőfi Exhibition** ◻ *by arrangement.*

IN 1696 THERE was a small Baroque palace on this site, which was extended by András Meyerhoffer between 1759–68. Subsequent rebuilding, which gave the palace a Neo-Classical appearance, was undertaken between 1832–41 by Anton Riegl. It is named after Mihály Károlyi, leader of the 1918–19 Hungarian Republic *(see p34)*, who was born here in 1875.

The palace now houses the Hungarian Museum of Literature and the Petőfi Exhibition, which is dedicated to the poet Sándor Petőfi *(see p31)*. Other Hungarian poets remembered here include Atilla József, Endre Ady and Mór Jókai.

University Library 🕭

EGYETEMI KÖNYVTÁR

Ferenciek tere 6. **Map** 4 F1. ☎ 266 58 66. Ⓜ *Ferenciek tere, Kálvin tér.* ◻ *9am–3:30pm Mon–Fri.*

THIS NEO-RENAISSANCE edifice, by Antal Szkalniczky and Henrik Koch, was built from 1873–6. It is distinguished by the dome on the corner tower. The library's two million works include 11 *Corviniani (see p72)* and 160 medieval manuscripts and miniatures. The reading room has sgraffiti by Mór Than and frescoes by Károly Lotz.

Franciscan Church 🕭

BELVÁROSI FERENCS TEMPLOM

Ferenciek tere 9. **Map** 4 F1.
☎ 317 33 22. Ⓜ *Ferenciek tere.*

A FRANCISCAN CHURCH and monastery have stood on this site, beyond the old city walls, since the 13th century. In 1541 the Turks rebuilt the church as the Mosque of Sinan, but after the liberation *(see pp26–7)* the monks regained the building. Between 1727–43 they remodelled the church in the Baroque style, which it still retains today.

The façade features a magnificent portal incorporating the Franciscan emblem, crowned by a figure of Mary being adored by angels. Sculptures of Franciscan saints also embellish the façade.

The interior of the church is decorated with frescoes, dating from 1894–5, by Károly Lotz and paintings by Victor Tardo Kremer, from 1925–6. The jewel of this church is the Baroque main altar with sculptures that date from 1741 and 1851. The side altars and the pulpit date from 1851–2.

AROUND VÁROSLIGET

VÁROSLIGET, OR CITY PARK, was once an area of marshland, which served as a royal hunting ground. Leopold I gave the land to the town of Pest, but it was in the mid-18th century, under Maria Theresa, that the area was drained and planted. Today's park was designed towards the end of the 19th century in the English style, which was the fashion of the

Statue of János Hunyadi

day. Városliget was chosen as the focus of the Millennium Celebrations in 1896 *(see p142)*, which marked the 1,000-year anniversary of the conquest of the Carpathian basin by the Magyars. A massive building programme was undertaken, which included the Museum of Fine Arts, Vajdahunyad Castle and the impressive monument in Heroes' Square.

SIGHTS AT A GLANCE

Museums
Ferenc Hopp Museum
  of Far Eastern Art **6**
Franz Liszt Museum **2**
*Museum of Fine Arts
  pp146–9* **9**
Palace of Art **8**
Zoltán Kodály Museum **4**

Parks and Zoos
Vidám Park **12**
Zoo **11**

Streets and Monuments
Andrássy Street **1**
Hermina Street **14**
Millennium Monument **7**
Városligeti Avenue **5**

Historic Buildings
Academy of Fine Art **3**
Erkel Theatre **15**
Széchenyi Baths **13**
Vajdahunyad Castle **10**

GETTING THERE
The M1 metro line runs under Andrássy út from Oktogon to Hősök tere, while bus 4 runs along the street above. Trams, buses and the metro operate in the south of the area, around Thököly út.

KEY

- 🔲 Street-by-Street map
  See pp142–3
- **P** Parking
- **M** Metro station
- 🚔 Police station
- ⊠ Post office
- 🚋 Tram stop

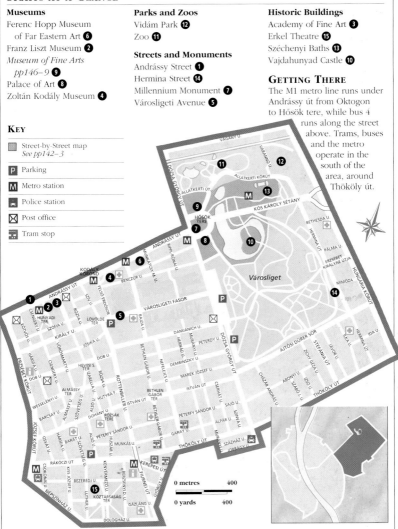

◁ **The picturesque façade of the Renaissance section of Vajdahunyad Castle, in Városliget**

Street-by-Street: Around Heroes' Square

H EROES' SQUARE is a relic of a proud
era in Hungary's history. It was
here that the Millennium Celebrations
opened in 1896. A striking example of this national pride is the
Millennium Monument. Its
colonnades feature statues of
renowned Hungarian leaders
and politicians, and the grand
central column is crowned by a
figure of the Archangel Gabriel.
Vajdahunyad Castle was built in Városliget, or
City Park, adjacent to the square. Probably the
most flamboyant expression of the celebrations,
it is composed of elements of the finest architectural works found throughout Hungary.

**Árpád, leader of
the Magyars**

★ **Museum of Fine Arts**
*This monumental museum building has
an eight-pillared portico supporting a
tympanum* **9**

**Entrance
to the Zoo**

Millennium Monument
Dominating Heroes' Square, this monument includes a figure of Rydwan, the
god of war, by György Zala.

Palace of Art
*The crest of Hungary
decorates the façade
of this building. Dat-
ing from 1895, it is
the country's largest
venue for artistic
exhibitions* **8**

**Secession
pavilion**

THE HUNGARIAN
MILLENNIUM CELEBRATIONS

The Millennium Celebrations in 1896 marked
a high point in the development of Budapest
and in the history of the Austro-Hungarian
monarchy. The city underwent modernization
on a scale unknown in Europe at that time.
Hundreds of houses, palaces and civic buildings were constructed, gas lighting was
introduced and continental Europe's first
underground transport system was opened.

**Archangel
Gabriel**

0 metres		200
0 yards		200

KEY

- - -   Suggested route

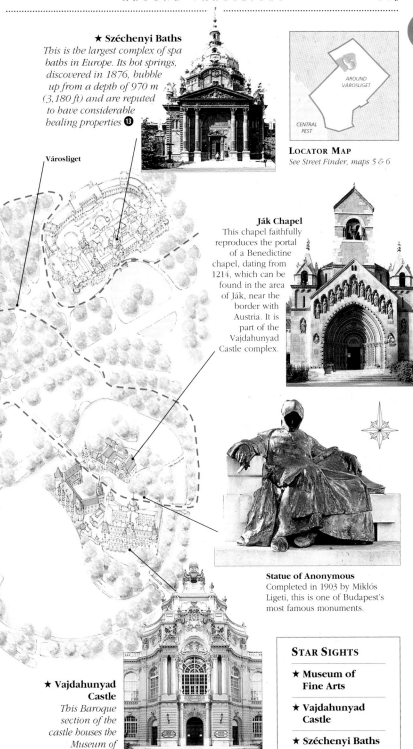

★ Széchenyi Baths
This is the largest complex of spa baths in Europe. Its hot springs, discovered in 1876, bubble up from a depth of 970 m (3,180 ft) and are reputed to have considerable healing properties ⑬

LOCATOR MAP
See Street Finder, maps 5 & 6

AROUND VÁROSLIGET

CENTRAL PEST

Városliget

Ják Chapel
This chapel faithfully reproduces the portal of a Benedictine chapel, dating from 1214, which can be found in the area of Ják, near the border with Austria. It is part of the Vajdahunyad Castle complex.

Statue of Anonymous
Completed in 1903 by Miklós Ligeti, this is one of Budapest's most famous monuments.

★ Vajdahunyad Castle
This Baroque section of the castle houses the Museum of Agriculture ⑩

STAR SIGHTS

★ **Museum of Fine Arts**

★ **Vajdahunyad Castle**

★ **Széchenyi Baths**

The former headquarters of the ÁVO at No. 60 Andrássy Street

Andrássy Street ❶
ANDRÁSSY ÚT

Map 2 F4, 2 F5. **M** Hősök tere.

AT OKTOGON TÉR, Andrássy Street intersects with the bustling Erzsébet körút and Teréz körút. From here, diplomatic and government offices line Andrássy Street, and it loses its commercial character as it leads to Heroes' Square. At No. 60, is the former headquarters of the secret police, the ÁVO, who actively enforced the repressive Stalinist regime of the 1950s.

Franz Liszt Museum ❷
LISZT FERENC EMLÉK MÚZEUM

Vörösmarty út 35. **Map** F4.
C 322 98 04. **M** Vörösmarty utca.
O 10am–6pm Mon–Fri, 9am–5pm Sat. free Mon. by arrangement.

THIS NEO-RENAISSANCE corner house was designed in 1877 by Adolf Lang. Above the windows of the second floor are bas-reliefs depicting famous composers – J S Bach, Wolfgang Amadeus Mozart, Joseph Haydn, Ferenc Erkel,

Ludwig van Beethoven, and Franz Liszt himself. Liszt not only lived in this house, but also established an Academy of Music in the city (see p129).

In 1986, 100 years after Franz Liszt's death, this museum was established in his house. Various items were assembled here, including documents, furniture and two pianos on which he composed and practised his work.

Academy of Fine Art ❸
KÉPZŐMŰVÉSZETI FŐISKOLA

Andrássy út 69–71. **Map** 2 F4.
C 342 17 38. **M** Vörösmarty utca.
Barcsay Gallery O 10am–6pm Mon–Fri, 10am–1pm Sat.

THE ACADEMY OF Fine Art began as a drawing school, later becoming a Higher School of Art. Since 1876, it has occupied these adjacent buildings on Andrássy Street.

The two-floor Neo-Renaissance building at No. 71 was designed in 1875, by Lajos Rauscher. Its façade is decorated with sgrafitti by Robert Scholtz. The Italianate Renaissance exterior of No. 69, designed by Adolf Lang from 1875–7, is distinguished by Corinthian pilasters and a full-length balcony. The entrance hall and first-floor corridor feature frescoes by Károly Lotz. Only the Barcsay Gallery is open to visitors, but the interior can be glimpsed from here.

Sgrafitto by Robert Scholtz

Zoltán Kodály Museum ❹
KODÁLY ZOLTÁN EMLÉK MÚZEUM

Kodály Körönd 1. **Map** 2 F4.
C 352 71 06. **M** Kodály Körönd.
O 10am–6pm Thu–Sat, 10am–2pm Sun, 10am–4pm Wed.

ZOLTÁN KODÁLY (1881–1967) was one of the greatest Hungarian composers of the 20th century. His profound knowledge of Hungarian folk music allowed him to use elements of it in his compositions, which reflected the fashion for Impressionism and Neo-Romanticism in music.

This museum was established in 1990 and occupies the house where he lived and worked from 1924 until his death in 1967. A plaque set into one of the walls of the house bears testimony to this fact. The museum consists of three rooms that have been preserved in their original style, and a fourth room that is used for exhibitions. An archive has also been created here, in which the composer's valuable handwritten music scores and a wealth of correspondence are kept.

Worthy of attention are the composer's piano in the salon and a number of folklore ceramics which Kodály collected in the course of his ethnographical studies. Portraits and busts of Kodály by Lajos Petri can also be viewed.

Városligeti Avenue ❺
VÁROSLIGETI FASOR

Map 5 C5. **M** Hősök tere.

THIS BEAUTIFUL street, lined with plane trees, leads from Lövölde tér to Városliget.

At the beginning of the avenue is a Calvinist church built in 1912–13 by Aladár Árkay. This stark edifice is virtually bereft of any architectural features. However, stylized, geometric folk motifs

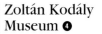

Original furnishings in the salon in the Franz Liszt Museum

Chinese gate at the Ráth György Museum on Városligeti Avenue

have been used as ornamentation and harmonize with the interior Secession decoration.

In front of the church is the Ráth György Museum, part of the Ferenc Hopp Museum of Far Eastern Art, displaying artifacts from China and Japan collected in the 19th century.

Further along the avenue is a Lutheran church. It was constructed between 1903–5 to a Neo-Gothic design by Samu Pecz, who also designed the interior detail. Worthy of note is the painting on the high altar, by Gyula Benczúr, entitled *The Adoration of the Magi.*

Ferenc Hopp Museum of Far Eastern Art ❻

Hopp Ferenc Keletázsiai Művészeti Múzeum

Andrássy út 103. **Map** 2 F5. **℡** 322 84 76. **Ⓜ** *Bajza utca.* ● *temporarily.*
Ráth György Museum **℡** 342 39 16. ○ *10am–6pm Tue–Sun.*

Ferenc hopp (1833–1919), a wealthy merchant and the proprietor of an opthalmic shop, was the first great Hungarian traveller. His collection of more than 20,000 items from countries such as India, China and Vietnam was left to the nation. This museum was established in Hopp's large villa and garden. The collection's smaller examples of art and handicrafts can be seen in the house, while the garden features large stone sculptures and architectural fragments.

The Chinese and Japanese collection is displayed in the Ráth György Museum at No. 12 Városligeti Avenue.

Millennium Monument ❼

Ezeréves emlékmű

Map 5 C4. **Ⓜ** *Hősök tere.*

This monument was designed by György Zala and Albert Schikedanz to commemorate Hungary's Millennium Celebrations in 1896, but was not completed until 1929.

At the centre of the monument is a 36-m (120-ft) high Corinthian column, upon which stands the Archangel Gabriel holding St István's crown and the apostolic cross. These objects signify Hungary's conversion to Christianity under King István *(see p22).* At the base of the column there are equestrian statues of Prince Árpád and six of the conquering Magyar warriors.

A stone tile set in front of the column marks the Tomb of the Unknown Soldier.

The column is embraced by two curved colonnades, featuring allegorical compositions at both ends. Personifications of War and Peace are nearest the column, while Knowledge and Glory crown the far end of the right-hand colonnade, and Labour and Prosperity crown the far end of the left. Statues of great Hungarians, including statesmen and monarchs, are arranged within the colonnades.

The right-hand colonnade of the Millennium Monument on Heroes' Square, completed in 1929

Museum of Fine Arts ❾

T HE ORIGINS OF the Museum of Fine Arts' comprehensive collection date from 1870, when the state bought a magnificent collection of paintings from the artistocratic Esterházy family. The museum's collection was enriched by donations and acquisitions, and in 1906 it moved to its present location.

Grimani jug

The building, by Fülöp Herzog and Albert Schickedanz, is Neo-Classical with Italian-Renaissance influences. The tympanum crowning the portico is supported by eight Corinthian columns. It depicts the Battle of the Centaurs and Lapiths, and is copied from the Temple of Zeus at Olympia, Greece.

First floor

Woman with a Jug
(c. 1810)
La Aquadora *demonstrates the full range of Francisco de Goya's artistic talent.*

Still Life with Turkey
This work is attributed to Jean-Baptiste-Siméon Chardin, a French painter who emulated the 17th-century Dutch masters' genre painting.

★ **Esterházy Madonna**
(c. 1508)
This unfinished picture by Raphael is so named because it became the property of the Esterházy family at the beginning of the 19th century.

Lower ground floor

KEY

- ☐ Egyptian artifacts
- ☐ Classical artifacts
- ☐ Sculpture
- ☐ German art
- ☐ Dutch and Flemish art
- ☐ Italian art
- ☐ Spanish art
- ☐ French and English art
- ☐ Drawings and graphic art
- ▨ 19th- and 20th-century works

St James Conquers the Moors *(1759)*
Giambattista Tiepolo portrayed this miraculous appearance of the saint during a battle at Clarijo in 844.

View of Amsterdam
(c. 1656)
Jacob van Ruisdael was a master of Dutch realist landscape painting. He greatly influenced the development of European landscape painting in the 19th century.

Mother and Child
(1905)
The rare subtlety of this intensely intimate picture, by Pablo Picasso, is achieved using watercolour.

Ground floor

★ **St John the Baptist's Sermon** *(1566)*
In this wonderful painting, Pieter Breughel the Elder, a renowned observer of daily life, depicts a preacher addressing a group of peasants from Flanders.

These Women in the Refectory *(1894)*
This pastel sketch by the artist Henri de Toulouse-Lautrec, an observer and protagonist in the Parisian demi-monde, depicts prostitutes in a bar.

MUSEUM GUIDE
Restoration work on the museum began in 1997 and is expected to continue until 2004. As a result, not all the rooms are currently open to the public. The works displayed are being moved as restoration work progresses.

STAR EXHIBITS

★ **Esterházy Madonna**

★ **St John the Baptist's Sermon**

Exploring the Museum of Fine Arts

Egyptian head (c. 1200 BC)

THE MUSEUM'S COLLECTION encompasses international art dating from antiquity to the 20th century. As well as Egyptian, Greek and Roman artifacts, the museum houses galleries dedicated to modern art. Alongside its interesting collection of sculptures, there are priceless drawings and works of graphic art. Over the next few years the museum will be undergoing a process of redevelopment scheduled to last until the year 2004. In spite of this, exhibits will continue to be open to the public throughout the duration of the restoration work. Individual collections will simply be moved to different locations as building work progresses.

Albrecht Dürer's simple yet beautiful *Portrait of a Young Man*

EGYPTIAN ARTIFACTS

EGYPTIAN ARTIFACTS have been exhibited in the museum since 1939. Principally, they are the result of 19th-century excavations that involved Hungarian archaeologists.

The rich collection includes stone sculptures from each historic period, from the Old Kingdom to the Ptolemy dynasty. A man's head, a fragment of a larger statue, dates from the New Kingdom and is a particularly beautiful example.

Also worthy of note is the collection of small bronze figures, which also date mainly from the New Kingdom, together with domestic objects that illustrate everyday life.

CLASSICAL ARTIFACTS

THE COLLECTION of Classical artifacts is rather varied. It encompasses works of Greek, Etruscan, and Roman works.

Detail of a hunting scene on a 3rd-century AD Greek sarcophagus

The collection of Greek vases ranks as one of the best of its kind in Europe. A black-figure amphora by Exekias and a kylix from the studio of the painter Andokides are very fine examples of this work.

Bronze work, which dates from various epochs, including the famous Grimani jug from the 5th century BC, gold jewellery, and marble and terracotta sculptures are all exquisite artifacts from this era.

SCULPTURE

UNDOUBTEDLY the most valuable element of this collection is a small bronze sculpture by Leonardo da Vinci (1452–1519). This is an unusually dynamic representation of King François I of France on his horse. Other superb examples of Italian sculpture, by masters such as Andrea Pisano of the Ronni family, can also be seen.

Leonardo da Vinci's figure of François I

GERMAN ART

AMONG THE most valuable works in the collection are the *Portrait of a Young Man*, by Albrecht Dürer, and the carefully composed painting of *The Dormition of Mary*, by Hans Holbein. The work of such masters as Hans Baldung Grien and Lucas Cranach are worth seeing, as is the collection of German and Austrian Baroque painting, which includes work by Franz Anton Maulbertsch.

DUTCH AND FLEMISH ART

THE MUSEUM'S Dutch and Flemish collection features works by the finest masters, including influential landscape artist, Jacob van Ruisdael, with *View of Amsterdam (see p147)*. The subtle *Nativity* by Gerard David and Pieter Breughel's detailed masterpiece *St John the Baptist's Sermon (see p147)*, depicting Dutch peasants listening to the saint's words, are exemplary exhibits.

The museum also boasts canvases attributed to Rembrandt, including *St Joseph's Dream*, portraits by Frans Hals and Jan Vermeer's *Portrait of a Lady*. Not to be missed are the magnificent 17th-century Dutch miniature paintings by artists including Adrien van Ostad, Jacob Ruisdael, Jan Steen and others.

The highlight of the Flemish collection is the 17th-century *Mucius Scaevola before Porsenna* by Peter Rubens and his then assistant, Anthony van Dyck. The latter was responsible for the picture of St John the Evangelist, also on display.

Also important are the paintings of Adam and Eve and *Satyr with Peasants* by Jacob Jordaens, who also worked as an assistant to Rubens.

ITALIAN ART

THIS VALUABLE collection of
Italian art, which was the
core of the Esterházy family's
collection, is often considered
the museum's biggest attraction. All the schools of Italian
painting, from the 13th to the
18th centuries, are on display
here. The Renaissance period is
perhaps the best represented.

Of particular note is the captivating *Esterházy Madonna
(see p146)*, an unfinished painting by Raphael. Another great
work by this outstanding artist
is the *Portrait of Pietro Bembo*.

There is no shortage of work
by famous 16th-century
Venetian artists among the
paintings collected here. Works
by Titian, Bonifazio Veronese,
Gentile da Fabriano, Antonio
Correggio, Jacopo Tintoretto,
Giorgione and Giovanni
Boltraffio are all exhibited
here. An excellent example
of Baroque art is Giambattista
Tiepolo's vast late 18th-century
painting, *St James Conquers
the Moors (see p146)*.

**Giovanni Boltraffio's *Madonna
and Child* (c. 1506)**

SPANISH ART

THE MOST IMPORTANT features
of this collection are seven
paintings by El Greco, including *The Annunciation, Christ
in the Garden of Gethsemane*
and *The Penance of St Mary
Magdalene*, a subtle though
fully expressive work.

The dramatic *Martyrdom of
St Andrew* by Jusepe de Ribera
should not be missed, nor the
work of artists such as Diego

**El Greco's *The Penance of St Mary
Magdalene* (c. 1576)**

Velázquez, Bartolomé Murillo
and Francisco Zurbarán. Similarly, Francisco de Goya's
observations of daily life produced paintings such as *Woman
with a Jug (see p146)*, which
also deserves special attention.

FRENCH AND
ENGLISH ART

WORKS BY French and
English artists are not as
numerous as Italian works, for
example, but represent the various styles of the two countries.

French works include the
well-composed *Resting on the
Journey to Egypt* by Nicolas
Poussin, *Villa in the Roman
Countryside* by Claude Lorrain,
and *Still Life with Turkey*,
thought to be by Jean-Baptiste-
Siméon Chardin *(see p146)*.

The collection of English
paintings includes portraits by
artists of the calibre of Joshua
Reynolds, William Hogarth
and Thomas Gainsborough.

DRAWINGS AND
GRAPHIC ART

THE COLLECTION of drawings
and graphic art combines
the work of old masters, including drawings by Leonard
da Vinci, Raphael, Albrecht
Dürer and Rembrandt, with
pieces from artists of the 19th
and 20th centuries. The collection is one of Europe's best.

19TH- AND 20TH-
CENTURY WORKS

FRENCH PAINTING is the
largest constituent of the
collection of 19th- and 20th-
century art. The visitor can
admire paintings such as
Pablo Picasso's *Mother and
Child (see p147)*, Henri de
Toulouse-Lautrec's *These
Women in the Refectory (see
p147)*, Gustave Courbet's
Wrestlers, Edouard Manet's
Woman with a Fan and
Camille Pissarro's *Pont-Neuf*.
Paul Gauguin's *Black Pigs*, one
of his first Tahitian canvases, is
on display here. The likes of
Eugène Delacroix, Claude
Monet, Pierre Bonnard, Pierre
Renoir and Paul Cézanne are
also represented.

In the section dedicated to
Austrian and German painting
there are pieces by Wilhelm
Leibl and Oskar Kokoschka.

The exhibition ends with
19th- and 20th-century sculptures. Particularly beautiful are
those by 19th-century French
sculptor, Auguste Rodin.

Paul Cézanne's still life, *Credenza*, dating from 1874–7

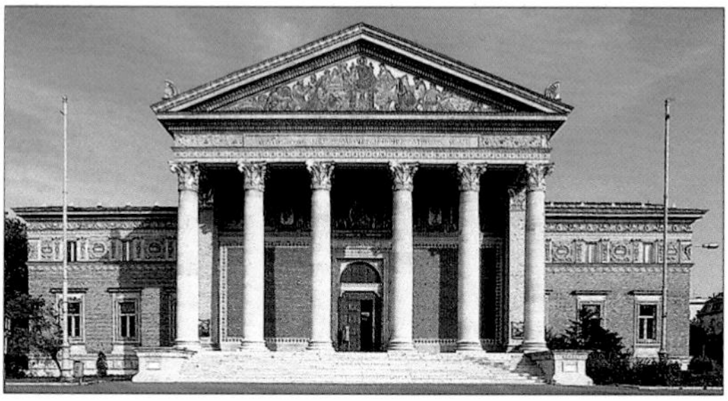

The façade of the Palace of Art, featuring a six-columned portico

Palace of Art 8

Műcsarnok

Dózsa György út 37. **Map** 5 C4. *343 74 01.* *Hősök tere.* *10am – 6pm Tue – Sun.*

On the southern side of Heroes' Square, opposite the Museum of Fine Arts *(see pp146–9)*, is the Palace of Art. This imposing Neo-Classical building was designed by Albert Schickedanz and Fülöp Herzog in 1895. It is Hungary's largest exhibition space. Temporary exhibitions of mainly contemporary painting and sculpture are held here.

The Palace of Art is fronted by a vast six-columned portico. The mosaic, depicting St István as the patron saint of fine art, was added to the tympanum between 1938–41. Behind the portico is a fresco in three parts by Lajos Deák Ébner, illustrating *The Beginning of Sculpture*, *The Source of Arts* and *The Origins of Painting*.

Museum of Fine Arts 9

Szépművészeti Múzeum

See pp146 – 9.

Vajdahunyad Castle 10

Vajdahunyad Vára

Városliget. **Map** 6 D4. *343 13 45.* **Museum of Agriculture** *343 13 98.* *mid-Nov–Mar: 10am–4pm Tue–Fri, 10am–5pm Sat & Sun; Apr–mid-Nov: 10am–5pm Tue– Fri, 10am–6pm Sat & Sun.*

This incredible, fairytale-like building is picturesquely located among the trees at the edge of the lake in Városliget. Not a genuine castle but a complex of buildings reflecting various architectural styles, it was designed by Ignác Alpár for the 1896 Millennium Celebrations *(see p142)*.

Alpár's creation illustrated the history and evolution of architecture in Hungary. Originally intended as temporary exhibition pavilions, the castle proved so popular with the public that, between 1904–6, it was rebuilt using brick to create a permanent structure.

The pavilions are grouped in chronological order of style: Romanesque is followed by Gothic, Renaissance, Baroque and so on. The individual styles were linked together to give the impression of a single, cohesive design. Each of the pavilions use authentic details copied from Hungary's most important historic buildings or are a looser interpretation of a style inspired by a specific architect of that historic period.

The Romanesque complex features a copy of the portal from a chapel in Ják *(see p143)* as well as a monastic cloister and palace. The details on the Gothic pavilion have been taken from castles like those in Vajdahunyad and Segesvár (both now in Romania). The architect Fischer von Erlach was the inspiration for the Renaissance and Baroque complex. The façade copies part of the Bakócz chapel in the cathedral at Esztergom *(see p164)*.

The Museum of Agriculture can be found in the Baroque section. It has exhibits on cattle breeding, wine-making, hunting and fishing.

The entire complex reflects more than 20 of Hungary's most renowned buildings. The medieval period, often considered the most glorious time in Hungary's history, is given greatest emphasis, while the controversial Habsburg era is pushed into the background.

Zoo 11

Állat-és Növénykert

Állatkerti körút 6–12. **Map** 6 D3. *343 60 75.* *Széchenyi fürdő.* *Apr–Aug: 9am– 6pm daily; Sep–Mar: 9am–3pm daily.*

Budapest's zoo is one of the city's great attractions. It was established in 1866 by the Hungarian Academy of Sciences *(see p114)*. In 1907 it was bought by the State and totally redeveloped, from 1909–11, by Károly

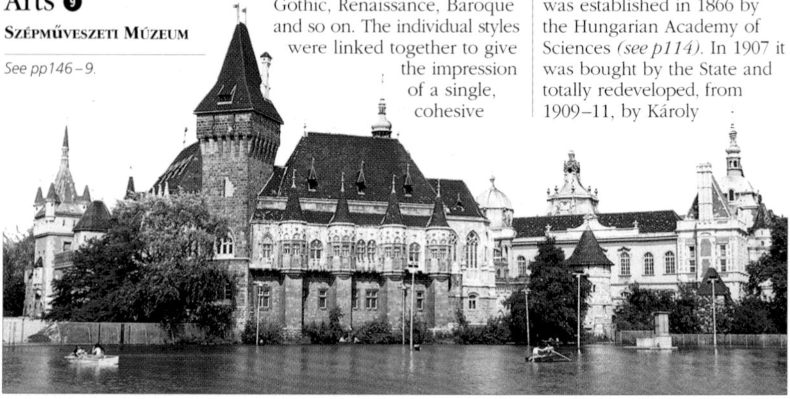

View across the lake of the Gothic (left) and Renaissance (right) sections of Vajdahunyad Castle

Kós and Dezső Zrumeczky as part of the 1896 Millennium Celebrations. At the time it was Europe's most modern zoo.

The animals, including lions, tigers, giraffes, bears and hippos, are housed in enclosures, most of which strive to mimic their natural habitat. The elephant house, however, by Kórnel Neuschloss-Knüsli, is a fine example of Secession style. Károly Kós, on the other hand, adopted a folk style for the aviary, in which a wide variety of birds fly freely.

Vidám Park **⑫**

VIDÁMPARK

Állatkerti körút 14–16. **Map** 6 D3.
C 343 09 96. **M** Széchenyi fürdő.
O Apr–Oct: 10am–8pm daily;
Nov–Mar: 10am–6pm daily.

IN 1878 THERE was already a carousel here, along with games and theatrical shows.

Today it is a charmingly unsophisticated amusement park with an assortment of old-fashioned rides. Next door is a smaller funfair for toddlers,.

There are numerous kiosks, bars and restaurants serving food, so it is easy to spend the entire day here.

Széchenyi Baths **⑬**

SZÉCHENYI STRANDFÜRDŐ

Állatkerti körút 11. **Map** 6 D3.
C 321 03 10. **M** Széchenyi fürdő.
O 6am– 6:45pm Mon–Fri,
6am–4pm Sat & Sun.

A STATUE STANDS at the main entrance to the Széchenyi Baths depicting geologist Vilmos Zsigmond, who discovered a hot spring here while drilling a well in 1879.

The Széchenyi Baths are the deepest and hottest baths in Budapest – the water reaches the surface at a temperature of 74–5° C (180° F). The springs, rich in minerals, are distinguished by their alleged healing properties. They are recommended for treating rheumatism and disorders of the nervous system, joints and muscles.

One of the outdoor pools at the beautiful Széchenyi Baths

The spa, housed in a Neo-Baroque building by Győző Cziegler and Ede Dvorzsák, was constructed in 1909–13.

In 1926, three swimming pools were added. Despite being open-air, the pools are popular all year due to the high temperature of the water.

Hermina Street **⑭**

HERMINA ÚT

Map 6 E3, 6 E4 & 6 F4. **🚌** 70.
Transport Museum
C 343 05 65. **O** 10am–5pm Tue–Fri, 10am–6pm Sat & Sun; Nov–Mar closes one hour earlier. **🅿** **♿**
📷 by arrangement.

THIS BEAUTIFUL street is worth walking along to experience the romantic atmosphere of the historic, elegant villas in this area. Particularly notable is the unusual Secession building at No. 47, Sipeky Balázs Villa (see p55), built in 1905–6 by architects Ödön Lechner, Marcell Komor and Dezső Jakab. The asymmetric design of the villa's façade includes features such as a domed glass conservatory,

A steam train exhibited at the Transport Museum, just off Hermina Street

an ironwork porch and a tall, narrow side tower. The villa's exterior decoration is inspired by Hungarian folk art.

Hermina Chapel at No. 23, by József Hild, was built in 1842–6 in memory of Palatine József's daughter, Hermina Amália, who died in 1842.

Backing onto Hermina Street, at No. 11 Városligeti körút, is the Transport Museum with exhibits on the evolution of air, sea, road and rail transport. Among the trains, helicopters and aeroplanes are some pre-World War II right-hand-drive cars from when Hungarians still drove on the left.

Poster for a gala ballet performance at the Erkel Theatre

Erkel Theatre **⑮**

ERKEL SZÍNHÁZ

Köztarsaság ter 30. **Map** 7 C3.
C 333 01 08. **M** Keleti pu.

AN ALTERNATIVE venue of the National Opera Company, this is the largest theatre in Hungary, seating 3,000 people. Designed in 1911 by Marcell Komor, Dezső Jakab and Géza Márkus, its current form dates from the 1950s. Concerts and operas are performed here.

FURTHER AFIELD

BUDAPEST IS A SPRAWLING city and several sights on its periphery are well worth a visit. North from the centre of Buda are the fascinating ruins of Aquincum, a town founded by the Romans in approximately AD 100. To the west, the city is skirted by wooded hills, which offer walks around beautiful nature reserves and exciting cave visits. Out

Roman urn from Aquincum

to the east of Pest is Kerepesi Cemetery, where a host of famous Hungarians are buried. To the south of the city is the Nagytétény Palace, one of the most beautiful Baroque palaces in Hungary. The new setting for Socialist-era statues, the Park of Monuments, is not far from the palace. All the sights can be reached easily using public transport.

SIGHTS AT A GLANCE

Museums
Aquincum **25**
Gizi Bajor Theatre Museum **19**

Historic Buildings and Monuments
Geology Institute **4**
Ludovika Academy **9**
Nagytétény Palace **23**
Park of Monuments **21**
Raoul Wallenberg
  Monument **1**
Technical University **16**
Törley Mausoleum **22**
Wekerle Estate **15**

Parks and Recreation Areas
Buda Hills **24**
Budapest Exhibition Centre **11**
Congress Centre **18**
Eagle Hill Nature Reserve **20**
People's Park **10**
People's Stadium **5**
Szemlő-hegy and Pál-völgy
  Caves **2**
University Botanical
  Gardens **8**

Cemeteries
Jewish Cemetery **14**
Kerepesi Cemetery **6**
Municipal Cemetery **13**

Churches
Cistercian Church of St Imre **17**
Józsefváros Parish Church **7**
Kőbánya Parish Church **12**
Újlak Parish Church **3**

KEY

▩	City centre
▢	Greater Budapest
✈	Airport
🚉	Train station
▭	Motorway
▬	Main road
—	Railway

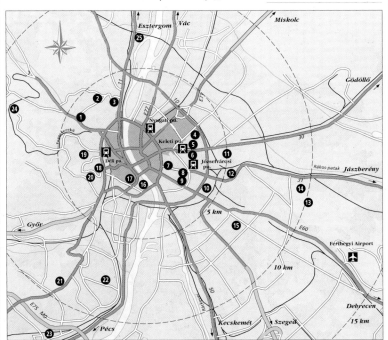

◁ **View of the ruins of the Roman town of Aquincum, founded in around AD 100**

Raoul Wallenberg Monument ❶

WALLENBERG RAOUL SZOBOR

Szilágyi Erzsébet fasr. **Map** 7 C3.
🚌 56.

TUCKED AWAY at the junction of Szilágyi Erzsébet fasor and Nagyajtai utca, is this monument to an heroic but little known figure of World War II. Raoul Wallenberg was a Swedish diplomat who used his position to save over 20,000 Hungarian Jews from the extermination camps. He set up safe houses in the city and obtained fake Swedish documents for them.

Following the liberation of Budapest by the Soviet army, Wallenberg disappeared. It is thought he was arrested by the KGB and sent to a prison camp where he died. The memorial, by sculptor Imre Varga, was erected in 1987.

Szemlő-hegy and Pál-völgy Caves ❷

SZEMLŐ-HEGYI-BARLANG ÉS PÁL-VÖLGYI-CSEPPKŐBARLANG

Szemlő-hegy Cave Pusztaszeri út 35.
📞 325 60 01. 🚌 29. ⏰ 10am–3pm Mon, Wed–Fri, 10am–4pm Sat–Sun. 🅿 ♿ 📷
Pál-völgy Cave Szépvölgyi út 162.
📞 325 95 05. 🚌 65. ⏰ 10am–4pm Tue–Sun. 📷 📷

TO THE NORTH of Budapest lies the Pilis mountain range, formed of limestone and dolomite. Natural geological processes which occur within these mountains have created some picturesque caves, two of which are unusual tourist attractions.

Szemlő-hegy Cave features extraordinary formations called "cave pearls", produced when hot spring waters penetrate its limestone walls. In Pál-völgy Cave strange formations protruding from the rock face resemble animals, including an elephant and a crocodile.

It is a good idea to wear warm clothes when visiting the caves as they are cold and damp. Some claim, however, that the atmosphere in the caves has a therapeutic effect on the respiratory system.

The Baroque interior of Újlak Parish Church, dating from 1756

Újlak Parish Church ❸

ÚJLAKI PLÉBÁNIATEMPLOM

Bécsi út 32. **Map** 2 E5.
🚌 17.

BAVARIAN SETTLERS first built a small church here early in the 18th century. The present church, designed by Kristóf Hamon and Mátyás Nepauer, was finished in 1756. Its tower was added some years later.

In the Baroque interior there is a depiction of the Madonna, a gift from the inhabitants of Passau to the church. The main altar, dating from 1798, also includes

a painting entitled *The Visitation*, which was the work of Francis Falkoner.

Not far away, at Zsigmond tér, stands the Holy Trinity Column, built in 1691 as a memorial to the city's earliest plague epidemic. The Baroque monument is the work of two Italian sculptors, Venerio Cresola and Bernard Feretti, and was moved from central Buda to Újlak in 1712.

Geology Institute ❹

FÖLDTANI INTÉZET

Stefánia út 14. **Map** 6 F5. 📞 251 09 99. 🚌 75, 77. **Museum** ⏰ 10am–4pm Thu, Sat & Sun. 📷

THIS BEAUTIFUL and unusual building, housing the Geology Institute, dates from 1898–9 and was designed by Ödön Lechner *(see p56)*.

Lechner's very individual Secession style, also known as the Hungarian National Style, is on show here including motifs drawn from Hungarian Renaissance architecture.

On the picturesque elevations and gables of the building pale yellow plaster walls form a striking contrast to the brick-work quoins and window frames. Here and there Zsolnay blue glazed ceramic ornaments adorn the walls and harmonize with the blue roof tiles. The central pitched roof is topped by three

The Geology Institute, with its stunning blue ceramic roof

human figures bent under the weight of a large globe.

Inside the Geology Institute, there is a small museum with rock and mineral exhibits. Lechner's Secession interiors have been carefully preserved in their original condition. The central hall, which is particularly magnificent, can be seen when visiting the museum or on its own with the caretaker's permission.

People's Stadium ❺

NÉPSTADION

Kerepesi út. **Map** 8 D2. 251 12 22. 23, 24, 36.

HUNGARY'S BIGGEST sports stadium was built between 1948–53, to a design by Károly Dávid. The roofless stadium seats 78,000, but is generally at least half empty, only filling to capacity when a major pop group plays here.

The stadium's entrance is at the end of Ifjúság útja, the Road of Youth, a broad avenue lined with Stalinist-era statues. Depicting various sports disciplines, the statues are the work of a number of well-known Hungarian sculptors including Imre Varga and István Tar.

Kerepesi Cemetery ❻

KEREPESI TEMETŐ

Fiumei út 16–20. **Map** 8 D2. 23, 24, 36.

FOR MORE THAN 150 years since it was established in 1847, the Kerepesi Cemetery has provided the resting place for many of Hungary's most prominent citizens. Fine tombstones mark the graves of some, while others were interred here inside monumental mausoleums.

The mausoleum of the leader of the 1848–9 uprising, Lajos Kossuth (see p106) is by Alajos Stróbl, while that of Lajos Batthyány, the first prime minister of Hungary (see p31) is the work of Albert Schickedanz.

Ferenc Deák, who formulated the Compromise with Austria (see p32), is among the other statesmen buried here.

Also at the cemetery are the graves of poets Endre Ady and Attila József (see p106), writers Kálmán Mikszáth Zsigmond Móricz and actors such as Lujza Blaha, whose tomb is particularly beautiful. Sculptors, painters and composers are buried close to great architects, including Alajos Stróbl, Ödön Lechner and Alajos Hauszmann.

Hungarian Communists, including László Rajk (see p34), who were sentenced to death in the show trials of 1949, were buried in a separate part of the cemetery. Their funerals inspired a revolutionary spirit which, a few years later, led to the 1956 Uprising (see p34).

Józsefváros Parish Church ❼

JÓZSEFVÁROS PLÉBÁNIATEMPLOM

Horváth Mihály tér 7. **Map** 7 C4. 313 61 26. 83. 9, 17.

THE BUILDING WORK on this Baroque church began in 1797. It was not completed until 1814, by Fidél Kasselik. At the end of 19th century further additions were made to the structure.

The main altar is by József Hild. A formidable architectural composition, it is based on a triumphal arch. This frames a magnificent painting, *The*

The late Baroque façade of Józsefváros Parish Church

Apotheosis of St Joseph, by Leopold Kupelwieser, an Austrian artist. The church also has two beautiful, late Baroque side altars.

University Botanical Gardens ❽

EGYETEMI BOTANIKUS KERT

Illés utca 25. **Map** 8 D5. 210 10 74. M Klinikák. 9am–4pm Sat–Thu. by prior arrangement.

GARDENS WERE first established on this 3-ha (8-acre) site by the Festetics family. Their modest, early-Neo-Classical villa is now the administration centre for the botanical gardens. It was built in 1802–3, most probably to a design by Mihály Pollack. The smoking room in the villa houses a huge collection of tropical plants. These include the striking *Victoria regia*, which flowers once a year.

The Hungarian author Ferenc Molnár (1878–1952) used the gardens as a setting in his novel, *The Paul Street Boys*, although the lake mentioned in the book no longer exists. Not far away are Pál utca (Paul Street) and Mária utca, the scene of a battle the boys fought. However, the Maria utca of the novel was prior to the invasion of tenement blocks.

The tomb of actress Lujza Blaha at Kerepesi Cemetery

Ludovika Academy **9**
LUDOVIKA AKADÉMIA

Üllői út 82 (off Ludovika tér).
M *Klinikák.* **(** *267 70 07.*
○ *10am– 5pm Wed– Mon.* **Natural
History Museum ○** *10am–6pm
Wed– Mon.*

THE HUGE Ludovika Academy
is in district IX, east of the
city centre. It was designed in
the 1830s by Mihály Pollack,
the famous architect of the
Hungarian National Museum
(see pp130– 33). A military
academy until 1945, it is an
impressive example of Neo-
Classical style. Rebuilding work
in 1880 left many original
features intact, including the
main hall and the chapel's
interior. Following refur-
bishment, the academy is
now home to the city's new
Natural History Museum.

**A children's playground
in People's Park**

People's Park **10**
NÉPLIGET

M *Népliget.* **Planetarium (** *265
07 25.* **○** *shows: 9:30am, 11am,
1pm, 2:30pm, 4pm Tue–Sun.*

LANDSCAPED IN THE 1860s, the
People's Park, about 5 km
(3 miles) southeast of central
Pest, is the city's largest park.
Its 112 ha (277 acres) consist of
large areas of grass and trees
interspersed with flowerbeds
and children's playgrounds.
  At one corner of the park is
the popular Planetarium. The
paths of the planets, as seen
from earth, are projected on to
the 23-m (75-ft) dome. Regular
evening laser shows with both
pop and classical soundtracks
also take place here.

Budapest Exhibition Centre **11**
BUDAPESTI NEMZETKÖZI
VÁSÁRKÖZPONT

Albertirsai út 10. **(** *263 61 01.*
□ *100.*

BUDAPEST HAS a long history
of trade fairs and exhi-
bitions, which began with the
hugely successful Millennium
Exhibition of 1896. Budapest
Exhibition Centre, also known
as HungExpo and built in 1980,
is just north of Kőbánya on the
city's eastern side. It is the
venue for several trade fairs,
including the IFABO computer
fair *(see p58).* Another popular
event is Budapest International
Fair, or BNV. Held annually in
September, this is a huge shop
window for consumer goods
from Hungary and other parts
of Europe. Visitors to the fair
include business people and
members of the public.

Kőbánya Parish Church **12**
KŐBÁNYAI PLÉBÁNIATEMPLOM

Szent László tér. **▣** *13, 28.*
□ *17, 32, 62, 185.* **&**

AN INDUSTRIAL SUBURB on
the eastern side of Pest,
Kőbánya is the unexpected
home of the beautiful Kőbánya
Parish Church. Designed by
Ödön Lechner *(see p56)* in the
1890s, the church makes magnificent use of the architect's
favourite materials, including
vibrant roof tiles developed
and produced at the now-
famous Zsolnay factory in
the town of Pécs. Like
much of Lechner's
work, including the
Museum of Applied
Arts *(see pp136–7),*
the church com-
bines motifs and
colours from
Hungarian folk
art with Neo-
Gothic elements.
Inside the church,
both the altar and
the pulpit are
superb examples
of early 20th-
century wood

**Schmidel family tomb at the
Jewish Cemetery**

**Gleaming ceramic tiles on the
roof of Kőbánya Parish Church**

carving. Somehow surviving
heavy World War II bombing,
a number of Miksa Roth's
original stained-glass windows
are still in place.

Municipal Cemetery **13**
RÁKOSKERESZTÚR

See pp158–9.

Jewish Cemetery **14**
ZSIDÓ TEMETŐ

Kozma út. **Map** 2 E3. **□** *37.*

NEXT DOOR TO the Municipal
Cemetery is the Jewish
Cemetery, opened in 1893.
The many grand tombs here
are a vivid reminder of the
vigour and success
of Budapest's pre-war
Jewish community. At
the end of the 19th
century, nearly a
quarter of the city's
inhabitants were
Jewish. Tombs
to look out for
as' you stroll
among the
graves include
that of the
Wellisch family,
designed in
1903 by Arthur
Wellisch, and
that of Konrád
Polnay, which

was designed five years later by Gyul Fodor. Perhaps the most eyecatching of all belongs to the Schmidel family. The startlingly flamboyant tomb, designed in 1903 by architects Ödön Lechner and Béla Lajta, is covered in vivid turquoise ceramic tiles. The central mosaic in green and gold tiles represents the Tree of Life.

Wekerle Estate ⑮

WEKERLE TELEP

Kós Károly tér. **M** *Határ út, then* **194**.

Façade of the Technical University, as seen from the Danube

O UT IN DISTRICT XIX, the Wekerle Estate was built between 1909 and 1926, and represents a bold and successful experiment in 20th-century social planning. Named after Prime Minister Sándor Wekerle, the estate was originally known as the Kispest Workers and Clerks Settlement and was built to provide better housing for local workers.

Designed by a group of young architects, students of Ödön Lechner, the buildings have a uniquely Hungarian style. Seeking inspiration from medieval peasant buildings, the architects would visit rural locations, gathering together architectural details in the same way that Béla Bartók and Zoltán Kodály *(see p144)*

collected folk songs. Other key influences were the English Arts and Crafts movement, and early English new towns such as Hampstead Garden Suburb in London.

Conceived as a self-contained village, the estate enjoys many of its own amenities, including a Catholic church, several schools, a cinema and a police station. Fanning out around Kós Károly tér, 16 types of family house and apartment block are separated by tree-lined streets. Wooden gables and balconies, and sharply pitched, brightly tiled roofs, contribute to the estate's lively and eclectic atmosphere.

Rents on the Wekerle Estate are now high, though the area manages to retain much of its working-class spirit.

Technical University ⑯

MŰSZAKI EGYETEM

Műegyetem rakpart 3. **Map** 4 F4. ☎ 463 11 11. 🚊 4, 6, 18, 19, 47, 49. 🚋 7, 86.

F OUNDED IN 1857, the city's Technical University moved to its present site in 1904. Built on reclaimed marshland, the imposing building overlooks the Danube just south of Gellért Hill *(see pp88–9)*. Extended at the end of World War II, it is now the largest higher education establishment in Hungary. Former students include Imre Steindl, the architect of the Parliament building *(see pp108–9)*, and the richest and most widely known graduate to date, Ernő Rubik, inventor of the Rubik Cube.

Cistercian Church of St Imre ⑰

CISZTERCIEK SZENT IMRE PLÉBÁNIATEMPLOM

Villányi út 25. **Map** 3 C4. 🚊 61. 🚋 27, 40. ♿

N OT FAR FROM the Technical University is the Cistercian Church of St Imre. The vast Neo-Baroque structure with its double tower was built in 1938 and is typical of the grand and rather sombre architecture in vogue in Budapest during the inter-war years.

Inside the church are relics of St Imre, canonized at the end of the 11th century. Other patron saints of the Cistercian order are depicted above the church's main entrance.

A police station on the early 20th-century Wekerle Estate

Municipal Cemetery ⓭

A NEW, HISTORIC significance was gained by the Municipal Cemetery following the 1956 Uprising *(see p35)*. Here, at Budapest southeastern limits, the leaders and victims of this bloody revolution against the oppressive Stalinist government were secretly buried in mass graves. During the 1970s, the country's democratic opposition began placing flowers on the site, at the far side of the cemetery. In 1990, after the fall of Communism, the revolutionary heroes were given a ceremonial funeral and reburied, and several memorials were set up to them.

View of Plot 300
Until 1989, the state militia guarded access to a thicket which covered the communal graves of the heroes of the 1956 Uprising.

Campanile
A wooden campanile is the type of decoration often found in old Hungarian cemeteries. It stands in front of panels listing the names of over 400 victims of the 1956 Uprising, giving the exact locations of their graves.

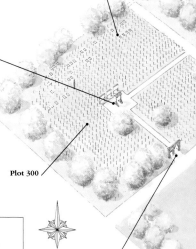

Plot 300

PLAN OF THE CEMETERY

In 1886, the city authorities opened a vast, new municipal cemetery in Rákoskeresztúr, on the outskirts of town. It became the largest cemetery in Budapest, occupying 30 sq km (12 sq miles).

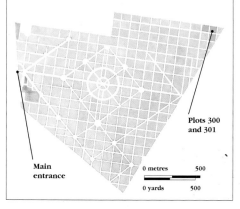

Plots 300 and 301

Main entrance

0 metres   500

0 yards   500

★ Transylvanian Gate
The 1956 Uprising Combatants' Association erected the carved Transylvanian Gate which stands at the beginning of one of the paths leading into plot 300. It is inscribed with the words: "Only a Hungarian soul may pass through this gate".

★ Imre Nagy's Grave
A marble slab bears the modest inscription: "Imre Nagy, Prime Minister of Hungary, 1956". Arrested after the uprising, Nagy was interned and shot dead on 16 June 1956 in Budapest, following a bogus political trial.

VISITORS' CHECKLIST

Kozma utca 8–10, Kőbánya.
210 15 00. 95 from Zalka Máté tér. **Plots 300 and 301** *30 mins walk from the main gate. Fee charged for cars.*

Plot 301

Christ the Sorrowful
A figure of Christ the Sorrowful is traditionally placed in a plot containing Protestant graves.

★ Heroes' Monument
This simple monument symbolizes the passage through purgatory. It was created by the leading modern Hungarian sculptor, György Jovánovics.

Protestant Graves
The tradition of Hungarian Protestants is to place a simple wooden post to mark each grave.

STAR SIGHTS

★ **Transylvanian Gate**

★ **Imre Nagy's Grave**

★ **Heroes' Monument**

The main entrance to the Congress Hall in the Congress Centre, a venue for international events and conferences

Congress Centre ⑱

KONGRESSZUSI KÖZPONT

Jagelló út 1–3. **C** 209 48 50.
🚌 61. ⭘ for events.

OPENED IN 1975, this large arts complex houses a concert hall, a cinema, conference rooms and several restaurants. It provides a venue for international conferences and events, as well as for the annual Hungarian Film Festival (see p61).

The Congress Centre, with the neighbouring Novotel Budapest Centrum (see p185), was designed by the architect József Finta. The Tree of Life, which decorates the main wall of the Congress Hall, is the work of József Király.

Gizi Bajor Theatre Museum ⑲

BAJOR GIZI SZINÉSZMÚZEUM

Stromfeld Aurél út 16.
C 356 42 94. 🚌 102. ⭘ noon–
4pm Tue, 2pm–6pm Thu, 10am–6pm
Sat & Sun. 🖼️ 📷

THIS MUSEUM was opened in 1952, in a garden villa which once belonged to Gizi Bajor, a leading Hungarian actress of her day. Its exhibits, which include furniture, portraits, theatrical props, fans and velvet gloves, transport visitors to the world of the theatre in the 19th century.

In 1990, the 200th anniversary of theatre in Hungary, the museum's collection was further extended, to include mementos of well-known

contemporary Hungarian actors, after whom some of the museum's rooms are named.

The garden features the busts of several writers and other leading figures in Hungary's cultural history.

Eagle Hill Nature Reserve ⑳

SASHEGY TERMÉSZET-VÉDELMI TERÜLET

Tajék utca 26. **C** 248 12 08.
🚌 8, 8A. ⭘ Mid-Mar–mid-June &
Sep–mid-Oct: 10am–4pm Sat & Sun.
📷 compulsory.

A NATURE RESERVE more or less in the centre of a city of two million inhabitants is a remarkable phenomenon.

Access to the summit of this steep, 266-m (872-ft) high hill to the west of Gellért Hill (see pp88–9) is strictly regulated to protect the extremely rare animal and plant species found here. A smart residential quarter, which lies on the lower slope of Eagle Hill, extends almost to the fence of the reserve and the craggy 30-ha wilderness that it encloses.

It is well worth taking a guided walk, particularly in spring or early autumn. Only here is it possible to see centaurea sadleriana, a flower resembling a cornflower but much bigger. The reserve is also home to a type of spider not found anywhere else in the world, as well as to extraordinary, colourful butterflies and to ablebharus kitaibeli, a rare lizard.

Park of Monuments ㉑

SZOBOR PARK

Balatoni út & Szabadkai utca.
C 227 74 46. 🚌 50. ⭘ Apr–Oct:
10am–6pm daily; Nov–Mar: 10am–
dusk Sat & Sun. 🖼️

IN 1991, BUDAPEST'S City Council decided to gather in one place 41 Communist monuments which had formerly occupied prestigious locations in the city. The park where they can be viewed is now a popular attraction for visitors to the city who are curious about its recent past.

The competition for the design of the park was won by architect Ákos Eleöd and it opened to the public in 1993. Behind a red-brick wall, six rings of monuments are arrayed on the site. Statues of Karl Marx, Friedrich Engels, VI Lenin and Hungarian Communist heroes stand side by side, headed by the leader of the 1919 revolution in Hungary (see p34), Béla Kun. A statue of a Russian soldier removed from the Liberation Monument (see p92) can also be seen in the park.

The park has its own shop which sells books and other paraphenalia connected with the Communist era.

Cubist-style statues of Marx and Engels in the Park of Monuments

The marble Törley Mausoleum

Törley Mausoleum ㉒

TÖRLEY MAUZOLEUM

Sarló utca 6. 3.

U NTIL 1880 Budafok had a number of vineyards, but their cultivation was destroyed in that year by a plague of phylloxera (American aphid). It was then that József Törley, who had studied wine-making in Reims, started to produce sparkling wine in Budafok using the French model *(see p192)*. His wines sold well abroad and he quickly expanded his enterprise, storing the wines in the local cellars.

József Törley died in 1900 and was laid to rest in this monumental mausoleum designed by Rezső Vilmos Ray. Constructed of white marble, it is adorned with Eastern motifs and bas-reliefs by József Damko.

Nagytétény Palace ㉓

NAGYTÉTÉNYI-KASTÉLY

Csókási Pál utca 9–11. 226 55 47. 41. *until 2000.*
Nagytétény Palace Museum
226 85 47. *until 2000.*

T HIS IS ONE OF THE best known Baroque palaces in Hungary. Nagytétény Palace was built in the mid-18th century, incorporating the remains of a 15th-century Gothic building. The work was started by György Száraz and completed by his son-in-law,

József Rudnyánszky, acquiring its final shape in 1766. Based on the typical Baroque layout – "between the courtyard and the garden" – it includes a main block and side wings. The coping features the Száraz and Rudnyánszky family crests.

The palace suffered severe damage during World War II, but the original wall paintings and furnishings survived. In 1949, the palace was rebuilt and turned into an interior design museum. Now it is a department of the Museum of Applied Arts *(see pp136–7)*. On display are fine pieces of Hungarian and European furniture from the 15th – 18th centuries, early 19th-century paintings and more functional items, such as tiled stoves.

Standing close to the palace is an 18th-century Baroque church, built on the remains of a medieval church. Original Gothic features incorporated in it include the window openings in its tower and three supports on the outer wall of the presbytery. In 1760, the Austrian artist Johann Gfall created the painting in the dome which features illusory galleries. The altars, pulpit and baptistries also date back to the mid-18th century.

Buda Hills ㉔

BUDAI-HEGYSEG

M *Moszkva tér, then cog-wheel railway or chair lift.*

T O THE WEST of the city centre are the wooded Buda Hills where Budapesters come to walk and relax.

The first station of a cog-wheel railway, built in 1874, is on Szilágyi Erzsébet fasor. This runs up Sváb Hill – named after the Germanic Swabians, who settled here under the Habsburgs *(see p28)* – and then Széchenyi Hill.

From Széchenyi Hill a narrow-gauge railway covers a 12-km (7-mile) route to the Hűvös Valley. As in the days of the Soviet Young Pioneers movement, the railway is entirely staffed by children, apart from the adult train drivers. At the top of János Hill stands the Erzsébet Look-Out Tower, designed by Frigyes Schulek in 1910. A chair lift also connects the summit of János Hill with Zugligeti út and is a good way of making the descent.

Aquincum ㉕

AQUINCUM

See pp162–3.

The Erszébet Look-Out Tower at the summit of János Hill

Aquincum ㉕

THE REMAINS OF the Roman town of Aquincum *(see p20–21)* were excavated at the end of the 19th century. Visitors are free to stroll along its streets, viewing the outlines of temples, shops, baths and houses, in what was once the centre of the town. This civilian town was founded at the beginning of the 2nd century AD, a couple of decades after a legionary fortress *(see pp170–71)* was established to its south. In the centre of the site there is a Neo-Classical museum displaying the most valuable Roman archaeological finds. On the other side of the road are the remains of an amphitheatre, where Aquincum's inhabitants once sought entertainment.

Roman Column

View towards the Museum
The area opened to visitors is only a fragment of a much bigger town.

★ **Public Baths**
The walls of the thermal baths are immaculately preserved. Visiting the baths was a social event for the Romans.

Central Heating System
Archaeologists have here unearthed the Roman version of central heating, an under-floor system in which hot air was circulated under mosaic floors.

★ **Macellum**
This was the covered market hall. Having shops or stalls positioned around a cool inner courtyard kept the produce fresh and made shopping comfortable all year round (see pp20–21).

STAR SIGHTS

★ **Museum**

★ **Public Baths**

★ **Macellum**

★ Museum
This Neo-Classical Lapidarium is part of the museum, which houses an exhibition of objects found at Aquincum and at other Roman sites nearby. These include weapons and in-scribed stone monuments.

VISITORS' CHECKLIST

Szentendrei út 139. **C** 250 16 50.
R Aquincum. **O** May– Aug:
9am–6pm; Apr, Sep & Oct: 9am
–5pm Tue–Sun. **Museum**
O Apr–Oct: from 10am.

Thoroughfare
Paving stones can still be seen on the network of streets that run across the town at right angles.

Double Baths
Built mainly of stone, the baths were once richly decorated. Traces of wall paintings and mosaics can still be seen in some places.

Drain Cover
Aquincum had a water supply system. Carefully crafted drain covers, such as this one, cut into the stone paving slabs, provided the required drainage.

Peristyle House
Surrounded by a colonnade, this courtyard once stood at the centre of a large town house.

Excursions from Budapest

BUDAPEST IS TEN TIMES BIGGER than any other Hungarian city. Sleepy and charming, the towns and villages on these pages are ideal for day or overnight trips. Coaches *(see p226)* and trains *(see p231)* are cheap and reliable. Esztergom, Visegrád and Szentendre to the north of the city can all be reached by boats *(see p227)*, which run throughout the summer along this beautiful stretch of the Danube. More off the beaten track, the towns and villages to the south offer a fascinating glimpse of traditional life.

KEY

▦	City centre
▢	Greater Budapest
══	Motorway
▬	Main road

Esztergom **1**

46 km (28 miles) NW of Budapest.
🚶 30,000. 🚍 from Árpád híd.
🚆 from Nyugati pu. 🚢 from Vigadó tér (summer only). 🛈 Lőrinc utca.
Cathedral Szent István tér 1.
📞 0633 41 18 95. ☐ Mar–Oct: 6am –6pm; Nov–Apr: 6am– 4pm.
🚻 **Treasury** ☐ May–Sep: 9am–5pm daily; Oct–Dec: 11am–3pm daily.
📷 🚫 **Castle** Szent István tér 1.
📞 0633 41 59 86. ☐ Apr–Oct: 9am –4:30pm Tue–Sun; Nov–Mar: 10am– 3:30pm Tue–Sun. 📷

ST ISTVÁN, HUNGARY'S first Christian King, was baptized in Esztergom and crowned here on Christmas Day 1000 AD. Almost completely destroyed by the Mongol invasion 250 years later, the city was gradually rebuilt in the 18th and 19th centuries.

Esztergom today is still the country's most sacred city, the seat of the archbishop of Hungary. Dominating the skyline is the huge Catholic **cathedral**, built in the early 19th century. By the southern entrance, built by 16th-century Florentine craftsmen, is the red marble Bakócz burial chapel.

On the northern side is the **treasury** containing a collection of ecclesiastical treasures rescued from the ruins of the 12th-century church that existed on the cathedral site.

Below the cathedral are the remains of the 10th-century **castle**, rebuilt several times. One of its best features is a 12th-century chapel. The picturesque old town is also well worth exploring. At its heart is the town square, which is home to several cafés.

Visegrád **2**

40 km (25 miles) N of Budapest.
🚶 1,800. 🚍 from Árpád híd.
🚢 from Vigadó tér (summer only).
🛈 Rév utca 15. 📞 0626 39 81 60.
Castle 📞 0626 39 81 01. ☐ Apr–Oct: 8:30am–6pm Tue–Sun; Nov–Mar: 10am–3pm Tue–Sun. 📷 🚻
Mátyás Museum & Visegrád Palace
📞 0626 39 80 26. ☐ 9am–4:30pm Tue–Sun. 📷 📷 by arrangement.

SET ON THE narrowest stretch of the Danube, the village of Visegrád is a popular tourist destination, thanks to its spectacular ruined **castle**.

A 25-minute walk, a bus, or a taxi, will take you up to the castle from Visegrád. Built in the 13th century by King Béla IV, this was once one of the finest royal palaces ever built in Hungary. The massive outer walls are still intact, and offer stunning views over the surrounding countryside.

Located halfway down the hill, in the Salamon Tower, is the **Mátyás Museum**, a collection of items excavated from the ruins of the **Visegrád Palace** in the village. Built by King Béla IV at the same time as the castle, the palace was renovated two centuries later, in magnificent Renaissance style, by King Mátyás Corvinus *(see pp24–5)*. Destroyed in the

Overlooking the Danube, the vast cathedral at Esztergom

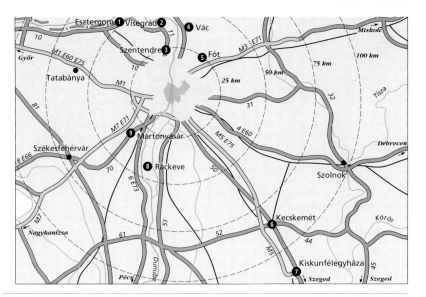

16th century after the Turkish invasion, then buried in a mud slide, the ruins of the palace were not rediscovered until 1934, when the excavations took place here.

Blagovestenska church in Fő tér, Szentendre's main square

Szentendre ❸

25 km (16 miles) N of Budapest.
🚶 20,000. 🚇 from Batthyány tér.
🚌 from Árpád hid. ⛴ from Vigadó tér (summer only). 🛈 Dumtsa Jenő utca 22. 📞 0626 31 79 66.
Belgrade Cathedral Pátriárka utca 5.
📞 0626 31 23 99. ⛪ **Museum of Serbian Art** Pátriárka utca 5.
📞 0626 31 23 99. ⏰ May–Sep: 10am–6pm Tue–Sun; Oct–Apr: 10am–4pm Tue–Sun (Jan–Feb: Fri–Sun). 📷 📷 **Margit Kovács Museum** Vastaggyörgy utca 1.
📞 0626 31 07 90. ⏰ mid-Mar–Oct: 10am–6pm Tue–Sun (Jun–Sep: daily); Nov–mid-Mar 10am–4pm Tue–Sun.
📷 📵 📷 by arrangement.

ONLY 25 KM (16 miles) outside Budapest, Szentendre is a town built and inhabited by a succession of Serbian refugees. A period of prosperity in the 18th-century led to a wave of house-building, and most of Szentendre's older buildings date from this time.

Orthodox religious tradition still lies at the heart of the town, which contains many Orthodox churches. The western European façades hide Slavic interiors filled with incense, icons and candlelight. **Blagovestenska Church** on Fő tér, the main square, is just one example. Look out for the magnificent iconstasis that separates the sanctuary from the nave. Sunday mass at **Belgrade Cathedral** is of interest to believers and non-believers alike. Next door is a **Museum of Serbian Art**, full of icons and other religious artifacts.

Since the 1920s, Szentendre has been home to a growing number of artists. As a result, the town contains many galleries exhibiting the work of local artists. At **Margit Kovács Museum**, off Fő tér, visitors can enjoy the work of one of Hungary's best-known ceramic artists. Throughout her life, Margit Kovács (1902–77) drew inspiration from Hungarian mythology and folk traditions, and her varied work includes statues and glazed wall panels.

Vác ❹

40 km (25 miles) N of Budapest.
🚶 36,000. 🚇 from Nyugati pu.
🚌 from Árpád hid. 🛈 Dr Csányi László körút 45. 📞 0627 31 61 60.

VÁC HAS STOOD on the eastern bank of the Danube since 1000 AD. Destroyed by war in the late 17th century, the town was rebuilt and today its centre, built around four squares, dates from the early 18th century. At its heart is Marcius 15 tér, where the **Town Hall** and **Fehérek Church** are located. At the northernmost end of the old town, on Kötársaság út, is Hungary's only **Arc de Triomph**. This was built in 1764, after a visit from the Habsburg Empress, Maria Theresa.

Arc de Triomph in Vác, built in honour of Empress Maria Theresa

Interior of Fót's Church of the Immaculate Conception

Fót **❺**

25 km (15 miles) NE of Budapest.
👥 *16,000.* 🚉 *Nyugati pu.* 🚌 *Árpád hid.* 🛈 Vörösmarty tér 3. 📞 *(0627) 35 81 03.* **Károlyi Palace and park** Vörösmarty tér 2. ◯ *by appt.* 📞 *(0627) 35 80 22.* 🚫 ♿ *ground floor only.* 📷 *obligatory.* **Church of the Immaculate Conception** Vörösmarty út 2. 📷

JUST OUTSIDE the Budapest city limits is the small town of Fót. Its main attraction is the fine **Károlyi Palace**, home to the aristocratic Károlyi family and birthplace of the country's first president, Mihály Károlyi. Károlyi became president in November 1918 at the end of World War I *(see p34)*. With the defeat of the Austro-Hungarian Empire, Hungary was quick to declare her independence, becoming instead the Hungarian Democratic Republic. Problems with the post-war peace treaty, however, led to the resignation of the Károlyi government less than six months later.

The Károlyi Palace was built in the 1830s, with a pavilion added on each side a decade later. A huge Károlyi family crest is emblazoned on the pediment, which is supported on massive Ionic columns. Surrounding the house are attractive landscaped gardens.

Also worth a visit is the town's attractive 19th-century **Church of the Immaculate Conception**, with its impressive many-columned nave.

Kecskemét **❻**

86km (52 miles) SE of Budapest.
👥 *110,000.* 🚉 *Nyugati pu.* 🚌 *Népstadion.* 🛈 Kossuth tér 1. 📞 *(0676) 48 10 65.* **Town Hall** Kossuth tér 1. 📞 *(0676) 48 36 83.* ◯ *7:30am–4pm Mon– Thu, 7:30am–1pm Fri.* 📷 *by appointment.* **Cifra Palace** Rákoczi utca 1. 📞 *(0676) 48 07 76.* ◯ *10am–6pm Tue–Sun.* 🚫 ♿ 📷 *by appointment.*

SPREADING OUT in a vast sweep around Budapest is the Great Hungarian Plain, or *Alföld*, which covers nearly half of modern Hungary. For hundreds of years, Kecskemét has been the major market town of the central-southern plain. Distributing and processing the products of the surrounding rich farmland, Kecskemét grew affluent, particularly towards the end of the 19th century. As a result, the town today boasts many gracious squares and splendid 19th and early 20th century buildings. The most famous is Ödön Lechner's massive **Town Hall**. Built between 1893–6, the building is a combination of both Renaissance and Middle-Eastern influences. The flamboyant **Cifra Palace** (Ornamental Palace), built as a casino in 1902, is a uniquely Hungarian variation of the Secession style *(see pp54–7)*.

Kecskemét Town Hall, designed by Ödön Lechner

Kiskunfélegyháza **❼**

110 km (66 miles) SE of Budapest.
👥 *40,000.* 🛈 Kossuth utca 1. 📞 *(0676) 46 32 20.* 🚉 *Nyugati pu.* 🚌 *Népstadion.* **Kiskunsági National Park (office)** Liszt Ferenc utca19. 📞 *(0676) 48 26 11.* ◯ *8am–3pm Mon–Thu, 8am–1pm Fri (park open permanently).* **Kiskun Museum** Dr Holló Lajos utca 9. 📞 *(0676) 46 14 68.* ◯ *late Mar– Oct: 9am–5pm Wed–Sun.* 🚫 📷

MUCH OF THE Great Hungarian Plain, once a vast expanse of marsh and grassland, is now used to grow maize and vines. Small areas, however, have been preserved as national parks. About 10 km (6 miles) to the east of Kiskunféleghyháza is

Detail of the ornate Town Hall façade at Kiskunfélegyháza

the **Kiskunsági National Park**. Many rare native animals and birds can be seen here, as well as the traditional way of life of the plains herdsman.

The poet and national hero, Sándor Petőfi, was born in Kiskunfélegyháza, and his childhood home is now part of the **Kiskun Museum**. Built in 1912, the **Town Hall** is a masterpiece, combining influences of the Secession style *(see pp54–7)* with motifs from Hungarian folk art.

Ráckeve ❽

43 km (26 miles) SW of Budapest.
🚶 *8,500.* 🚌 *Soroksári út.*
🚌 *Népstadion.*

Well-preserved frescoes in the Orthodox church at Ráckeve

THE VILLAGE OF Ráckeve is built on Csepel Island, which extends 54 km (34 miles) south along the middle of the Danube from Budapest. Ráckeve (Rác means Serb in Hungarian) was founded in the 15th century by Serbs from Keve, who fled Serbia after the Turkish invasion *(see pp26–7)*.

The oldest building in the village is the **Orthodox church**, built by some of the first of the Serbian refugees. Dating back to 1487, this is the oldest Orthodox church in Hungary. Its walls are covered in well-preserved frescos, the first telling the story of the Nativity and the last showing the Resurrection. The church also boasts a beautiful iconostasis separating the sanctuary from the nave.

Ráckeve's peaceful and convenient situation made it the country home of one of Europe's greatest military strategists, Prince Eugene of Savoy *(see p26)*. Credited with the expulsion of the Turks from Hungary at the end of the 17th century, Prince Eugene built himself a country **mansion** on what is now Kossuth Lajos utca. Now used as a hotel, the interior of the house has been modernized, but the elegant façade has been preserved and is well worth a look. The formal gardens can be seen from the river.

Martonvásár ❾

30 km (18 miles) SW of Budapest.
🚶 *4,900.* 🚏 Buda út 13. 📞 *(0622) 46 00 16.* 🚌 *Déli pu.* 🚌 *Erzsébet tér.* **Brunswick Palace** Brunswick utca 2. ☐ *8am–dusk daily (park only).* 📷 **Beethoven Museum** ☐ *10am–noon, 2–6pm Tue–Sun.* 📷 📷

THE VILLAGE OF Martonvásár has existed here since medieval times, but its principal tourist attraction is now the **Brunswick Palace**. Towards the end of the 18th century the whole village was bought by the German Brunswick family, and the original palace was built for Anton Brunswick in grand Baroque style. A century later, in 1875, the palace was totally rebuilt, this time in the Neo-Gothic style. Little evidence of the original palace remains today, among the flamboyant turrets and pinnacles. The magnificent parklands, however, are open to the public and are much as they always have been. The estate's church, built in 1775, also remains largely unaltered. The interior of the church is decorated with well-preserved frescoes.

Ludwig van Beethoven was a regular visitor to the original palace. He gave music lessons to the daughters of the house, Thérèse and Josephine, with whom he is said to have fallen in love. Some of the palace rooms have been converted into a small **Beethoven Museum**. Occasional concerts are held in the gardens during the summer months.

The Neo-Gothic Brunswick Palace at Martonvásár

TWO GUIDED WALKS

Anchor at the
Vasmacska
restaurant

BUDAPEST IS A CITY made for exploring on foot. From Turkish bathhouses to Baroque palaces, evidence of the city's long and colourful past is visible at every turn. The following guided walks take you through two fascinating areas: Óbuda to the north of the city centre, once the site of a Roman garrison and now a residential district, and Margaret Island, a park in the middle of the Danube.

Óbuda has yielded a wealth of archaeological discoveries including some of the earliest to be made in Hungary. This walk takes in the ruins of a Roman military camp and amphitheatre, as well as the area's more modern attractions. In contrast, the two-hour walk around the wonderfully car-free Margaret Island includes an exotically landscaped garden and the remains of several historic churches.

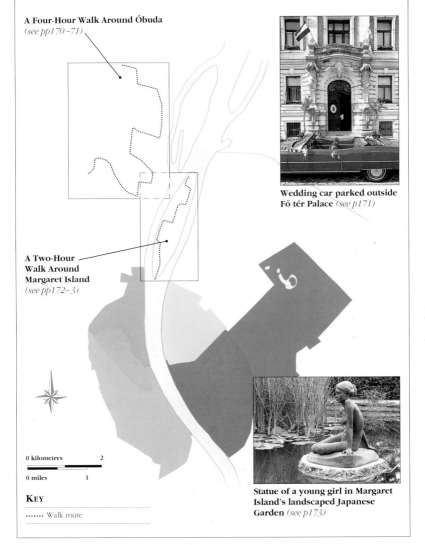

A Four-Hour Walk Around Óbuda
(see pp170–71)

A Two-Hour Walk Around Margaret Island *(see pp172–3)*

Wedding car parked outside Fő tér Palace *(see p171)*

0 kilometres   2

0 miles   1

KEY

······ Walk route

Statue of a young girl in Margaret Island's landscaped Japanese Garden *(see p173)*

◁ **The courtyard of the exclusive Ramada-Grand Hotel on Margaret Island** *(see p173)*

A Four-Hour Walk Around Óbuda

A T FIRST GLANCE ÓBUDA TODAY seems little more than a concrete jungle of tower blocks and flyovers. Behind the grey façade, however, there is a strong local identity and clues to the area's long and colourful past abound. Arriving here in AD 89, the Romans built a garrison in this district shortly before founding the civilian town of Aquincum *(see pp162–3)* to the north. After the departure of Romans in the 5th century AD, successive waves of invaders, including the Magyars *(see pp22–3)* all left their mark on Óbuda (literally "Old Buda"). By the end of the 16th century, Óbuda was a thriving market town, eventually forming part of the city of Budapest in 1873.

A section of Óbuda's impressive Roman amphitheatre ②

The elegant, Neo-Baroque Fő tér Palace with its sentry box ⑫

From the Kiscelli Museum to the Roman Camp Museum

Begin the walk at the hill-top Kiscelli Museum ①. A mixture of historical items on show here includes printing presses and a collection of 19th-century street statuary from around the city. Upstairs is an important collection of 19th- and 20th-century Hungarian painting. The building was erected in the mid-18th century as a cloister for monks of the Trinitarian order. Following the dissolution of the order in 1783, it was turned into a barracks and hospital, finally becoming a museum in 1935. Leaving the museum, continue along Kiscelli utca, then turn right into Bécsi út and left at

Nagyszombat utca. At the corner of Pacsirtamező út is the Roman amphitheatre ②. The Romans arrived in the region soon after the time of Christ, building this impressive amphitheatre in the middle of the 2nd century AD, by which time Aquincum was the thriving capital of the province of Lower Pannonia *(see pp20–21)*. Originally used by the Roman soldiers from the nearby garrison, it became a fortress in the 9th century for the invading Magyar army. Not much remains of its once huge walls, but the scale of the theatre, which was designed to seat 14,000, is still awe inspiring. From the amphitheatre, continue along Pacsirtamező út to No. 63, the Roman Camp (Táborváros) Museum ③. In the 1950s, this modern residential district, built on top of a Roman military camp complex, was found to be enormously rich in Roman artifacts. The museum,

the first of four on this walk route housing Roman finds from the area, displays ceramics, glassware and a variety of household tools.

Old Óbuda Synagogue to Flórián Tér

Now turn right down Perc utca, up Mókus utca, then Jós utca, turning left into Lajos utca. At No. 163 is the former Óbuda Synagogue ④, now a television studio. Built in the early 1820s to serve the area's growing Jewish community, this is a Neo-Classical building with a six-columned portico. Also on

The former home of novelist and colourful local figure, Gyula Krúdy ⑥

Lajos utca, at No. 168, is Óbuda Parish Church ⑤. Constructed in 1744–9 on the site of the Roman military camp, the church has survived since then largely unchanged. The interior includes a magnificently carved pulpit showing the Good Shepherd and Mary Magdalene. Turning left up Óbudai utca, you will pass the house where the popular novelist, bon viveur and local

Zichy Mansion, built in the 18th century for an aristocratic family ⑪

character, Gyula Krúdy once lived ⑥. Writing in the early 20th century, much of Krúdy's work looks back at an idealized rural Hungary and is extremely popular in his country. From here, turn right along Tanuló utca and pass the ruins of the 14th-century St Clare's Nunnery ⑦. Then continue along the south side of Flórián tér to Kálvin köz. At No. 2 is the 18th-century Óbuda Calvinist Church ⑧. Next door is the presbytery, built in 1909 to a design by Károly Kós, better known for his work on the innovative Wekerle Estate *(see p157)*. Next, walk back up to busy Flórián tér, where in 1778 some Roman thermal baths were discovered. Hidden in the underpasses beneath the square are the Roman Baths Museum and the Roman Settlement Museum ⑨.

Imre Varga Gallery

Zichy Mansion

Gyula Krúdy's house ③

Óbuda Synagogue

Roman amphitheatre

0 metres   400

0 yards   400

Szentlélek Tér and Fő Tér

Tavasz utca, off to the the right from north of Flórián tér, leads to Szentlélek tér. In the south wing of the Zichy Mansion, on Szentlélek tér, is the Vasarely Museum, opened in 1987 ⑩. The 20th-century artist Victor Vasarely is remembered as the founder of the Op-Art movement, producing work full of bright colours, geometric shapes and optical illusions. The crumbling Zichy Mansion ⑪ itself was built for the Zichy family in 1757. Continue north up to Fő tér, one of the few areas of 18th- and 19th-century architecture remaining in Óbuda. On one side of the square stands the Neo-Baroque Fő tér Palace ⑫, its entrance still guarded by an 18th-century sentry box.

Imre Varga Gallery to the Hercules Villa

From Fő tér Palace walk up Laktanya utca, where on the right there is a group of statues, *Women with Umbrellas*, by contemporary sculptor Imre Varga ⑬. At No. 7 Laktanya utca is the Imre Varga Gallery ⑭, where further examples of the sculptor's work can be seen. Finally, make your way up to Szentendre út and cross it at the underpass. Turn right into Kerék ut, then left into Herkules utca to finish the walk at No. 21, the ruins of the Hercules Villa ⑮. Once a lavish Roman home, it takes its name from some stunning mosaics *(see p21)*.

One of several *Women with Umbrellas* by Imre Varga ⑬

TIPS FOR WALKERS

Starting point: Kiscelli utca 108.
Getting there: Bus 60 or tram 17.
Length: 5 km (3 miles).
Stops: The Kéhli Restaurant (see p199) on Mókus utca, or the Régi Sipos Étterem (see p199) on Lajos utca for the city's freshest fish.

A Two-Hour Walk Around Margaret Island

H ISTORICALLY INACCESSIBLE in the middle the Danube, Margaret Island was a retreat for religious contemplation from at least the 11th century onwards. Relics of the island's past include the remains of two monastic churches and also the ruins of the convent home of Princess Margit, daughter of King Béla IV, who gave the island its name. Opened to the public in 1869, Margaret Island is today Budapest's most beautiful park, a car-free haven of greenery in the middle of the city and the ideal location for a peaceful stroll. On the western shore, the Palatinus Strand bathing complex makes use of the mineral-rich hot springs rising on the island.

The Water Tower

A relief of Archangel Michael on
St Michael's Church ⑧

Centenary Monument to Palatinus Strand

The walk begins amid the peace and greenery of the southern tip of Margaret Island. Proceeding to the north, the first landmark is the Centenary Monument ① (see p62), which stands in front of a sizable fountain. Designed by István Kiss, the monument was made in 1973, to commemorate the centenary of the unification of the towns of Buda, Óbuda and Pest (see p32). At night the fountain is dramatically illuminated. Taking a left turn ahead, the Hajós Olympic Pool Complex (see p53) ② is soon reached. Built in 1930, the complex was designed by the multi-talented Alfréd Hajós. He won gold medals in swimming events in the 1896 Olympic Games and

was also a member of the Hungarian football team. Continuing northwards, there is a rose garden to the right before the ruins of the early 14th-century Franciscan Church ③ come into view. Constructed in the Gothic style of the time, the church was originally attached to a monastery. Still clearly visible in the west wall is the doorway which once led to the organ loft, as well as a spiral staircase and fine arched window. A little further on is the busy Palatinus Strand ④ (see p53). In front of the entrance to its pools there stands a statue by French sculptor Emile Guilleaume.

Water Tower to St Michael's Church

Clearly visible to the northeast of Palatinus Strand, is the 57-m (187-ft) high Water Tower ⑤. Built in 1911 and now protected by UNESCO, this graceful tower is currently used as an exhibition space for a variety of previously un-exhibited modern crafts and artworks, ranging from puppets to paintings. At the foot of the Water Tower is the Summer Theatre, a large modern amphitheatre seating 3,500 people, which hosts a summer season of operatic performances. To the southeast

Ruins of the 14th-century Franciscan Church ③

Stepped pathway through the lush foliage of the Japanese Garden ⑪

of the Water Tower are the ruins of a 13th-century Dominican Church and Convent ⑥ The latter was once home to Princess Margit, after whom the island is named. King Béla IV (see p23) swore that if he succeeded in repelling the Mongol invasion of 1241 that he would offer his daughter to God. He kept his oath, building the church and convent, to which the 9-year-old Princess Margit was sent in 1251. She led a godly and ascetic life and died here at the age of 29. Nearly 300 years later, in 1541, the nuns of the convent fled to Pozsony (now Bratislava, capital of the Slovak Republic) in the face of the Turkish invasion, (see pp26–7), leaving the church and the convent to be destroyed. Severe floods in 1838 led to the discovery of the ruined church and its underground vaults. The tomb of the now-canonized Margit was also excavated here 20 years later. Just to the north of the Dominican Church and Convent, near to the Water Tower, is the beginning of Artist's Avenue ⑦. A collection of contemporary busts of Hungarian writers, painters and musicians lines this promenade leading up to the Ramada-Grand Hotel. A little way before the hotel is

Bust of Zsigmond Móricz on Artists' Avenue ⑦

St Michael's Church ⑧. Originally built by members of the Premonstratensian Order, this is the oldest building on the island. In addition, the foundations of an 11th-century chapel have been excavated inside the 12th century church. Destroyed by the invading Turks in 1541, the church was eventually reconstructed in the 1930s, using materials from the original building. In the bell tower hangs a bell which, unusually, survived the Turkish invasion. Probably buried by the monks at the time of the invasion, the bell dates from the early 15th century. It was discovered in 1914 when its walnut-tree hiding place was uprooted during a violent storm.

Ramada-Grand Hotel to Arpád Bridge

The Ramada-Grand Hotel ⑨ (see p185) was designed in 1872 by Miklós Ybl (see p119). For many years it was the most fashionable hotel in Budapest, known simply as "The Grand". After World War II, the hotel was modernized and became the Ramada-Grand, and in the 1970s the luxurious Thermal Hotel ⑩ (see p185) was built nearby. The two hotels are joined by an underground walkway and offer thermal baths and a variety of spa treatments (see p52). Heading west from the Thermal Hotel, the final stretch of the walk passes beside the Japanese Garden ⑪. A variety of exotic plants, a rock garden, waterfalls and streams crossed on rustic bridges all contribute to the garden's atmosphere. The final stopping point on the walk is an unusual musical well, known as the Bodor Well ⑫. The original well was designed and constructed by Transylvanian Péter Bodor in 1820 and stood in the town of Marosvásárhely (modern-day Tirgu Mures, in Romania), which was then part of the Austro-Hungarian Empire. In 1936 this copy was built on Margaret Island. Continuing past the well, at the northern tip of Margaret Island the Árpád Bridge provides another link from the island to the city.

The musical Bodor Well ⑫

TIPS FOR WALKERS

Starting point: Southern end of Margaret Island, reached from Margaret Bridge.
Getting there: Bus 26 or 106.
Length: 3.3 km (2 miles).
Stops: There are numerous take-away kiosks and several cafés on Margaret Island, selling drinks, snacks and ice creams in summer. The Ramada-Grand Hotel and the Thermal Hotel also have a choice of restaurants and cafés.

KEY

Walk route

0 metres   500
0 yards   500

Arpád híd

la-Grand Hotel

⑨

heal's rch

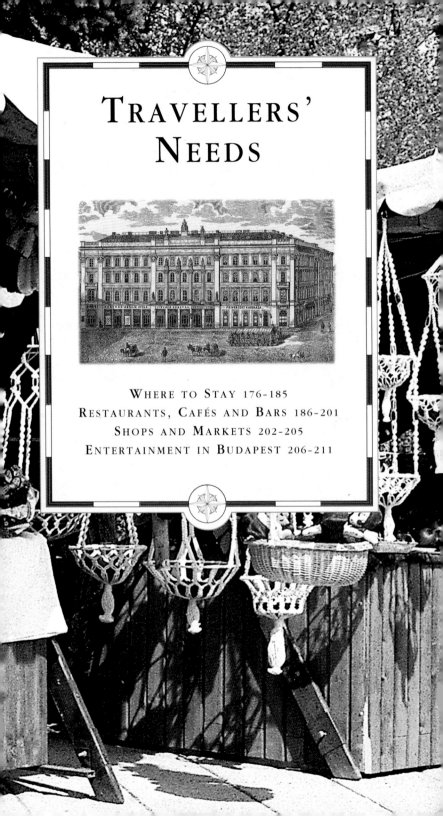

TRAVELLERS'
NEEDS

WHERE TO STAY

Budapest has a broad range of accommodation from top-class hotels, some with spa facilities, and private apartments to campsites and hostels. The larger hotels often belong to well-known groups and meet international standards, but are more expensive. Cheaper accommodation can be found in hostels or bed and breakfasts, or outside the city centre.

Travel agents and tourist information offices (see p179) will provide information on these options. Of the 200 hotels and pensions we surveyed, over 50 have been selected from across the price catagories and are, in our opinion, the best on offer. Each is listed, with a short description, on pages 182–5. The chart on pages 180–81 will help you choose the right hotel.

The exterior of the Kempinski Corvinus Hotel (see p183)

WHERE TO LOOK

When deciding on accommodation, first choose the general location: Buda or Pest, or maybe even the picturesque suburbs further afield. In low-lying Pest, many hotels are literally only a few steps away from most of the major tourist attractions, while visitors staying in hilly Buda can enjoy cool, fresh air and quiet surroundings.

Good value for money can be found by renting a room in one of the small pensions or private hotels in and around Budapest. The more exclusive hotels offer an ideal environment for a luxurious stay, but at a much greater price – as much as 40,000 Hungarian forints and above per night.

Most luxury hotels, such as the Atrium Hyatt (see p183), are located along the eastern bank of the Danube. Others, such as the Marriott (see p184) or the Kempinski Corvinus (see p183) are situated nearer

to the centre of Pest, close to the theatres and shops. Those located further out of town are usually an easy journey from the city centre, particularly since hotels are often situated close to metro stations.

Tourinform (see p179) is one of the tourist offices in Budapest that provide information (in Hungarian, English, French, German, Russian and Italian) on accommodation and places to eat, as well as on tourist and cultural events.

Maps can be found on sale here, as well as free booklets and pamphlets. The office is open daily, from 8am to 8pm during the peak tourist season and at weekends, and from 8am to 3pm during the winter months. Should visitors need any further information to supplement this guide, this office can offer details of alternative accommodation, from hotels to camp sites. The *Tourist Almanac*, available from most bookshops, is also a useful publication.

The Atrium Hyatt (see p183), with its famous suspended model plane

Reception desk at the Hilton Hotel (see p182) in the Castle District

HOTEL AND PENSION CLASSIFICATION

Hotels are classified in five categories from one to five stars and there are two categories of pension.

At the luxury end of the scale – the five-star and four-star hotels – all rooms have a bathroom, a telephone, a TV, a radio and a refrigerator, and many will be air-conditioned. The majority of these hotels will also offer business and fitness facilities. Three-star hotels have at least one restaurant and one bar, and staff are expected to speak at least one foreign language. Two thirds of the rooms in two-star hotels have their own shower or bath, while rooms in one-star hotels simply have washbasins with hot and cold running water.

Pensions have a standard minimum room size, and every room has a shower or a bath. The accommodation is clean and simple, and all the necessary services and amenities should be provided by friendly and helpful staff.

The Radisson Béke Hotel (see p183), featuring György Szondi's mosaic

HOTEL PRICES

ROOM TARIFFS reflect the hotel classification, but it is always wise to double check the price at the time of booking. Accommodation in a centrally located, higher category hotel will be much more expensive than in an out-of-town, lower category hotel. Relatively cheap rooms can be found in pensions and hostels. Hotel prices usually include breakfast, which in hotels with three stars or more typically means a self-service buffet. Pensions also offer good value, substantial meals.

Many luxury hotels, such as the Aquincum (see p185), offer substantial weekend reductions in the low season (mid-September to mid-March). During this period a three-night stay would cost the same as one-night stay during the high season.

In spa hotels, such as the Gellért (see p182), which offer hydrotherapy, the fee for using the pools and sauna is included in the room price. However, any treatments, such as massage, will incur an extra charge. Check these details with the hotel in advance.

Prices in Budapest's hotels and pensions are often quoted in foreign currencies, usually Deutschmarks or US dollars, although payment is made in Hungarian forints.

HIDDEN EXTRAS

BOTH VAT AND resort tax are included in the price of the room (resort tax is charged because Budapest is classed as a health resort), but there are often hidden surcharges that can greatly increase the overall cost of a stay. For example, many hotels have currency exchange desks, but these offer a poor rate of exchange. It is better to change money at a bank or *bureau de change* where rates are much more favourable.

Telephone calls, particularly international calls, cost almost twice as much when made from hotel rooms as opposed to public telephones. There are plenty of these in Budapest, although it may be necessary to buy a phone card (see p222).

Most hotels have their own car parks. Some, such as the Inter-Continental (see p183), the Atrium Hyatt (see p183) or the Victoria (see p182), offer off-street or garage parking, for which a modest fee may be charged.

HOW TO BOOK

THE BUDAPEST tourist season starts in the middle of June and lasts until the beginning of September. During this period, as well as around New Year and the Hungarian Grand Prix weekend (see p210), hotels become fully booked very quickly.

It is advisable to book at least two weeks ahead. Most hotels will accept bookings made by fax and will reply in the same way. Guests should confirm their reservations with a follow-up phone call a few days before arrival.

It is possible to find accommodation if an advance booking has not been made, but rooms in the right location or price range may be harder to come by, especially in the high season. Bookings can be made at Ferihegy 1 and 2 airports (see pp224–5) and at Nyugati pu, the city's western train station (see p226–7).

Stained-glass window in the Gellért Hotel (see p182)

The entrance to the Ramada Grand Hotel *(see p185)* on Margaret Island

SERVICE

THE SERVICES and amenities offered by each hotel will vary according to price. Rooms are cleaned regularly, and most higher category hotels offer 24-hour service, including meals that can be brought to the room. This usually incurs an extra charge, but tips are always welcome.

Most reception personnel will speak some foreign languages, most commonly English and German. The hotels with an outstanding level of service are indicated on the chart on pages 180–81.

TRAVELLING WITH CHILDREN

MOST HOTELS welcome children and offer free accommodation to those up to the age of four travelling with their parents. Additional beds can often be provided for older children in the parents' room for a small extra charge. Many hotels also offer a child-minding service.

DISABLED TRAVELLERS

BUDAPEST IS TRYING to make up for the neglect that disabled travellers to the city have suffered. Specialist facilities are gradually being introduced throughout the city. For example, most recently built hotels have facilities enabling disabled guests to have as pleasant and easy a stay as able-bodied people. Such hotels will display information about their facilities for disabled guests. Further information can be obtained from **Budapesti Turisztikai Hivatal** and travel agents.

SELF-CATERING

A FEW HOTELS in Budapest, especially those in the embassy district, such as the Radio Inn *(see p184)*, offer accommodation in suites with kitchenettes. This type of accommodation is particularly good for families as it gives them the option of eating "at home", rather than taking every meal at a restaurant. Another advantage is, of course, the extra space, which allows greater freedom of movement; often hotel suites are equal in size to an apartment.

There are also some specially converted buildings that consist solely of self-catering apartments. The **Charles Apartment House** is a good example of this type of accommodation; the apartments are spacious and well equipped.

HOSTELS

BUDAPEST HAS a few hostels that stay open all year. For visitors on a tight budget, these provide good, if basic, low-cost accommodation. The **Express**, the **Universitás** and the **Citadella** *(see p182)*, which is situated in the Citadel *(see pp92–3)* on Gellért Hill, are just some examples. Hostels often provide guests with a choice of staying in a dormitory or a single or double room.

SEASONAL HOSTELS

THE CLOSEST THING to youth hostels that Budapest has are the college halls of residence, which are only available during the summer vacation in July and August. Many students' halls of residence are turned into hostels, adding approximately 4,000 beds to Budapest's accommodation list and providing tourists with a convenient and inexpensive place to stay.

Given their popularity, it is advisable to book a room in advance. This is best done via the **Express Központi Iroda**, rather than contacting individual hostels directly. International Youth Hostels Organisation membership will enable guests to get a discount on room rates.

The interior of the recently restored Astoria Hotel *(see p183)*

STAYING IN PRIVATE ROOMS AND APARTMENTS

SOME VISITORS choose to stay in a private home. Accommodation usually consists of a separate bedroom and use of a kitchen and bathroom. The price depends on the facilities and the area, and varies from 700–3,000 Hungarian forints per day for a double room and upwards of 300 forints per day for a single room. **Skála Metro** is a reputable agency through which this type of accommodation can be booked.

Renting an apartment is probably the most economical way of having a longer stay in Budapest. As well as using agencies to find private apartments, it is worth checking the *albérlet* (to rent) advertisements in newspapers such as *Expressz* and *Hirdetés*.

CAMPING

CAMPING IS only permitted at designated campsites. There are several of these situated on the outskirts of Budapest. The biggest and most picturesque of them all is **Római Camping**, which is located on the road leading from Óbuda to Szentendre. Campsites are open, in general, from May until the end of October. Some operations, such as the **EXPO**, are open only from 1 July to 31 August, while others are open throughout the year.

The restaurant of the Erzsébet Hotel *(see p183)*, in the city centre

---

DIRECTORY

INFORMATION

Hungarian National Touist Office (UK)
Embassy of the Republic of Hungary
46 Eaton Place
London SW1X 8AL
(0171 823 1032.
FAX 0171 823 1459.

Hungarian National Touist Office (US)
150 East 58th Street
33rd Floor
New York
NY 10155-3398
(212 355 0240.
FAX 212 207 4103.

Budapesti Turisztikai Hivatal
1056 Budapest,
Marcius 15 tér 7.
Map 4 E1. (266 04 79.

Budapest Tourist
1051 Budapest,
Roosevelt tér 5. Map 2 D5.
(317 35 55.
FAX 318 60 62.

Tourinform
1051 Budapest,
Sütő utca 2. Map 2 E5.
(317 98 00.
FAX 317 96 56.

AGENCIES

Express Központi Iroda
1052 Budapest,
Semmelweis utca 4.
Map 4 F1.
(317 66 34.

Hungarian Youth Hostels Federation
1121 Budapest,
Konkoly Thege M út 21.
(395 65 37.
FAX 395 73 27.

IBUSZ
1051 Budapest,
Petőfi tér 3. Map 4 E1.
(318 48 48.
FAX 317 90 99.

SELF-CATERING

Charles Apartment House
1016 Budapest,
Hegyalja út 23. Map 3 B2.
(201 17 96.
FAX 202 29 84.

HOSTELS

Citadella
118 Budapest,
Citadella sétany. Map 4 D3.
(466 57 94.
FAX 386 05 05.

Diák Sport Hostel
1134 Budapest,
Dózsa György út 152.
Map 5 A1.
(340 85 85.
FAX 320 84 25.

Express
1126 Budapest,
Beethoven utca 7–9.
(375 25 28.
FAX 375 30 82.

Martos Hotel
1111 Budapest,
Stoczek utca 5–7.
(463 36 51.
FAX 463 36 50.

Rózsa Kollégium
1117 Budapest,
Bercsényi utca 28.
Map 4 E5.
(463 42 50.
FAX 463 42 59.

Universitás
1111 Budapest,
Irinyi József utca 9–11.
Map 4 F5.
(463 29 22.

SEASONAL HOSTELS

Schonherz Kollégium
1117 Budapest,
Irinyi József utca 42.
Map 4 E5.
(372 51 00.

ELTE Kőrösi Csoma Sandor Kollegium
1118 Budapest,
Dayka Gabor utca 4.
(319 09 99.

PRIVATE ROOMS AND APARTMENTS

Skála Metro
1068 Budapest,
Bajcsy-Zsilinszky út 17.
Map 2 E4.
(312 36 21.
FAX 312 71 26.

CAMPING

Autoskemping Porta
1044 Budapest,
Üdülő sor 7.
(FAX 233 34 13.

EXPO
1101 Budapest,
Albertirsai út 10.
(263 76 00.
FAX 263 76 11.

Hárshegyi Camping
1021 Budapest,
Hárshegyi út 5–7.
(391 23 00.

Római Camping
1031 Budapest,
Szentendrei út 189.
(368 62 60.
FAX 250 04 26.

Choosing a Hotel

THIS CHART PROVIDES a quick and easy-to-use reference guide to the hotels, pensions and hostels that we have selected in and around Budapest. They range from the basic to the luxurious, but the standard of each is high within its category. For further information on each entry see pages 182–5.

Hotel	Price	NUMBER OF ROOMS	LARGE ROOMS	BUSINESS FACILITIES	CHILDREN'S FACILITIES	RECOMMENDED RESTAURANT	CLOSE TO SHOPS AND RESTAURANTS	QUIET LOCATION	24-HOUR ROOM SERVICE	OUTSTANDING SERVICE
CASTLE DISTRICT *(see p182)*										
Alba	●●●	95	●	●	●		●	●		●
Hilton	●●●●●	322	●	●	●	●	●	●	●	●
GELLÉRT HILL AND TABÁN *(see p182)*										
Citadella	●	15	●	●				●		
Orion	●●	30	●		●	●		●	●	
Flamenco Parkhotel	●●●	358	●	●	●	●		●	●	
Gellért	●●●●●	233	●	●	●	●			●	●
NORTH OF THE CASTLE *(see p182)*										
Buda Center	●●	37			●			●		
Dunapart	●●●	32	●			●	●	●		●
Mercure Buda	●●●	399		●		●				
Victoria	●●●	30	●		●			●		
AROUND PARLIAMENT *(see pp182–3)*										
City Panzió Ring	●●	39	●	●	●		●			
Medosz	●●	72	●		●		●			
K + K Opera	●●●●	115		●	●		●	●		
Radisson Béke	●●●●	247		●	●	●	●			
Atrium Hyatt	●●●●●	344	●	●		●	●	●	●	●
CENTRAL PEST *(see pp183–4)*										
City Panzió Mátyás	●●	55					●			
EMKE	●●	74				●	●			
King's Hotel Kosher	●●	100		●			●	●		
Ibis Centrum	●●●	126		●	●		●	●	●	
Nemzeti	●●●	76	●	●		●	●		●	
Astoria	●●●●	130		●		●	●			
Erzsébet	●●●●	123		●	●	●	●			
Mercure Korona	●●●●	433		●	●		●			●
Taverna	●●●●	230	●	●			●			
Inter-Continental	●●●●●	398	●	●	●	●	●	●	●	●
Kempinski Corvinus	●●●●●	369	●	●			●		●	●
Marriott	●●●●●	362	●	●	●	●	●	●	●	●
AROUND VÁROSLIGET *(see p184)*										
Park	●	170					●			
Radio Inn	●	31	●					●		
Liget	●●	139	●	●	●			●		

Price categories for a double room with bathroom, including breakfast and service:
ⓦ below 10,000 HUF
ⓦⓦ 10,000 – 20,000 HUF
ⓦⓦⓦ 20,000 – 30,000 HUF
ⓦⓦⓦⓦ 30,000 – 40,000 HUF
ⓦⓦⓦⓦⓦ over 40,000 HUF

LARGE ROOMS
A significant proportion of standard rooms are larger than average.

BUSINESS FACILITIES
Facilities such as a message-taking service, fax machine and meeting room are available.

CHILDREN'S FACILITIES
See p178.

OUTSTANDING SERVICE
Service is of a consistently high standard.

	Price	NUMBER OF ROOMS	LARGE ROOMS	BUSINESS FACILITIES	CHILDREN'S FACILITIES	RECOMMENDED RESTAURANT	CLOSE TO SHOPS AND RESTAURANTS	QUIET LOCATION	24-HOUR ROOM SERVICE	OUTSTANDING SERVICE
Benczúr	ⓦⓦⓦ	93	▦	●	▦			●		
Ibis Volga	ⓦⓦⓦ	315	▦		▦					
Grand Hungaria	ⓦⓦⓦⓦ	499	▦	●	▦		▦			
FURTHER AFIELD *(see pp184–5)*										
Expressz	ⓦ	31	▦					▦	●	
Agro	ⓦⓦ	149	▦	●		●			●	
Griff	ⓦⓦ	108		●	▦	▦				
Mohácsi Panzió	ⓦⓦ	9	▦		▦	▦		●		
Molnár Panzió	ⓦⓦ	23	▦	●	▦	●		●		●
Normafa	ⓦⓦ	70	▦		▦	●		●	▦	
Olympia	ⓦⓦ	166	▦	●	▦			●	▦	
Panda	ⓦⓦ	28			▦	●		●	▦	
Platánus	ⓦⓦ	128	▦		▦			●	▦	
Rege	ⓦⓦ	164	▦	●				●	▦	
Budapest Szálloda	ⓦⓦⓦ	289	▦		▦	●		●	▦	
Ibis-Aero	ⓦⓦⓦ	139	▦		▦	●	▦			
Novotel Budapest Centrum	ⓦⓦⓦ	321	▦	●	▦			●		
Rubin Aktiv	ⓦⓦⓦ	85	▦	●	▦			●		
Vadvirág Panzió	ⓦⓦⓦ	18	▦					●		
Villa Korda	ⓦⓦⓦ	21	▦	●	▦	●		●		●
Ramada-Grand	ⓦⓦⓦⓦ	499	▦	●	▦	●		●		●
Aquincum	ⓦⓦⓦⓦⓦ	312		●	▦	●	▦	●	▦	●
Thermal Helia	ⓦⓦⓦⓦⓦ	262		●	▦	●		●	▦	●

USING THE LISTINGS

The hotels on pages 182–5 are listed according to area and price category. These symbols summarize the facilities in each hotel.

🛁 Room with bath or shower

1 Single-rate rooms available
🛏 Rooms for more than two people
24 24-hour room service
TV Television in all rooms
🗄 Business facilities
🚭 No-smoking rooms available
🗎 Air conditioning in all rooms

🏋 Gym/fitness facilities
🏊 Swimming pool in hotel
👶 Caters for children
P Hotel parking available
🍸 Bar
💳 Credit cards accepted:
AE American Express
DC Diners Club
JCB Japanese Credit Bureau
MC MasterCard/Access
V Visa

CASTLE DISTRICT

Alba

1011 Budapest, Apor Péter utca 3.
Map 1 C5. **C** 375 92 44.
FAX 375 98 99. **Rooms:** 95.

This comfortable hotel is situated beneath the Royal Palace, just off Fő utca and close to Clark Ádám tér (*see p100*). It has good-sized, if slightly basic, single, double and triple rooms, all with large, bright bathrooms. A hearty buffet breakfast is available.

Hilton

1014 Budapest, Hess András tér 1–3.
Map 1 B4. **C** 214 30 00. **FAX** 214 21 85. **Rooms:** 322.

The Hilton (*see p81*), one of the most modern and luxurious hotels in Budapest, is located in a recent building that incorporates parts of a Gothic church and Jesuit monastery. In the heart of the Castle District, it offers a bar, a café and three restaurants serving Hungarian and international cuisine. Prices are high but guests are rewarded with magnificent views over the Danube and the Pest cityscape.

GELLÉRT HILL AND TABÁN

Citadella

1118 Budapest, Citadella sétány.
Map 4 D3. **C** 466 57 94.
FAX 386 05 05. **Rooms:** 15.

This one-star hostel-style hotel occupies the casements of the Citadel (*see pp92–3*). It offers inexpensive, neat and clean double and multiple-occupancy rooms. A popular wine bar, restaurant and nightclub are nearby

Orion

1013 Budapest, Döbrentei utca 13.
Map 4 D1. **C** 356 85 83. **FAX** 375 54 18. **Rooms:** 30.

Hidden in a secluded spot, this pleasant hotel offers clean but plainly decorated rooms, all complete with bathrooms, controlled air conditioning and colour televisions. A small restaurant serves a good range of inexpensive Hungarian and international cuisine.

Flamenco Parkhotel

1113 Budapest, Tas vezér utca 7.
Map 3 C5. **C** 372 20 00.
FAX 365 80 07. **Rooms:** 358.

This hotel is adjacent to a park with a lake and is close to Buda's main sights. Built during the 1960s, the interior of the Flamenco Parkhotel depicts Spanish themes. The Solero restaurant and La Bodega wine bar offer Spanish specialities. Further facilities include a terrace café, business centre and sauna.

Gellért

1111 Budapest, Szent Gellért tér 1.
Map 4 D2. **C** 385 22 00. **FAX** 466 66 31. **Rooms:** 233.

The Gellért is a famous spa hotel (*see pp90–91*) that was built at the beginning of the 20th century. Its indoor and outdoor pools provide an attractive environment in which to relax at any time of the year. Treatments such as massage and water-jet massage are also available. Other facilities include a restaurant, a bar and a beer bar, a nightclub and banqueting halls. Rooms range from luxury suites to more modest attic rooms.

NORTH OF THE CASTLE

Buda Center

1027 Budapest, Csalogány utca 23.
Map 1 B3. **C** 201 63 33. **FAX** 201 78 43. **Rooms:** 37.

This hotel stands at the foot of Castle Hill, close to Batthyány tér. It offers modest rooms with their own bathrooms, air conditioning if requested and a child-minding service. There is also a reasonable Chinese restaurant off the foyer.

Dunapart

1011 Budapest, Szilágyi Dezső tér.
Map 1 C4. **C** 355 90 01. **FAX** 355 37 70. **Rooms:** 32.

This quirky hotel is located on a boat moored off the western bank of the Danube, close to the Calvinist Church (*see p100*). Accommodation in the Dunapart is in air-conditioned cabins, some of which offer an interesting view of Parliament (*see pp108–9*). The facilities are good and there is a restaurant on board, from which diners can enjoy the view of the Chain Bridge and Elizabeth Bridge (*see pp62–3*).

Mercure Buda

1013 Budapest, Krisztina körút 41–3.
Map 1 A4. **C** 356 63 33.
FAX 355 69 64. **Rooms:** 399.

Built during the 1960s, this hotel is close to the Vérmező park and has a large car park. Some of the rooms have beautiful views overlooking the Castle District. The facilities include a swimming pool, a vegetarian restaurant, a bar and a beer bar. Dogs are welcome.

Victoria

1011 Budapest, Bem rakpart 11.
Map 1 C4. **C** 457 80 80.
FAX 457 80 88. **Rooms:** 30.

Situated in a secluded spot on the western bank of Danube, the Victoria is in easy reach of Buda's main tourist sights. This hotel provides big, comfortable air-conditioned rooms, many with views of the Chain Bridge, the Elizabeth Bridge and Pest. The hotel does not have a restaurant so breakfast is served in the bar. The hotel's facilities include a sauna, a child-minding service and an in-house doctor.

AROUND PARLIAMENT

City Panzió Ring

1137 Budapest, Szent István körút 22.
Map 2 E2. **C** 340 54 50. **FAX** 340 48 84. **Rooms:** 37.

The City Hotel is a new establishment situated in a well-chosen location within easy reach of Parliament (*see pp108–9*). All rooms are spotlessly clean and subtly decorated in neutral shades. There are few facilities and services at this hotel, and this is reflected in its very reasonable prices. Although there is no restaurant here, there are many places to eat nearby. However, the hotel does have a cheerful breakfast room.

Medosz

1061 Budapest, Jókai tér 9.
Map 7 A1. **C** 353 17 00.
FAX 332 43 16. **Rooms:** 67.

This former trade union hostel has been successfully converted into an inexpensive and basic hotel. The modesty of its rooms is more than made up for by its excellent location close to Liszt Ferenc tér and Oktogon tér.

K + K Opera

1065 Budapest, Révay utca 24.
Map 2 F4. 269 02 22.
FAX 269 02 30. **Rooms:** 205. 1
TV AE, DC, MC, V.

This hotel belongs to the K + K group and is situated close to the State Opera House *(see pp118–19)*. It offers guests comfortable accommodation in very modern, clean and spacious rooms. There is also a café, a pub, a bar and secure car parking facilities for hotel guests.

Radisson Béke

1067 Budapest, Teréz körút 43.
Map 2 F3. 301 16 00. FAX 301 16 15. **Rooms:** 247. 24 TV
AE, DC, MC, V.

This old, magnificent hotel *(see p115)*, situated close to Nyugati pu metro station, has a beautiful mosaic on its façade. The hotel has, in fact, been restored and is now equipped with the latest facilities, including the new Orfeum Casino, which is open from 5pm. The restaurants serve European and Hungarian delicacies, while the first-floor Zsolany café serves tea and coffee from Zsolany porcelain *(see p56)*.

Atrium Hyatt

1051 Budapest, Roosevelt tér 2.
Map 2 D5. 266 12 34. FAX 266 91 01. **Rooms:** 344. 1 24 TV
AE, DC, MC, V.

Located close to the Danube, the modern Atrium Hyatt has views of the Castle District and the Pest cityscape. There are stylish restaurants, serving international and Hungarian cuisine, terrace cafés and a cocktail bar. Souvenir boutiques and the Las Vegas Casino *(see p206)* are on the ground floor. The hotel gets its name from its central atrium, where a huge model plane is suspended.

CENTRAL PEST

City Panzió Mátyás

1056 Budapest, Marcius 15 tér 8.
Map 4 E1. 318 05 36.
FAX 367 90 86. **Rooms:** 55. 1
TV AE, DC, V.

This small, neat pension offers basic rooms, with showers, at affordable prices. There is no bar or restaurant at the pension, but breakfast is available. The City Panzió Mátyás is well located and many of Budapest's attractions are within walking distance or are easily reached on public transport.

EMKE

1072 Budapest, Akácfa utca 1–3.
Map 7 B3. 322 92 30. FAX 322 99 33. **Rooms:** 74. 1 TV
AE, DC, V.

Situated in the city centre, in a quiet side street close to Blaha Lujza tér, the EMKE offers pleasant rooms, including non-smoking ones. The service is friendly.

King's Hotel Kosher

1072 Budapest, Nagy Diófa utca 25–27. **Map** 7 A2. 352 76 75.
FAX 352 76 75. **Rooms:** 100.
TV AE.

Right in the heart of the Jewish Quarter *(see p134)*, this wonderfully restored 19th-century building has been a hotel since 1995. The rooms are modern and plain, but many have small balconies overlooking the quiet residential street. The restaurant offers a tasty range of strictly Kosher meals.

Ibis Centrum

1092 Budapest, Ráday utca 6.
Map 7 A5. 215 85 83.
FAX 215 57 14. **Rooms:** 126. 1
24 AE, DC, MC, V.

This new hotel is located close to the Hungarian National Museum *(see pp130–33)*, Kálvin tér and several restaurants. The comfortable rooms and friendly service ensure a restful stay.

Nemzeti

1088 Budapest, József körút 4.
Map 7 B3. 303 93 10.
FAX 314 00 19. **Rooms:** 76.
1 24 TV
JCB.

Built at the end of 19th century, this hotel features a wonderful grand staircase. Its main attraction is the Secession-style restaurant, which offers good food. The rooms are comfortable, and those facing the courtyard are particularly pleasant.

Astoria

1053 Budapest, Kossuth Lajos u. 19–21.
Map 4 F1. 317 34 11.
FAX 318 67 98. **Rooms:** 130.
1 TV AE, DC, MC V.

This old hotel, designed in the Secession style *(see pp54–7)*, but with a Neo-Baroque breakfast room, has been refurbished to recreate its original interior. Even if not staying at the hotel, it is worth visiting the café *(see p201)* to see the beautiful interior. The rooms at the front tend to be noisy. The hotel has facilities for wheelchair users.

Erzsébet

1364 Budapest, Károlyi Mihály utca 11–15. **Map** 4 F1. 338 21 11.
FAX 328 57 63. **Rooms:** 123. 1
TV DC, JCB, MC.

This modern hotel is located close to the shops on Váci utca *(Váci Street, see p127)*. The hotel has a restaurant, café and bar, which have a friendly atmosphere and a high standard of cuisine.

Mercure Korona

1053 Budapest, Kecskeméti utca 14.
Map 4 F2. 317 41 11. FAX 318 38 67. **Rooms:** 433. 1 TV
AE, DC, MC, V.

The Mercure Korona is situated in a small street off Kálvin tér, close to cafés and restaurants. The hotel has a wide range of amenities, including its own swimming pool, gymnasium, sauna and solarium.

Taverna

1052 Budapest, Váci utca 20.
Map 4 E1. 338 49 99.
FAX 318 71 88. **Rooms:** 230. 1
TV AE, DC, MC, V.

Situated on Váci utca *(Váci Street, see p127)*, the Taverna offers all the facilities associated with four-star hotels. The elegant rooms create oases amid the noise and bustle of this busy commercial district.

Inter-Continental

1052 Budapest, Apáczai Csere János utca 12–14. **Map** 2 D5. 327 63 33. FAX 327 63 57. **Rooms:** 398.
1 24 TV
AE, DC, V.

This luxury hotel, situated close to Pest's riverside promenade, offers a magnificent view across the Danube to the Castle District. The facilities include a cocktail bar and a buffet restaurant. The beautifully decorated Viennese Café is located on the first floor.

Kempinski Corvinus

1051 Budapest, Erzsébet tér 7–8.
Map 2 E5. 429 37 77.
FAX 429 47 77. **Rooms:** 369.
1 24 TV
AE, DC, MC, V.

This exclusive hotel often welcomes heads of state and other notable personalities among its guests. The large and luxuriously furnished rooms are enormously relaxing. The hotel has fitness facilities, two restaurants, bars and a pub.

Marriott

1052 Budapest, Apáczai Csere János utca 4. **Map** 4 E1. (266 70 00.
FAX 266 50 00. **Rooms:** 362.
⬛⬛⬛⬛⬛⬛⬛⬛⬛⬛
⬛⬛⬛⬛ AE, DC, MC, V.
⬛⬛⬛⬛⬛

All the rooms in this luxury hotel overlook both the Danube and the Buda skyline. The Marriott's excellent facilities include banqueting rooms, three restaurants, a business centre, a sauna and a fitness centre. The rooms are of a high standard and the staff provide an exemplary level of service. It was here, in 1991, that the decision was taken to dissolve the Warsaw Pact and Comecon (see p35).

AROUND VÁROSLIGET

Park

1087 Budapest, Baross tér 10.
Map 7 C2. (313 14 20.
FAX 313 56 19. **Rooms:** 170. ⬛⬛
⬛⬛⬛⬛ AE, MC, V. ⬛

This is a typical low-budget hotel located on a busy square that provides good public transport links to Budapest's major sights. The Park has basic facilities, which are adequate for a short stay.

Radio Inn

1068 Budapest, Benczúr utca 19.
Map 5 C4. (322 04 37.
FAX 322 82 84. **Rooms:** 31. ⬛⬛⬛
⬛⬛⬛⬛⬛ MC, V. ⬛

This pension-style hotel is the official guesthouse of Hungarian National Radio and entertains many visiting personalities. The Radio Inn offers accommodation to tourists in spacious suites with well-equipped kitchens. Although the facilities are fairly basic, the Radio Inn is ideal for families as it is situated in the peaceful embassy quarter and there is a garden. It is just a short walk away from Andrássy út (Andrássy Street, see p144) and Hősök tere (Heroes' Square, see pp142–3).

Liget

1068 Budapest, Dózsa György út 106.
Map 5 C3. (342 57 60.
FAX 259 53 29. **Rooms:** 139. ⬛⬛
⬛⬛⬛⬛⬛⬛⬛
⬛ AE, DC, MC, V. ⬛⬛

Situated on the edge of the Hősök tere (Heroes' Square, see pp142–3), close to the Museum of Fine Arts (see pp146–9), the Liget offers pleasant rooms. Its facilities include a sauna, a solarium and a rent-a-bike scheme. It does not have a restaurant, but breakfast is available.

Benczúr

1068 Budapest, Benczúr utca 35.
Map 5 C4. (342 79 70.
FAX 342 15 58. **Rooms:** 93.
⬛⬛⬛⬛⬛⬛⬛⬛
⬛⬛⬛ MC, V. ⬛⬛⬛⬛

Situated in a quiet street close to Városliget (see pp142), this hotel offers small but comfortable rooms. In addition, there is a good restaurant, as well as a terrace and a garden. Guests are also able to make use of the services of an in-house dentist. Prices are sometimes considerably reduced out of the high season, so it is worth making enquiries.

Ibis Volga

1134 Budapest, Dózsa György út 65.
Map 5 C4. (350 21 77.
FAX 340 83 16. **Rooms:** 315.
⬛⬛⬛⬛⬛⬛⬛⬛⬛
⬛⬛ AE, DC, JCB, MC, V. ⬛⬛⬛

This reasonable hotel complex caters for both tour groups and individuals. It offers functional rooms and good car parking facilities. There are a good range of entertainment options, which include a restaurant, a café, a bar and a nightclub. Medical care can also be obtained here.

Grand Hungaria

1074 Budapest, Rákóczi út 90.
Map 7 C2. (322 90 50.
FAX 351 06 75. **Rooms:** 499.
⬛⬛⬛⬛⬛⬛⬛⬛⬛
⬛⬛⬛⬛⬛ AE, DC, JCB,
MC, V. ⬛⬛⬛⬛

Budapest's largest hotel, the Grand Hungaria offers both single and double rooms. All rooms are clean and functional, but since they vary considerably in size it is worthwhile asking to view the room before checking in. The facilities include a café, a restaurant and several bars, as well as a child-minding service. Dogs are permitted to stay, but there is an extra charge.

FURTHER AFIELD

Expressz

1126 Budapest, Beethoven utca 7–9.
(375 30 82. FAX 375 30 82.
Rooms: 31. ⬛⬛⬛⬛ ⬛

This well-located one-star hotel is situated just outside Buda. It is more like a hostel and offers two- and four-person rooms with bunk beds. It is especially suitable for people on a low budget, although the low prices are reflected in the facilities available, which are clean and functional but rather limited.

Agro

1121 Budapest, Normafa út 54.
(375 40 11. FAX 375 61 64.
Rooms: 149. ⬛⬛⬛⬛⬛⬛
⬛⬛⬛⬛⬛⬛⬛ AE, DC,
JCB, MC, V. ⬛⬛

This out-of-town hotel, situated on Sváb Hill (see p161), still retains echoes of Budapest's Communist past. However, the Agro's relaxing surroundings and good food are matched by excellent facilities. These include a swimming pool, a bowling alley, tennis courts, a gymnasium and a sauna. There are splendid views, and walking in the Buda Hills (see p161) is an enjoyable pastime.

Griff

1113 Budapest, Bartók Béla út 152.
(204 26 66. FAX 204 00 62.
Rooms: 108. ⬛⬛⬛⬛⬛
⬛⬛⬛⬛⬛⬛⬛ AE, MC.
⬛⬛

This two-star hotel offers adequate facilities, including colour television in all rooms and a child-minding service. The restaurant regularly features a live Hungarian band.

Mohácsi Panzió

1022 Budapest, Bimbó út 25a.
(326 77 41. FAX 326 77 84.
Rooms: 9. ⬛⬛⬛⬛⬛⬛⬛⬛

This small, pleasant and inexpensive pension is located just off Margit körút, in the Rózsadomb area. The pension offers clean rooms with either a shower or a bath, and all rooms have a television.

Molnár Panzió

1124 Budapest, Fodor utca 143.
(395 18 73. FAX 395 18 72.
Rooms: 23. ⬛⬛⬛⬛⬛⬛⬛
⬛⬛⬛⬛ AE, MC, V. ⬛⬛

This mid-range pension is situated in a residential district on the slopes of the Buda Hills (see p161). Its green surroundings add to the homely atmosphere and offer guests complete peace. Family rooms are available. The amenities include a bar, fitness facilities and parking.

Normafa

1121 Budapest, Eötvös út 52–54.
(395 65 05. FAX 395 65 04.
Rooms: 70. ⬛⬛⬛⬛⬛⬛⬛
⬛⬛⬛⬛⬛⬛⬛⬛
⬛ AE, MC, V. ⬛⬛

Guests have the option of indulging in complete relaxation at the Normafa, or exploring the beautiful scenery on foot. All rooms have terraces, and there is also a swimming pool, a sauna, tennis courts, a restaurant, a café and a beer bar.

Olympia

1121 Budapest, Eötvös utca 40.
[395 64 47. **FAX** 395 64 43.
Rooms: 166. 🛏 1 🛗 24 TV
🛢 🍴 ♨ 🏋 P 🅿 🅱 Y 🔧 ♿ ⬆
🅮 AE, DC. 🅮🅮

Built in beautiful surroundings on
the slopes of Sváb Hill *(see p161)*,
this hotel was originally the Olympic athletes' centre. The air is clean
and during the week it is very
peaceful. At weekends the area is
packed with day-trippers.

Panda

1026 Budapest, Pasaréti út 133.
[394 19 32. **FAX** 394 10 02.
Rooms: 28. 🛏 1 24 TV 🖥 🏋
P 🅿 Y ⬆ 🅮 AE, DC, JCB, MC, V.
🅮🅮

This small hotel is situated in
Pasarét, a quiet residential district
of Buda. It offers a family atmosphere and a substantial, tasty
breakfast. Bus 5 provides quick
transport into the centre.

Platánus

1087 Budapest, Könyves Kálmán
körút 44. **[** 333 65 05.
FAX 210 43 86. *Rooms:* 128. 🛏 1
🛗 24 TV 🖥 P 🅿 Y ⬆
🅮 AE, DC, JCB, MC, V. 🅮🅮

The Platánus is a comfortable,
inexpensive hotel situated on the
edge of the People's Park *(see
p156)* and close to the Népliget
metro station. The hotel has clean,
functional rooms, and offers good
food. Other facilities available
include a sauna, a solarium and
an in-house doctor.

Rege

1021 Budapest, Pálos utca 2.
[200 88 16. **FAX** 200 88 24.
Rooms: 164. 🛏 1 🛗 24 TV
🛢 ♨ 🏋 P 🅿 Y 🔧 ⬆
🅮 AE, DC, MC, V. 🅮🅮

Situated in a high-rise building in
the Buda Hills *(see p161)*, this
hotel is often patronized by actors.
It offers peace and quiet, beautiful
views and recreational facilities.

Budapest Szálloda

1026 Budapest, Szilágyi Erzsébet fasor
47. **[** 202 00 44. **FAX** 202 08 08.
Rooms: 289. 🛏 1 🛗 24 TV 🖥
🍴 🏋 P 🅿 Y 🔧 ⬆ 🅮 AE, DC, JCB,
MC, V. 🅮🅮🅮

This establishment was built in the
late 1960s and was the pride of the
local hotel industry for many years.
Its location in the Buda Hills *(see
p161)* and the magnificent view
from the roof terrace remains
unrivalled. The facilities include
two restaurants and a wine cellar.

Ibis-Aero

1091 Budapest, Ferde utca 1–3.
[280 60 10. **FAX** 280 64 03.
Rooms: 139. 🛏 🛗 TV 🖥 🛢 🍴
P 🅿 Y 🔧 ⬆ 🅮 AE, DC, JCB,
MC, V. 🅮🅮🅮

Situated close to Ferihegy airport,
this hotel is particularly convenient
for those making only a short stop
in Budapest. The rooms are cosy
and tastefully decorated, and
include some suites for families
and rooms for non-smokers. All
rooms have balconies. In the
evening a Gypsy band plays in
the restaurant, while during the
summer months barbecues are
held in the garden.

Novotel Budapest Centrum

1444 Budapest, Alkotás utca 63–67.
Map 3 A2. **[** 209 19 90.
FAX 466 56 36. *Rooms:* 321. 🛏 🛏
🛗 TV 🖥 🛢 🍴 ♨ 🏋 P 🅿
Y ⬆ 🅮 AE, DC, JCB, MC, V.
🅮🅮🅮

Situated in the immediate vicinity
of the Congress Centre *(see p160)*,
the Novotel Budapest Centrum
offers modern rooms. The facilities
include a swimming pool, a sauna,
a bowling alley and a cocktail bar.
The hotel also has a large car
park. The reception rooms and
banqueting halls can accommodate approximately 1,000 people.

Rubin Aktiv

1118 Budapest, Dayka Gábor utca 3.
[319 32 31. **FAX** 319 26 56.
Rooms: 85. 🛏 1 🛗 TV 🛢
🛢 🍴 ♨ 🏋 P 🅿 Y ⬆
🅮 AE, DC, MC, V. 🅮🅮🅮

This modern hotel offers various
relaxation and sporting facilities.
Its sauna, swimming pool, tennis
courts and bowling alley have
been tastefully incorporated in the
overall architectural design. The
hotel is in a quiet location close to
the M1 and M7 motorways. The
accommodation range includes
some suites with kitchenettes and
some maisonettes for families
with children.

Vadvirág Panzió

1025 Budapest, Nagybanyai út 18.
[394 42 42. **FAX** 275 02 00.
Rooms: 18. 1 TV P 🅿 DC, JCB,
MC, V. 🅮

This privately owned pension,
located in a quiet and green district
of the Buda Hills *(see p161)*, has a
homely atmosphere. Its facilities
include comfortable rooms with
balconies, a dining room, a terrace
and a sauna. Close by is where the
composer Béla Bartók once lived.

Villa Korda

1025 Budapest, Szikla utca 9.
[325 91 23. **FAX** 325 91 27.
Rooms: 21. 🛏 1 🛗 TV
🛢 🖥 🍴 🏋 P 🅿 Y 🔧
🅮 AE, DC, MC, V. 🅮🅮🅮

This exclusive pension-style hotel
was built in a smart residential
district on the slopes of Mátyás
Hill by the popular Hungarian
singer, György Korda. It offers
a high standard of service and
exclusive company. It is best
reached by car due to its location
and the steep road that leads to it.

Ramada-Grand

1138 Budapest, Rákösi út 90.
[322 90 50. **FAX** 352 18 58.
Rooms: 499. 🛏 1 🛗 TV 🛢
🖥 🍴 🏋 P 🅿 Y ⬆
🅮 AE, DC, V. 🅮🅮🅮🅮

Built before World War II, this
hotel on Margaret Island *(see
pp172–3)* is favoured by visitors
from all over the world who come
in search of balneological
treatments. Other attractions
include the shaded terrace cafés
and restaurants, and the numerous
possibilities for taking tranquil
walks around the island. Tennis
courts, a swimming pool and bike
hire are also available.

Aquincum

1036 Budapest, Árpád fejedelem útja
94. **[** 250 33 60. **FAX** 250 46 72.
Rooms: 312. 🛏 1 🛗 24 TV 🛢 🖥
🖥 🍴 ♨ 🏋 P 🅿 Y 🔧 ⬆
🅮 DC, JCB, MC, V. 🅮🅮🅮🅮

This hotel offers guests everything
to pamper themselves or to improve
their health. Facilities include an
excellent swimming pool, hot- and
warm-water spas, a jacuzzi, a sauna,
massage and a gymnasium. The
hotel also has a resident doctor and
staff dedicated exclusively to the
needs of disabled guests who come
here for treatment. Some rooms
have beautiful views of the Danube.

Thermal Helia

1133 Budapest, Kárpát utca 62–64.
[350 32 77. **FAX** 452 58 01.
Rooms: 262. 🛏 1 TV 🛢 🖥 🍴
🍴 ♨ 🏋 P 🅿 🅱 🔧 ⬆
AE, DC, JCB, MC, V. 🅮🅮🅮🅮

This is a light and airy hotel
located on the bank of Danube,
opposite Margaret Island *(see
pp172–3)*. From the rooms overlooking the river, guests can watch
boats cruising along it. The most
modern spa hotel in Budapest, the
Thermal Helia offers a full range
of health and beauty facilities,
including massage, thermal waters
and the services of a qualified
medical practitioner.

RESTAURANTS, CAFÉS AND BARS

FOLLOWING A VISIT to Budapest, the Nobel Prize-winning Latin American writer Miguel Ángel Asturias said that "the exquisite taste of Hungarian cuisine is a language understood by all". The numerous restaurants, cafés and bars in Budapest give the visitor ample opportunity to sample the delights of this distinctive cuisine. The most typical examples of traditional Hungarian cooking can be seen on pages 190–91, while information on what to drink is given on pages 192–3. A detailed guide to around 50 of the city's best restaurants, covering all price categories, is provided on pages 196–9, and the choosing chart on pages 194–5 summarizes the information, highlighting such attractions as Hungarian specialities and live music.

WHERE TO LOOK

THERE ARE a great many eating establishments in Budapest and the surrounding suburbs. Good traditional Hungarian dishes can be found within all price ranges in restaurants and inns, but in recent years Budapest has seen the arrival of cuisine from all over the world. Among the ethnic eating options now available are Italian, Greek, Chinese and Thai restaurants. American-style fast food chains are also appearing and are rapidly becoming popular.

The city's main tourist areas are well off for places to eat, but may not offer the best fare or prices. It is often worth looking off the the main roads or away from popular areas to find establishments frequented by local Budapest residents. The restaurants, cafés and bars on Váci utca (Váci Street, see p127) are notorious for overcharging, especially at night.

Entrance to Ruszwurm Cukrászda (see p201), in the Castle District

TYPES OF RESTAURANTS, CAFÉS AND BARS

BUDAPEST OFFERS a variety of places to eat and a range of prices to suit most budgets. The differences between the types of establishments can be subtle, but they break down roughly into the following types. An étterem is a restaurant that offers Hungarian and international cuisine. A csárda comes in various forms. Most are folky restaurants typically offering interesting local specialities. A fisherman's csárda, known as a halászcsárda, will offer mainly fish dishes and soups. There are two types of inn, a vendéglő, which has an informal ambience, and a kisvendéglő, (literally a "small inn"), which is similar to a cosy pub. Cafés range from a kávéház (coffee house) to a cukrászda (patisserie), and types of bars include a borozó, a söröző and an eszpresszó (see pp200–1).

WHAT TO ORDER

ORDERING A Hungarian meal may not be as simple as it may first seem. There are many different varieties of Hungarian soups, some of which are a meal in themselves. Bogrács, which is often served in a kettle, and bean soups are the heartiest soups and would normally be followed by a light, hot pudding or pancakes. Hungarian fish soup is a particular speciality and owes its red colour to paprika. This should be followed by delicate homemade noodles served with crackling, cheese and cream. There are also many light soups, or small portions of the more substantial soups, which can be eaten as a starter, thus leaving room for the main course.

The archetypal Hungarian main dish is goulash and there are several versions of the basic thick meat stew. Another Hungarian speciality is pörkölt (a paprika stew very similar to goulash). This stew is made with lean meat such as veal, poultry or fish, with sour cream added at the end of cooking. Almost all meals are eaten with bread; the white wheat variety is particularly delicious.

Food served in bars or bought from street kiosks is a different matter. More akin to fast food, it is often eaten standing up or on the move. Spicy sausages, liberally seasoned with paprika and garlic are served grilled or boiled. Grilled chicken and various smoked meats are also widely available. Another alternative is the delicious lángos (pronounced "langosh"), which is sold at markets. This flat, savoury, yeast cake is served with cream or cheese.

More detailed information on this subject is contained in What to Eat in Budapest on pages 190–91.

Lantern outside the Gerbeaud Cukrászda

VEGETARIAN FOOD

VEGETARIAN cuisine *per se* is not found in abundance in Budapest. There are very few vegetarian restaurants, of which one, the Vegetárium, is recommended in this guide *(see p197)*. Ethnic restaurants may offer a wider vegetarian choice.

Nevertheless, meat-free dishes can be found on most Hungarian menus. *Főzelék*, a vegetable dish that normally accompanies steak, sausage or a hamburger, can be ordered on its own or with egg. *Lecsó (see p191)* is another popular vegetable side dish that makes a substantial meal by itself. Other specialities include *túrós csusza*, a pasta dish served with cottage cheese and sour cream. There are also many sweet and savoury varieties of *palacsinta* (pancake).

RESERVING A TABLE

IN HUNGARY it is customary to join other guests at a table, especially during the busy lunch period. To secure a private table, it is advisable to book in advance. This applies equally to Budapest's exclusive restaurants and cheaper establishments.

MENUS AND PRICES

ALL HUNGARIAN restaurants display a menu by the entrance, and, as a rule, this is translated into English or German. The name of the dish is followed by a brief description. The day's "specials" – a set meal consisting of a soup, a main course and a dessert –

A charming outdoor café on Margaret Island

are listed at the head of the menu. Set menus are often very good value and provide an ideal opportunity to sample several Hungarian specialities.

The prices should also be displayed. If they are not, it is wise to go elsewhere or at least see the prices, including any surcharges, before ordering the meal. The introduction of printed and itemized bills has made it more difficult for hidden "extras" to be added to the final bill.

In most Hungarian restaurants the waiters tend to round up the bill, particularly when serving foreign customers. This practice led to a minor scandal in 1997 when several embassies, including the American and British delegations, compiled a blacklist of dishonest restaurants, after receiving numerous complaints, and published it on the Internet. The government closed the offending establishments and the situation has

now improved. Visitors should still be cautious, however. By selecting a restaurant from those listed in this guide *(see pp196–9)*, this problem should be easily avoided.

TIPPING

IN SOME restaurants a service charge is included in the final bill, in others it is customary to tip. If a service charge is added, this should be stated on either the menu or the bill; this could be up to 15 per cent. However, if there is any doubt, it is courteous to leave a tip. In general, an acceptable tip is between 10–15 per cent of the cost of the meal.

CHILDREN

CHILDREN ARE welcomed in all restaurants without exception. If children's portions do not appear on the menu, the chef will prepare suitable dishes to order. These are usually charged at half price. The only exception is dessert, but this can often be shared. However, the desserts in Hungarian restaurants are so delicious that most children will happily eat a whole portion.

USING THE LISTINGS

🅷🅵	fixed-price menu
V	vegetarian dishes
	outdoor eating
🎵	live music
	good wine list
★	highly recommended
	credit cards accepted:
AE	American Express
DC	Diners Club
JCB	Japanese Credit Bureau
MC	MasterCard
V	VISA

Price categories for a three-course meal with half a bottle of wine, including service:

🅷🅵	under 2,000 HUF
🅷🅵🅷🅵	2,000–3,000 HUF
🅷🅵🅷🅵🅷🅵	3,000–4,000 HUF
🅷🅵🅷🅵🅷🅵🅷🅵	4,000–5,000 HUF
🅷🅵🅷🅵🅷🅵🅷🅵🅷🅵	over 5,000 HUF

The underwater world of the Nautilius Étterem *(see p198)*, in Pest

Budapest's Best: Restaurants and Cafés

BUDAPEST'S restaurants and cafés are a source of pride. Some of the more famous establishments date back to the 19th century and have become part of the city's history, adding to its character and ambience. As well as traditional Hungarian fare, many different styles of cuisine can be found in Budapest. The following restaurants, taken from the list of over 50 establishments on pages 196–201, give a selection of the best the city can offer.

Garvics Vendéglő
This restaurant serves modern international dishes, as well as some unusual Hungarian fare. Located in attractive surroundings, it is one of Budapest's most exclusive restaurants (see p199).

Régi Sipos Halászkert
Good wines and a choice selection of fish dishes, including an excellent fish soup, are on offer here (see p199).

North of the Castle

Castle District

DANUBE

Arc Parli

Szindbád Étterem
A large variety of dishes and excellent desserts are on offer in this formal yet charming restaurant (see p198).

Fortuna Étterem
This restaurant is one of the best to be found in the Castle District. It occupies the cellars of an historic house (see p196).

Gellért Hill and Tabán

| 0 metres | 500 |
| 0 yards | 500 |

Pest Buda Vendéglő
Behind this modest entrance, a selection of Hungarian and international culinary delights awaits the visitor (see p196).

Irén Légrádi Antique Restaurant
Resembling an elegant drawing room, this up-market restaurant is located right in the centre of Pest (see p197).

Gundel Étterem
A house speciality of flambéed pancakes (see p191) is just one of the many mouth-watering dishes that have given the Gundel its international reputation (see p198).

Around Városliget

Central Pest

New York Café
It is worth enjoying a meal or just a coffee in this magnificent Neo-Baroque restaurant (see p201).

Gerbeaud Cukrászda
Established in the 19th century, this pâtisserie has an beautifully decorated Secession interior and serves wonderful cakes (see p201).

Mátyás Pince Étterem
Located in a cellar, this restaurant specializes in meat dishes served on wooden plates. There is also an authentic Gypsy band that plays while diners enjoy their meal (see p197).

What to Eat in Budapest

Hungarian peppers

HUNGARIAN CUISINE is similar to that of its neighbours, Austria, Slovakia and the Czech Republic. However, it does have one unique characteristic: paprika. This spicy pepper can be found in a many robust Hungarian soups and sauces, and is used as a seasoning for meat and fish dishes. Meat, especially pork and beef, forms the basis of the majority of main course dishes, which are served with potatoes or dumplings. Peppers, which until the mid-19th century were used only as a fever remedy, onions and tomatoes are among the most common vegetable accompaniments.

Libamáj Zsirjában
Goose liver, fried in its own fat, is a Hungarian speciality and is considered a great delicacy.

Hortobágyi Palacsinta
Eaten as a hot starter, these pancakes are filled with paprika-seasoned meat and served in a cream sauce.

Jókai Bableves
This thick bean soup contains smoked gammon, sausage and small dumplings.

Halászlé
Carp filets are the main ingredient of this paprika-seasoned fisherman's soup.

Töltött Paprika
These peppers are stuffed with rice and meat and served in a tomato sauce.

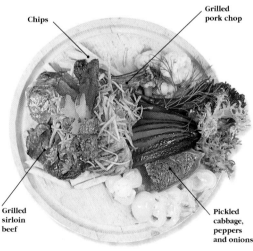

Chips

Grilled pork chop

Grilled sirloin beef

Pickled cabbage, peppers and onions

Borjúpaprikás Galuskával
Pieces of veal in a cream and paprika sauce are served with small flour dumplings.

Fatányéros
This selection of grilled beef and pork is richly garnished with pickles, peppers and chips. It is served in traditional Transylvanian style on a large wooden plate, and each portion is intended for two people. A popular option, fatányéros is available on almost all restaurant menus.

Bélszinszelet Budapest Módra
Sirloin beef steak Budapest-syle is served in a peppery sauce with mushrooms.

Marhapörkölt Tarhonyával
Beef goulash in hot, paprika sauce is often accompanied by soft noodles (tarhonya).

Brassói Aprópecsenye
Pieces of pork, strongly seasoned with garlic and paprika, are stewed and served with fried potatoes.

Bakonyi Sertésborda
A pork chop is served in a creamy mushroom sauce.

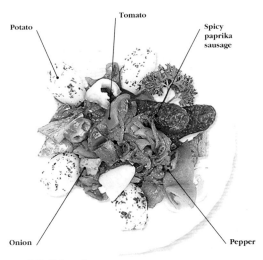

Tomato

Potato

Spicy paprika sausage

Onion

Pepper

Borjúbélszin Gundel Módra
A rich mushroom sauce accompanies these medallions of beef.

Lecsó Kolbásszal
Peppers braised in fat with onions and tomatoes is called lecsó, and provides the basis for many Hungarian dishes. Here it is accompanied by spicy sausages, but it can often be ordered on its own as a vegetable dish.

Gundel Palacsinta
Almond-filled flambéed pancakes are accompanied by a dark chocolate sauce.

Dobos Torta
Delicate slices of sponge cake, layered with a coffee filling, are covered with a golden brown icing.

Rétes
Light French pastry is filled with an apple and raisin, a cherry or a cheese filling, and sprinkled with icing sugar.

What to Drink in Budapest

HUNGARY IS FAMOUS for its excellent wines and, although it is not a big country, it has as many as 13 vine-growing regions. These regions produce all the characteristic wine styles, from *pezsgő* (sparkling wine) and light whites that come from Mátra, near Lake Balaton, to dry reds from Villány or Eger, as well as Tokaji, a distinctive sweet dessert wine. Many wines from different vineyards are matured in a maze of underground of cellars in Budafok. They are all widely available in Budapest's many restaurants, wine bars and wine shops. As well as being a prominent wine producer, Hungary also makes beer, *pálinka* (a drink distilled from different orchard fruits), several types of brandy and a bitter herb liqueur called Unicum.

American-style drinks cabinet

Light Hungarian beers

PÁLINKA

KECSKEMÉT IS the largest region that produces the alcoholic drink *pálinka*, which is distilled from fruit grown in the orchards situated on the Great Hungarian Plain, some 100 km (60 miles) southeast of Budapest. *Pálinka* is a spirit native to Hungary and comes in a variety of flavours including *barack* (apricot) and *cseresznye* (cherry). The best of them, however, is *szilva* (plum) which comes from the Szatmár district and is much favoured by the Hungarians.
Pálinka is not the only spirit indigenous to Hungary. Other examples include Törköly, a spirit distilled from rape, which possesses a very delicate flavour, and Vilmos, a brandy made from Williams pears.

Barack pálinka

SPARKLING WINES

SPARKLING WINE, called *pezsgő* (the Hungarian word for "sparkling"), enjoys a good reputation in Hungary. The classic method of producing these wines was introduced to Hungary from France by József Törley, in 1881. It was Törley *(see p161)* who built

Pezsgő by Törley and Hungaria

the first production plant in Budafok, which continues to produce excellent sparkling wines over 100 years on. Today, Hungary has several other vineyards producing *pezsgő*, mainly concentrated around Budapest, in the Pannonia and Balatonboglár regions. As well as Törley, Hungaria is another good label to look out for.

HUNGARIAN BEERS

IN RECENT YEARS Hungarians have been turning increasingly to beer as their chosen drink as it goes exceptionally well with many traditional, paprika-flavoured Hungarian dishes, goulash among them. There are three remaining authentic Hungarian breweries. These are Arany Ászok, Kőbányai (which was established in the Kőbánya district of Budapest some 150 years ago) and the excellent Dreher. Unfortunately, many other formerly Hungarian breweries have now been taken over by large foreign corporations. However, many of these brands are also well known and all are widely available in Budapest.

HUNGARIAN WINES

THE CHOICE OF good wine available in Hungary has increased dramatically over the past few years. This is thanks to the ever-improving wines being matured in private cellars. The styles currently

One of Budafok's cellars, where wines are aged in barrels

Egri Bikavér, "Bulls' Blood", a full-bodied red wine

A dry white wine from the Budacsona vineyards

favoured by the producers include dry white Chardonnay and Reisling, medium-dry Zödszilváni, Harslevelű and Szürkebarát, medium-sweet Tramini and the aromatic Muskotály, which is produced in Budascona, Balatonboglár, Csopak and Somló.

Among red wines, the dry Kékfrankos, Burgundi, Oportó, Cabernet and Pinot Noir are popular, as is the medium-dry Merlot, which is produced in Silkós, Sopron, Szekszárd, Tihány and Villány.

Another vine-growing district is Eger, which is famous for its aromatic, robust red Egri Leányka and the dry red Egri Bikavér, or "Bulls' Blood", which is produced from a combination of three grape varieties. Other Hungarian wines take their names from their place of origin or the variety of grape from which they are produced.

TOKAJI

THE DESSERT WINE Tokaji has a very different style. Its bouquet and flavour come from a mould that grows only in the fork of the Bodrog and Tisza rivers and the volcanic soil in which the vines grow.

Tokaji ranges from sweet to dry and is full-bodied and rich. Particularly worth sampling is Aszú, which is made with the addition of over-ripe grapes harvested after the first frost. The proportion of these grapes added to the must (grape juice) determines the wine's body and sweetness. The more of these grapes used, the sweeter and richer the Aszú.

Although cheap varieties of Tokaji do exist, they do not share the quality of the genuine article.

UNICUM

FOR OVER 150 years, a blend of 40 Hungarian herbs has been used to create Unicum. The herbs, which are gathered in three separate areas, are combined to produce this bitter liqueur. Unicum can be drunk either as an apéritif before a meal or afterwards as a digestif with coffee.

The recipe has been held by the Zwack family, and remained a secret, since the reign of King Franz I (*see p19*). Originally, Unicum was prescribed as a remedy for the king by the court physician, who was himself a member of the Zwack family.

Unicum herb liqueur

Sweet Tokaji Szamorodni

Dry Tokaji Szamorodni Száraz

Tokaji Aszú, a renowned golden dessert wine

Pear-flavoured Vilmos liqueur

Sisi, an apricot liqueur

Choosing a Restaurant

THIS CHOOSING CHART is designed to show at a glance the location and price range of each establishment, and what facilities they have to offer. More information is given about each in the listings on pages 196–9. The restaurants have been chosen for their atmosphere and service as well as for the quality of the food.

	Price	Fixed-Price Menu	Attractive Location	Outdoor Tables	Live Music	Late Opening	Recommended	Hungarian Specialities
CASTLE DISTRICT *(see p196)*								
Aranyhordó Restaurant	©©	●			●	●		●
Fekete Holló	©©©				●	●		●
Pest Buda Vendéglő	©©©	●	●			●		●
Fortuna Étterem	©©©©	●	●		●	●		●
Alabárdos Étterem	©©©©©	●	●		●	●		●
GELLÉRT HILL & TABÁN *(see p196)*								
Tabáni Kakas Vendéglő	©					●		●
Aranyszarvas	©©	●			●	●	●	●
Citadella Étterem	©©	●			●	●		●
Búsuló Juhász	©©©©	●			●	●	●	●
Casino-Valentine Restaurant	©©©	●	●		●		●	●
NORTH OF THE CASTLE *(see p196)*								
Dunaparti	©	●			●			
Paksi Halászcsárda	©©		●		●	●		
Margitkert Étterem	©©©	●	●		●	●	●	●
AROUND PARLIAMENT *(see p197)*								
Gresham Borozó	©				●		●	●
Tüköry Étterem Söröző	©	●			●			
Barokk Étterem	©©©		●		●			●
Gambrinus Étterem	©©©©	●			●	●	●	●
Szindbád Étterem	©©©©		●				●	●
CENTRAL PEST *(see pp197–8)*								
Fülemüle Étterem	©	●				●		●
Kádár Étkezde	©							●
Alföldi Étterem	©©				●			●
Apostolok Étterem	©©		●		●			●
Duna Corso Étterem	©©	●			●	●		●
Hanna Ortodorkóser Étterem	©©	●	●					●
Kaltenberg Bajor Királyi Söröző	©©		●			●		●
Vegetárium Étterem	©©					●		
Mátyás Pince Étterem	©©©	●	●		●	●	●	●
Fészek Művész Club	©©©©				●	●	●	●
Százéves Étterem	©©©©		●		●	●		●
Irén Légrádi Antique Restaurant	©©©©©		●		●		●	●
Légrádi Testvérek Vendéglője	©©©©©		●			●	●	●
Nautilius Étterem	©©©©©		●		●	●		●
AROUND VÁROSLIGET *(see p198)*								
Media Klub	©	●			●	●		●
Bagolyvár Étterem	©©	●			●		●	●

Price categories for a three-course meal with half a bottle of wine, including service:
- ⓌⒻ under 2,000 HUF
- ⓌⓌ 2,000–3,000 HUF
- ⓌⓌⓌ 3,000–4,000 HUF
- ⓌⓌⓌⓌ 4,000–5,000 HUF
- ⓌⓌⓌⓌⓌ over 5,000 HUF

FIXED-PRICE MENU
Restaurants offering a full dinner, for a fixed price.
ATTRACTIVE LOCATION
Restaurants in unusual or historic settings.
OUTDOOR TABLES
Food can be served outside.
LATE OPENING
Last orders accepted after 11:00pm.

	Price	Fixed-Price Menu	Attractive Location	Outdoor Tables	Live Music	Late Opening	Recommended	Hungarian Specialities
Robinson Restaurant Café	ⓌⓌⓌ	■	●	■	●			■
Gundel Étterem	ⓌⓌⓌⓌⓌ	■	●	■	●		●	■
FURTHER AFIELD *(see pp198–9)*								
Fenyőgyöngye Vendéglő	Ⓦ	■		■	●			■
Söröző a Szent Jupáthoz	Ⓦ	■		■		■		■
Sport Vendéglő	Ⓦ	■		■	●			■
Náncsi Néni Vendéglője	ⓌⓌ		●	■	●			■
Régi Sipos Halászkert	ⓌⓌ		●	■	●		●	■
Borkatakomba Étterem	ⓌⓌⓌ				●			■
Kéhli Vendéglő	ⓌⓌⓌ	■	●	■	●		●	■
Kalocsai Paprika Csárda	ⓌⓌⓌ				●			■
Kisbuda Gyöngye Étterem	ⓌⓌⓌ		●	■	●		●	■
Remíz Kávéház	ⓌⓌⓌ	■	●	■	●	■		■
Garvics Vendéglő	ⓌⓌⓌⓌ		●				●	■
Mágnáskert Restaurant	ⓌⓌⓌⓌ	■	●	■	●		●	■
Udvarház	ⓌⓌⓌⓌ	■	●	■	●		●	■
Vadrózsa Étterem	ⓌⓌⓌⓌ	■	●	■	●		●	■

Aranyhordó Restaurant

Tárnok utca 16. **Map** 1 B4.
(356 13 67. **○** 11am – midnight
daily. ▮▯▮ **V** 🍴 🎵 🍽 MC, V.
🔤🔤

The Aranyhordó inn is one of
the cheapest places to eat in the
Castle District. It is located in a
16th-century house, which once
belonged to a wine merchant who
supplied the royal court. The wine
bar can be found in the old wine
cellar. The walls of the restaurant
are adorned with well-preserved
medieval paintings. The menu
mainly offers Hungarian fish
dishes, and live Gypsy music is
played throughout the evening.

Fekete Holló

Országház utca 10. **Map**1 B4.
(356 23 67. **○** 11am – 11pm
daily. **V** 🍴 🎵 🍽 MC, V. 🔤🔤🔤

The "Black Raven Inn" serves fine
Hungarian specialities including
a selection of fish, game, cheese
and wine. It also offers some
international dishes. This is
a small establishment with a
unique atmosphere.

Pest Buda Vendéglő

Fortuna utca 3. **Map** 1 B4.
(212 58 80. **○** noon – midnight
daily. ▮▯▮ **V** 🎵 🍽 AE, MC, V.
🔤🔤🔤

This luxurious restaurant hides
behind an unassuming exterior.
The extensive menu of Hungarian
and international choices and
good wines will please even the
most discerning gourmet palate,
and all for a very reasonable
price. Traditional Gypsy musicians
provide the entertainment.

Fortuna Étterem

Hess András tér 4. **Map** 1 B4.
(175 68 57. **○** noon – 4pm,
7pm – 1am (kitchen until midnight)
daily. ▮▯▮ **V** 🍴 🎵 🍽 ♟ AE,
JCB, MC, V. 🔤🔤🔤🔤

One of the best-known restaurants
in the Castle District, the Fortuna
is located in a medieval building.
The restaurant occupies two main
areas: the cellar is the most interesting, while the ground floor is
the smartest. In the summer, tables
are also set for dining outside. The
favourite speciality house dishes
are sirloin steak, *shashliks* (kebabs)
and pancakes Fortuna-style. This
restaurant also offers an excellent
choice of Hungarian wines. Live
music and floor shows provide
the evening's entertainment.

Alabárdos Étterem

Országház utca 2. **Map** 1 B4.
(356 08 51. **○** 7 – 11pm Mon –
Sat. ▮▯▮ **V** 🍴 🎵 🍽 AE, DC,
JCB, MC, V. 🔤🔤🔤🔤

Decorated with armour, swords
and halberds, this restaurant serves
Hungarian dishes prepared in a
medieval style. These include flame-
grilled *shashliks* (kebabs), roast
sirloin beef and dishes prepared by
the chef directly at the table. The
Alabárdos has a medieval-style garden, in which an authentic Gothic
atmosphere prevails. A Gypsy band
often plays here.

· GELLÉRT HILL
AND TABÁN

Tabáni Kakas Vendéglő

Attila út 27. **Map** 3 C1. **(** 375 71 65.
○ noon – 11pm daily. **V** 🎵
🍽 AE, MC, V. 🔤

Patrons of the inexpensive and
excellent, though little-known,
Tabáni Kakas inn appreciate its
good food. Authentic Hungarian
poultry dishes, cooked with paprika or a cream and paprika sauce,
are a speciality. Vegetarian options
are also available.

Aranyszarvas

Szarvas tér 1. **Map** 3 C1 – 4 D1.
(375 64 51. **○** May – Sep: noon –
11pm daily; Oct – Apr: 4 – 11pm Mon –
Fri, noon – 11pm Sat & Sun. ▮▯▮ **V**
🍴 🎵 ♟ AE, DC, MC, V. 🔤🔤

This restaurant enjoys a charming
location in the Golden Stag House
(see p95) at the foot of Castle Hill.
Visitors can see the stag that gives
the inn its name over the entrance.
Excellent game dishes, particularly
pörkölt (stew) and the roast venison, are the house specialities. The
cellar houses a pleasant wine bar
with a large selection of wines.

Citadella Étterem

Gellérthegy, Citadella sétány.
Map 4 D3. **(** 466 77 36. **○** May –
Sep: noon – 11pm daily; Oct – Apr:
noon – midnight daily. ▮▯▮ **V** 🍴
🎵 🍽 AE, DC, JCB, MC, V. 🔤🔤

The casements of the Citadel (see
pp92 – 3), built by the Habsburgs,
have been turned into a restaurant.
The Citadella consists of several
spacious rooms and a separate banqueting hall. In summer, tables are
also set so that guests can enjoy a
meal on the outdoor terrace. The
restaurant offers Hungarian and
international cuisine and, for an
extra charge, dinner can be served
on Herend porcelain (see p204).

Búsuló Juhász

Kelenhegyi út 58. **Map** 3 C3.
(209 16 49. **○** noon – midnight
daily. ▮▯▮ **V** 🍴 🎵 🍽 AE, MC, V.
🔤🔤🔤🔤

This restaurant is situated on the
slopes of Gellért Hill and has wonderful views over the southern part
of Buda. Hungarian food, including
some vegetarian shepherds' dishes,
is served here.

Casino-Valentine
Restaurant

Ybl Miklós tér 9 – 11. **Map** 4 D1.
(202 42 44. **○** 7pm – 2am daily.
▮▯▮ **V** 🍴 ♟ ★ 🔤🔤🔤🔤

This exclusive restaurant is one
of Hungary's best. It is situated in
the Neo-Renaissance Várkert Kiosk
(see p95) designed by Miklós Ybl.
Sophisticated international cuisine,
a good wine list and excellent
service all command a high price,
but are worth it to experience a
memorable night out in Budapest.

NORTH OF
THE CASTLE

Dunaparti

Halász utca 1. **Map** 1 C4.
(212 38 17. **○** noon – 11pm
daily. ▮▯▮ **V** 🍴 🔤

This inn, situated on the western
bank of Danube and overlooking
Pest, offers simple yet hearty meals
of fish or meat and a wide choice
of vegetable dishes. It is very
popular with local people.

Paksi Halászcsárda

Margit körút 14. **Map** 1 B2.
(212 55 99. **○** noon – midnight
daily. **V** 🍴 🎵 🍽 AE. 🔤🔤

This fisherman's *csárda* (small inn),
with its stylish setting, is near to
Margaret Bridge. It offers several
fish soups, including an exceptionally hot variety, which is eaten
with dumplings to dilute the taste.
A Gypsy band plays here.

Margitkert Étterem

Margit utca 15. **Map** 1 B1.
(326 08 60. **○** noon – midnight
daily. ▮▯▮ **V** 🍴 🎵 ★ 🍽 AE, DC,
MC, V. 🔤🔤

Located in a traditional house, this
restaurant is just a short walk from
Margaret Bridge (see pp62 – 3). It
offers wonderful Hungarian cuisine, which includes platters of
cold meats such as garlic sausage,
salami and bacon, as well as the
characteristic goulash and *palacsinta* (pancakes).

AROUND PARLIAMENT

Gresham Borozó

Mérleg utca 2. **Map** 2 D5.
[317 44 45. ◯ 7am–10pm
Mon–Fri, 8am–4pm Sun. V 🔲 ★
🍴 AE, DC, JCB, MC, V. (LP)

This is an excellent restaurant
with low prices, quick service and
a menu that changes daily. The
splendid food includes mushrooms
fried in breadcrumbs, goulash,
pörkölt (stew) and pancakes with
sheep's cheese and dill. Good,
inexpensive wines are available.

Tüköry Étterem Söröző

Hold utca 15. **Map** 2 E4.
[269 50 27. ◯ 11am–midnight
Mon–Fri. ● public hols. 🍴 V
🔲 🍴 MC, V. (LP)

Although regarded as a beer house,
this small inn also offers tasty, inexpensive food. Specialities include
sausage soup and Hungarian-style
meat cutlets served with *lecsó* (see
p191). Dreher beer is served in
tankards, and seating is in booths
or at long tables. It is always busy
but worth the wait for a table.

Barokk Étterem

Mozsár utca 12. **Map** 2 F4.
[331 89 42. ◯ noon–midnight
daily. V 🔲 🍴 AE, JCB, MC, V.
(LP)(LP)(LP)

This elegant restaurant lives up to
its name not only with its Baroque
interior but also with its cuisine. The
owner has collected many recipes
created by an 18th-century aristo-
crat, Count Radvánszky, and
included them on the menu. Hence,
many of the dishes have unusual
names and are also liberally flavoured with a variety of herbs.

Gambrinus Étterem

Váci utca 20. **Map** 7 A1.
[338 41 99.◯ 7pm–midnight
daily. 🍴 V 🔲 🎵 ★ 🍴 AE, DC,
JCB, MC, V. (LP)(LP)(LP)

This smart, Parisian-style restaurant
has catered for state receptions for
Queen Elizabeth II of the United
Kingdom and Russian president
Boris Yeltsin. Diners can expect
to be served by waiters wearing
tail coats and white cotton gloves.

Szindbád Étterem

Markó utca 33. **Map** 2 E3.
[332 29 66. ◯ 11:30am–3:30pm,
4:30–midnight Mon–Fri, 6pm–
midnight Sat & Sun. V ★ 🍴 AE,
DC, JCB, MC, V. (LP)(LP)(LP)(LP)

The Szindbád is a formal restaurant
offering Europeanized Hungarian
cuisine. Of its many original and
stylishly presented dishes, the hot
consommé served with toast is
particularly worth trying. This restaurant is one of the most exclusive and expensive in Hungary.

CENTRAL PEST

Fülemüle Étterem

Kőfaragó utca 5. **Map** 7 B3.
[266 78 80. ◯ 11am–11pm
Mon–Fri, 11am–6pm Sat & Sun.
🍴 V 🎵 🍴 DC, V. (LP)

This small inn, with its enormous
menu, can be found in the narrow
streets behind the Hungarian
National Museum (see pp130–33).
Goose livers, a Hungarian delicacy,
are served here, prepared in a
variety of ways. A Gypsy band
often plays in the evenings.

Kádár Étkezde

Klauzál tér 9. **Map** 7 A2.
[321 36 22. ◯ 11:30am–3:30pm
Tue–Sat. (LP)

This tiny restaurant has a simple
interior with white kitchen tables
set with old-fashioned soda siphons.
The walls are hung with photographs of famous patrons, including
Hungarian sports and arts personalities. On Saturdays, the best
czulent in Budapest is served, and
it is often difficult to find a table.

Alföldi Étterem

Kecskeméti utca 4. **Map** 4 F2.
[267 02 24. ◯ 11am–11pm daily.
V 🔲 (LP)(LP)

This small restaurant serves tasty
Hungarian food, including dishes
from the Debrecen *puszta*. The delicious *alföldi* (a mutton goulash)
takes the restaurant's name and is a
popular choice. The large helpings
and low prices mean that the house
specials go very quickly. The pep-
pered *pogácsa* (a heavy savoury
bread) is especially tasty and is
well complemented by a light or
dark Hungarian beer (see p192).

Apostolok Étterem

Kígyó utca 4–6. **Map** 4 E1.
[267 02 90. ◯ noon–11pm daily.
V 🔲 🍴 AE, JCB, MC. (LP)(LP)

The Apostolok restaurant has an
intimate atmosphere and a very
good menu. Here guests can enjoy
such delicacies as *paté de foie gras*,
as well as tasty soups and desserts
such as flambéed pancakes. The
restaurant takes its name from the
woodcarvings of the 12 Apostles
that hang above the alcoves. It is
advisable to book a table for dinner.

Duna Corso Étterem

Vigadó tér 3. **Map** 4 D1.
[267 02 62. ◯ noon–midnight
daily. 🍴 V 🔲 🎵 🍴 AE, DC, JCB,
MC, V. (LP)(LP)

Situated on the eastern bank of
Danube, the Duna Corso attracts
people with its good food and its
view of the Royal Palace (see pp70
–71). The Hungarian favourite of
pörkölt (stew) with dumplings is
served here as well as the Austrian
speciality Wienner schnitzel, which
is popular with the restaurant's
many German-speaking patrons.

Hanna Ortodorkóser Étterem

Dob utca 35. **Map** 7 A2.
[342 10 72. ◯ 11am–4pm daily.
🍴 V (LP)(LP)

This kosher restaurant occupies
part of the Orthodox Synagogue in
the Jewish Quarter (see p134). The
Hanna serves excellent food, but is
open only for lunch. Its clientele
consists mainly of Orthodox Jews,
and men are requested to cover
their heads. A skullcap will be
offered to men not suitably attired.

Kaltenberg Bajor Királyi Söröző

Kinizsi utca 30–36. **Map** 7 A5.
[215 97 92. ◯ noon–midnight
daily. V 🎵 🍴 AE, DC, JCB, MC, V.
(LP)(LP)

This attractively furnished Bavarian
beer cellar is located close to the
Museum of Applied Arts (see
pp136–7). It offers a rich choice
of Hungarian and German cuisine
to complement the Hungarian and
Bavarian beer. Servings are huge,
and the platters for two include
pork cooked in beer. Advanced
booking is recommended.

Vegetárium Étterem

Cukor utca 3. **Map** 4 F2.
[267 03 22. ◯ noon–10pm daily.
V 🎵 🍴 AE, JCB, MC, V. (LP)(LP)

This is one of the few vegetarian
restaurants in Budapest. Particularly recommended is the *hamis
gulyás* – a potato dish with an
authentic Hungarian flavour.

Mátyás Pince Étterem

Március 15 tér 7. **Map** 4 E1.
[318 16 93. ◯ 6am–1am daily.
🍴 V 🔲 🎵 🍴 AE, DC, JCB,
MC, V. (LP)(LP)(LP)

For many years Budapest's smartest
restaurant, the Mátyás Pince's interior features stained-glass windows
that depict episodes from the reign
of King Mátyás Corvinus (see p18).
The menu offers Hungarian

dishes, including Serbian-style *Dorozsma* carp, as well as Transylvanian platters, laden with cooked meats, serving two people. Although the restaurant has maintained its beautiful interior, the standard of cuisine and service do not match their former standards.

Fészek Művész Club

Kertész utca 36. **Map** 7 A2.
[322 60 43.] noon–1am daily.
V 🔲 🎵 ★ 🗐 AE, V. 🆎🆎🆎🆎

The house specialities in this restaurant, belonging to the Actors' Club, include duck braised in red wine and served with a spicy sauce, and chicken fried in breadcrumbs. The inner courtyard garden, lit with old-fashioned gas lamps, provides a particularly pleasant setting.

Százéves Étterem

Pesti Barnabas utca 2. **Map** 4 E1.
[267 02 88.] noon–midnight daily. 🔲 🎵 ★ 🗐 AE, DC, JCB, MC, V. 🆎🆎🆎🆎

Located in the Péterffy Palace *(see p122)*, the oldest secular Baroque building in the city, this restaurant was established in 1831. Its rooms are furnished with antiques and seat over 100 diners. The menu offers Hungarian and international cuisine, including good fish and game options, in particular the delicious venison cutlet with cranberries.

Irén Légrádi Antique Restaurant

Bárczy István utca 3–5. **Map** 2 E5.
[266 49 93.] noon–3pm, 7pm–midnight Mon–Fri, 7pm–midnight Sat. V 🎵 ★ 🗐 AE, DC, JCB, MC, V. 🆎🆎🆎🆎

This smart restaurant is entered through an antique shop owned by the restaurateur Irén Légrádi. The antique furniture and table settings recreate the ambience of an elegant French drawing room. The menu includes fish, lobster, various meat dishes, desserts and excellent wines, and pleases even the most sophisticated of palates. In recent years, the restaurant has been acclaimed as the best in Hungary.

Légrádi Testvérek Vendéglője

Magyar utca 23. **Map** 4 F2.
[318 68 04.] 6pm–midnight Mon–Sat. V 🎵 ★ 🗐 AE, MC, V. 🆎🆎🆎🆎

At the end of the 1980s the Légrádi brothers opened another small restaurant, again serving fine cuisine. Its customers can enjoy superb Hungarian and international food, which is eaten from the finest porcelain plates using silver cutlery.

Nautilus Étterem

Váci utca 72. **Map** 4 F2. [338 48 30.
] 11:30am–12:30pm daily. 🔲 🗐 AE, DC, JCB, MC, V. 🆎🆎🆎🆎🆎

This exclusive and unusual restaurant is arranged in the manner of Captain Nemo's submarine from the novel *Ten Thousand Leagues Under the Sea* by Jules Verne and creates the impression of an underwater world. A rich selection of sea food and fish dishes, such as creamed fish with oranges, spiny lobster in garlic, lobster beer pie and caviar on toast, can be enjoyed here.

AROUND VÁROSLIGET

Media Klub

Andrássy út 101. **Map** 5 B5.
[322 16 39.] noon–midnight Mon–Sat, noon–4pm Sun. 🍴 V 🔲 🎵 🗐 AE, DC, MC, V.

This low-priced complex includes a café, a restaurant and a beer house. The Media Klub is set in the garden of the Hungarian Journalists' House and is also frequented by well-known politicians and artists. The restaurant has an extensive menu that offers almost every kind of Hungarian food.

Bagolyvár Étterem

Allatkerti út 2. **Map** 5 C3.
[351 63 95.] noon–11pm daily. 🍴 🔲 🎵 ★ 🗐 AE, DC, V. 🆎🆎

Located next door to the famous Gundel restaurant, the Bagolyvár attracts its own clientele with its good food and charming garden. Its reasonable prices are much lower than those of its neighbour, which is another appealing feature of this restaurant. The all-female staff provide friendly service.

Robinson Restaurant Café

Városliget. **Map** 5 C3. [343 09 55.
] noon–4pm, 6pm–midnight daily. 🍴 V 🔲 🎵 🗐 AE, DC, JCB, MC, V. 🆎🆎🆎

The Robinson is set on a tiny island at the northern end of the lake in Városliget *(see pp142–3)*. It occupies a light, two-floor pavilion, which has a pretty waterside terrace from which patrons can enjoy a view of Vajdahunyad Castle *(see p150)*. The menu offers a huge selection of Hungarian dishes, prepared with a French twist, and fine wines. Once one of the most popular restaurants in Budapest, its famous guests have included the rock star David Bowie and the film actor Arnold Schwarzenegger.

Gundel Étterem

Allatkerti út 2. **Map** 5 C3.
[321 35 50.] noon–4pm, 6:30pm–midnight daily. 🍴 V 🔲 🎵 ★ 🗐 AE, DC, JCB, MC, V. 🆎🆎🆎🆎

This renowned restaurant was established as the Wampetics in 1894. In 1910 it was taken over by chef Károly Gundel, originally from Bavaria, who renamed it. During its long history the Gundel has introduced into Hungarian cuisine such specialities as *Zander Gundel-style* and flambéed pancakes with an almond filling covered in chocolate sauce *(Gundel palacsinta, see p192)*. The delicate and delicious paprika goulashes and excellent meat dishes flavoured with a variety of herbs have a distinctive French accent. The Gundel also has perhaps the most extensive selection of wines in Hungary. This excellent cuisine is served in a magnificent historic building.

FURTHER AFIELD

Fenyőgyöngye Vendéglő

Szépvölgyi út 155. [325 97 83.
] noon–11pm daily 🍴 V 🔲 🎵 🗐 AE, DC, JCB, MC, V. 🆎🆎

This friendly, homely inn is situated on a road leading into the Buda Hills and offers Hungarian dishes. It serves particularly delicious traditional meat dishes and pancakes. In the summer, it is pleasant to sit on the terrace and enjoy the greenery of the garden.

Söröző a Szent Jupáthoz

Retek utca 16. **Map** 1 A3.
[212 29 23.] 24 hours daily.
🍴 V 🔲 🆎

Culinary creations, dominated by the distinct flavours of paprika and garlic, are served in huge portions and accompanied by low prices. The menu includes tasty soups, strips of roast pork a la Brassó, veal cutlets fried in breadcrumbs, pork knuckle for two people and many desserts.

Sport Vendéglő

Csömöri út 154. [405 33 64.
] 10am–10pm Tue–Sun. 🍴 🔲 🎵 🗐

This is considered to be one of the best restaurants in Budapest and is worth the trip to the suburb of Rákosszentmihály. The restaurant offers a vast selection of dishes, particularly poultry. A rare delicacy of cock's combs and testicles, fried in breadcrumbs, or served in the form of a paprika goulash, is on the menu. Added to this are a large selection of wines, splendid service and very affordable prices.

Náncsi Néni Vendéglője

Ördögárok utca 80. **C** *397 27 42.*
○ *noon – 11pm daily.* **V** 🏢 🎵
🍽 *AE, MC, V.* 🈯🈯

It is worth the trip to the Hűvös Valley *(see p161)*, in the outskirts of Buda, to enjoy a good meal in this charming inn. The surroundings are homely, with kitchen dressers full of old appliances and tables covered with chequered cloths. Particulary good dishes from their traditional menu are the bean goulash, ham pasta, hot *lecsó* and giant cheese dumplings, although all dishes are of a good standard and are charged at reasonable prices.

Régi Sipos Halászkert

Lajos utca 46. **C** *368 64 80.*
○ *noon – midnight daily.* 🏢 🎵 ★
🍽 *AE, DC, JCB, MC, V.* 🈯🈯

This is the best fish restaurant in Budapest and boasts a 100-year-old tradition of preparing boneless fish soup. Its owner, Károly Sipos, was the first chef to fillet the carp for the soup, and to this day they serve the best fish soup in town. Fresh fish are often brought to the table before cooking, so that the guests may choose the best looking specimen. The restaurant has been recently refurbished and tables are available in the garden during the summer. There is a Gypsy band that plays all year round.

Borkatakomba Étterem

Nagytétényi út 64. **C** *226 09 97.*
○ *10am – midnight daily.*
V 🎵 🍽 🍽 *AE, V.* 🈯🈯

This unique and moderately priced restaurant occupies one of Budafok's wine cellars *(see p192)*. The Borkatakomba offers traditional Hungarian cuisine, and meals are eaten at tables with benches, which are are actually set inside huge wine barrels. There is a great atmosphere, particularly when the Gypsy band is playing. As one would expect from such a location, there is also an excellent wine list.

Kéhli Vendéglő

Mókus utca 22. **C** *250 42 41.*
○ *5pm – midnight daily Mon – Fri, noon – midnight Sat & Sun.* 🍴 **V**
🏢 🎵 ★ 🍽 *AE, JCB, MC, V.* 🈯🈯🈯

This is the restaurant where Gyula Krúdy *(see p171)* used to eat. Krúdy is one of Hungary's best-loved 20th-

century writers but is little-known outside the country. The menu therefore features several dishes named after him, including *roast a la Krúdy*, which is heavily flavoured with garlic. Particularly recommended is a bone marrow soup – a consommé flavoured with saffron and pepper and consisting of vegetables, mushrooms and a chunk of beef bone, which is served with garlic toast. Some of the best traditional Hungarian dishes in Budapest are served at the Kéhli, and they are available at reasonable prices. It is advisable to book in advance as the main dining room fills up quickly.

Kalocsai Paprika Csárda

Bláthy Ottó utca 13–15. **C** *333 59 72.*
○ *noon – midnight Mon – Sat.* 🎵
🈯🈯🈯

The best Hungarian peppers come from the Kalocsa region and this *csárda* (small inn) uses this homegrown variety exclusively. The interior of the restaurant has been decorated with patterns and laces from the same Kalocsa region. There are also folk dancers, who treat customers to a lively display of the Hungarian national dance.

Kisbuda Gyöngye Étterem

Kenyeres utca 34. **C** *368 64 02.*
○ *noon – midnight Mon – Sat.* **V**
🏢 🎵 ★ 🍽 *AE, DC, MC, V.*
🈯🈯

This restaurant in Óbuda is not only a gourmet but an aesthetic delight. The interior is carefully fitted with old furniture in the style of a drawing room. The Kisbuda Gyöngye has a wide selection of food and wine on offer. The venison fillet with wild mushrooms in a brandy sauce is especially good. This restaurant invariably ranks highly among the city's top culinary establishments.

Remíz Kávéház

Budakeszi út 5. **C** *275 13 96.*
○ *noon – midnight Mon – Sat.* 🍴
V 🏢 🎵 🍽 *AE, DC, MC, V.*
🈯🈯🈯

This smart restaurant-cum-bar has a very pleasant atmosphere and a secluded garden, which is the venue for summer barbecues. The locals visit the Remíz for its roasted ribs, grilled meats and draught beer. Another attraction is the Russian caviar, which is the cheapest to be found in Budapest. It also offers a good selection of vegetable dishes and a wide choice of salads, as well as delicious desserts. Discrete piano music is played.

Garvics Vendéglő

Ürömi köz 2. **C** *326 38 78.*
○ *noon – midnight Mon – Fri.*
V ★ 🍽 *AE, DC, JCB, MC, V.*
🈯🈯

This restaurant is considered to be the new star of Budapest's restaurant scene. It offers dishes that are new to Hungary, including choices such as salmon mousse and crab. The service is excellent, but the prices are high. Due to its exclusive reputation, this restaurant has become a favourite haunt of Budapest's wealthy elite and visiting foreign business people.

Mágnáskert Étterem

Csatárka út 58. **C** *325 99 67.*
○ *noon – midnight daily.* **Bar**
○ *6pm – 3am daily.* 🍴🈯 **V** 🏢 🎵
🍷 ★ 🍽 *CD, MC, V.* 🈯🈯🈯🈯

This recently built, luxurious restaurant, which has both wine cellars and terraces, stands on top of Rózsadomb. It enjoys a beautiful setting in a picturesque garden and offers discrete elegance and comfort. There is an enormous selection of fine food and drink, and the champagne bar stays open late. The prices at this top class establishment are high.

Udvarház

Hármashatárhegyi út 2. **C** *388 69 21.*
○ *Apr – Oct: 11am – 11pm daily; Nov – Mar: 6pm – 11pm Mon – Fri, 11am – 11pm Sat & Sun.* 🍴🈯 **V** 🏢 🎵 ★
🍽 *AE, Dc, JCB, MC, V.* 🈯🈯🈯🈯

Standing on a peak in the Buda Hills is the Udvarház. It specializes in game and fish, and has a magnificent view over Budapest. Here, patrons can also enjoy Hungarian music, have a dance or just relax in the terrace café with a coffee.

Vadrózsa Étterem

Pentelei Molnár utca 15. **C** *326 58 17.*
○ *noon – 3pm, 7pm – midnight daily.*
● *last 2 weeks of Jul & Dec.*
🍴🈯 **V** 🏢 🎵 ★ 🍽 *AE, DC, JCB, MC, V.* 🈯🈯🈯

This restaurant is situated in one of three small, picturesque villas half way up Rózsadomb. It is entered through a garden, which is full of roses in the summer and beautifully floodlit at night. Although now past its best, the Vadrózsa still produces its rich cuisine in an unconventional way. Instead of choosing from a written menu, diners are asked to select the raw ingredients, which can include goose liver, wild boar, venison and caviar, and these are then prepared by the chef. The ambience of the restaurant is added to by the playing of a pianist.

Cafés, Wine Bars and Beer Houses

To sample the true atmosphere of Hungary, it is essential to visit the smaller eating and drinking establishments that are scattered across the city and into the suburbs. Behind even the most ordinary of buildings there could be hiding a timeless pocket of old Hungarian culture. Equally, bright neon and loud music signify the culture favoured by Budapest's contemporary youth. Between these extremes, visitors can also find a taste of 19th-century opulence in the old coffee houses and patisseries that were once at the heart of the city's life.

CAFÉS AND COFFEE HOUSES

Hungary has one of the oldest coffee-drinking traditions in Europe. Introduced to Hungary by the Turks during their occupation (see pp26–7), the coffee culture blossomed towards the end of the Habsburg era (see pp32–3), when there were almost 600 kávéházes in the city.

The 19th-century café scene was a hotbed of intellectual activity dominated by literary and artistic circles. The **New York Café** (see p129), which opened in 1894, was for many years the centre of this creative scene; its walls were even adorned with frescoes painted by the leading artists of the day. And it was at the former Café Pilvax that the seeds of the uprising of 1848–9 (see pp30 –31) were first sown.

Today's café scene is much changed. Almost every luxurious cukrászda and kávéház has closed down, giving way to a new variety of coffee bar. Eszpresszó bars first appeared in the 1930s but were most popular in the 1960s. Much cheaper than their predecessors, they catered for teenagers with a taste for western culture. These have subsequently been replaced by more modern cafés, such as **Talk Talk**.

There are many styles of coffee in Budapest. A kávé is an espresso with milk and sugar, and a dupla is a double espresso. French-style milky coffee is called a tejeskávé, while cappuccinos are often served with whipped cream or Viennese-style, without either chocolate or cinnamon. Order a koffeinmentes for a decaffeinated coffee.

WINE BARS

Wine and wine bars occupy a very different positon in the social hierarchy in Hungary than they do in, say, Britain or the United States. Whereas the latter regard wine drinking as something of a middle-class pursuit, it was considered a workers' pastime in Hungary. Despite the fact that young men are starting to adopt beer as their favoured drink, the old tradition of wine-drinking is still reflected today in the borozó in Budapest.

A borozó is an unglamorous, cheap wine cellar, where wine is served straight from the barrel and sold by the decilitre. Few places have tables and chairs. The **Grotta** is a charming example of such a bar, which serves a selection of Hungarian dishes at good prices. In the city centre there is the stylish **Rondella Borbár**, where wine is drawn from the barrels and served in curious jugs with a tap at the bottom.

The Castle District is home to a range of borozós. The Hattyú, meaning "Swan", at No. 1 Hattyú utca, and the Varfok Borozó, at No. 9 Varfok utca are of the simple kind. At the other end of the spectrum, the **Fortuna Restaurant** (see p196), the **Alabárdos Étterem** (see p196) and the **Hilton Hotel** (see p182) have stylish wine bars located in authentic medieval cellars. Such establishments tend to serve expensive, bottled wine rather than wine from a barrel.

Tokaji (see p193) also has a number of wine bars dedicated to it. The best is found in **Tokaji Borozó**, at No. 20 Andrássy út, where customers drink standing up.

BEER HOUSES

In recent years, beer has become very popular in Hungary. It is beginning to take over from wine as the favoured drink. Driven by this fashion, many wine bars have now been turned into beer houses, called sörözős. Several new places have also opened, modelled on the German bierstube and the English pub. As a result of this, beer-drinking in Budapest is considered an aspirational pastime, and prices are much higher than in borozós, especially in popular tourist areas.

As well as Hungarian világos (light) and barna (dark) beers (see p192), it is now possible to get virtually all the major international brands. Beer is measured by the korsó, the equivalent of a pint, and the pohár, a smaller glass. Sörözős differ from borozós as they offer a variety of good and moderately priced snacks and hot dishes, including smoked knuckle. Also, a söröző will serve wine, while a borozó would never serve beer.

FOOD AND CUSTOMS

Wine bars, where people can pop in for a glass of wine or a spritzer (see p193) at any time of day, do not generally serve food. Occasionally, however, light snacks are available. Typically these consist of a slice of bread and dripping with raw onion, sprinkled with paprika, or pogácsa, a yeast pan-bread with crackling, cheese, caraway seeds or paprika. Wine bars with tables sometimes serve frankfurters or knuckle.

It is extremely rare to see a woman in a wine bar, and those who do attend will always be accompanied by a man. It is wise to follow this custom rather than attract unwanted attention. An acceptable "women's drink" is a small glass of wine or spritzer.

When in Hungary, it is not done to clink beer glasses. This seemingly innocent practice was adopted by the Austrians as they executed Hungarian generals after the uprising of 1848–9, and is frowned upon.

DIRECTORY

CASTLE DISTRICT

Cafés
Pierrot
Fortuna utca 14.
Map 1 B4. 375 65 71.
11am–1am daily.

Ruszwurm Cukrászda
Szentháromság utca 7.
Map 1 B4. 375 52 84.
10am–10pm daily.

Wine Bars
Fehér Galamb
Szentháromság utca 9–11.
Map 1 B4. 375 69 75.
noon–midnight daily.

Gretta
Táncsics Mihály utca 10.
Map 1 B4. 155 91 89.
11am–11pm daily.

Móri Borozó
Fiáth János utca 16.
Map 1 A3. 214 92 16.
2–11pm Mon–Sat,
2–9pm Sun.

Beer Houses
Budavári
Hess András tér 4.
Map 1 B5. 375 61 75.
10am–10pm daily.

GELLÉRT HILL AND TABÁN

Wine Bars
Egri Gödör Borozó
Villányi út 4.
Map 4 D5. 466 73 94.
10am–10pm Mon–Fri.

NORTH OF THE CASTLE

Wine Bars
Bástya Borozó
Székely utca 2–4.
Map 1 C4. 212 38 19.
10am–10pm daily.

Kékfrankos Borozó
Keleti Károly utca 4.
Map 1 A2.
212 53 86. 6
10am–9pm daily.

Pincecsárda
Török utca 1.
Map 1 B1. 212 45 08.
11am–10pm Mon–Fri.

Vincellér Borozó
Erőd utca 10.
Map 1 B3. 201 15 61.
10am–6pm Mon–Fri,
5pm–midnight Sat.

Beer Houses
Alagút
Alagút utca 4.
Map 1 B5. 212 37 64.
24 hours daily.

AROUND PARLIAMENT

Cafés
Anna Café
Váci utca 7.
Map 4 E1. 266 90 80.
8:30am–
midnight daily.

Café Firenze
Szalay utca 5a.
Map 2 E3.
331 83 99.
9am–9pm daily.

Művész Cukrászda
Andrássy út 29.
Map 2 F4. 352 13 37.
9am–midnight daily.

Wine Bars
Tokaji Borozó
Falk Miksa utca 32.
Map 2 D2. 269 31 43.
noon–10pm Mon–Fri,
4pm–11pm Sat.

Beer Houses
Tóth Kocsma
Falk Miksa utca 17.
Map 2 D2.
302 40 20.
11am–11pm daily.

CENTRAL PEST

Cafés
Auguszt Cukrászda
Kossuth Lajos utca 14–16.
Map 4 F1.
316 89 31.
10am–6pm Tue–Fri,
10am–2pm Sat.

Café Károlyi
Károlyi Mihály utca 19.
Map 4 F2. 267 02 06.
9am–1am daily.

Café Mozart
Erzsébet körút 36.
Map 7 B2. 352 06 64.
9am–11pm Sun–Fri,
9am–12am Sat.

Söröző a Szent Jupáthoz
Retek utca 16.
Map 1 A3. 212 29 23.
24 hours daily.

Gerbeaud Cukrászda
Vörösmarty tér 7.
Map 2 E5. 318 13 11.
9am–9pm daily.

New York Kávéház
Erzsébet körút 9–11.
Map 7 B2. 322 38 49.
9am–10pm daily.

Talk Talk
Magyar utca 12–14.
Map 4 F1. 317 45 13.
24 hours daily.

Grinzingi Borozó
Veres Pálné utca 10.
Map 4 F2.
317 46 24.
9am–1am Mon–Sat,
3pm–11pm Sun.

Rondella Borozó
Regiposta utca 4.
Map 4 E1. 267 02 87.
noon–midnight daily.

Villányi-Siklósi Borozó
Gerlóczy utca 13.
Map 4 F1.
267 02 41.
6am–11pm Mon–Fri.

Beer Houses
Aranyászok
József nádor tér 12.
Map 2 E5.
317 00 54.
11am–11pm daily.

Astoria Hotel Bar
Kossoth Lajos utca 19.
Map 4 F1.
317 34 11.
7am–11pm daily.

Bécsi Söröző
Papnövelde utca 8.
Map 4 F2. 267 02 25.
10am–10pm Mon–
Fri, 10am–4pm Sat & Sun.

Fregatt
Molnár utca 26.
Map 4 E2. 318 99 97.
11am–11pm daily.

Gösser
Régiposta utca 4.
Map 4 E1. 318 26 08.
11am–11pm.

Beckett's Irish Pub
Bajcsy Zsilinszky út 72.
Map 2 E3. 269 10 64.
noon–2am daily.

AROUND VÁROSLIGET

Cafés
Lukács Café
Andrássy út 70.
Map 5 A5. 302 87 47.
9am–8pm daily.

Beer Houses
Liget
Állatkerti út 8.
Map 5 C3. 321 10 27.
11am–10pm daily.

Bajor Sörsátor
Kós Károly sétany.
Map 6 D3. 343 15 04.
10am–11pm daily.

FURTHER AFIELD

Wine Bars
Vidog Borozó
Lajos utca 98.
388 83 14. noon–
11pm Mon–Thu, noon–
midnight Fri–Sun.

John Bull Pub
Apáczai Csere János utca
17. **Map** 2 D5.
338 21 68.
noon–11pm daily.

Badacsonyi Borozó
Károlyi István utca 24 .
Map 4 F2.
370 42 61.
6am–9pm Mon–Fri.

SHOPS AND MARKETS

SHOPPING IN BUDAPEST has changed dramatically since the more spartan days of Communism. A huge variety of consumer goods, both foreign and home produced, are now available here. Major shopping streets include the pedestrianized and fashionable Váci utca (Váci Street, *see p127*) good for folk art and Zsolnay porcelain, and the less fashionable, but much cheaper

String of paprika peppers

Nagykörút, where locals come to do their shopping. For a more traditional shopping experience, don't miss a visit to some of Budapest's many markets. These range from stunning 19th-century food halls such as the Great Market Hall (Nagy Vásárcsarnok), to flea markets such as the huge and lively Ecseri Flea Market, for everything from bric-a-brac to furniture and antiques.

OPENING HOURS

MOST SHOPS in Budapest open from 9am to 5:30 or 6pm Monday to Friday, and from 9am to 1pm on Saturday. Department stores open at 10am, while green-grocers, bakeries and super-markets are open from 7am until 8pm. Many shops stay open until 8 or 9pm on Thursday, closing for an hour at lunchtime. Indoor markets and department stores open on Sunday, and most cafés sell milk and bread on Sunday morning. One result of the increase in private enterprise since 1989 is a large number of small shops which open 24 hours a day and sell groceries, cigarettes and alcohol.

Duna Plaza Shopping Centre on Váci út

HOW TO PAY

CREDIT CARDS and Euro-cheques can be used to pay for goods and services in many of the more touristy parts of Budapest. Outside these areas it is best to carry plenty of cash in Hungarian forints.

VAT EXEMPTION

THE PRICE OF ALL goods in Hungary includes a value-added tax of 25% (ÁFA). With the exception of works of art and antiques, it is possible to claim back the value-added tax on anything costing more than 50,000 forints when you leave the country. First, present your goods at customs within 90 days of purchase to receive your customs certification and a refund claim form. You will need your sales receipt and currency exchange or credit card receipt, plus the customs certification, to apply for your refund within 183 days of your return home.

DEPARTMENT STORES AND MALLS

THERE ARE A number of department stores in the city, many housed in spec-tacular old buildings. The Secession-style **Luxus** on Vörösmarty tér offers three floors of smart men's and women's clothing, as well as accessories and perfumes. Nearby on Váci út, the **Fontana** is a slightly down-

Traditional folk crafts, on sale around Váci utca

market version of the Luxus, selling clothing, luggage and children's toys, and with an excellent rooftop café.

More of a mall than a department store, the **Duna Plaza** on Váci út is smart but overpriced. Gleaming with glass and nickel, the Duna Plaza is equipped with an ice-skating rink, a video arcade and a bowling alley. The now refurbished **Corvin** on Blaha Lujzha tér is the closest you can get to the kitsch treasure troves of the Communist era. Shoes and clothes here are Hungarian-made and offer fantastic value. The old-fashioned payment system involves taking an invoice and paying at a booth before going to claim your purchase. Other popular stores worth a look include the busy **Skála Metro** on Nyugati tér opposite the railway station, and on Flórián tér in Óbuda.

Sausages on sale at the Central Market Hall

huge variety of vegetables, fruit, meat and cheese, under a gleaming roof of brightly-coloured Zsolnay tiles. The market opens from 7am–6pm Mon–Fri and 7am–1pm Sat.

In addition to the covered market halls, there are open-air food markets in every Budapest neighbourhood. In many you will see country women in traditional costumes selling fruit and vegetables, as well as local cheeses, honey and sausages. Some of the best markets are at Lehel tér (district XIII), Bosnyák tér (XIV) and Fehérvári út (IX). Delicious hot sausages with mustard and fresh bread, or *lángos*, a flat bread served with cream or grated cheese, are traditional and widely available market snacks.

Beginning at 156 Nagykőrösi út in district XIX, is the **Écseri Flea Market**. Outside, a maze of wooden tables is covered in Communist artifacts, second-hand clothes and all sorts of bric-a-brac, while from tiny cubicles inside the market, serious antique dealers sell porcelain, icons, silverware, jewellery and much more. It is necessary to obtain permission from the Museum of Applied Arts *(see pp136–7)* before you can take antiques out of the country. The flea market is open 8am–3:30pm Mon–Fri and 8am–2pm Sat.

Another market well worth a visit is the extremely busy **Józsefvárosi Market**, situated close to Józsefváros pu on Kőbányai út and open 7am–6pm daily. Many of the traders here are Chinese, often with Roma assistants, using the Trans-Siberian railway to transport a huge variety of new goods from China, southeast Asia, the former Soviet Union and eastern Europe, all sold at knock-down prices. Look out for all sorts of entertaining and obvious southeast Asian fashion fakes, as well as electronic goods, Chinese silks, Russian caviar and vodka, and Stalinist memorabilia. Authentic Chinese, Vietnamese or Turkish food stalls offer a tasty lunch.

Delicate lace, an example of traditional Hungarian folk art

MARKETS

MARKETS OF ALL sorts are an essential part of life in Budapest, and offer a delightfully traditional shopping experience to visitors. Perhaps the most spectacular are the five cavernous market halls which dot the city. All were built in the late 19th century and several are still used as markets. The three-level **Great Market Hall** (Nagy Vásárcsarnok) on Fővám tér is the largest of all. More than 180 stalls display a

Marks & Spencer, which has now made it to Budapest

What to Buy in Budapest

DESPITE PRICE RISES since the return to a free-market economy, many Hungarian goods are still great bargains. Embroidered peasant blouses and wooden carvings make unique souvenirs, as does the distinctive porcelain produced at the world-famous Zsolnay and Herend factories. Cheap, good quality CDs and records are widely available, and Hungarian wines, salamis and other foodstuffs can be bought in the city's many lively markets. Clothes and shoes made to your specifications represent one of the city's most luxurious bargains.

FOLK ART

HUNGARIAN FOLK culture is still alive and well in many parts of rural Hungary. You can buy textiles, ceramics and woodwork from flea markets (see p203) and from street vendors around Moszkva tér and Parliament (see pp108–9). Folk art shops such as **Folkart Centrum**, sell machine-made products, and, for genuine Transylvanian textiles there is **Judit Folklór**. For the cheapest authentic folk costumes, head to the second floor of the **Central Market Hall** (Nagy Vásárcsarnok).

ANTIQUES

DOMINATED BY 18th- and 19th-century pieces in the Habsburg style, the Budapest antiques scene is concentrated in the Castle District, around Falk Miksa utca and on Váci utca (Váci Street, see p127). **Moró Antik** is a tiny shop specializing in 18th-century weapons, while the huge **Nagyházi Gallery** sells everything from jewellery to furniture. The **Écseri Flea Market** (see p203) is also a good place for antiques.

PORCELAIN

THERE ARE TWO major porcelain manufacturors in Hungary, **Herend** and **Zsolnay**. Herend enjoys a reputation as the producer of the country's finest porcelain, while Zsolnay's brightly-glazed tiles can be seen on many of the city's notable buildings. Second-hand porcelain can be bought in antique shops and markets. Both companies have shops selling new pieces.

CLOTHES AND SHOES

MADE-TO-MEASURE clothes and shoes, and ready made designer clothes offer some of the best bargains to be had by visitors to Budapest. With a luxurious array of velvets, silks and wools, **Merino** is both a fabric shop and a workshop, where you can choose your fabric and have it made up either here or by a local designer, most of whom are happy to oblige for a fairly modest fee. Six young designers make up **Rakpart Divattervező**, where good value dresses and jackets are simple and stylish. For more classic clothes, the highly-respected **Greti** is the oldest of the city's design houses, making elegant and beautifully tailored clothes for women. Shoemaker's in Budapest tend to make only men's shoes. **Vass** will make you a one-off pair of dress shoes in about a month. They cost around 50,000 Hungarian forints.

FOOD AND WINE

FOOD AND WINE in Hungary are great value and make excellent souvenirs of your stay. Sausage is a national passion and can be bought in shops and markets all over the city. Some of the most popular types include spicy sausages from Debrecen, smoked sausages from Gyulai and a whole range of world-famous salamis. Also worth bringing home are dried mushrooms, paté de foie gras, a string of paprika or some fresh sheep's cheese. All these can be bought in Budapest's markets and in supermarkets such as **Közert**, **Pick** and **Julius Meinl**. Hungary's national drink is wine (see pp192–3). Bottles to look out for include fine desert wines from the Tokaji region, Muscats from Kiskunhalas on the central plain and Chardonnays from Mátraalja. Also popular are the herbal liqueur Unicum, and the strong, fiery pálinka, made from plums, cherries or apricots. Wines and spirits are available in supermarkets and in specialist shops such as **Wine City** and **Borház**.

MUSIC

HUNGARY'S RICH folk and classical music traditions make low-priced CDs, tapes and vinyl a tempting purchase in Budapest. For Hungarian folk music, from traditional Roma (Gypsy) music to recordings of village folk music, the old-style **Rózsavölgyi Zeneműbolt** is a good choice. In nearby Dob utca, **Concerto Records** offers a selection of new and second-hand vinyl and CDs, specializing in classical and opera, with some jazz, folk and funk. The state label, **Hungaroton**, has a shop in Vörösmarty tér that sells a wide range of classical music as well as some pop.

BOOKS

FOR ILLUSTRATED BOOKS and English-language guidebooks, try the **Litea Bookstore and Café**, where you can brouse through the books while enjoying coffee and cakes at tables set among the shelves. The large **Studium Libri** stocks many books in English. A wide range of English-language newspapers, magazines and novels are available at **Bestsellers**. **Irók Boltja** sells art books and some English-language books, while **Pendragon** stocks a varied assortment of fiction in English. One of the best places for maps and English-language guide books is **Párizsi Udvar**. **Librotrade-Kodex** stocks books in English, French and German. For antique books, etchings and maps a good place to try is **Központi Antiqvárium**.

DIRECTORY

DEPARTMENT STORES

Corvin
Blaha Lujza tér 1.
Map 7 B3.
338 41 60.

Duna Plaza
Váci út 178.
Map 2 F1.
465 12 20.

Fontana
Váci utca 16.
Map 4 E1.
266 64 00.

Luxus
Vörösmarty tér 3.
Map 2 E5.
318 22 77.

Skála Metro
Nyugati tér 1–2.
Map 2 F2. 318 22 22.

MARKETS

Bosnyák tér Market
Bosnyák tér.

Central Market Hall (Központi Vásárcsarnok)
Vámház Körút 13.
Map 4 F3.

Écseri Flea Market
Nagykörösi út 156.

Fehérvári út Market
Fehérvári út 20.
Map 4 D5.

Fény utca Market
Mammut Shopping Centre, near Moszkva tér.
Map 1 A3.

Great Market Hall (Nagy Vásárcsarnok)
Fővám tér.
Map 4 F3.

Inner City Market Hall (Belvárosi Vásárcsarnok)
Hold utca 13.
Map 2 E3.

Józsefvárosi Market
Kőbanyai út.
Map 8 F4.

Lehel tér Market
Lehel tér.
Map 2 F1.

FOLK ART

Folkart Centrum
Váci utca 14.
Map 4 E1.
318 58 40.

Judit Folklór
Váci utca 23.
Map 4 E1.
317 32 97.

ANTIQUES

Moró Antik
Szent István körút 1.
Map 2 E2.
312 78 77.

Nagyházi Gallery
Balaton utca 8.
Map 2 D2.
357 05 21.

PORCELAIN

Herend Shops
József Nádor tér 11.
Map 2 E5.
267 46 26.

Szentháromság utca 5.
375 58 57.

Kigyó utca 5.
Map 4 E1.
266 51 11.

Zsolnay Shops
Kigyó utca 2.
Map 4 E1.
318 37 12.

Bajcsy-Zsilliszky út 23.
Map 2 E4.
311 40 94.

CLOTHES AND SHOES

Greti
Bárczy István utca 3.
Map 2 E5.
317 85 00.

Merino
Petőfi Sandór utca 20.
Map 4 E1.
318 44 78.

Rakpart Diverttervező
Bem rakpart 38–39.
Map 1 C2.
214 09 40.

Vass
Haris köz 2.
Map 4 E1.
318 32 75.

FOOD AND DRINK

Borház
Jókai tér 7.
Map 2 F3.
353 48 49.

La Boutique des Vins
Józef Attila utca 12.
Map 2 E5.
317 59 19.

Közert
Batthyány tér 5–7.
Map 1 C3.
202 50 44.

Szentháromság tér 1–3.
Map 1 B4.
356 81 84.

Julius Meinl
Margit körút 6.
Map 1 A3.
212 54 07.

Rákóczi út 50.
Map 7 B3.
322 00 69.

Pick
Kossuth Lajos tér 9.
Map 2 D3.
331 77 83.

Wine City
Párizsi utca 1.
Map 4 E1.
266 24 46.

MUSIC

Concerto Records
Dob utca 33
Map 2 F5
268 96 31.

Hungaroton
Vörösmarty tér 1.
Map 2 E5.
338 27 32.

Liszt Ferenc Zeneműboltja
Andrássy út 45.
Map 2 F5.
322 40 91.

Rózsavölgyi Zeneműbolt
Szervita tér 5.
Map 4 E1.
266 83 37.

Zenáruház
Jókai utca 40.
Map 2 F3.

BOOKS

Bestsellers
Október 6 utca 11.
Map 2 E4.
312 12 95.

Írók Boltja
Andrássy út 45.
Map 2 F4.
322 16 45.

Központi Antiqvárium
Muzeum Körút 15.
Map 4 F1.
327 35 14.

Librotrade-Kodex
Honvéd utca 5.
Map 7 C3. 332 73 85.

Litea Bookstore and Café
Hess András tér 4.
Map 1 B4.
375 69 87.

Párizsi Udvar
Petőfi Sándor utca 2.
Map 4 E1.
118 31 36.

Pendragon
Raoul Wallenberg utca 9–11. 340 44 26.

Studium Libri
Váci utca (main pedestrian precinct).
Map 4 E1. 318 56 80.

ENTERTAINMENT IN BUDAPEST

B UDAPEST HAS BEEN known as a city of entertainment since the late 19th century, when people would travel here from Vienna in search of a good time. Its buzzing nightclubs were frequented for their electric atmosphere and the beautiful girls that danced the spirited *csárdás* and the cancan. Nowhere else did fiddlers play such heartrending music or were the gambling casinos witness to such staggering losses as in Budapest. Between the wars the city was as famous for its glittering society balls as for its libertine delights. The half-century of Communist rule dampened the revelry, but since 1990 the Budapest music scene has flourished and theatres, cabarets, festivals, cinemas and discotheques are all buzzing. Above all, the renowned nightclubs have risen convincingly from their ashes.

ENTERTAINMENT HIGHLIGHTS

B UDAPEST HAS two opera houses, an orchestral concert hall at the **Franz Liszt Academy of Music** *(see p208)*, several other concert halls, an operetta theatre, numerous cabarets and more than 50 theatres, including the fringe. Among them is the **Merlin Theatre** *(see p209)*, which performs only in English.

The greatest concentration of theatres is in district V, in Nagymezö utca, which has been nicknamed "Budapest's Broadway". Along this 100-m (328-ft) stretch there are two theatres, the **Operetta Theatre** *(see p208)*, the satirical cabaret **Mikroszkóp** *(see p209)*, which is reputed to be the best in Hungary, and the **Moulin Rouge** *(see p209)* revue theatre. Film lovers are also spoilt for choice, as Budapest boasts a large number of cinemas.

Városliget *(see pp142–3)* offers numerous attractions,

including a permanent circus, funfair and zoo, complete with a number of small bars and beer tents in the summer.

The youth entertainment centre, **Petöfi Csarnok** *(see p209)*, stages rock concerts and hosts the largest discotheque in town. Casinos and striptease clubs are the latest addition to the city's nightlife. Budapest also has its own red-light district, whose activities, although illegal, form part of a long-standing tradition.

PRACTICAL INFORMATION

T HE TOURIST BUREAU publishes two monthly bulletins. The *Programme* contains information in English and German, while the *Budapest Panorama* is in four languages, with Italian and Russian as well. Both bulletins are free and can be found in hotels and tourist information centres. They also include free-entry coupons to some casinos and nightclubs.

The *Programme* gives full information on cultural events and entertainments being held throughout the whole of Hungary, while *Budapest Panorama* informs the reader only about what is happening in Budapest. Pamphlets and bulletins are often issued in connection with festivals and other special events, and it is worth keeping an eye out for the numerous poster pillars throughout the town. The Saturday editions of all newspapers carry a calendar of events; however, this is only of use to those who understand Hungarian.

CASINOS

B UDAPEST HAS several casinos. Given their relatively recent reappearance, it is interesting that most of them occupy historical buildings next to smart hotels. Players can try their hand at roulette, Black Jack, poker and the wheel of fortune at any one of them. Bear in mind that only one – the **Las Vegas Casino** – is run American-style, which means that guests do not have to wear evening dress.

Entrance to a popular casino, at No. 13 Deák utca

CASINO ADDRESSES

Casino Budapest (Hilton Hotel)
Hess András tér 1–3. 📞 *240 30 00.*
Casino Budapest Gresham
Roosevelt tér 5. 📞 *267 31 45.*
Casino City
Váci utca 14. 📞 *338 20 69.*
Casino Vigadó
Vigadó utca 2. 📞 *317 08 69.*
Las Vegas Casino
(Atrium Hyatt Hotel)
Roosevelt tér 2. 📞 *266 20 81.*

Lavishly staged opera at the State Opera House *(see p208)*

BUYING TICKETS

Tickets for all theatre productions and concerts can be purchased in advance, either at the booking offices or by telephoning the venue in question direct. Addresses and telephone numbers can be found on pages 208–9. The most difficult to obtain are tickets to the **Franz Liszt Academy of Music** concerts, as these tend to be sold many days in advance. Similarly, seats at opera and operetta performances sell out quickly. The best way of securing a seat, particularly for summer performances, is via the **Central Booking Office**, which is located right in the centre of town at Vörösmarty tér 1. In Budapest, like anywhere else, you can risk it and try buying returned tickets at the last minute. A cheap alternative, but not one for the foot weary, is to buy a standing-room pass.

Poster pillar

NIGHT LIFE

At the centre of Pest, particularly along Váci utca, numerous hawkers push pamphlets on passers-by, advertising the best places for striptease and erotic dancing. The experience can be quite unpleasant financially, as even a small beer and a packet of peanuts can set you back a fortune. There are now scores of such

places to choose from. None of them are cheap, but some are quite smart and offer relatively modest prices. When choosing where to go, you should consider the places that advertise in the official information bulletins published by the tourist agencies. These include: Caligula, Dolce Vita, Tiamo bár and Aphrodite Night Club. In the last-named, scantily dressed girls dance behind the glass of the display window to lure in potential guests walking by.

CIRCUS, FUNFAIR AND ZOO

Budapest's **Great Capital Circus** (see p211) has been present in Városliget since 1878, but was given a permanent home only in 1971. The building is both comfortable and functional. Shows are held twice a day during the week, in the afternoon and evening, with additional morning performances on Saturdays and Sundays. It is possible to purchase tickets on the day, but it is better to book them in advance.

The **Funfair** (see p211) has an enormous merry-go-round, a scenic railway and scores of other diversions to entertain visitors. You have to pay separately for all the individual attractions, in addition to buying the entry pass, which can make it a relatively expensive outing. There is

Pelicans at the Zoo

enough to do here for many hours, from visiting the haunted house to playing one-arm bandits.

On the 12-ha area occupied by the **Zoo** (see p211), you will find over 500 animal species, as well as hundreds of exotic trees and shrubs. There is also a palmhouse and a special enclosure for elephants and hippos.

JAZZ

Jazz was very late in reaching Hungary. The best known and revered Hungarian jazz band is the Benkő Dixieland Band, which during Spring Festivals (see p58) plays in various theatres and large halls. It is worth keeping an eye out around town for notices advertising their performances. The **Hades Restaurant** is a highly atmospheric venue where jazz is performed five nights a week. A large and invariably crowded club is the **Közgaz Jazz Klub** (see p208), which is located at the University of Economics.

LATE-NIGHT TRANSPORT

Budapest's metro (see p230) runs until just after 11pm. Buses marked with black numbers and the letter E provide the night transport on busy routes. There are also night trams running on some routes, though their frequency varies from between one and three an hour. Night buses must be boarded through the front door, showing your ticket to the driver. On approaching the required stop, press the request button above the door. The HÉV train (see p231) that connects Budapest with its suburbs stops running at about 11:30pm.

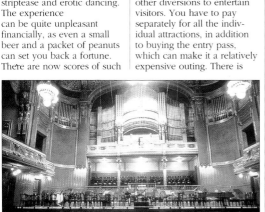

The elegant interior of the Vigadó concert hall (see p208)

Classical and Folk Music

THANKS TO THE GREAT composers such as Franz Liszt *(see p144)*, Béla Bartók and Zoltán Kodály *(see p144)*, as well as to the great wealth of its folk tradition, Hungary is famous throughout the world for its music. Hungarians always were, and remain to this day, a nation of music lovers and song-singers. In addition to the performances by leading Hungarian artists and ensembles, Budapest is frequently visited by revered musicians from around the world.

OPERA AND OPERETTA

THE STANDARD OF opera in Budapest is very high. Performances are at either the **State Opera House** *(see pp118–19)* or the **Erkel Theatre** *(see p151)*. At both there is a mainly classical repertoire, sung in Italian with Hungarian subtitles. The secondary focus is on Hungarian works, such as Ferenc Erkel's *Bánk Bán* and Béla Bartók's *Miraculous Mandarin*.

During its season the **Operetta Theatre** *(see p115)* generally tends to stage Hungarian operettas by Imre Kálmán and Ferenc Lehár.

CLASSICAL MUSIC

THE LARGE HALL of the **Franz Liszt Academy of Music** *(see p129)*, with performances by top orchestras every night of the week, is the leading venue for classical music

concerts. The city's largest concert hall is at the **Congress Centre** *(see p160)*. Unfortunately the acoustics of the **Vigadó** *(see p126)* do not match the beauty of its décor. It is sometimes used as a venue for classical concerts, but more often hosts operatic medleys.

It is worth keeping an eye out for the classical music concerts that are sometimes held in the domed hall of Parliament *(see pp108–9)*, where the acoustics are excellent.

Budapest also has a strong tradition of music festivals, including the Budapest Contemporary Music Weeks *(see p60)*.

SACRED MUSIC

CONCERTS OF organ music are held between March and December in the magnificent setting of the **Mátyás Church** *(see pp82–3)*. Among the composers whose works are featured, Bach is the most

popular. **St Stephen's Basilica** *(see pp116–17)* serves sporadically as the venue for concerts of choral music. Lastly, between March and October the Musica Sacra Agency organizes concerts in the **Great Synagogue** *(see p134)*.

FOLK AND GYPSY MUSIC

PERFORMANCES OF folk and gypsy music are regularly held at the **Duna Palota** and the **Budai Vigadó**. Watch out for shows by the Hungarian State Song and Dance Ensemble and a Gypsy band that is part of the ensemble but also stages independent concerts. Its players include top Gypsy artists and their music and dance shows are a magnificent display of Hungarian Romany folklore.

During July and August the city is visited by folk troupes from all over the country. Folklore evenings are held in the Casino-Valentine Restaurant *(see p196)* on Margaret Island.

From October to May, the city's dance houses rock to the sounds of fiddles and flutes. Some of the most renowned are **Fonó Budai Zenéház**, which stages peasant and Gypsy bands from Transylvania, the Kalamajka Dancehouse at the **Inner City Arts Centre** and the **Gyökér Klub-Vendéglő**.

DIRECTORY

TICKETS

Central Booking Office
Vörösmarty tér 1.
Map 2 E5.
(266 31 08.

OPERA AND OPERETTA

Erkel Theatre
Köztársaság tér 30.
Map 7 C3.
(333 01 08.

Operetta Theatre
Nagymező útca 1.
Map 2 F3.
(269 38 70.

State Opera House
Andrássy út 22. **Map** 2 F4.
(331 25 50.

CLASSICAL MUSIC

Congress Centre
Jagelló út 1–3.
(209 48 50.

Franz Liszt Academy
Liszt Ferenc tér 8.
Map 7 A1. (341 47 85.

Vigadó
Vigadó ter 2. **Map** 4 D1.
(318 91 67.

SACRED MUSIC

Great Synagogue
Dohány utca 2–8.
Map 7 A3. (342 89 49.

Mátyás Church
Szentháromsag tér 2.
Map 1 B4. (355 56 57.

St Stephen's Basilica
Szent István tér.
Map 2 E4. (332 17 90.

FOLK AND GYPSY MUSIC

Budai Vigadó
Corvin tér 8. **Map** 1 C4.
(201 37 66.

Duna Palota
Zrínyi utca 5. **Map** 2 E5.
(317 27 90.

Fonó Budai Zenéház
Sztregova utca 3.
Map 2 E5.
(206 53 00.

Gyökér Klub-Vendéglő
Eötvös utca 46.
Map 2 F3.
(302 40 59.

Inner City Arts Centre
Molnár utca 9. **Map** 4 E2.
(317 59 28.

JAZZ

Közgáz Jazz Klub
Kinizsi utca 2–6.
Map 7 A5.
(217 30 33.

Hades Restaurant
Vörösmarty utca 31.
Map 5 A5.
(352 15 03.

Theatre, Cinema and Nightclubs

B UDAPEST HAS many theatres, which are worth visiting not only for their impressive repertoires, but also because they are invariably located in beautiful historic buildings. Cinemas show the latest films soon after their world premieres, although not many retain the original soundtrack. For late-night dancing the city has a wealth of popular clubs to choose from.

THEATRE

T HE FIRST THEATRE to stage plays in Hungarian was the **Castle Theatre** *(see p73)*. Other established theatres include the **Madách Theatre, Nemzeti Theatre, Pesti Theatre** and **Lézerszínház**. Of interest to English speakers is the **Merlin Theatre**, sponsored by the city council, which performs in English.

Budapest has over 30 drama and cabaret theatres. Among the most prestigious is the **József Katona Theatre**, which became famous following performances in Paris and London. Its repertoire includes Shakespeare and Gogol.

Another interesting theatre is the **Vígszínház**, meaning "comedy theatre", which specializes in musicals. During the summer memorable rock-operas are staged on Margaret Island. These shows are highly prized for their good music performed in a magnificent setting.

CINEMA

M OST OF BUDAPEST'S cinemas were built during the 1920s and 1930s. They are therefore old-fashioned and heavily ornamented, which unfortunately does not add up to luxury. The smarter and more comfortable ones include **Broadway, Corvin Film-palota** and **Uránia**.

Apart from foreign films, which are often dubbed into Hungarian, the cinemas also show native Hungarian films. The range covers both the latest releases and vintage films from a time of Hungarian cinematic glory, notably when Miklós Jancsó and István Szabó received international awards for directing. The Broadway cinema regularly shows these undubbed masterpieces of a bygone era. All cinema tickets can be bought in advance on the same day and Corvin Film-palota will also sell you tickets for the next day.

NIGHTCLUBS

M ANY OF BUDAPEST'S clubs and discotheques are associated with colleges and universities. **Petőfi Csarnok**, a youth entertainment centre built in 1984 during the Communist era, occupies a cavernous hall at the rear of Városliget *(see pp142–3)*. It is a stage and disco complex that traditionally serves as a venue for local and international rock bands. Here it is possible to listen to music and dance the night away every day of the week.

Other student discos that are worth recommending include the **E-Klub**, which is housed next to the Planetarium *(see p211)*. It is open on Fridays and Saturdays and is always crowded with Technical University students. One really vibrant student club is the **Közgáz Pince Klub**, which is held in the huge hall of the University of Economics *(see p138)*.

Budapest's chic set meet in the exclusive **Made Inn**, where the attractive patio and garden are full to bursting in summer. It boasts two dance floors and a room for live bands. Equally popular among the young and trendy is **Picasso Point**, where crowds dance furiously to rock bands once a week.

DIRECTORY

THEATRE

Castle Theatre
Disz tér 17.
Map 1 B5.
 375 86 49.

József Katona Theatre
Petöfi Sándor utca 6.
Map 4 E1.
 318 65 99.

Lézerszínház
Népliget,
Planetarium.
 263 08 71.

Madách Theatre
Erzsébet körút 31.
Map 7 A2.
 322 20 15.

Merlin Theatre
Gerlóczy utca 4.
Map 4 F1.
 317 93 38.

Mikroszkóp
Nagymező utca 22–24.
Map 2 F3.
 311 33 22.

Nemzeti Theatre
Hevesi Sándor tér 4.
Map 7 B1.
 341 38 49.

Pest Theatre
Váci utca 9. **Map** 4 E1.
 266 55 57.

Vígszínház
Szent István körút 14.
Map 2 E5.
 269 53 40.

CINEMA

Broadway
Károly körút 3. **Map** 2 F5.
 321 40 03.

Corvin Filmpalota
Corvin köz 1.
 303 15 25.

Uránia
Rákóczi út 21. **Map** 7 A3.
 318 89 55.

NIGHTCLUBS

E-Klub
Népliget út 2.
 263 16 14.

Közgáz Pince Klub
Fövam tér 8. **Map** 4 F3.
 218 68 55.

Made Inn
Andrássy út 112.
Map 7 A1.
 311 34 37.

Petőfi Csarnok
Zichy Mihály utca 14.
Map 6 E4.
 251 72 66.

Picasso Point
Hajós utca 31. **Map** 2 F4.
 302 32 68.

Sports

HUNGARIANS ARE FINE athletes, as is testified by their consistently outstanding performances at competitive events, such as the Olympic Games. Budapest's world-class sports facilities serve as venues for many of these international events, including European and World championships. Sporting opportunities for visitors to the city are both varied and accessible.

SPECTATOR SPORTS

MOST COMPETITIVE sporting events are held either in the magnificent **People's Stadium** (see p155), which seats 80,000 spectators, or in the modern, indoor **Budapest Sportcsarnok**.

Soccer remains the most popular spectator sport, although Hungarian fans can only look wistfully back to the time when their national side was highly successful. In the 1950s, for instance, Hungary beat England 6–3 at Wembley. League matches in Budapest attract big crowds. The atmosphere is particularly electric when local favourites Ferencváros, FTC, take to the pitch.

Two of the three great events regularly held in Budapest are the Welcom Marathon Hungary (see p58) and the Budapest Marathon. These are run on the last Sundays of April and September respectively. The third big sporting event of the year is the Hungarian Grand Prix (see p59), which takes place during August at the Mogyoród racing circuit.

Hungarians achieve impressive results in boxing, canoeing, swimming, water polo and fencing, which are all widely supported.

HORSE RACING AND RIDING

AS A NATION of former nomads, the Hungarians have retained a great love of horses. In Budapest this passion finds its expression in horse racing, which is enormously popular. A few hours spent at a racetrack can be a cheap and fun way of soaking up the local atmosphere. Near Keleti pu (see p227) is the Trotters' Racecourse, the **Ügetőpálya**. A little further on is **Kincsem Park**, one of the loveliest flat-racing courses in Europe. Races are held all afternoon from 1:30pm, every day from Wednesday to Sunday. On both courses the totalizator betting system is operated.

Those wishing to be rather more energetic and ride themselves instead of watch horses, should contact the **National Riding School**, the **Petneházy School** or the **Budapest Riding Club**.

SPORTING ACTIVITIES

PRACTISING SPORT for fitness and pleasure is both cheap and popular in Budapest.

Strolling through the city's parks, particularly on Margaret Island, you will encounter scores of eager joggers, both young and not so young. The indoor and outdoor swimming pools are full of regular visitors, who come here for an hour of healthy exercise. Particularly popular is the **Hajós Olympic Pool** on Margaret Island, which is named after Hungary's first Olympic gold winner for swimming, who was also the pool's architect. Busy open-air options inlcude **Császár Baths** and the neighbouring **Lukács Baths**, both of which can be enjoyed even in winter as the hot spring water creates a steamy atmosphere over the water's surface. For the hottest spa water in the city, head to the **Széchenyi Baths** (see p151), which is the largest bathing complex in Europe. The most atmospheric and beautiful baths are undoubtedly the 16th-century Turkish **Rudas Baths** (see p93).

Cycling is gaining in popularity, particularly since the advent of cycling lanes (see p228). There are many tennis courts, but these tend to be monopolized by Hungarians. Your best bet is to either to befriend a local tennis player, or to use the courts found in some hotels.

Despite the moderate climate, it is also possible to undertake winter sports in Budapest. From December until March the Városliget lake (see pp142–3) is turned into a skating ring. Sváb Hill (see p161) is generally snow-covered from December to March and has several ski runs and ski lifts.

DIRECTORY

STADIA

Budapest Sportcsarnok
Hungária körút.
Map 6 F4.
☎ 251 12 22.

People's Stadium
Stefánia út 3–5.
Map 6 F5.
☎ 251 12 22.

HORSE RACING AND RIDING

Budapest Riding Club
Kerepesi út 7.
☎ 313 52 10.

Kincsem Park
Albertirsai út 2.
☎ 263 78 18.

National Riding School
Kerepesi út 7.
☎ 313 04 15.

Petneházy School
Feketefej utca 2–4.
☎ 376 59 92.

Ügetőpálya
Kerepesi út 9–11.
☎ 334 29 58.

SWIMMING POOLS

Császár Baths
Árpád fejedelem út 7.
☎ 369 03 44.

Lukács Baths
Frankel Leó út 25.
Map 1 C1. ☎ 326 16 95.

Hajós Olympic Pool
Margitsziget.
☎ 340 49 46.

Rudas Baths
Döbrentei tér 9.
Map 4 D2. ☎ 375 88 73.

Széchenyi Baths
Frankel Leó út 25.
Map 1 C1. ☎ 321 03 10.

Children's Budapest

VISITING BUDAPEST can be great fun for children. There are several options in the way of energetic outdoor pursuits, including a funfair, a zoo and a variety of swimming venues. If the weather is poor then there are a number of historical monuments that will entertain and inform. Alternatively, there are two puppet theatres that cater specifically for younger audiences.

SIGHTSEEING WITH CHILDREN

THE BUSY AND crowded centre of Pest is likely to be a difficult area in which to entertain children. However, the glittering opulence of the **Postal Museum** can provide a good morning's distraction.

Of more interest is the Royal Palace *(see pp70–71)* and the Castle District *(see pp68–85)* of Buda, where children can appreciate a sense of the city's history and tradition. Having visited the **Hungarian National Gallery** *(see pp72–5)* children usually enjoy seeing the palace courtyard with its fabulous *turul*, the giant bird that is so steeped in myths. The *Mátyás Fountain (see pp72–3)* is also worth a look. A must, of course, is the ride up and down Castle Hill by the funicular railway, the *Budavári Sikló (see p231)*.

Especially fun for children is the **Labyrinth** in Lords' Street *(see p85)*, an underground exhibition of the town's early history that really appeals to a child's imagination.

The **War Museum** will absorb those who like to see old weapons, armours and the mock-ups of battles.

RECREATION FACILITIES

THE MOST SUITABLE swimming complex for children is the **Palatinus Strand** *(see p172)* on Margaret Island. Not only does it have a number of pools with varying water temperatures, but there are also slides, artificial waves and other fun and games. Numerous nearby kiosks sell snacks, ice cream and fruit.

During the winter season take the children to the **Gellért Hotel and Baths Complex** *(see pp90–91)* instead. The large swimming pool here has artificial waves and the paddling pool's very warm water is particularly enjoyed by toddlers.

Children and adults alike love the **Zoo** *(see pp150–51)*, which is one of the largest in Europe. Attractions of particular interest for children include the large sea-water aquarium, a terrarium with splendid specimens of snakes and an impressive aviary.

The **Great Capital Circus** is an ideal way to keep youngsters occupied. Shows, which often star international artists, are held daily.

Children will also spend many happy hours at the

INDOOR ATTRACTIONS

THERE ARE TWO puppet theatres in Budapest, which in addition to Hungarian classics also stage such favourites as *The Jungle Book*, *Cinderella* and *Snow White*.

A great attraction, and not only for children, is the **Planetarium**, situated in the People's Park *(see p156)*. Opened in 1977, it has been equipped with Zeiss Jena optical systems, thereby creating a fascinating laser world.

SCENIC RAILWAYS

CHILDREN LOVE the trip up into the Buda Hills *(see p161)*. The first leg is a cogwheel railway up to the top of Széchényi Hill. The track is 3,730 m (12,240 ft) long and climbs to 315 m (1,035 ft).

At the top of the hill is a playground and the first stop of the Children's Railway, on which all the signalmen and conductors are children. The train follows the ridge of the Buda Hills, taking children to the Hűvös Valley.

The Libegő chair lift has run to the top of János Hill since 1970. Its lower station is located in Zugliget, which can be reached by taking bus 158 from Moszkva tér.

Vidám Park funfair *(see p151)* at Városliget, riding on the merry-go-rounds or the railway and zooming down the slides. Older children will enjoy testing their marksmanship in the shooting galleries and their luck at the game machines.

DIRECTORY

MUSEUMS

Hungarian National Gallery
Szent György tér 2.
Map 3 C5. (375 75 33.

Labyrinth
Úri utca 9. **Map** 1 A4.
(375 68 58.

Postal Museum
Andrássy út 3. **Map** 2 F4.
(269 68 38.

War Museum
Kapisztrán tér. **Map** 1 A4.
(356 95 22.

RECREATION FACILITIES

Vidám Park
Állatkerti körut 14–16.
Map 5 C3. (343 09 96.

Gellért Hotel and Baths Complex
Kelenhegyi út 4–6.
Map 3 C3.
(466 61 66.

Great Capital Circus
Állatkerti körut 7.
Map 5 C3.
(343 83 00.

Palatinus Strand
Margitsziget.
(340 45 05.

Zoo
Állatkerti körut 6–12.
Map 5 C3.
(343 60 75.

INDOOR ATTRACTIONS

Állami Bábszínház
Andrássy út 69.
Map 5 A5.
(341 21 66.

Kolibri Színház
Jókai tér 10. **Map** 2 F3.
(312 06 22.

Planetarium
Népliget.
(265 09 96.

SURVIVAL
GUIDE

PRACTICAL INFORMATION

BUDAPEST was always famous for its hospitality and the Hungarians, particularly in recent years, have been emphasizing tourism as an important part of the national economy. The biggest problem in its development is the formidable barrier posed by the Hungarian language, which hinders access to information. The Hungarians are therefore trying hard to learn foreign languages.

TOURIST

i

SERVICE

Tourist
information
sign

In all tourist offices, bigger hotels and most restaurants either English or German is spoken. Information brochures and tourist pamphlets are now published in several languages. It is difficult to get lost in Budapest as the road sign system is easy to follow. The historic monuments in the city centre are best visited on foot, while the more distant sights can be easily reached by public transport *(see pp228– 33)*.

TOURIST INFORMATION

PRIOR TO YOUR arrival in Budapest it is worthwhile getting in touch with your nearest **Hungarian National Tourist Office**, who can supply you with endless useful information and put you in touch with reputable tour operators.

Agencies that specialize in organizing tours and individual trips to Hungary include **Danube Travel**, **Budapest Breaks** and **Paul Laifer Tours**. They can all provide you with detailed information on meals and accommodation and help you to make reservations.

Tourist information centres in Budapest can be found at the **Agip Office** in a petrol station by the M7 motorway, at **Nyugati pu** railway station and at **Ferihegy 2** airport. General tourist information, regarding accommodation,

meals, sightseeing and entertainment are provided, in foreign languages, by **Tourinform Budapest** and **Budapest Tourist**. Tourinform is described in greater detail on page 176.

Since 1997, computer information terminals have been introduced in Budapest. These are can be found in eight locations throughout the city. They provide an "info-touch" facility, giving the addresses of museums, theatres and hotels, together with instructions on the best method of getting there, either on foot or by public transport. This information is provided in Hungarian, English and German. More information on these computer information terminals and their locations is given on pages 216–17.

IBUSZ
TRAVEL

PROGRAM

Logo of IBUSZ tourist
information office

One of several IBUSZ tourist information offices in Budapest

ADVICE FOR VISITORS

BUDAPEST IS best visited between March and the end of June, and from the middle of August until October. July is generally so hot that it is almost unbearable to stay in the city, particularly in Pest. The only way to enjoy such weather is by escaping to a swimming pool during the day and relaxing in a restaurant garden at night. The end of the year is also a fun time, when visitors can experience Budapest's exhilarating New Year's Eve street party.

On arriving in Budapest it is a good idea to get hold of the foreign language information booklets. The *Budapest Panorama* and the *Programme* each contain the calendar of cultural and tourist events for the month. They are free and are easily available from tourist centres, airline offices and hotel reception desks. Both bulletins contain accurate maps of Budapest.

It is also worth investing in the Budapest Card *(see p216)*, which, as well as entitling cardholders to unlimited use of public transport, gives reductions on the price of tickets for various cultural events.

OPENING HOURS

MUSEUMS AND galleries are open all year round. Opening times for specific venues are given under their individual entries.

Horses on a tourist carriage

As a general rule, the winter season from November until March sees museums offering shorter opening hours. In the summer, from April until October, they tend to stay open a couple of hours longer, typically from 10am until 6pm. Museums remain closed on Monday, except for the National Jewish Museum (see p134), which is closed on Saturday instead. Most museums, both state and private tend to charge an entrance fee, though it is worth checking to see if there are any applicable discounts.

Although several shops in Budapest are open 24 hours a day, grocery stores are open from 7am to 7pm and other shops from 10am until 6pm during the week, though shops still tend to close for lunch at 1pm. On Saturdays shops close at 1pm, while on Sundays some department stores and market halls are open, often until 2pm. Detailed information on the opening hours of particular shops and markets is given on pages 202–5. Hungarians take lunch early, between noon and 1pm.

ENTRY TICKETS

TICKETS TO museums and historical monuments can be purchased on the spot. Average prices vary from 200 to 400 fortints per person, but can be as much as 700 forints. Students and school children are entitled to reductions. Opera, concert and other tickets can be bought at the Central Booking Office (see p208). Theatre tickets are also sold at individual box offices, either for shows on the same day or in advance. Ticket prices can vary from 500 to 5,000 forints.

ETIQUETTE

CASUAL CLOTHES are often worn to the theatre, particularly during summer. By comparison classical music concerts and operas are much smarter affairs and even tourists will feel more comfortable wearing evening dress. Traditionally, Hungarians attach great importance to being properly dressed when going to an opera or concert hall.

Tickets to two of Budapest's museums

DIRECTORY

DIALLING CODES FOR BUDAPEST

From US and Australia
(00 11 361.
From Great Britain and most of Europe
(00 361.

TOURIST OFFICES IN BUDAPEST

AGIP Office
2040 Budaörs.
(0623 417 518.
FAX 0623 417 518.

American Express
1052 Budapest,
Deák Ferenc utca 10.
Map 4 E1.
(235 43 00.
FAX 235 43 03.
Hilton Hotel

Hess András tér 1–3.
Map 1 B4.
(214 30 00.
FAX 214 21 85.

Budapest Tourist
1051 Budapest,
Roosevelt tér 5. **Map** 2 D5.
(318 66 00.
FAX 318 60 62.

Ferihegy 2
1185 Budapest.
(296 70 00.
FAX 296 82 22.

IBUSZ
1053 Budapest,
Ferenciek tere 10.
Map 4 F1.
(318 68 66.
FAX 318 77 23.

Welcome
1052 Budapest,
Apáczai Csere János utca 1.

Map 2 D5.
(318 48 48.
FAX 317 90 99.

Nyugati pu
1062 Budapest,
Teréz körút 52. **Map** 2 F3.
(302 85 80.

Tourinform Budapest
1052 Budapest,
Sütő utca 2. **Map** 2 E5.
(317 98 00.
FAX 356 19 64.

TOURIST OFFICES ABROAD

United Kingdom
Hungarian National
Tourist Office
Embassy of Hungary
46 Eaton Place
London SW1X 8AL.
(0171 823 1032.

United States
Hungarian National
Tourist Office
150 East 58th Street
33rd Floor
New York
NY 10155-3398
(212 355 0240.

TRAVEL AGENTS ABROAD

Budapest Breaks
10 Hatton Garden
London EC1N 8AH
(0171 831 7626.

Danube Travel
45 Great Cumberland Place
London W1H 7LH
(0171 724 7577.

Paul Laifer Tours
106 Parsippany Road
Parsippany
New Jersey 07054
(973 887 1188.

Additional Information

Tourists in Szentháromság tér

COMPUTER INFORMATION

TOWARDS THE END of 1997 tall yellow boxes, equipped with computer screens, appeared on the streets of Budapest. These state-of-the-art **computer information terminals** have been acquired by the town authorities and placed in eight locations. There are plans to provide even more such computers in the future, thereby making Budapest one of the first European cities with a developed computerized tourist information network. The terminal will allow tourists not only to check the addresses of various hotels and other establishments, but also to find their desired

A yellow "info-touch" computer information terminal

destination in Budapest and the shortest possible route for getting there, including travelling by public transport.

PASSPORT AND CUSTOMS REGULATIONS

TO ENTER HUNGARY, visitors must have a valid passport. The loss or theft of a passport should be reported to the appropriate consulate or embassy. To meet international regulations, Hungary has reduced to a minimum the formalities of currency and customs regulations. As well as personal belongings, visitors are now allowed to bring in 200 cigarettes, 2 litres of wine, 1 litre of liqueur, 1 kilogram each of coffee, tea and cocoa and an unlimited quantity of beer.

TAX-FREE GOODS

FOREIGN TOURISTS can apply for the refund of VAT (ÁFA in Hungarian) charged on goods purchased in Hungary. To reclaim it, visitors need to present the ÁFA invoice at the border. This only applies to sums in excess of 50,000 Hungarian forints, and does not apply to works of art. The exported goods must be new and not previously used in Hungary. They must also have been bought within the last 90 days.

BUDAPEST CARD

THIS SPLENDID new facility was introduced in 1997, designed for tourists visiting the city for three days. The Budapest Card entitles visitors to use all city transport free of charge, as well as providing free entry to 55 museums, the zoo and the funfair. It also entitles the holder to a 50 per cent discount on all guided tours of the city organised by IBUSZ, a 30 per cent discount on tickets to selected swimming centres and cultural events, a 20 per cent discount on opera tickets and a 10 per cent discount in five recommended restaurants. The card costs about 2,900 Hungarian forints for adults and 2,000 forints for children up to 14 years of age.

Cards can be purchased at tourist offices, hotel reception desks, museums and at the ticket offices of the larger metro stations. Enclosed with the card is an information pamphlet, in four languages, listing the benefits available to the cardholder.

Budapest Card

PRESS, RADIO AND TV

IN BUDAPEST all the world's top newspapers and magazines are easily accessible at hotels and the larger news stands. Bear in mind that the foreign daily newspapers on sale tend to be yesterday's editions, but even so they often sell out by lunchtime. For English-speaking tourists there are also three Hungarian weekly magazines – *Budapest Week*, *Buda and Pest* and *Budapest Sun*. These all provide comprehensive information on world events as well as full entertainment guides. Radio Bridge broadcasts in English daily, on frequency FM 102.1, from 5am until 10pm. In addition to the state and independent

English language magazines, published in Budapest

Hungarian television channels, most larger hotels offer at least one channel in English and another in German.

DISABLED TRAVELLERS

BUDAPEST IS NOT the most accessible city for disabled visitors. Public transport is virtually impossible, except for the airport bus. For special travel advice and help, contact the **Hungarian Disabled Association**. Many museums and monuments are also beset with difficulties for the disabled, although increasingly they are being renovated to be wheelchair-friendly.

BUDAPEST TIME

BUDAPEST USES Central European time, in keeping with the rest of mainland Europe, which means it is two hours ahead of Greenwich Mean Time (GMT) in the summer and one hour ahead in the winter.

Examples of the winter time differences between Budapest and other major cities are as follows: London: -1 hour; New York: -6 hours; Dallas: -7 hours; Los Angeles: -9 hours; Perth: +7 hours; Sydney: +9 hours; Auckland: +11 hours; Tokyo: +8 hours.

PUBLIC TOILETS

THERE ARE NOT many public toilets in Budapest. The cubicle type is found in some squares and parks and these are usually free.

In cafés and restaurants there are toilet attendants and the price for using the facility is clearly displayed. In wine bars and beer houses toilets tend to be free, which is all too often reflected in their poor level of cleanliness.

There are no public toilets in metro stations, except for Batthyány tér. Apart

Sign for the ladies' toilet

Sign for the gentlemen's toilet

from the generally understood picture symbols, the toilets are signed in Hungarian: *Hölgyek* (ladies) and *Urak* (gentlemen), or *Nök* (women) and *Férfiak* (men).

ELECTRICAL AND GAS APPLIANCES

HUNGARIAN ELECTRICITY supply is 220 V and the plugs needed are the standard continental type. Adapters can be purchased in most countries. Since sockets are generally earthed, the most commonly used plugs are the flat type.

Hungarian gas cookers are equipped with a bimetal safety device, which means that after lighting the knob should be held down until the burner warms up. This is an effective means of preventing the escape of any unlit gas.

Hungarian plug with two pins

Security and Health

BUDAPEST IS NOT JUST a beautiful city, it is also one with efficient and well-maintained services which help to ensure the safety and well-being of its residents. The public telephones generally work, telephone booths are equipped with a directory, the bus and tram stops display timetables and public transport is both clean and reliable. Nevertheless, as with all other central European countries, there are a growing number of negative social phenomena. Local people are increasingly complaining about rising crime rates, the plague of pickpockets and incidences of car theft. Visitors to Budapest will also be sadly aware of the growing numbers of people living on the streets.

Police Symbol

Policeman   **Policewoman**

SECURITY

Police car

ADVICE TO VISITORS

DOCUMENTS AND money should be carried in secure, inside pockets or in special money belts. Since traveller's cheques are now commonly used, there is actually no need to carry much cash on you.

Money should be exchanged at either a bank or an exchange bureau, never on the black market. Do not leave valuables in your car.

There are three multistorey car parks in the city centre, at Nos. 4–6 Aranykéz utca, No. 20 Nyár utca and on Szervita tér. Cars parked improperly are towed away to a car park outside the centre. To find out where a car has been taken, call the **Removed Cars Information** enquiries line.

Pickpockets operate mainly during rush hours, targeting crowded metro stations, buses and shopping centres. Extra care should be

Police badge

taken at the metro stations at Keleti pu railway station, and at Moszkva tér, Batthyány tér and Örs vezér tér, which tend to be target areas for those seeking to take advantage of distracted tourists. It is a good idea to have a photocopy of your passport and your travel insurance. If a passport is lost call the police in Kecskeméti utca on 317 07 11, where English is spoken. Once the appropriate police certificate is obtained, report the loss to your embassy (see p217).

Road policeman on a motorbike

HUNGARIAN POLICE are frequently seen patrolling the streets on motorbikes, on foot or in cars. In addition, every district has its own police station. The Hungarian word for police is *rendőrség*. In the event of anything going missing, because of loss or theft, a report should be made immediately to the police. In the event of a lost passport, see the above section under the heading *Advice to Visitors*.

American and Australian tourists will need a visa to enter Hungary, but European tourists can stay in Hungary without a visa for three to six months. However, after one month check the registration requirements at the local police station. In reality, this applies mainly to tourists staying in private accommodation or with friends, since all hotels, hostels and pensions automatically register foreign guests.

Tourists driving to Budapest are obliged to have the green insurance card, while those hiring a car need just their dirving licences. Hitchhiking, although not against the law, is not a recommended way of travelling in Hungary.

Women should not walk unaccompanied late at night in poorly lit areas and should avoid deserted streets. Rakóczi tér and Mátyás tér, in district VIII, have been imfamous for their brothels since the 19th century and have a long-standing tradition as hangouts for prostitutes. Prostitution has been officially outlawed in Hungary since 1950. In recent years, however, it has been tolerated and the authorities of district VIII are in the process of trying to legalize it.

MEDICAL MATTERS

WHEN TRAVELLING to Hungary it is highly recommended that visitors take out travel insurance.

Foreign nationals are only entitled to free medical help in emergencies, such as accidents or a sudden illness requiring immediate medical intervention. Any other medical care, including hospitalization, must be paid for. The cost depends on the type of insurance policy held

Pharmacy sign

and the relevant agreement between Hungary and the visitor's home country. Most insurance companies expect policy holders to pay for their treatment as they receive it and then apply for a refund on their return home. All the relevant bills and police reports must be submitted with any insurance claim. Remember that, where applicable, a report must be made to the police within seven days of any incident.

Budapest's pharmacies (*Gyógyszertár* or *Patika*) are well stocked and, in case of a minor ailment, the chemist will be able to recommend a

suitable treatment. Some drugs require a prescription, while others can be sold over the counter. If your nearest pharmacy is closed, there should be a list displayed, either on the door or in the window, of all the local chemists and it will indicate which ones are on 24-hour emergency duty.

No special vaccinations are required for Hungary and the general standard of hygiene in the country is reasonably good. That said, allergy sufferers and people with breathing difficulties should take account of the summer smog conditions, which are particularly acute in the crowded streets of Pest. Those susceptible should consider staying in the Castle District, from which cars are banned, or retreating to the wooded Buda Hills *(see p161)* or the greenery of Margaret Island *(see pp170–71)*.

Pharmacy shop front

The water supply in Budapest is of a good quality. It is generally considered safe to drink water straight from the tap.

There are also the many thermal baths *(see pp50–53)*, which can be an excellent way to relax or to treat rheumatism. However, people suffering from heart conditions should use them with caution and are advised to talk to their own doctors before departure, or to consult a duty doctor at any of the spas.

Ambulance

DIRECTORY	**Gas Emergency Service**	**Alcoholics Anonymous**	**International Vehicle Insurance**
EMERGENCY SERVICES	(334 40 00 (24-hour).	(352 89 48.	(061 209 07 30.
	Electricity Emergency Service	**BRV Lost Property**	**Removed Cars Information**
Ambulance	(350 14 01 (ask for number of local service).	(267 52 99 (lost today). (461 65 00 ext. 11346 (lost prior to today).	(307 52 08.
(104 (also 311 16 66).	**Water Emergency Service**	**Falck Emergency Medical Service**	**Telefon-doktor** (317 21 11.
Fire (105 (also 321 62 16).	(329 60 93.	(275 15 35.	**Vehicle Assistance and Breakdown Emergency Service**
Police (107.	**HELPLINES**	**Foreigners' Registry Office** Izabella utca 61.	(088. Mak-Magyar Autóklub
Metropolitan Police (318 08 00.	**Aids Helpline** (366 92 83 🕒 8am–4pm Mon, Wed & Thu, 9am–noon Tue & Fri.	(311 86 42. 🕒 8am–noon Mon–Wed & Fri, 8am–6pm Thu.	(345 16 87 (English spoken).

Local Currency and Banking

Bureau de change sign

THE HUNGARIAN CURRENCY system is rapidly approaching the European standard. Budapest now boasts many modern banks, both Hungarian and foreign, which are located in smart and spacious buildings. The service is efficient and courteous. There are many automatic cash dispensers and bureaux de change in the town centre and around the railway stations. An increasing number of shops and restaurants now accept credit cards, but it is still more common in Budapest to pay for goods and services in cash. Most banks will now also advance money on a credit card.

Cash dispenser

CURRENCY REGULATIONS

FOREIGNERS are allowed to bring 350,000 Hungarian forints into Hungary, which at the beginning of 1998 was equal to about US $1,600 (970 pounds sterling). The same amount of money can be taken out of the country. There are no restrictions concerning the denominations of the Hungarian currency brought in or taken out.

Tourists who bring in foreign currencies totalling in excess of 100,000 Hungarian forints should declare them on arrival and ask the customs official for a receipt. This can then be presented when leaving the country, as the same limit applies to foreign currencies brought in and taken out of the country, without the need for an additional licence.

Foreign currencies can be easily exchanged into forints in banks, bureaux de change and hotels, but there is a limit of 20,000 Hungarian forints per day. To exchange any unspent forints back into a

Entrance to a branch of the Budapest Bank, in Váci utca

convertible currency, visitors have to present the proof of purchase. So keep all the exchange receipts until the end of the visit. Otherwise, tourists will find themselves at home with forints that devalue quite rapidly, at a rate of 10–15 per cent relative to the major foreign currencies.

BANKS AND BUREAUX DE CHANGE

FOR THE BEST rate of exchange, take foreign currency to a bank or bureau de change, which are generally run by Hungarian banks. Before changing money, check the rate of exchange, as they do tend to vary quite widely. The rates quoted by some exchange offices can be misleading as they could apply only to sums in excess of 200,000 forints, which is stated in a very small print. The least favourable rates are in hotels and at the airport, while the best are offered by the bureaux de change near the railway stations and in the town centre, in Petőfi Sándor utca. A reasonable, average rate can usually be found at Hungarian banks.

The branches of the **National Bank of Hungary** and **Budapest Bank** are open Monday till Friday, from 10:30am until 2pm. Merchant banks, such as **Kereskedelmi**, the **Magyar Hitel Bank** and the **Postbank**, are open Monday till Thursday, between 8am and 3pm, and on Friday between 8am and 1pm. All banks are closed on

Saturdays and Sundays, but the bureaux de change and automatic cash dispensers remain open.

Most hotels, large stores, smart shops and restaurants accept credit cards. The most widely accepted are VISA, American Express, MasterCard and Diners Club. As elsewhere, the logos of accepted credit cards appear on the doors of establishments.

DIRECTORY

BANKS

Budapest Bank
Alkotmány utca 3. **Map** 2 E3.
269 23 58.
Honvéd utca 10. **Map** 2 E3.
269 23 53.
Hercegprímás utca 5. **Map** 2 E4.
266 32 22.

Kereskedelmi
Vigadó tér 1. **Map** 4 D1.
328 90 00.

Magyar Hitel Bank
Szent István tér 15. **Map** 2 E5.
Türr utca 9. **Map** 2 E1.
Apáczai Csere János utca 7.
Map 2 D5.
267 06 50.

National Bank of Hungary
1054 Budapest, Szabadság tér 8/9.
Map 2 E4.
269 47 60.

Postbank
József nádor tér 1 &10. **Map** 2 E5.
Andrássy út 5. **Map** 2 F4.
Erzsébet körut 17. **Map** 7 A2.
318 08 55.

Hungarian currency

The Hungarian currency unit is the forint (HUF or Ft), which formerly divided into 100 fillérs. Although fillér coins are now no longer in use, prices are still sometimes quoted in them and then rounded up when payment is made.

500 HUF

1,000 HUF

5,000 HUF

Banknotes
Hungarian banknotes are issued in denominations of 200, 500, 1,000, 2,000, 5,000 and 10,000 forints. Both an old and a new style of some banknotes are currently legal tender.

200 HUF

500 HUF

1,000 HUF

2,000 HUF

10,000 HUF

Coins
Currently in circulation are coins of 1, 2, 5, 10, 20, 50 and 100 forints. As with the banknotes, new coins are gradually being phased in – the new 100 forint coin, with a brass disc inside a nickel ring, is now the only legal version.

1 HUF

2 HUF

5 HUF

10 HUF

20 HUF

50 HUF

100 HUF

Telephone and Postal Services

Telephone symbol

To OBTAIN your required telephone number in Budapest demands enormous patience. In recent years the numbering has been changed several times, due to the increase in subscribers. Generally speaking, telephones are not Budapest's strongest point, although there are many telephone boxes, even on the outskirts of town. Most of the telephone boxes have a telephone directory secured with a chain, but it is still not easy to obtain the right number.

Telephone box

USING THE TELEPHONE

TELEPHONE CARDS are the best option when making calls. The cards can be bought in either 50 or 120 units. They are widely available from tobacconist shops, post offices, street vendors and some newspaper kiosks. Alternatively, coin phone boxes accept 20, 50 and 100 forint coins. To make an international telephone call you need to dial 00, wait for the dialing signal and then dial the country code, followed by the rest of the number. Ironically, international telephone calls are much easier to make than domestic ones.

Budapest telephone numbers consist of seven digits (when combined with the dialing code there are eight digits). There is no advantage in using the services of a hotel operator, as this only makes the call very much more expensive.

Cheaper off-peak rates apply throughout the night and on public holidays.

USING A CARD TELEPHONE

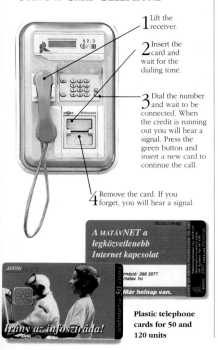

1 Lift the receiver.

2 Insert the card and wait for the dialing tone.

3 Dial the number and wait to be connected. When the credit is running out you will hear a signal. Press the green button and insert a new card to continue the call.

4 Remove the card. If you forget, you will hear a signal.

Plastic telephone cards for 50 and 120 units

USING A COIN TELEPHONE

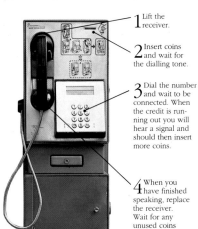

1 Lift the receiver.

2 Insert coins and wait for the dialling tone.

3 Dial the number and wait to be connected. When the credit is running out you will hear a signal and should then insert more coins.

4 When you have finished speaking, replace the receiver. Wait for any unused coins to be returned.

| 5 HUF | 10 HUF | 20 HUF |

Budapest's Districts

Budapest is divided into 23 districts. Streets of the same name may appear in several different districts, so it is important when addressing a letter to quote the four-digit postal code.

Hungarian stamps

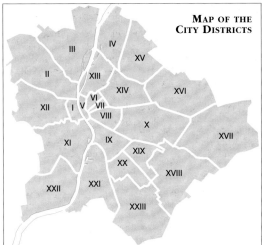

MAP OF THE CITY DISTRICTS

POSTAL SERVICES

WHEN GOING TO a post office in Budapest, you must be prepared to spend some time there. The Hungarian post is not very reliable, but all letters and parcels are carefully examined and weighed. The cheapest postage stamp is 65 Hungarian forints for sending a postcard. Apart from ordinary stamps, all post offices sell various special issues that are very pretty. Ask the cashier if you can see the different designs.

On weekdays, post offices are open from 8am until 6pm. They close at 2pm on Saturday and are closed all day Sunday. In the town centre, at No. 13 Petőfi Sándor utca, is a large post office selling postcards and stamps. It also has several telephones. If you know the values of the stamps you require, it is easier to buy them from a *trafik* (a

Post office logo

tobacconist shop or a newspaper kiosk), as there are usually long queues at post offices.

Post offices cannot be avoided, however. Airmail (*légiposta*) or registered letters have to be posted at a post office and poste restante mail has to be collected there. Telegrams can also be sent by telephone from post offices. Public fax machines can be found at the Telecommunication Trade Office, at Nos. 17–19 Petőfi Sándor utca.

Budapest postal codes are four-digit numbers. The first digit refers to Budapest, the second and third digits refer to the district number and the fourth digit defines the postal area within the district.

Post boxes are emptied daily at the times indicated on the front of the box.

MAIN POST OFFICE

Petőfi utca 13. **Map** 4 E1.
📞 *318 48 11.*

POST OFFICES OPEN 24 HOURS

Nyugati
Teréz körút 51. **Map** 2 F3.
📞 *312 12 00.*

Keleti
Baross tér 11c. **Map** 8 D2.
📞 *322 10 99.*

Red post box for national and international mail

USEFUL TELEPHONE NUMBERS AND DIALLING CODES

- Sending telegrams: 192
- International operator calls: 190
- Inland operator calls: 191
- Inland information: 198
- International information: 199
- Wake-up call: 193
- Speaking clock: 080

- SDC for international calls: 00
- SDC from Budapest to other Hungarian towns: 06
- SDC from Budapest to Australia: 00 61
- SDC from Budapest to France: 00 33
- SDC from Budapest to New Zealand: 00 64
- SDC from Budapest to South Africa: 00 27
- SDC from Budapest to the UK: 00 44
- SDC from Budapest to the US: 00 1

GETTING TO BUDAPEST

Hungarians like to boast that Budapest is the heart of central Europe – a claim with some justification as the city acts as a major crossroads linking north to south and west to east. It has excellent rail links with the whole of Europe and its two largest railway stations, Keleti pu and Nyugati pu *(see p227)* are conveniently situated in the centre of town. The country's motorway network has undergone improvements in recent years, successfully making up for decades of neglect. Budapest can now be reached by motorway from all but the northern direction. Travelling down by car from Slovakia and Poland, via Vác, is not recommended. The poorly maintained and narrow road makes for a very tedious journey, particularly at peak travelling times, such as in high season and at weekends. For sheer comfort and convenience, it is far better to make use of the air links Budapest has with major cities throughout Europe. The journey from London to Budapest, for example, takes just two and a half hours.

A plane owned by the Hungarian airline, Malév

ARRIVING BY AIR

Airlines from around 40 towns and cities, in 27 different countries, now fly to Budapest. The city's Ferihegy airport is used by all the major international airlines, including **Air France**, **Alitalia**, **British Airways**, **Delta Air Lines**, **Lufthansa** and, of course, the Hungarian national carrier, **Malév**.

British Airways and Malév each operate two daily scheduled flights between London's Heathrow airport and Budapest. There are also four code-share flights a week from Gatwick airport, which are a joint operation between British Airways and Malév. It is possible to fly to Budapest from other airports in the UK, including Manchester, but only by taking a connecting flight from another European city, such as Brussels or Frankfurt.

Consequently, the flight time and cost are both greater.

Delta flights from the United States involve a transfer or touch down in Frankfurt or Zurich, but there is a daily direct code-share flight from New York's JFK airport with Delta reservations on a Malév-owned plane. The flight takes around ten hours.

TICKETS AND CONCESSIONS

When planning to travel to Budapest by air, bear in mind that substantial savings can be made by purchasing APEX tickets, although they do carry certain conditions. The tickets require fixed dates for departure and return, and the stay must include at least one Saturday and last no longer

Malév stewardess

than one month. APEX tickets usually need to be bought in advance but it is worth checking purchasing arrangements with individual airlines.

For those aged 2–24, British Airways offer youth fares to Budapest which, although nominally higher than the lowest APEX fare, carry none of the restrictions. Autumn and winter is an opportune time to look around for special offers, as the low season brings with it some very good deals. Look out for excellent low-price weekend flight-plus-hotel deals between September and March.

FERIHEGY AIRPORT

Budapest's international airport at Ferihegy is 15 km (9 miles) from the city centre and has two terminals. Ferihegy 1 was opened in 1950 and has been constantly modernized ever since. Situated a little further away from the city is Ferihegy 2. Originally built in 1985, it was extended to accommodate more flights in 1997–8.

Ferihegy 2 deals with the arrivals and departures of the Hungarian carrier, Malév, and other airlines including Air France, Alitalia, Delta and Lufthansa. Ferihegy 1 is used by all other airlines.

Both terminals offer comfort and good amenities to passengers. Catering facilities

Check-in desk at Budapest's modern Ferihegy 2 air terminal

A Malév aircraft parked outside Ferihegy 2 terminal

include bars, cafés and restaurants, and there are numerous boutiques and shops. Having passed through passport control you will find duty-free shops offering attractive prices on all kinds of goods – not only Hungarian products. Both terminals have information centres where accommodation can be booked (see p215). All the major car rental firms have desks in the arrival halls of both Ferihegy 1 and Ferihegy 2. The main names to look out for are Avis, Budget, Europcar and Főtaxi (see p228).

Airport car rental company logo

Malév airlines' logo

GETTING TO THE CENTRE

For around 1,200 Hungarian forints the **Airport Minibus Shuttle** will take passengers from either terminal to any address in the city centre. As well as being wheelchair-accessible, they also run a pick-up service for the return journey. Every half an hour from 6am–10pm a minibus with "Centrum-Airport" on the side leaves for Erzsébet tér bus station. You can also take bus 93 to Kőbánya-Kispest metro station, followed by the blue M3 metro line.

Taxis from the airport are very costly – ensure that the driver starts the meter or you may well be overcharged.

BUDAPEST'S AIR LINKS WITH EUROPE

Budapest has air links with major cities in every European country. From each of the locations marked on the map you can travel to Budapest in under three hours.

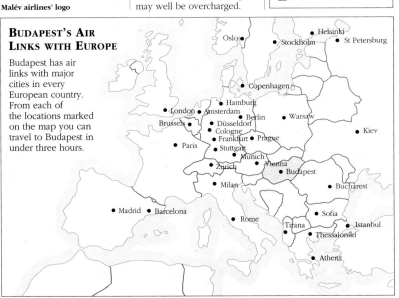

Ticket offices at a main railway station in Budapest

RAIL TRAVEL

BUDAPEST has direct rail links with 25 other capital cities. Every day, more than 50 international trains, many of them express services, arrive and depart from the city's four railway stations. Some trains terminate here, others enable passengers to join connecting services. Hungarian trains are widely considered a very efficient means of getting around, and with good reason. They invariably depart and arrive at the right time.

Trains from Budapest to Vienna, the main communication hub for western Europe, depart approximately every three hours. The fastest trains run at top speeds of 140–160 km/h (85–100 mph). The travelling time is an efficient 2 hours 25 minutes. The "Hellas" train, which also has car carriages, runs from Keleti pu to Thessaloníki in Greece three times a week (Tuesdays, Fridays and Sundays) between June and September and twice a week (Tuesdays and Fridays) between October and May.

Detailed information on all domestic and international rail travel running to and from Budapest can be obtained from either Keleti pu or the MÁV (Hungarian Railways) ticket sales office, which is centrally located at No. 35 Andrássy út.

It is worth knowing that there are several concessionary fares available. Foreign visitors to Hungary can buy a season ticket that is valid for

between seven and ten days of unlimited travel throughout the country. Passengers up to 26 years old are entitled to a 30 per cent discount on fares. For those working abroad or possessing dual nationality, the BIGT cut-price tickets are available. People over 60 years of age who buy the RES card, which is valid for one year, will receive a 30 per cent discount on most European rail travel. In addition, the Hungarian rail companies generally offer a number of cheap tickets to travellers coming from outside Europe.

Local trains can be either "slow" (*személy*) or "speedy" (*sebes*), but both invariably make frequent stops. A much better option if time is **Railwayman** tight is the fast (*gyors*) train. There are also 29 modern Intercity trains, which will take passengers to Pécs, Miskolc, Debrecen, Szeged and Békéscsaba in around 1–3 hours. Seat reservations, costing a small extra charge, are required on these clean and comfortable trains.

RAILWAY STATIONS

THERE ARE three main railway stations in Budapest – Keleti pu (East), Nyugati pu (West) and Déli pu (South). A fourth station, Józsefvaros pu, handles mainly domestic traffic. Most international trains run from Keleti pu. The express train to Croatia ("Maestral") and trains to the Lake Balaton resorts leave from Déli pu, almost every hour during the high season. The international express trains to Amicus, Aquincum, Caliudopolis, Corona, Partium, Gerecse and Baia Mare depart from Nyugati pu.

The easiest way to get to Keleti pu is by the M2 metro. The same line connects Keleti pu with Déli pu. For Nyugati pu take the M3 metro line, or trams 4 or 6. A special minibus runs between the various railway stations.

Rail information

℃ *461 55 00* (international).
℃ *313 68 35* (national).

COACH TRAVEL

BUDAPEST has two international coach stations. The scheduled coaches to western Europe depart from Erzébet tér station, while the Népstadion út station handles the eastern European traffic. The former is situated right in the town centre, near Deák tér, and can be easily accessed from any of the three metro lines. The latter, situated near the People's Stadium at Nos. 45–52 Hungária körút, is best reached by the M2 metro line. The international routes are served by luxury coaches, which have all the usual

The imposing exterior of one of Budapest's main railway stations

Luxury air-conditioned tourist coach

facilities. The domestic traffic is served by Volánbusz coaches, which operate routes to most of the major towns throughout Hungary.

Coach information
📞 317 29 66.

TRAVELLING BY BOAT

FROM APRIL UNTIL October hydrofoils run along the Danube between Vienna and Budapest, via Bratislava.

It is also possible to take a hydrofoil or pleasure boat along the Danube bend, to towns such as Esztergom and Visegrád (see p164). See the timetable at the departure point at Vigadó tér for exact times.

TRAVELLING BY CAR

THE LACK OF parking makes arriving by public transport preferable to travelling by car. Driving distances to Budapest are: from Vienna, 250 km (155 miles); from Prague, 560 km (350 miles); and from Frankfurt, 950 km (590 miles).

Motorways are marked by the letter "M" and international highways with the letter "E". The speed limit is 120 km/h (75 mph). Seven main roads lead out of Budapest and one, the A8, starts in Székésfehérvár. The M1 stretches from Budapest to the Hegyeshalom border crossing, where it joins the Austrian motorway network.

Tolls are payable up to Györ. The M3 links Budapest to Gyöngyös and is being extended to join up with the Slovak road network. From Budapest the M5 leads to Kecskemét (see p166), while the M7 links to the Balaton resorts.

Minor roads have three or four digits, with the first digit indicating the number of the connecting main road.

The police patrol right from the Hungarian border, so it is worth studying the traffic regulations displayed on information boards. These include: driving with the headlights on, wearing seatbelts in the back and keeping to the speed limit of 50 km/h (30 mph) in built-up areas.

Vehicle assistance
📞 0 88.

A road sign directing traffic to Margaret Bridge and the M3

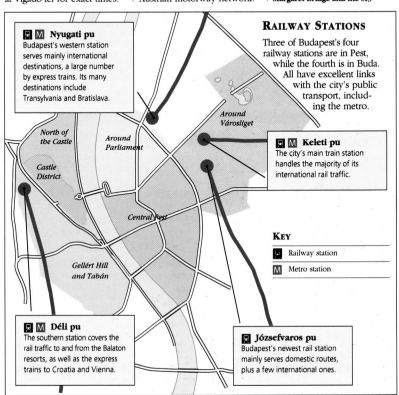

🚉 Ⓜ **Nyugati pu**
Budapest's western station serves mainly international destinations, a large number by express trains. Its many destinations include Transylvania and Bratislava.

Around Városliget

North of the Castle

Around Parliament

Castle District

Central Pest

Gellért Hill and Tabán

RAILWAY STATIONS

Three of Budapest's four railway stations are in Pest, while the fourth is in Buda. All have excellent links with the city's public transport, including the metro.

🚉 Ⓜ **Keleti pu**
The city's main train station handles the majority of its international rail traffic.

KEY

🚉 Railway station

Ⓜ Metro station

🚉 Ⓜ **Déli pu**
The southern station covers the rail traffic to and from the Balaton resorts, as well as the express trains to Croatia and Vienna.

🚉 **Józsefvaros pu**
Budapest's newest rail station mainly serves domestic routes, plus a few international ones.

GETTING AROUND BUDAPEST

BUDAPEST IS a sprawling city with many suburban districts. However, most of its main tourist attractions are centrally located and can be easily reached by the city's public transport system, or on foot. The many choices of transport by rail, road and even water provide the visitor to Budapest with ample opportunity to travel through and around the city to reach their chosen

One of Budapest's environmentally-friendly city buses

destinations. The infrastructure of Budapest is chiefly determined by the *körúts* (ring roads), which radiate out from the city centre and into the city's suburbs. The metro system mainly operates in Pest, although the red M2 line crosses the Danube at Batthyány tér and runs just north of the Castle District. The overland HÉV train provides a service from the city centre to the suburbs.

DRIVING IN BUDAPEST

THE LARGE number of one-way streets in Budapest make it a very difficult city for visitors to navigate by car. The many changes of direction often result in unfamiliar drivers becoming lost. Any confusion brought about by the complex system of roads is further aggravated by the heavy rush-hour traffic. There are also few places to park in the city, so it is much better to sightsee on foot or by public transport.

In Hungary it is strictly forbidden to drive following

One-way traffic in direction indicated

Stop sign at road junction

End of pedestrian and cycle zone

any alcohol consumption. If any trace of alcohol is found in the bloodstream, the fine for drink-driving can be as high as 30,000 Hungarian forints (approximately US $180) and is only payable in forints.

All car occupants, both in the front and the back seats, are required by law to wear seat belts. Motorcycle drivers and passengers must wear helmets at all times.

In built-up areas the speed limit is 50 km/h (30 mph), and most of the road signs follow the European pattern. In towns the use of the horn is legally restricted to cases of imminent danger. Despite this, Hungarian drivers hoot loudly and often at both pedestrians and other drivers.

New regulations permit the use of mobile telephones by drivers only when the car is fitted with a hands-free system. Otherwise, it is advisable to pull over and stop if you wish to make or receive a call.

BUDAPEST ON FOOT

Budapest is a city in which every pedestrian will find something of interest. Visitors who enjoy rambling along leafy trails should take the railway or bus 21 from Moszkva tér to the Buda Hills (*see p161*). Those who prefer to stroll through picturesque streets and alleyways should go to Buda's Castle District, which is closed to traffic. Váci utca (Váci Street, *see p127*) is fully pedestrianized and has seats where weary walkers can rest and watch the bustle. The promenade along the Danube is one of the most pleasant walks in Budapest.

Pedestrian zone

V. Kerület, Lipótváros
Báthori utca
2 — 2

New street name plate

OKTÓBER 6. UTCA

Old street name plate

Pedestrian crossing

Walk signal at a pedestrian crossing

HIRING A CAR

CARS CAN BE HIRED from the airport on arrival in Budapest (*see p225*), or from one of several car hire offices, such as Budget Hungary (214 04 20) who give discounts to Budapest Card holders (*see p216*). Be prepared to leave a credit card deposit of between 50,000 and 300,000 forints and pay US $20–30 per day plus 30 cents per mile or US $100 per day for unlimited mileage.

PARKING

Budapest's car parks, indicated by a blue "P", reduce the problem of on-street parking (and also relieve traffic congestion). There are four covered car parks in the centre, at Nyár utca, Aranykéz utca, Osvát utca and Szervita tér. There are a further 15 attended and 30 unattended car parks situated in other busy parts of town. Several hotels also have car parks, which offer spare parking spaces to non-guests. Parking charges vary from 80 to 250 Hungarian forints per hour.

Parking at the main tourist attractions, for example, near Hősök tere (Heroes' Square, see pp142–3) or the Citadel (see pp92–3), is free for the duration of the visit. These car parks cannot be used by people not visiting the particular sight.

Stopping and parking prohibited

FIZETŐ ÖVEZET
H–P: 08.00–18.00
Szo : 08.00–12.00
MAXIMUM 2 óra
Fizetés a jegykiadó automatánál.

Parking of cars allowed in this zone for a maximum of two hours

CLAMPING AND TOWING

Wheel-clamping is growing in Budapest; all illegally parked vehicles are subject to clamping. As well as paying a fine, it costs around 8,000 forints (US $35) to release a car from a clamp. Parking meters often give the telephone number to contact in the event of wheel-clamping. It is also worth asking a car park attendant for advice, or going personally to No. 5 Károly körút to pay the fine and get declamped. If the car has been towed away, details on its whereabouts and retrieval can be obtained by telephoning 307 52 08.

CYCLING

Cycling around Budapest is difficult and fairly dangerous. Cyclists have to be careful of the tram rails and the uneven, cobble-stoned surface of some roads. Budapest's main roads are closed to

A wheel-clamped car

cyclists and designated cycle lanes continue to be in short supply. Until recently, Szentendrei út was the only road with anything resembling a cycle lane. However, the provision of three new cycle routes in Budapest has made cycling an increasingly popular and safe pastime.

The best way to see some of Budapest on a bicycle is by taking a cycling trip around Margaret Island (see pp172–3). There are several bike-hire shops on the island, which can provide everything that is needed for a day's cycling. The range of bicycles includes children's bikes, thus enabling family groups to explore the paths and avenues of this picturesque, quiet island. Numerous kiosks selling food and drinks are to be found on the island, so cyclists can spend the whole day there.

PARKING METERS

When parking in a metered parking bay, the length of stay must be specified in advance. Parking without a valid ticket or overstaying the allocated time can lead to a parking fine or wheel-clamping. In 1997 parking meters were installed between Nagykörút and the Danube, allowing cars to park here for a limited period.

Road sign indicating parking meters

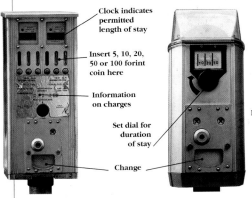

Clock indicates permitted length of stay

Insert 5, 10, 20, 50 or 100 forint coin here

Information on charges

Set dial for duration of stay

Change

Card slot

Coin slot

Clock

Press green button after inserting coins

Press red button to set required parking time

Ticket appears here

Getting Around by Metro

BUDAPEST HAS THREE METRO LINES *(see inside back cover)*, which intersect only at Deák tér station. Here passengers can change trains (stamping their tickets once again), by following the clearly marked passageways. The oldest line, the yellow M1 line, runs just beneath the surface of the city. Built in 1894, it is known as the Millennium Line after the celebrations that took place two years later *(see p142)*. Recently it has been modernized and extended. Two more lines – the red M2 and blue M3 lines – have been added since 1970, serving the rest of the city.

Sign over the entrance to the M1 metro line at Oktogon tér station

Signs for the M2 and M3 lines

THE METRO SYSTEM

TWO WORDS to remember when using Budapest's metro system are *bejárat*, meaning entrance and *kijárat*, meaning exit, both of which are always clearly marked.

To plan a journey, consult the map at the back of this guide. Most metro stations display maps of the local area, and maps of each line are placed over the doors inside the trains. A recorded voice message announces when the door is closing and gives the name of the next station.

Smoking and eating are not permitted on the trains, and music can only be listened to through headphones. Dogs are allowed to travel on the metro, but only when muzzled. They are required to have a franked ticket for the normal fare. This rule applies to all forms public transport, whatever the size or breed of the dog.

The metro service runs from 4:30am until just after 11pm.

Metro Museum
Deák tér. ☐ *10am – 6pm Tue – Sun.*

A typical station on the original M1 metro line

USING A TICKET

Tickets are bought in advance and need to be franked in a machine before a journey is made. On the machines, the machines are located outside the platforms on the all the lines. Tickets are checked frequently, and there is a fine of 1,000 Hungarian forints for travelling without a valid ticket.

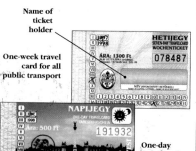

Name of ticket holder

One-week travel card for all public transport

One-day travel card for all public transport

BKV TICKET PRICES

75 forints: single ticket valid for one journey, without an interchange, by bus, tram, metro, trolley bus, funicular or HÉV.
675 forints: 10-ticket book.
1,250 forints: 20-ticket book.
600 forints: one-day travel card.
1,550 forints: one-week travel card.
900 forints: family weekend ticket.
3,000 forints: monthly ticket (photocard).

SINGLE METRO FARES

50 forints: valid for three stations, without interchange (30 minutes' travel)
80 forints: valid for five stations, with interchange (1 hour's travel)
120 forints: valid for more than five stations, with one interchange (1 hour's travel).

Single ticket for all public transport

Travelling on the HÉV

The suburban railway logo

THE OVERLAND HÉV RAILWAY provides an essential means of transport that connects Budapest with its suburban districts. It carries residents to and from work and tourists to attractions located 20–30 km (10–20 miles) away from the city centre. The standard tickets *(see p230)* used on other forms of transport can be used to travel to the central destinations on the HÉV line, but additional fares are payable to more distant destinations. Tickets can either be bought at stations before travelling or from the conductor while on the train.

A standard HÉV train carriage

SUBURBAN RAIL LINES

THE HÉV LINE most commonly used by tourists runs north from Batthyány tér *(see p100)* towards Szentendre *(see p165)*, taking in such sights as Aquincum *(see pp162–3)* along the way. Many of the trains on this line terminate at Békásmegyer rather than running on to Szentendre. Check the destination on the front of the train before boarding. Another line runs from Örs vezér tere (at the eastern terminus of the M2 metro line)

to Gödöllő, passing the *Hungororing* Grand Prix race track *(see p59)* near Mogyoród en route. Gödöllő, a small Baroque town, was once the summer residence of the Habsburgs *(see pp28–9)*.

The third HÉV line begins at Közágóhíd and terminates at Ráckeve *(see p167)*. Tourists who make this long journey can enjoy a visit to the palace of Prince Eugene of Savoy.

The HÉV service between Boráros tér and Csepel Island is the longest at approximately 50 km (30 miles).

OTHER TOWN TRANSPORT

THE BUDAVÁRI SIKLÓ is an old funicular railway, which takes passengers from the head of the Chain Bridge in Buda to the top of Castle Hill.

Several modes of transport operate in the Buda Hills *(see p161)*. A cog-wheel railway connects Szilágyi Erszébet fasor with Széchenyi Hill, with its picturesque walking trails, while the Children's Railway runs from there to the Hűvös Valley. A chair lift, or *libegö*, descends from the top of János Hill down onto Zugligeti út.

Getting Around by Taxi

Taxi sign

IT HAS ALWAYS BEEN EASY to find a taxi in Budapest, and now, with over 15,000 registered cabs, the competition for passengers is fierce. Nevertheless, not all taxi drivers read the meter correctly and they have been known to exploit foreign visitors, especially those unfamiliar with Budapest who are travelling to the city centre from airports or railway stations. To reduce this risk, choose a taxi whose tariffs and meters are clearly displayed.

A typical taxi meter

FARES

TAXI RANKS can be found throughout Budapest and are seldom empty. Taxis can also be hailed on the street but it is often better to book one from your hotel. The current fare for official taxis is a flat

rate of 50 Hungarian forints plus a further 140–50 forints for every kilometre travelled. But before getting in to the taxi, ask what the fare will be.

A licenced Budapest taxi

USEFUL TAXI NUMBERS:

Budataxi 233 33 33.
City Taxi 211 11 11.
Főtaxi 0680 22 22 22.
Palota Taxi 221 11 11.
Rádiótaxi 377 77 77.
Taxi 2000 200 00 00.
Tele5 355 55 55.
Volán Taxi 466 66 66.
6x6 Taxi 266 66 66.

Ensure that the meter is set at the beginning of the journey and get a receipt for the fare. Fares increase from year to year but can be negotiated with unlicenced taxis. This price should always be agreed in advance.

Getting Around by Tram

Budapest tram logo

THERE ARE OVER 30 tram lines in Budapest, which extend to practically every part of the city. These yellow trams are an efficient and speedy means of getting around Budapest, as they avoid traffic and run very frequently. Services start early in the morning, at around 4:30am, and run regularly throughout the day until 11pm or midnight, depending on the route. Night trams operate only on certain routes, at an average of four trams per hour. Timetables are displayed at each stop. It is worth knowing that *utolsó indul* means "last tram".

THE TRAM SYSTEM

TICKETS FOR trams can be bought at metro stations, tobacconist shops *(trafiks)* and some newspaper kiosks. Passes valid for a week or

Yellow Budapest tram

more require a photograph and can only be bought at metro stations.

When ticket offices are closed, tickets should be bought from the metro station guard. Tickets are valid for a single journey where no changes are involved, and can be used on any form of public transport. It can be cheaper and more convenient to buy books of 10 tickets.

TRAVELLING WITH LUGGAGE

EVERY PASSENGER on the tram, just as on the bus or trolley bus, is entitled to carry two pieces of luggage. These should not exceed 40 by 50 by 80 cm (16 by 20 by 30 inches) or 20 by 20 by 200 cm (8 by 8 by 80 inches) in

TRAM STOP

Every tram stop displays the appropriate tram numbers and the timetable.

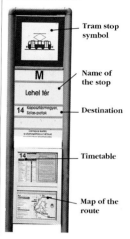

- Tram stop symbol
- Name of the stop
- Destination
- Timetable
- Map of the route

size. You can also carry one pair of ice skates and one pair of skis, providing they are clean, as well as a child's buggy. If you need to transport a bicycle or a larger item of luggage, up to 100 by 100 by 200 cm (40 by 40 by 80 inches) in size, then the rack railway or the designated carriages of the HÉV trains should be used. Any items left on public transport can be traced at the Lost Property Office, at No. 18 Akácfa utca *(see p219)*.

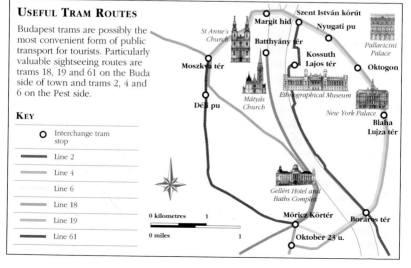

USEFUL TRAM ROUTES

Budapest trams are possibly the most convenient form of public transport for tourists. Particularly valuable sightseeing routes are trams 18, 19 and 61 on the Buda side of town and trams 2, 4 and 6 on the Pest side.

KEY

O	Interchange tram stop
▬	Line 2
▬	Line 4
▬	Line 6
▬	Line 18
▬	Line 19
▬	Line 61

Szent István körút
Margit hid
Nyugati pu
St Anne's Church
Battyány tér
Pallavicini Palace
Moszkva tér
Kossuth Lajos tér
Oktogon
Ethnographical Museum
Mátyás Church
Déli pu
New York Palace
Blaha Lujza tér
Gellért Hotel and Baths Complex
Móricz Körtér
Boráros tér
Oktober 23 u.

0 kilometres   1
0 miles   1

Getting Around by Bus

Budapest bus logo

BUDAPEST HAS ABOUT 200 different bus routes, which altogether cover most of the city. The blue Ikarus buses generally run from 4:30am until 11pm, with departures on most routes every 10–20 minutes. Times and a list of destinations are on display at most stops. Ordinary buses are indicated by black numbers and stop at every stop. Buses with red numbers follow express routes and omit a number of stops.

THE BUS SYSTEM

BUDAPEST's bus transport is extremely efficient and makes exploring the city easy, even for first-time visitors. Tickets can be purchased at metro stations and from tobacconist shops *(trafiks)*. They must be punched upon entering the bus.

The driver always announces the next stop, often informing the passengers about any interchanges. To ensure that the bus stops, passengers should press the button located by the door before their required stop, otherwise the bus may carry on. When arriving at or leaving a bus stop, most drivers will welcome or bid farewell to passengers. Remember that Budapest's bus drivers tend to drive fast and that the streets, particularly in Buda, can be steep. This combination makes it advisable to hang on tightly to the hand grips when standing on a bus.

BUS STOP

The layout of bus stops is very similar to that of trams and trolley bus stops.

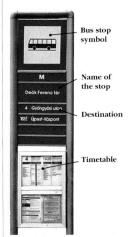

Bus stop symbol

Name of the stop

Destination

Timetable

A clean and efficient Ikarus bus in Budapest

Getting Around by Trolley Bus

TROLLEY BUSES SERVE mainly the suburbs and as such are little used by tourists. They are a particularly uncomfortable form of transport, as they move slowly along narrow streets. In addition, their pantographs often get dislodged, causing short breaks in the journey.

Trolley bus stop symbol

THE TROLLEY BUS SYSTEM

THE SAME RULES apply to travelling on a trolley bus as to travelling on a bus. Again, remember to signal to

the driver by pressing the button located above the door when approaching your stop. Otherwise, if there are no passengers waiting at the stop, the driver will not automatically come to a halt.

Trolley buses are numbered from 70 upwards and there are about 15 different routes in Budapest. Tickets must be punched upon entering the bus, and are the same type as for other forms of public transport. Failure to punch the ticket may result in a fine of 1,000 Hungarian forints. A particularly pleasant route is trolley bus 70, which runs between Kossuth Lajos tér and Erzsébet Királyné útja.

TICKET VENDING MACHINE

Tickets are sold at tobacconist shops (trafiks), *metro stations and the vending machines at major transport junctions and HÉV railway stations.*

Insert 1, 2, 5, 10, 20, 50 or 100 HUF coins

Press button to receive ticket

Check the amount paid

Collect the ticket and change

STREET FINDER

THE MAP REFERENCES for all the sights, hotels, bars, restaurants, shops and entertainment venues described in this book refer to the maps in this section. A complete index of street names marked on the maps appears on the following pages. The map below shows the area of Budapest covered by the *Street Finder* and is colour-coded by area. The *Street Finder* also includes bus and tram routes, major sights and places of interest together with other useful information listed in the key below.

As an aid to navigation, all street names, both on the *Street Finder* and in the index, are in Hungarian. Slightly confusing are the terms *utca* (often abbreviated to *u*), which means street, and *út* meaning avenue, a term mainly applied to wide, busy roads. Another commonly used term is *körút* which means ring road.

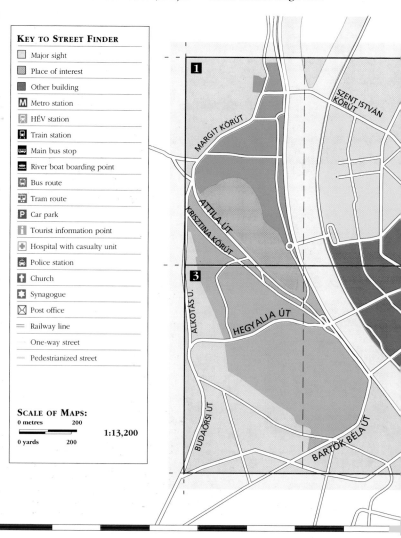

KEY TO STREET FINDER

▢	Major sight
▢	Place of interest
▢	Other building
M	Metro station
▢	HÉV station
▢	Train station
▢	Main bus stop
▢	River boat boarding point
▢	Bus route
▢	Tram route
P	Car park
i	Tourist information point
✚	Hospital with casualty unit
▢	Police station
✚	Church
✚	Synagogue
⊠	Post office
═	Railway line
—	One-way street
—	Pedestrianized street

SCALE OF MAPS:

0 metres   200

0 yards   200

1:13,200

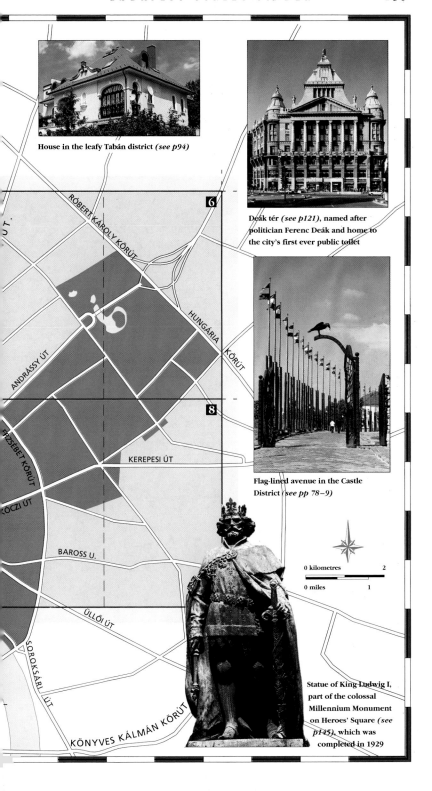

House in the leafy Tabán district *(see p94)*

Deák tér *(see p121)*, named after politician Ferenc Deák and home to the city's first ever public toilet

Flag-lined avenue in the Castle District *(see pp 78–9)*

RÓBERT KÁROLY KÖRÚT

6

ANDRÁSSY ÚT

HUNGÁRIA KÖRÚT

8

ERZSÉBET KÖRÚT

KEREPESI ÚT

RÁKÓCZI ÚT

BAROSS U.

0 kilometres   2

0 miles   1

ÜLLŐI ÚT

SOROKSÁRI ÚT

Statue of King Ludwig I, part of the colossal Millennium Monument on Heroes' Square *(see p145)*, which was completed in 1929

KÖNYVES KÁLMÁN KÖRÚT

Street Finder Index

HUNGARIAN USES the following letters not found in English: á, ó, ö, ő, ú and ű. As in the Hungarian alphabet, they are listed here as letters in there own right, following a, o and u respectively. Á is pronounced like 'a' in father while ó is a long version of the 'ou' in 'ought'. Ö is like 'ur' in 'pleasure', ő is a longer version of ö, ü is like the French 'tu' and ű is a longer version of ü. Most sights, buildings and places of interest are marked on the maps in their Hungarian forms only.

USEFUL WORDS

utca	street
út	avenue
körút	ring road
köz	lane
fasor	alley
tér	square
körtér	circus
ház	house
palota	palace
templom	church
kápolna	chapel
torony	tower
hid	bridge
hegy	hill

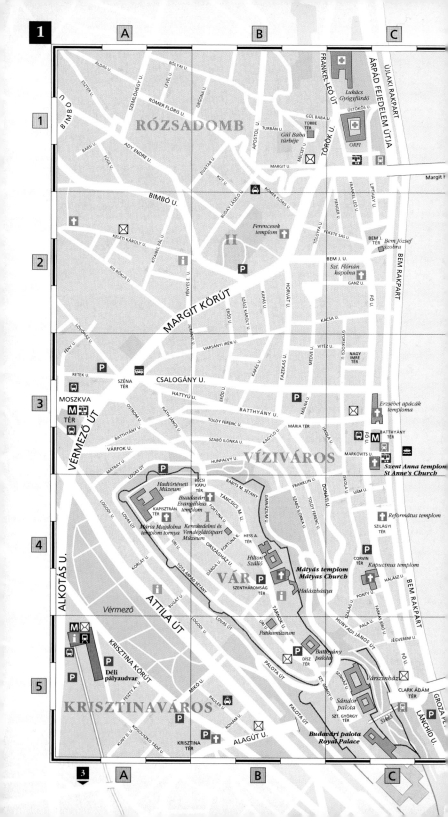

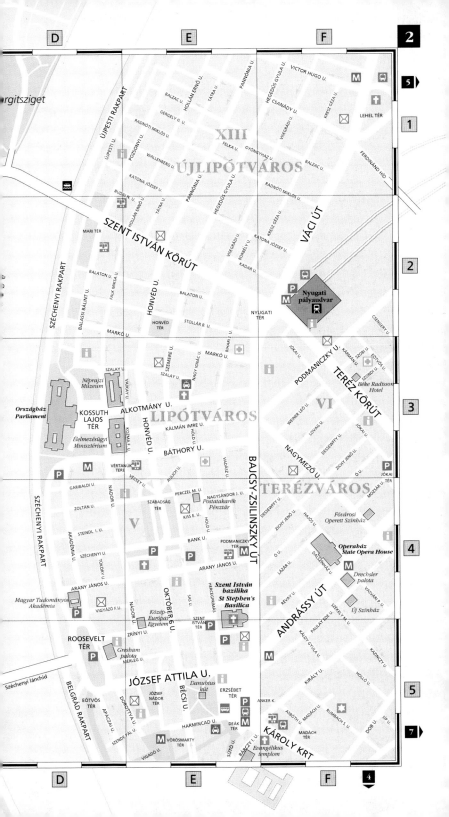

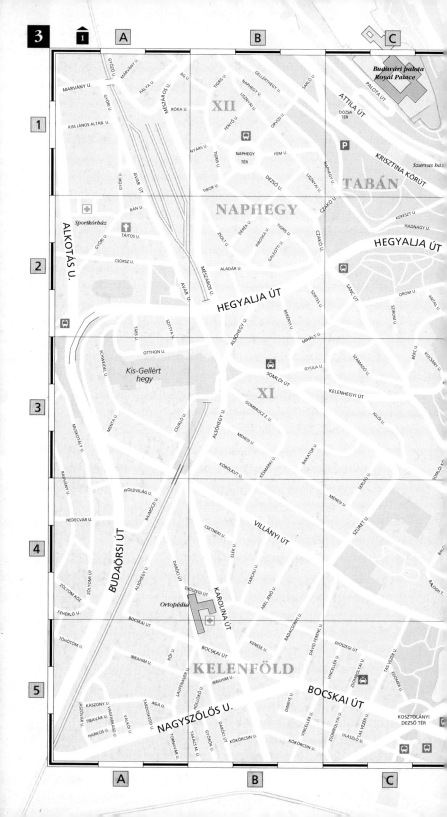

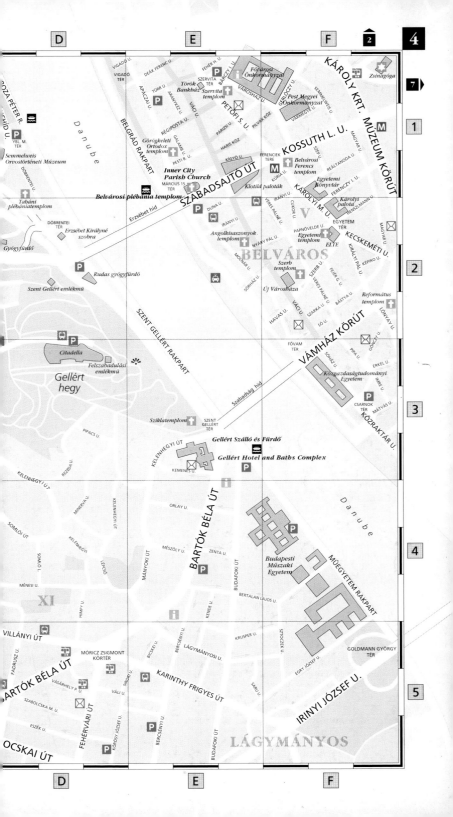

KÁROLY KRT. MÚZEUM KÖRÚT

VIGADÓ U.
VIGADÓ TÉR
DEÁK FERENC U.
FEHÉR H. U.
SZERVITA TÉR
Zsinagóga

TÜRR U.
APÁCZAI U.
Török Bankház
Szervita templom

Fővárosi Önkormányzat

Pest Megyei Önkormányzat

ARANYKÉZ U.
VÁCI U.
RÉGIPOSTA U.
PETŐFI S. U.
VÁROSHÁZ U.
BÁRCZY U.
PILVAX KÖZ
VÁRMEGYE U.
SEMMELWEIS U.
MAGYAR U.

Danube

BELGRÁD RAKPART

Semmelweis Orvostörténeti Múzeum

Görögkeleti Ortodox templom

PESTI B. U.
GALAMB U.
PÁRZSI U.
HARIS KÖZ
KÍGYÓ U.
FERENCIEK TERE
KURIA U.

KOSSUTH L. U.

Belvárosi Ferenc templom
Egyetemi Könyvtár

SZEP U.
REÁLTANODA U.
FERENCZY I. U.
HENSZLMANN U.

M

Tabáni plébániatemplom

Inner City Parish Church
MÁRCIUS 15 TÉR
Belvárosi plébánia templom

SZABADSAJTÓ ÚT

Klotild paloták

DUNA U.
IRÁNYI U.
VERES PÁLNÉ U.
CUKOR U.

KÁROLY M. U.

Károlyi palota
Károlyi palota

EGYETEM

V

M

Erzsébet híd

DÖBRENTEI TÉR
Erzsébet Királyné szobra

Gyógyfürdő

Angolkisasszonyok temploma

NYÁRY PÁL U.
MOLNÁR U.
PAPNÖVELDE U.
Egyetemi templom
ELTE

KIRÁLYI PÁL U.
KÉPIRÓ U.

KECSKEMÉTI U.

MAGYAR U.

BELVÁROS

Szent Gellért emlékmű

Rudas gyógyfürdő

SZENT GELLÉRT RAKPART

Szerb templom

VÁCI U.
SZARKA U.
FEHÉR G. U.
BÁSTYA U.
LÓNYAY U.

Református templom

1

2

Új Városháza
HAVÁS U.
SÓ U.

Citadella

Felszabadulási emlékmű

Gellért hegy

VÁMHÁZ KÖRÚT

FŐVÁM TÉR
SOMLÓI U.
PIPA U.
ERKEL U.
GÖNCZY U.

Közgazdaságtudományi Egyetem

CSARNOK TÉR
MÁTYÁS U.

KÖZRAKTÁR U.

Szabadság híd

Sziklatemplom
SZENT GELLÉRT TÉR

PIPACS U.

Gellért Szálló és Fürdő
Gellért Hotel and Baths Complex
KEMENES U.

KELENHEGYI ÚT

3

KELENHEGYI ÚT
RÉZDA U.

ORLAY U.

BARTÓK BÉLA ÚT

Danube

MINERVA U.
KELENHEGYI ÚT
KELENHEGY

MÉSZÖLY U.
ZENTA U.
MÁNYOKI ÚT
BUDAFOKI ÚT

Budapesti Műszaki Egyetem

MŰEGYETEM RAKPART

SOMLÓI ÚT
SOMLÓ U.
LÉPCSŐ

MÉNESI U.

HIMFY U.

BERTALAN LAJOS U.

XI

4

VILLÁNYI ÚT

FADRUSZ U.
MÓRICZ ZSIGMOND KÖRTÉR

BECSKŐ U.
BERCSÉNYI U.
LÁGYMÁNYOSI U.
KRUSPER U.
STOCZEK U.

GOLDMANN GYÖRGY TÉR

BARTÓK BÉLA ÚT
VÁSÁRHELY U.
VÁLI U.
SZABOLCSKA M. U.

SIROKI U.

KARINTHY FRIGYES ÚT

EGRY JÓZSEF U.
SARU U.
BUDAFOKI ÚT

IRINYI JÓZSEF U.

ESZÉK U.
FEHÉRVÁRI ÚT
KŐRÖSY JÓZSEF U.
BERCSÉNYI U.

KENDE U.

5

OCSKAI ÚT

LÁGYMÁNYOS

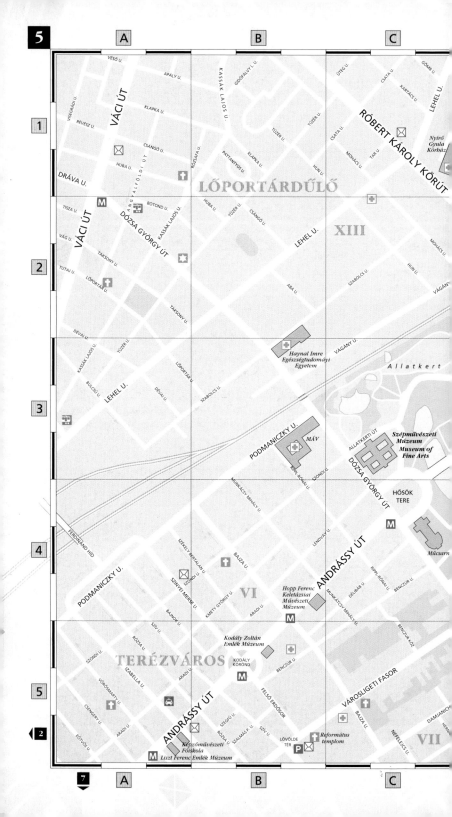

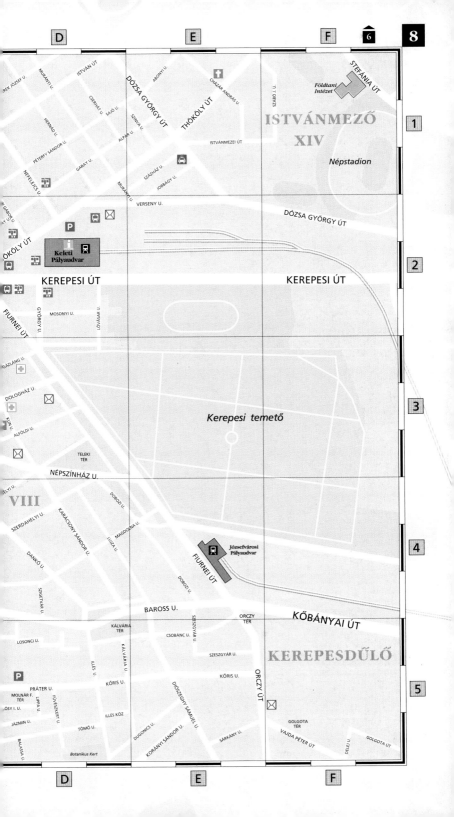

1

STEFÁNIA ÚT

Földtani
Intézet

ISTVÁNMEZŐ
XIV

Népstadion

SZABÓ J. U.

DÓZSA GYÖRGY ÚT

ÁBONYI U.

CSÁSZÁR ANDRÁS U.

ISTVÁNMEZEI ÚT

SZÁZHÁZ U.

JOBBÁGY U.

MURÁNYI U.

VERSENY U.

ISTVÁN ÚT

IREK JÓZSEF U.

MURÁNYI U.

CSERHÁT U.

SAJÓ U.

HERNÁD U.

PÉTERFY SÁNDOR U.

GARAY U.

NEFELEJCS U.

DÓZSA GYÖRGY ÚT

SZINVA U.

ALPÁR U.

DÓZSA GYÖRGY ÚT

THÖKÖLY ÚT

2

P

**Keleti
Pályaudvar**

KEREPESI ÚT

KEREPESI ÚT

KÖKÖLY ÚT

GÁBOR U.

FIUMEI ÚT

GYÖRGY U.

MOSONYI U.

LÓVÁSÁR U.

3

GÁZLÁNG U.

DOLOGHÁZ U.

KUN U.

ALFÖLDI U.

Kerepesi temető

TELEKI
TÉR

NÉPSZÍNHÁZ U.

4

VIII

SZERDAHELYI U.

KARÁCSONY SÁNDOR U.

DANKÓ U.

SZIGETVÁR U.

DOBOZI U.

MAGDOLNA U.

LUIZA U.

FIUMEI ÚT

**Józsefvárosi
Pályaudvar**

DOBOZI U.

BAROSS U.

KÁLVÁRIA
TÉR

CSOBÁNC U.

SZÉSZGYÁR U.

ORCZY
TÉR

KŐBÁNYAI ÚT

5

LOSONCI U.

KÁLVÁRIA U.

ILLÉS U.

KŐRIS U.

SZESZGYÁR U.

KŐRIS U.

ORCZY ÚT

KEREPESDŰLŐ

P

PRÁTER U.

MOLNÁR F.
TÉR

ÓSY I. U.

LIPPA U.

FÜVESKERT U.

DÓSZEGHY SÁMUEL U.

ILLÉS KÖZ

JÁZMIN U.

TÖMŐ U.

DUGONICS U.

KORÁNYI SÁNDOR U.

SÁRKÁNY U.

BALASSA U.

Botanikus Kert

GOLGOTA
TÉR

VAJDA PÉTER ÚT

DELEJ U.

GOLGOTA ÚT

Index

Thermal Hotel Helia 53, 181, 185
Thermal Hotel 52–3, 173
Thonet House 127
  Street-by-Street map 122
Tickets
  air travel 224
  Budapest Card 216
  for concerts 208
  for entertainments 207, 215
  HÉV railway 231
  Metro 230
  to museums 215
  trolley buses 233
Tiepolo, Giambattista 40
  St James Conquers the Moors 146,
  149
Tierney Clark, William 62
Tiffany workshop 137
Tildy, Zoltán 19
Time zones 217
Tintoretto, Jacopo 40, 149
Tipping 187
Titian 40, 149
Toilets, public 217
Tokaji
  What to Drink in Budapest 193
Tokaji Borozó 201
Tomb of Gül Baba 101
Törley, József 161
Törley Mausoleum 161
Török, Richárd 73
Tóth Kocsma 201
Toulouse-Lautrec, Henri de 149
  These women in the Refectory 147
Tourinform Budapest 179, 215
Tourist information 214, 215
  computer terminals 216, 217
Tourist Offices 215
Tradesco 215
Trading on the Pest Embankment
  (Ligeti) 32–3
Trains 226
  Buda Hills 161
  funicular railways 231
  HÉV railway 231
  railway stations 226, 227
  scenic railways 213
Trams 232
  night trams 207
Transport Museum 41, 151
Travel 224–33
  air travel 224–5
  around Parliament 105
  boats 227
  buses 233
  cars 227
  Castle Hill and the Old Town 69
  Central Pest 121
  coach travel 226–7
  cycling 210, 229
  driving in Budapest 228–9
  Gellért Hill and Tabán 87
  HÉV railway 231
  late-night transport 207
  Metro 230
  North of the Castle 97
  railways 226
  taxis 231
  trams 232
  trolley buses 233

Városliget 141
  walking 228
Travel agents 215
Traveller's cheques 218
Trinitarian Monastery 48
Trolley buses 233
Tüköry Étterem Söröző 194, 197
Tunnel 32, 100
Turinform Budapest offices 217
Turkish Bank 128
Turkish baths *see* Baths
Turkish occupation 26–7

U
Udvarház 195, 199
Ügetőpálya 210
Újlaki Parish Church 154
Ullmann, Gyula 111
UNESCO 35, 172
Ungleich, Philipp 80
Ungradt, Fülöp 124
Unicum
  What to Drink in Budapest 193
United Kingdom Embassy 217
United Kingdom tourist office 215
United States Embassy 217
United States tourist office 215
Universitás 179
Universities
  Lóránd Eötvös University 138–9
  Technical University 64, 157
  University of Central Europe 111
  University of Economics 65, 138
  University of Nagyszombat 28, 29
University Botanical Gardens 155
University Church 44, 139
University Library 139
Uprising (1956) 34, 35
  Municipal Cemetery 158
  Remembrance Day 60
Uránia 209

V
Vác 165
Vaccinations 219
Váci Street 15, 127
  Street-by-Street map 122–3
Vadrózsa Étterem 195, 199
Vadvirág Panzió 181, 184
Vágó, József and László 54, 114, 129
Vajdahunyad Castle 141, 150
  Street-by-Street map 143
Van Dyck, Anthony 148
Varga, Imre 40
  Holocaust Memorial 134
  Imre Varga Gallery 171
  People's Stadium 155
  Raoul Wallenberg Monument 154
  sculpture of King István I 22
  Women with Umbrellas 171
Várkert Kiosk
  Budapest's Best: Palaces and
  Historic Buildings 46
Varna, Battle of (1444) 25
Városliget 141–51
  area map 141
  cafés, wine bars and beer houses
  201
  hotels 180–81, 184
  Museum of Fine Arts 146–9

  restaurants 194–5, 198
  Street-by-Street map: Around
  Heroes' Square 142–3
Városliget Calvinist Church 45, 57
Városligeti Avenue 144–5
Vasarely, Victor 40, 171
Vasarely Museum 40, 171
Vass 205
Vaszary, János 56
VAT (value-added tax) 202
  in hotels 176
  tax-free goods 216
Vegetarian food 187
Vegetárium Étterem 194, 197
Vehicle Assistance and Road
  Emergency Service 219
Velázquez, Diego 149
Vermeer, Jan 148
Veronese, Bonifazio 149
Veronese, Paolo 40
  Portrait of a Man 39
Vezekény, Battle of 136
Victoria (hotel) 180, 182
Vidám Park 151, 213
Vidog Borozó 201
Vienna, Treaty of (1624) 27
Vienna Gate Square 48, 84
  Budapest's Best: Palaces and
  Historic Buildings 46
View of Amsterdam (Ruisdael) 147
Vigadó 49, 208
Vigadó Square 126
Vígszínház 209
Villa Korda 181, 185
Villányi-Siklósi Borozó 201
Vincellér Borozó 201
Visas 218
Visegrád 164–5
The Visitation (Master MS) 74, 76
"Vitam et Sanguinem" (Szentpetery)
  28–9
Víziváros 97
  Street-by-Street map 98–9
Vogl, Gergely 103
Volán Taxi 231
Vörösmarty, Mihály 72–3
  monument 122, 126
Vörösmarty Square
  Street-by-Street map 122
Vox Pacis 60

W
Wagenschön, Franz 103
Wagner, Otto 45
Wagner, Richard 115
Walesa, Lech 35
Walks 169–73, 228
  Four-Hour Walk around Óbuda
  170–71
  Two-Hour Walk Around Margaret
  Island 172–3
Wallenberg, Raoul
  Raoul Wallenberg Monument 154
War Museum 213
Warsaw Pact 35
Warsch, Jakab 135
Water, drinking 219
Water Emergency Service 219
Water Tower 172
Weather 58–61, 214

Acknowledgments

DORLING KINDERSLEY would like to thank the following people whose contributions and assistance have made this book possible:

MAIN CONTRIBUTOR
TADEUSZ OLSZANSKI was born in 1929 in Poland. During World War II, he fled with his parents to Hungary, where he attended a Polish school in Balatonboglar. He has since visited Hungary many times as a journalist and is the author of five books about the country. These include a volume of articles, *Budapesztanskie ABC*. In addition, he has translated over 30 Hungarian novels and dramas into Polish. From 1986 to 1994, he lived in Hungary, working both as the manager of the Institute of Polish Culture and as a correspondent for Polish Radio and TV. In recognition of his activities in promoting Hungarian literature and culture, he was awarded the Pro-Hungarian Culture Award and the Tibor Derye Literary Prize.

ADDITIONAL CONTRIBUTORS
Sławomir Fangrat, Mariusz Jarymowicz, Iza Mościcka, Barbara Olszańska, Ewa Roguska.

DESIGN AND EDITORIAL ASSISTANCE
Elizabeth Atherton, Arwen Burnett, Maite Lantaron, Rachel Symons, Anna Streiffert, Sophie Warne.

RESEARCHER
Julia Bennett.

INDEXER
Hilary Bird.

SPECIAL ASSISTANCE
THE PUBLISHER would like to thank the staff at museums, shops, hotels, restaurants and other organizations in Budapest for their invaluable help. Particular thanks go to: the Ambassador for the Republic of Hungary in Warsaw; the Ambassador for the Republic of Poland in Budapest; Gábor Bányai; Katalin Bara and the rest of the staff at the Hungarian airline, Malév; Beatrix Basics, Tibor Kovács and Péter Gaál at the Hungarian National Museum; Éva Benkő at the Museum of Fine Arts; Zoltan Fejős and Endre Stefana Szemkeő at the Ethnographical Museum; Béla Juszel and Éva Orosz at the Hungarian National Bank; the staff of the Kiscelli Museum; Imre Kiss, Zsuzsa Mátyus and Tivadar Mihalkovics at the State Opera House; Konrad Adenauer Stifung; the staff of the Franz Liszt Museum; Zsuzsa Lovag at the Museum of Applied Arts; the Meteorological Office of the Republic of Hungary; the staff at the Hungarian Post Office; Katalin Neray at the Ludwig Museum; Anita Obrotfa at the Budapesti Turisztikai Hivatal; Csilla Pataky at Cartographia Ltd; Géza Szabó; Mária Vida at the Semmelweis Museum of Medical History; Annamária Vigh at the Budapest History Museum.

PHOTOGRAPHY PERMISSIONS
DORLING KINDERSLEY would like to thank the following for their kind permission to photograph at their establishments: Ágnes Bakos, Margit Bakos and Bence Tihanyi at the Budapest History Museum; the staff of the Budapesti Turisztikai Hivatal; Eszter Gordon; István Gordon at the Kurir Archive; Astoria Hotel; Dénes Józsa at the Museum of Fine Arts; Ágnes Kolozs at the Museum of Applied Arts; the Ludwig Museum; the Hungarian National Museum; the Hungarian Academy of Sciences; Tibor Mester at the Hungarian National Gallery; Béla Mezey; the Imre Varga Gallery; András Rázsó at the Museum of Fine Arts; the Semmelweis Museum of Medical History; Judit Szalatnyay at the Kiscelli Museum; Ágnes Szél; Ferenc Tobias and Erzsébet Winter at the Ethnographical Museum; Richard Wagner at the Museum of Applied Arts; the Hungarian airline, Malév.

Dorling Kindersley would also like to thank all the shops, restaurants, cafés, hotels, churches and public services who aided us with our photography. These are too numerous to mention individually.

Particular thanks are due to Marta Zámbó at the Gundel Étterem, who provided the Hungarian cuisine photographed for this guidebook.

PICTURE CREDITS
t=top; tc=top centre; tr=top right; tl=top left; cla=centre left above; ca=centre above; cra=centre right above; cl=centre left; c=centre; cr=centre right; clb=centre left below; cb=centre below; crb=centre right below; bl=bottom left; bc=bottom centre; br=bottom right; b=bottom.

Every effort has been made to trace the copyright holders and we apologize in advance for any unintentional omissions. We would be pleased to insert the appropriate acknowledgments in subsequent editions of this publication.

The publisher is grateful to the following individuals, companies and picture libraries for permission to reproduce their photographs:

ASTORIA HOTEL: 178b.

BUDAPEST HISTORY MUSEUM: 32c, 33c, 38cb, 38b, 72t.
BUDAPESTI TURISZTIKAI HIVATAL: 50cr, 50clb, 50br, 51tc, 51b, 58t, 59b, 60b, 156b.

ESZTER GORDON: 35ca.

HUNGARIAN NATIONAL GALLERY: 16, 23b, 24cb, 26ca, 37br, 38ca, 54cla, 56cl, 74tl, 74tr, 75ca, 75cr, 75cra, 75b, 76t, 76c, 76b, 77t, 77c, 77b;
HUNGARIAN NATIONAL MUSEUM: 8, 20t, 20ca, 20cr, 20cb, 20b, 21t, 21cra, 21c, 21crb, 22t, 22c, 22cl, 22br, 23t, 23c, 23cra, 23crb, 23b, 24cl, 24c, 25t,

25c, 26t, 26b, 27t, 27cra, 27crb, 27cla, 28t, 28ca, 28c, 28cb, 29t, 29c, 29cra, 29crb, 30cl, 31tr, 32t, 32cra, 32cl, 32crb, 33cr, 37cl, 130tr, 130tl, 130ca, 130cb, 131t, 131ca, 131cb, 131bc, 133t, 133c, 133b.

JEWISH MUSEUM: 39cr.
KURIR ARCHIVE: 34tr, 34br, 35br.

LUDWIG MUSEUM: 40b, 73b; LUTHERAN MUSEUM: 41b.

BÉLA MEZEY 34ca; MUSEUM OF APPLIED ARTS: 5br, 56tr, 57bl, 136tr, 136tl, 136c, 137g, 137ca, 137c, 137cb, 137b; MUSEUM OF FINE ARTS: 39tr, 146tl, 146tr, 146ca, 146cb, 146b, 147t, 147ca, 147cb, 147b, 148tl, 148tr, 148c, 148bl, 149t, 149c, 149b.

SZÉCHENYI NATIONAL GALLERY: 39tl, 106tr, 110t; SZÉCHENYI NATIONAL LIBRARY: 24c, 25c, 26c, 27c, 72b; ÁGNES SZÉL: 34tl, 37br, 41c, 78bc, 84b, 160b, 190b.

COVER: ROBERT HARDING PICTURE LIBRARY: G Hellier front cover tc.

Phrase Book

PRONUNCIATION

When reading the literal pronunciation given in the right-hand column of this phrase book, pronounce each syllable as if it formed part of an English word. Remember the points below, and your pronunciation will be even closer to correct Hungarian. The first syllable of each word should be stressed (and is shown in bold). When asking a question the pitch should be raised on the penultimate syllable. "R"s in Hungarian words are rolled.

a	as the long 'a' in father
ay	as in 'pay'
e	as in 'Ted'
ew	similar to the sound in 'hew'
g	always as in 'goat'
i	as in 'bit'
o	as in the 'ou' in 'ought'
u	as in 'tuck'
y	always as in 'yes' (except as in ay above)
yub	as the 'yo' in 'canyon'
zh	like the 's' in leisure

IN EMERGENCY

Help!	Segítség!	shegeetshayg
Stop!	Stop!	shtop
Look out!	Tessék vigyázni	teshayk vidyahzni
Call a doctor	Hívjon orvost!	heevyon orvosht
Call an ambulance	Hívjon mentőt!	heevyon menturt
Call the police	Hívya a rendőrséget	heevya a rendur shayget
Call the fire department	Hívya a tűzoltókat!	heevya a tewzoltowkot
Where is the nearest telephone?	Hol van a legköze-lebbi telefon?	hol von uh legkurze-lebbi telefon
Where is the nearest hospital?	Hol van a legköze-lebbi kórház?	hol von a legkurze-lebbi koorhahz

COMMUNICATIONS ESSENTIALS

Yes/No	Igen/Nem	igen/nem
Please (offering)	Tessék	teshayk
Please (asking)	Kérem	kayrem
Thank you	Köszönöm	kurssurnurm
No, thank you	Köszönöm nem	kurssurnurm nem
Excuse me, please	Bocsánatot kérek	bochanutot kayrek
Hello	Jó napot	yow nopot
Goodbye	Viszontlátásra	vissontlatashruh
Good night	Jójszakát/jóéjt	yaw-ayssukat/yaw-ayt
morning (4–9 am)	reggel	reggel
morning (9am–noon)	délelőtt	daylelurt
morning (midnight–4am)	éjjel	ay-yel
afternoon	délután	daylootan
evening	este	eshteh
yesterday	tegnap	tegnup
today	ma	muh
tomorrow	holnap	holnup
here	itt	it
there	ott	ot
What?	mi	mi
When?	mikor	mikor
Why?	miért	miayrt
Where?	hol	hol

USEFUL PHRASES

How are you?	Hogy van?	hod-yuh vun
Very well, thank you	köszönöm nagyon jól	kurssurnurm nojjon yowl
Pleased to meet you	Örülök hogy megis-merhettem	ur-rewluk hod-yuh megishmerhettem
See you soon	Seia!	seeyuh
Excellent!	Nagyszerű!	nud-yusserew
Is there ... here?	Van itt ... ?	vun itt
Where can I get ...?	Hol kaphatok ...-t?	hol kuphutok ...-t
How do you get to?	Hogy lehet ...-ba eljutni?	hod-yuh lehet ...-buh el-yootni
How far is ...?	milyen messze van ...	meeyen messeh van ...
Do you speak English?	Beszél angolul?	bessayl ungolool
I can't speak Hungarian	Nem beszélek magyarul	nem bessaylek mud-yarool
I don't understand	Nem értem	nem ayrtem
Can you help me?	Kérhetem a segítségét?	kayrhetem uh shegeechaygayt
Please speak slowly	Tessék lassabban beszélni	teshayk lushubbun bessaylni
Sorry!	Elnézést!	elnayzaysht

USEFUL WORDS

big	nagy	noj
small	kicsi	kichi
hot	forró	meleg
cold	hideg	hideg
good	jó	yow
bad	rossz	ross
enough	elég	elayg
well	jól	yowl
open	nyitva	nyitva
closed	zárva	zarva
left	bal	bol
right	jobb	yob
straight on	egyenesen	ejeneshen
near	az ... közel	kurzel
far	messze	messeh
up	fel	fel
down	le	leh
early	korán	koran
late	késő	kayshur
entrance	bejárat	beh-yarut
exit	kijárat	ki-yarut
toilet	WC	vaytsay
free/unoccupied	szabad	sobbod
free/no charge	ingyen	injen

MAKING A TELEPHONE CALL

Can I call abroad from here?	Telefonálhatok innen külföldre?	telefonalhutok innen kewlfurldreh
I would like to call collect	Szeretnék egy R-beszélgetést lebonyolítani	seretnayk ed-yuh er-bessaylgetaysht lebon-yoleetuni
local call	helyi beszélgetés	hayce bessaylgetaysht
I'll ring back later	Visszahívom később	vissuh-heevom kayshurb
Could you leave a message?	Hagyhatnék egy üzenetet?	hud-yuhutnayk ed-yuh ewzenetet
Hold on	Várjon!	vahr-yon
Could you speak up a little please?	kicsit hangosab-ban, kérem!	kichit hungosh-shob-bon kayrem

SHOPPING

How much is this?	Ez mennyibe kerül?	ez menn-yibeh kerewl
I would like ...	Szeretnék egy ...-t	seretnayk ed-yuh ...-t
Do you have ...?	Kapható önöknél ...?	kuphutaw urnurknayl
I'm just looking	Csak körülnézek	chuk kur-rewlnayzek
Do you take credit cards?	Elfogadják a hitelkártyákat?	elfogud-yak uh hitelkart-yakut
What time do you open?	Hánykor nyit az nyitva?	Hahnkor nyit oz ewzlet
What time do you close?	Meddig van nyitva.	Meddig van nyitva?
this one	ez	ez
that one	az	oz
expensive	drága	drahga
cheap	olcsó	olchow
size	méret	mayret
white	fehér	feheer
black	fekete	feketeh
red	piros	pirosh
yellow	sárga	sharga
green	zöld	zurld
blue	kék	cake
brown	barna	borna

TYPES OF SHOP

antique dealer	antiqvárius	ontikvahrioosh
baker's	pékség	paykshayg
bank	bank	bonk
bookshop	könyvesbolt	kurn-yuveshbolt
cake shop	cukrászda	tsookrassduh
chemist	patika	putikuh
department store	áruház	aroo-haz
florist	virágüzlet	virag-ewzlet
greengrocer	zöldséges	zurld-shaygesh
market	piac	pi-uts
newsagent	újságos	oo-yushagosh
post office	postahivatal	poshta-hivatal
shoe shop	cipőbolt	tsipurbolt
souvenir shop	ajándékbolt	uy-yandaykbolt
supermarket	ábécé/ABC	abaytsay
travel agent	utazási iroda	ootuzashi iroduh

STAYING IN A HOTEL

Have you any vacancies?	Van kiadó szobájuk?	vun ki-udaw soba-yook
double room with double bed	francia-àgyas szoba	frontsia-ahjosh sobuh
twin room	kétágyas szoba	kaytad-yush sobuh
single room	egyágyas szoba	ed-yad-yush sobuh
room with a bath/shower	fürdőszobàs/ zuhanyzós szoba	fewrdur-sobahsh/ zoohonzahsh soba
porter	portás	portahsh
key	kulcs	koolch
I have a reservation	Foglaltam egy szobát	foglultum ed-yuh sobat

SIGHTSEEING

bus	autóbusz	owtawbooss
tram	villamos	villumosh
trolley bus	troli(busz)	troli(booss)
train	vonat	vonut
underground	metró	metraw
bus stop	buszmegálló	boossmegallaw
tram stop	villamosmegálló	villomosh-megahllaw
art gallery	képcsarnok	kayp-chornok
palace	palota	polola
cathedral	székesegyház	saykesh-ejhajz
church	templom	templom
garden	kert	kert
library	könyvtár	kurnvtar
museum	múzeum	moozayoom
tourist information	túristahivatal	toorishta-hivotol
closed for public holiday	ünnep van zarva	ewn-nep von zarva

EATING OUT

A table for ... please	Egy asztalt szeretnék... személyre	ed-yuh usstult seretnayk ... semayreh
I want to reserve a table	Szeretnék uszatnék foglalni	Sveretnayk ostolt foglolni
The bill please	Számla, kérem	samluh kayrem
I am a vegetarian	Vegetáriánnus vagyok	vegetari-ahnoosh vojok
I'd like ...	Szeretnék egy ...-t	seretnayk ed-yuh ...-t
waiter/waitress	pincér/pincérnő	pintsayr/pintsaymur
menu	étlap	aytlup
wine list	itallap	itullup
chef's special	konyhafőnök ajánlata	konha-furnurt oyahu-lotta
tip	borravaló	borovolo
glass	pohár	pohar
bottle	üveg	ewveg
knife	kés	kaysh
fork	villa	villuh
spoon	kanál	kunal
breakfast	reggeli	reg-geli
lunch	ebéd	ebayd
dinner	vacsora	vochora
main courses	főételek	fur-aytelek
starters	előételek	elur-aytelek
vegetables	zöldség	zurld-shayg
desserts	édességek	aydesh-shaydek
rare	anglosan	ongloshan
well done	àtsütve	ahtshewtveh

MENU DECODER

alma	olma	apple
àsvàny-víz	ahshvahn-veez	mineral water
bab	bob	beans
banán	bonahn	banana
barack	borotsk	apricot
bárány	bahrahn	lamb
bors	borsh	pepper
csirke	cheerkeh	chicken
csokoládé	chokolahday	chocolate
cukor	tsookor	sugar
ecet	etset	vinegar
fagylalt	fodyuhloot	ice cream
fehérbor	feheerbor	white wine
fokhagyma	fokhodyuhma	garlic
főtt	furt	boiled
gomba	gomba	mushrooms
gulyàs	gooyahsh	goulash
gyümölcs	dyewmurlch	fruit
gyümölcslé	dyewmurlch-lay	fruit juice
hagyma	hojma	onions
hal	hol	fish
hús	hoosh	meat
kávé	kavay	coffee
kenyér	ken-yeer	bread

krumpli	kroompli	potatoes
kolbász	kolbahss	sausage
leves	levesh	soup
máj	my	liver
marha	marha	beef
mustár	mooshtahr	mustard
narancs	noronch	orange
olaj	oloy	oil
paradicsom	porodichom	tomatoes
pàrolt	pahrolt	steamed
pite	piteh	pie
ràncott	rahntsott	fried in batter
rizs	rizh	rice
rostélyos szelet	bifstek	steak
roston/rostonsült	roshton/roshton-shewlt	grilled
sajt	shoyt	cheese
saláta	sholahta	salad
sertéshüs	shertaysh-hoosh	pork
só	shaw	salt
sonka	shonka	ham
sör	shur	beer
sült	shewlt	fried/roasted
sült burgonya	shewlt boorgonya	chips
sütemény	shewtemayn-yuh	cake, pastry
szendvics	sendvich	sandwich
szósz	sowss	sauce
tea	tay-uh	tea
tej	tay	milk
tejszín	taysseen	cream
tengeri hal	tengeri hol	seafood
tojás	toyahsh	egg
töltött	turlturt	stuffed
vörösbor	vur-rurshbor	red wine
zsemle	zhemleh	roll
zsemlegombóc	zhemleh-gombowts	dumplings

NUMBERS

0	nulla	noolluh
1	egy	ed-yuh
2	kettő, két	kettur, kayt
3	három	harom
4	négy	nayd-yuh
5	öt	urt
6	hat	hut
7	hét	hayt
8	nyolc	n-yolts
9	kilenc	kilents
10	tíz	teez
11	tizenegy	tizened-yuh
12	tizenkettő	tizenkettur
13	tizenhárom	tizenharom
14	tizennégy	tizen-nayd-yuh
15	tizenöt	tizenurt
16	tizenhat	tizenhut
17	tizenhét	tizenhayt
18	tizennyolc	tizenn-yolts
19	tizenkilenc	tizenkilents
20	húsz	hooss
21	huszonegy	hoossoned-yuh
22	huszonkettő	hoossonkettur
30	harminc	hurmints
31	harmincegy	hurmintsed-yuh
32	harminckettő	hurmintskettur
40	negyven	ned-yuven
50	ötven	urtven
60	hatvan	hutvun
70	hetven	hetven
80	nyolcvan	n-yoltsvun
90	kilencven	kilentsven
100	száz	saz
110	száztíz	sazteez
200	kétszáz	kayt-saz
300	háromszáz	haromssaz
1000	ezer	ezer
10,000	tízezer	teezezer
1,000,000	millió	milliaw

TIME

one minute	egy perc	ed-yuh perts
hour	óra	awruh
half an hour	félóra	faylawruh
Sunday	vasárnap	vusharnup
Monday	hétfő	haytfur
Tuesday	kedd	kedd
Wednesday	szerda	serduh
Thursday	csütörtök	chewturturk
Friday	péntek	payntek
Saturday	szombat	sombut

EYEWITNESS *TRAVEL GUIDES*

TITLES PUBLISHED TO DATE

THE GUIDES THAT SHOW YOU WHAT OTHERS ONLY TELL YOU

COUNTRY GUIDES

AUSTRALIA • FRANCE • GREAT BRITAIN • GREECE:
ATHENS & THE MAINLAND • THE GREEK ISLANDS
IRELAND • ITALY • PORTUGAL
SPAIN • THAILAND

REGIONAL GUIDES

CALIFORNIA • FLORENCE & TUSCANY
FLORIDA • HAWAII • LOIRE VALLEY
NAPLES WITH POMPEII & THE AMALFI COAST
PROVENCE & THE COTE D'AZUR • SARDINIA
SEVILLE & ANDALUSIA • VENICE & THE VENETO

CITY GUIDES

AMSTERDAM • ISTANBUL • LISBON • LONDON
MOSCOW • NEW YORK • PARIS • PRAGUE
ROME • SAN FRANCISCO • ST PETERSBURG
SYDNEY • VIENNA • WARSAW

TO BE PUBLISHED IN SPRING 1999
MADRID • BUDAPEST • DUBLIN

CONTINUALLY UPDATED

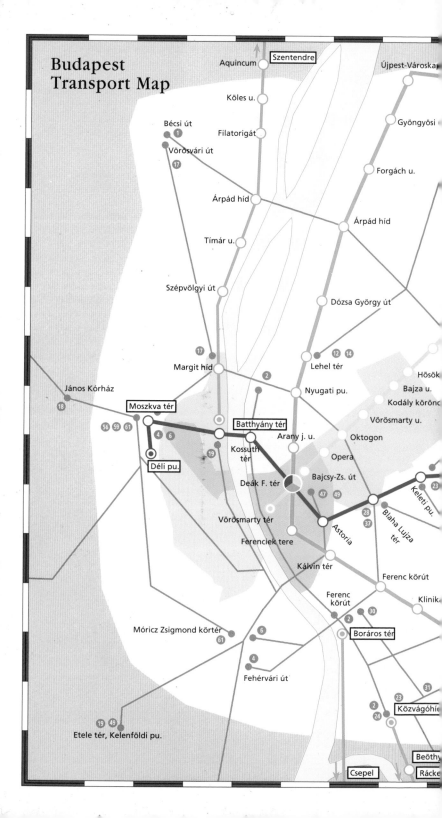

Budapest
Transport Map

Szentendre

Aquincum

Újpest-Városka

Köles u.

Gyöngyösi

Bécsi út ①

Filatorigát

Forgách u.

Vörösvári út ⑰

Árpád híd

Árpád híd

Tímár u.

Szépvölgyi út

Dózsa György út

⑰

Margit híd

⑫ ⑭

Lehel tér

Hősök

② Nyugati pu.

Bajza u.

János Kórház

Kodály körönd

⑱

Moszkva tér

Vörösmarty u.

㊅㊈㉑

④ ⑥

Batthyány tér

Arany j. u.

Oktogon

⑲

Kossuth tér

Opera

Déli pu.

Deák F. tér

Bajcsy-Zs. út

⑳ Keleti pu.

Vörösmarty tér

� ㊼

㊽ ㉓

㉘

Blaha Lujza tér

Ferenciek tere

Astoria ㊲

Kálvin tér

Ferenc körút

Ferenc körút

Klinik

㉚

Móricz Zsigmond körtér

Boráros tér

㊳ ⑥

㉑

④

Fehérvári út

㉛

② ㉓

Közvágóhi

⑲ ㊾

㉔

Etele tér, Kelenföldi pu.

Beöthy

Csepel

Rácke